From Everlasting to Everlasting

American University Studies

Series VII
Theology

Vol. 65

PETER LANG
New York · San Francisco · Bern
Frankfurt am Main · Paris · London

David Ingersoll Naglee

From Everlasting to Everlasting

John Wesley on Eternity and Time
Vol. 1

PETER LANG
New York · San Francisco · Bern
Frankfurt am Main · Paris · London

Library of Congress Cataloging-in-Publication Data

Naglee, David Ingersoll
    From everlasting to everlasting : John Wesley on
eternity and time / David Ingersoll Naglee.
        p. cm. — (American university studies. Series VII,
Theology and religion ; v. 65-66)
    Includes bibliographical references.
    1. Wesley, John, 1703-1791.   2. Eternity-History of
doctrines—18th century.   3. Time—Religious aspects—
Christianity-History of doctrines—18th century.   I. Title.
II. Series.
BX8495.W5N28   1991   236'.21—dc20   90-47316
ISBN 0-8204-1113-2 (v. 1)
        0-8204-1183-3 (set)   CIP
ISSN 0740-0446

© Peter Lang Publishing, Inc., New York 1991

TABLE OF CONTENTS

Preface

John Wesley, an eighteenth century priest in the Church of England, became famous as one of the chief founders of a religious movement called Methodism. He was its primary leader - its chief inspiration, its galvanizing organizer, its tireless evangelist, its thoughtful apologist, its ubiquitous pastor, its erudite teacher, its prolific author, its moral and spiritual conscience, its social idealist, its finagling financier, its critical interpreter of Scripture and history, its model of duty, its visionary of destiny, its effervescent example of zeal and courage, and, hardly least of all, he was Methodism's embodiment of primitive Christianity. Yet, he never intended that his followers should leave the Church of England and begin a new church. Many did, however. The War of Independence in the colonies severed the American Methodists from Mother Church, and Wesley felt obligated to help them organize into a church after that conflict. In England, on the other hand, he kept a tight reign on his Methodists and kept them from separation. However, within several decades of his death, British Methodism also departed the Anglican communion to become a church on its own terms.

Presently, the Methodist bodies worldwide number well in excess of eleven million communicants. This contemporary phase of the movement, in the past few years, has shown a renewed interest in discovering the meaning of John Wesley - the man, the message, and the mission. The bicentennial of American Methodism in 1984 thrust that large denomination into the process. One important result has been the broadened understanding of Wesley's religious thought. Traditionally, Wesley's theology was treated in the narrow confines of soteriology, with emphasis on such themes as justification, regeneration, sanctification, and assurance. Seldom did scholarly works seriously treat subjects as eternity, creation, Christian living in terms of pilgrimage, stewardship, marriage, or eschatology.

In December 1980, I was in London finishing research on another Wesleyan manuscript. While at Evensong in Westminster Abbey, as the choir sang a beautiful Advent anthem, a most unorthodox thought came to mind - "When you return home, read Wesley's JOURNAL in reverse, from end to beginning." This idea was preposterous at first. However, two months later, when the reading was completed, a radically broadened understanding of Wesley and his thought emerged. No great emphasis existed on the famous "Aldersgate Experience." Traditional treatments always stressed that religious experience as being formative for Wesley's thought, practice, and mission. Aldersgate, even for me, colored everything Wesley said and did after 1738. But, in the reversed flow of his JOURNAL, it plays a very minimal part, covering less than a few years at most. If Aldersgate salvation, then, is not the meaning of his theology, what is? This book seeks to answer that radical question, but the answer is not that radical. The answer shows Wesley's commitment to a rather systematic theology - not of his creation - but of his preference, inherited from late seventeenth century Anglicanism.

There are persons of infinite worth who have made this book possible. Without their expertise and cooperation, my efforts would have been quite minimal - Mr. Ian Pierson, Librarian of the Society for the Propagation of the Gospel in Foreign Parts, London; Mrs. Charlene Baxter, Catalog Librarian at LaGrange College; and Stephen C. Hemphill, Director of Educational Seminars - Cokesbury Bookstore, Atlanta, Georgia, who served as my reader and literary adviser. To such belongs the kingdom of God!

> David I. Naglee, Ph.D.,
> Professor of Religion and Philosophy
> LaGrange College
> LaGrange, Georgia

"How advisable, by every possible means, to connect the ideas of time and eternity, so to associate them together, that the thought of one may never recur to your mind, without the thought of the other! It is our highest wisdom to associate the ideas of the visible and invisible world; to connect temporal and spiritual, mortal and immortal being."
- John Wesley, February 19, 1790

To Elfriede, My Wife

Beloved pilgrim with me,
Loved to all Eternity!

Introduction - Wesley's Bible

"The Scripture. . . of the Old and New Testament is a most solid and precious system of divine truth. Every part thereof is worthy of God; and also together are one entire body, wherein is no defect, no excess. It is the fountain of heavenly wisdom, which they who are able to taste prefer to all writings of men, however wise or learned or holy."[1]

The study of John Wesley's theology is essentially the study of the Bible. At the root of every presupposition, of every affirmation, lies some biblical passage or principle. As in the thought of Socrates - "The whole universe is shot through with connections although many are not easily discernible" - so the universe of Wesley's thought is shot through with biblical connections, many not quickly discernible, at least to some contemporary readers, who are frequently alarmed that Wesley is out-of-tune with secularity. Nevertheless, Wesley remains popular with a great number of persons who are biblically literate. Moreover, there is presently a Renaissance of interest in Wesley, and the place of the Bible in his theology is being rediscovered.

FROM EVERLASTING TO EVERLASTING is a study of John Wesley's understanding of eternity and time. It is grounded in his interpretation of the Bible. It is an over-view of his theology - an *Heilsgeschichte* (Salvation History). Its scope is nearly infinite because Wesley began in that boundless duration of "eternity" and shifted to the linear dimension of the spatiotemporal that he called "time." He placed time within the boundary of six thousand years, having the material universe share its duration. With the dissolution of time, following the Great Judgment, Wesley held that a divine metamorphosis will lift matter to an eternal state of pure substance and being - the New Creation. It is the "Great I Am, the Alpha and Omega" who works all and in all to accomplish such a remarkable plan.

This grand motif is rooted by Wesley in the Scriptures, being shot through with biblical connections that seem almost inexhaustible. What some would regard as obscure passages, Wesley found explicit by virtue of his hermeneutical methodology, and he wove all the strands together. This is not to claim that he was a systematic theologian. Hardly, but he had a systematic understanding of eternity and time, and he subordinated all other theological concerns to this understanding. Actually, he inherited this understanding from the seventeenth century Church of England in which both Anglicans and Puritans were preoccupied with it. What Wesley did with the theme, however, was to "Wesleyanize" it for the spiritual strengthening of his Methodists. Consequently, his sermons, tracts, treatises, letters, essays, prayers, and hymns abound with explicit and implicit references to the theme - Eternity and time are filled with the love and presence of a God who never slumbers nor sleeps, who is always at work accomplishing His will, creating, sustaining, governing, redeeming, restoring, and finally renewing the work of His hands - all in love.

Of his numerous writings, Wesley's *EXPLANATORY NOTES UPON THE OLD TESTAMENT* and the *EXPLANATORY NOTES UPON THE NEW TESTAMENT* provide a skeletal outline for this theme. His other writings add sinew, flesh, skin, hair, and spirit to make the theological creature come alive. In a sense, Wesley's treatment is an Anglican rewriting of St. Augustine's *CIVITAS DEI* (City of God). In fact, his reliance on the thought of Augustine is overwhelmingly obvious. In a far greater sense, his theology of eternity and time represents an improvement on John Milton's *PARADISE LOST* and John Bunyan's *PILGRIM'S PROGRESS*.

Before searching out the depths of eternity and time, however, we must understand Wesley's commitment to the Bible, his hermeneutical and exegetical methods, and his determination to keep close to biblical religion.

THE WESLEY FAMILY BIBLE

Born of Samuel and Susanna Wesley, on June 17, 1703, the fifteenth of nineteen children, John inherited more than a share in a parson's family and rectory. While his family endured the economic outrage laid upon ministers with large families and small parishes, the Wesley family thrived on piety, character, and learning. Susanna was a main communicator to the children of the family values and traditions. While Samuel tended to the business of St. Andrews Parish of Epworth (Lincolnshire), Susanna conducted a week-day school in the rectory for her children. Their biblical education, however, began years before they entered her classroom on their fifth birthday. When a child began to speak, Susanna began to guide the child in memorizing verses of Scripture.[2] By the time the child was five, it knew a large number of biblical passages. Susanna's school met Monday through Friday, from nine in the morning until noon, and from two to five in the afternoon. The alphabet was mastered the first day of school, then the Bible was used for learning to read. Ten verses were to be covered per day by the five year old student. Susanna claimed that Jacky (John) "quickly did" his Bible lessons. To help the younger children, an older brother or sister read a chapter from the Old Testament and a Psalm before the end of the morning session, and then read a chapter from the New Testament and a Psalm before the close of the afternoon session.[3] By the time John was ten years of age, he had read the Bible through several times - quite a biblical exposure!

Unfortunately, many studies of John Wesley leave his father out of his educational molding. Samuel Wesley, Senior, was a priest in the Church of England, and he was a High Churchman at that. Writing to Lord North (June 15, 1775), John Wesley stated, "I am a High Churchman, the son of a High Churchman, bred up from my childhood in the highest notions of passive obedience and nonresistance."[4] He could have added, "And in biblical understanding." As a High Churchman, Samuel Wesley conducted daily prayer services at St. Andrews Church, matins in the morning and evensong in the evening, featuring the reading of the entire book of Psalms every month and select passages from the Old and New Testaments according to the lectionary. Moreover, he was a biblical preacher of unusual learning. His sermons were carefully and thoroughly prepared, designed to conquer the minds of his hearers and lead them into scriptural religion. In addition, he regularly preached the *HOMILIES OF THE CHURCH OF ENGLAND*, standard sermons on selected subjects, composed entirely of Scripture and sound reasoning. Young Wesley heard his father read the various services in *THE BOOK OF COMMON PRAYER* (1662), in which Scripture, prayer, and hymn were masterfully blended. By the age of ten, when John left Epworth for school at Charterhouse in London, the biblical impact of his father's life and ministry made a tremendous contribution to his spiritual development. Later in his youth, John Wesley followed in his father's steps and entered the priesthood, incorporating much of the *HOMILIES* and *THE BOOK OF COMMON PRAYER* into his biblically oriented ministry.

THE STUDENT AND THE BIBLE:
CHARTERHOUSE AND OXFORD

On January 28, 1714, John left the rectory at Epworth for Charterhouse in London - a school that prepared boys for university education. He was not yet eleven years old. Susanna's educational program brought out the glimmerings of a future scholar in him, and the Duke of Buckingham nominated him for Charterhouse.[5] His masters there remembered him as a studious fellow, who worked his way through Hebrew and Greek with an exacting thoroughness.[6] These linguistic studies brought him into the heart of the Bible, and from henceforth he could never be satisfied with any English translation of the Bible. He was also trained at Charterhouse as a choirboy, and his clear, high soprano voice graced many an anthem drawn from the Bible.

On his seventeenth birthday, in 1720, young Wesley entered Christ Church College at Oxford University.[7] Stevens has argued that Wesley was but sixteen years old,[8] but Baker's dating is to be preferred. Wesley's older brother, Samuel, who was a master at the Westminster School in London, recommended him for admission, believing him to be academically mature. His father secured the financial support needed, and John began his studies.

What kind of student was Wesley at Oxford? One of his diaries speaks eloquently of "scholarship" as a Christian virtue. He also placed great emphasis upon "method" and "industry".[9] He conceived scholarship to be his duty as a developing Christian. His understanding of "virtue and duty" were clearly Stoical in a Medieval Scholastic sense - It was both virtuous and dutiful to be loyal to scholarship inspite of well-being, sickness, or adiaphora. John Wesley never departed from these qualities.

His studies at Christ Church College followed the liberal arts tradition, with a heavy concentration in the Classics, languages, theology (the Queen of the Sciences), philosophy (the Handmaid of Theology), and natural philosophy. In literature he read and annotated Horace, Juvenal, Homer, Shakespeare, Spenser, and Milton, to cite a few.[10] Among the many theological works he studied, the writings of Bishop Bull were especially important to him.[11] His theological interests ran the entire span of the history of the Church. In linguistics, he advanced in his mastery of Hebrew and Greek and also learned Latin and French.[12] In the summer of 1724, he proudly received his Bachelor of Arts degree.[13]

THE BIBLE AND THE POSTGRADUATE WESLEY: 1725-1791

On September 19, 1725, John Wesley was ordained a deacon in the Church of England by John Potter, Bishop of Oxford. The following March 17th, he was elected to the fellowship of Lincoln College at Oxford. During the six months intervening, Wesley had read and annotated the following works: Drake and LeClerc, *PHYSICS*; Burnet, *THE REFORMATION*; Dennis, *AGAINST POPE*; Salmon, *REVIEWS*; Hickes, *ON SCHISM*; Lee, *AGAINST LOCKE*; Welstead, *POEMS*; *THE GREAT ATLAS*; Halley, *MAGNETISM AND GRAVITY*; Ditton, *MATTER'S THINKING*, *THE SOULS OF BRUTES*; Watts; Keil, *PRINCIPIA*; Cowley;

Locke; Norris, *HEAUTONTIMORUMENOS*; Cheyne, *FEVERS*;
EZRA in Hebrew; Horace, *ODES, EPODES AND SATIRES, DE
ARTE POETICA*, and *EPISTLES*; *LIFE OF WHITEWAYS*;
SAINT MATTHEW; Part of chapter 15 of *PROVERBS*, and trans-
lated by Wesley into Latin verse; Virgil, *ECLOGUE, LOGIC,
GEORGICS*; *SAINT MARK*; *SAINT LUKE, ANEIDS*; *LIFE OF
PLUTRARCH*; Epictetus; *THE ACTS*; *THE ILLIAD*; *ROMANS*;
Xenophon; *COLOSSIANS*; *THESSALONIANS*; *ECCLESI-
ASTES*; *PROVERBS*; Cornelius Nepos; Jackson; Cowley and
Watts, *ON THE CASE OF SUBSCRIBING*; Prior; Berkeley;
SATIRE OF JUVENAL; Vertol, *THE REVOLUTIONS OF
ROME*; Synge, *ON TOLERATION*; Clarendon; Milton; Rapin, *ON
ELOQUENCE*; *EPHESIANS*; and *THE TWELVE ODES OF
ANACRON*.[14] With this intellectual exposure, Wesley began his
fellowship at Lincoln College and took his Master of Arts degree
on February 14, 1727.[15]

One might suppose that all this learning would quickly and thoroughly extinguish the flame of biblical fervor. But not so, according to Wesley. If anything, the phenomenal increase in learning
fanned the flame of biblicism. His most pressing project now became how to relate all knowledge to the Bible. Wesley, in describing his biblical pilgrimage, said -

> "In 1730, I began to be *homo unius libri*, to study (comparatively) no book
> but the Bible. I then saw, in a stronger light than ever before, that only one
> thing is needful, even faith that worketh by the love of God and man, all in-
> ward and outward holiness; and I groaned to love God with all my heart, and
> to serve Him with all my strength."[16]

In one of his sermons, Wesley continued this theme of being "a
man of one book" - stressing the Bible is a map that shows the way
to heaven. As such, it shows "how to land safe on that happy
shore." God has condescended to show us the way, by coming
down from heaven, and writing the way in a book - the Bible.
Wesley implored, "O give me that book!" No matter what the
price, he would have the Bible because he knew its "knowledge is
enough for me."[17]

Colin Williams has observed that by Wesley's being *homo unius libri* he did not reject all other writings as being of no value.[18] On the contrary, he continued to study "subjects such as logic, in order to develop the faculty of thought, and in fields of medicine, history and literature, in order to become a more effective servant of God through better health, better understanding of the human situation, and better powers of expression."[19] The conclusion is incontestible: Wesley's "man of one book" meant a reliance upon that book for the way of salvation. The Bible is the textbook, the final authority in matters of religion, and all other books must be judged by this once-for-all revelation.[20]

Moreover, Wesley's acquisition of knowledge increased dramatically from 1730 onward. His Georgia experience was marked by studies in biblical, theological, devotional, linguistic, historical, musical, biographical, and even philosophical subjects.[21] But the one most constant area of study in Georgia was the Greek New Testament, with which he spent hours daily in solitude.[22] This preoccupation with the Greek New Testament began when he was a member of the Holy Club at Oxford. He retained this study practice throughout his life. At Savannah, he read the Bible and select books to numerous groups of persons, the German colonists in particular.[23]

Months after his return to England from Georgia, May 24, 1738, brought Wesley an experience of "assurance of faith" - and, in his words, "My heart was strangely warmed."[24] The place was a gathering center for a small Bible society, located on Aldersgate Street, London. As the reader intoned the Preface to Martin Luther's commentary on Romans, at about 8:45 p.m., Wesley gained the assurance that he possessed faith, saving faith of which the Bible speaks as being necessary for salvation. The years of searching the Bible, studying, and groaning after the primary message of the Bible seemed suddenly to be rewarded. Wesley now believed that salvation had come to him because he had an assurance that this faith was saving faith. Within six months, however, he lacked that assurance and frequently admitted to being spiritually "dead and cold." Unfortunately, this stage of Wesley's pilgrimage is often neglected but the following letters of Wesley about this condition are irrefutable - To Benjamin Ingham and James Hutton, November 16, 1738; To James Hutton and the Fetter Lane Society, July 2, 1739. The point to be made here is obvious - after the Aldersgate experience and its apparent break-down, Wesley depended more on the Bible than ever before.

In a letter to John Smith, dated December 30, 1745, Wesley exclaimed - "I desire none to receive my words, unless they are confirmed by Scripture and reason."[25] The inclusion of "reason" in understanding Scripture was no new addition. Wesley learned its application to Holy Writ from his mother, Susanna. The Moravians had convinced Wesley, before Aldersgate, to discard reason as a tool for discovering the meaning of the Bible. Wesley did what they advised, tried their bibliomancy, and from the Autumn of 1738 onward paid a bitter price for it. When he broke with the Moravians, and returned to a biblicism that included the use of reason, his spiritual life improved almost immediately. So in writing to John Smith, he included reason in the pursuit of knowing the Bible.

What is the origin of the Bible? Wesley saw a paradox in the answer to that question: In one sense, God is the author of the Bible because He inspired it; in another sense, holy men of old were the authors of it, having been inspired by God. An examination of these two poles of the paradox is appropriate. (1) Wesley's starting point was "divine inspiration." God chose men to do the writing and then inspired them. If there had not been inspiration, there would have been no Scripture. In speaking to young Timothy, the Apostle Paul affirmed, "All Scripture is inspired of God" (II Timothy III, 16). In the *EXPLANATORY NOTES UPON THE NEW TESTAMENT*, Wesley explained -

"The Spirit of God not only once inspired those who wrote it, but continually inspires, supernaturally assists, those that read it with earnest prayer. Hence it is profitable for doctrine, for the instruction of the ignorant, for the reproof or conviction of them that are in error or sin, for the correction or amendment of whatever is amiss, and for instructing or training up the children of God in all righteousness."[26]

One indication that God inspired the Scriptures is that persons continue in all ages to be inspired by the Holy Spirit as they read them, and the Scriptures, in turn, accomplish all that God designed when He initially gave them. Another aspect of the initial inspiration is linguistic in nature -

> "God speaks, not as man, but as God. His thoughts are very deep, and thence His words are of inexhaustible virtue. And the language of His words which are given them accurately answered the impression made upon their minds; and hence Luther says, 'Divinity is nothing but a grammar of the language of the Holy Ghost.'"[27]

In other words, the thoughts of God transcend the thoughts and language of man whom God inspires. Nevertheless, God gave His thoughts through inspiration, and inspired men received these thoughts as "impressions." The Holy Spirit, the agent by whom God inspires, enabled these men to translate the divine impressions into human thoughts and words, without exhausting God's thoughts. The Scriptures then are an approximation of God's revealed thoughts, being expressed in human thought-forms and language. But, they are not equal to the inexhaustible source from whence they spring. Nevertheless, they are inspired by God and suited for His divine purposes. By them God said more than his human instruments could imagine. So, in this sense, God is the true author of the Bible.

Another argument advanced by Wesley, for the divine authorship of the Bible, proceeds on the claim that the Scriptures contain no mistakes or falsehoods, which they would surely possess if written exclusively by men. This line of reasoning was used by Wesley against Soame Jenyns. In August of 1776, Wesley read *INTERNAL EVIDENCE OF THE CHRISTIAN RELIGION* by Jenyns. The author was once a Christian, then an apostate to either Deism or Atheism, and finally a Christian once more. In the tract, Jenyns asserted that the "Scripture is not given by inspiration of God, but the writers of it were sometimes left to themselves, and consequently made some mistakes." Wesley, no doubt, bristled as he retorted, "Nay, if there be any mistakes in the Bible, there may as well be a thousand. If there be one falsehood in that book, it did not come from the God of truth."[28]

It would be a serious mistake to write-off Wesley as a simplistic devotee of the Bible because of this position. Actually he was keenly aware of textual problems in the Bible. He recognized Synoptic differences and other apparent contradictions. Some differences, when rightly understood, occur because of the "intention" of God or the human author - Matthew said, "Blessed are the poor in spirit" and Luke said, "Blessed are ye poor." Though vastly different in meaning, both express the truth of God. More seriously, however, are those differences and contradictions which arise out of corrupted Hebrew and Greek texts, which are copies of copies of original texts. Then too, translators are to blame for some errors in Scripture. The scholar must pick his way through the received texts with prayer and redeemed reason, believing that behind them were original texts that were free from errors, mistakes, and contradictions. But one might ask Wesley, "Since Patristic times who has seen and read an original text from the pen of Paul, Peter, Matthew, Mark Luke, or John? Let alone Moses, David, Baruch, or Ezra?"

However frail this argument may be, it is significant that Wesley recognized and compensated for textual difficulties in the received texts from whence comes many modern translations. Colin Williams has captured the real Wesley at this point - "Wesley was open to textual criticism and was quite sure there were corruptions in the received texts."[29] Wesley occasionally referred to these corruptions as "the glosses of men."

Wesley's final argument for the divine authorship of Scripture is a remarkable bit of creative theologizing - "We believe, indeed, that 'all Scripture is given by inspiration of God;' and herein we are distinguished from Jews, Turks, and Infidels."[30] The Bible, as a means of grace,[31] makes Christians, not Jews, not Turks, nor Infidels. Unless it were inspired, it could not perform this transforming work. In particular, Methodist Christians are Bible Christians in two ways: First, they have been brought to faith in Christ through the Bible as a means of grace; and, secondly, they hold the

Scriptures to be the inspired word of God. For these reasons, Wesley incorporated the affirmation of divinely inspired Scripture into the opening paragraph of his *THE CHARACTER OF A METHODIST*.[32] For the student of Patristics, Ole Borgen notes, "Wesley's celebrated *'THE CHARACTER OF A METHODIST'* was patterned after Clement of Alexandria's drawing of the character of a perfect Christian."[33] (2) While it was true for Wesley that God inspired the Bible, it was equally true that certain men were inspired and wrote the books of Scripture accordingly. In the *EX-PLANATORY NOTES UPON THE NEW TESTAMENT*, Wesley spoke of the need to discover the individual personality of each biblical writer -

> "To understand thoroughly, we should observe the emphasis which lies on every word - the holy affections expressed thereby, and the tempers shown by every writer. But how little are these, the latter especially, regarded! Though they are wonderfully diffused through the whole New Testament, and are in truth a continued commendation of him who acts or speaks or writes."[34]

While inspired by God, the New Testament authors were free to use the vocabulary and literary style peculiar to each. Moreover, the "holy affections" differ from author to author. One of Paul's holy affections (wonderment) emerges in a common device - the question! "Who shall deliver me from the body of this death?"[35] The Apostle John's holy affections radiate through his warm and fatherly writings, "My little children, let us love not in word, neither in tongue; but in deed and in truth."[36] The Wesleyan principle of discovering the "tempers" of biblical authors is a clear indication that divine inspiration did not negate their personalities in any way. Inspiration did not make these persons robots, devoid of thought, will, emotions, or the like. Wesley observed that St. Paul had a temper for boasting,[37] and he defended it as being holy rather than vain.[38] But it was part of Paul, and Paul's alone. Peter, Wesley explained, had the temper to be "forward" and "speak" powerfully, revealing this tendency in his writings.[39] The humble temper of John caused him, in writing his gospel, to avoid "with great care the expressly naming himself."[40] James, the author of the Epistle, showed his temper by mentioning the name of Christ but twice, so that others would not think him vain for being "the brother of the Lord."[41] Jude wrote his short letter with the Second Epistle of Peter "in mind," but "he passes over some things mentioned by St. Peter. . . Thus St. Peter cites and confirms St. Paul's writings, and is himself cited and confirmed by St. Jude."[42] Colin Williams also concludes that this inspiration of authors was not "passive inspiration" but that it "used their memories, accepting traditions not necessarily accurate, and quoted Scripture without exactness."[43] A study of Wesley's *EXPLANATORY NOTES UPON THE NEW TESTAMENT* reveals this situation. (a) "Accepting traditions not necessarily accurate" - Wesley treated Hebrews II, 7 - "Thou hast made him a little lower than the angels." The author of this Epistle used the Greek Septuagint version when quoting from Psalm VIII. Wesley reminded his Methodist readers that the Psalm was originally written in Hebrew and reads correctly as "Thou has made him a little lower than God." Wesley argued that the Hebrew is preferable over the Greek translation, but the author of the Epistle used the inaccurate Greek rendering because his readers disliked the Hebrew idea of man being a little less than God. If the author had used the Hebrew he would "have occasioned disputes without end."[44]

Another "tradition" of dubious accuracy, not found in the Old Testament but only in the New, involves the Old Testament character Enoch. His brief citation in Genesis V states his father's name, that of his son, his length of years, that he walked with God, and that God took him. Two books of the New Testament, Hebrews and Jude, indicate a special prophetic tradition of Enoch which is not implicit in the Genesis account, and John Wesley recognized this fact. In Hebrews XI, 5, Enoch is depicted as having faith and consequently enjoyed a translation into heaven without death - repeated later in biblical history to reward the prophet Elijah, as Wesley noted. This translation established the idea of a prophetic link - Enoch was the first great prophet, and Elijah the second. Wesley, in his commentary on Hebrews I, 1, elaborated on this prophetic theme -

"*God who at sundry times* - the creation was revealed in the time of Adam; the last judgment in the time of Enoch; and so at various times, and in various degrees, more explicit knowledge was given.
In divers manners - in visions, in dreams, and by revelations of various kinds."[45]

As for the inclusion of the prophet Enoch in the Epistle of Jude, the text speaks for itself -

"Enoch the seventh from Adam, prophesied saying, 'Behold, the Lord cometh with ten thousand of his holy ones. To execute judgment upon all, and to convict all the ungodly of all their ungodly deeds which they have impiously committed, and of all the grievous things which ungodly sinners have spoken against him." (Verses 14-15)

Where did Jude get this information about Enoch? Wesley speculated - "St. Jude might know this (about Enoch) either from some ancient book, or tradition, or immediate revelation."[46] Contemporary scholarship recognizes this Enoch tradition as having been popularized in the pseudepigraphal work THE BOOK OF ENOCH, dated by some scholars as early as B.C. 150. Although Wesley could not determine the origin and historical accuracy of the Enoch theme, he recognized that extra-biblical material found its way into the New Testament. Nevertheless, he regarded this inclusion "worthy" of the New Testament.[47] (b) "Quoting Scripture without exactness" - One notable instance of this, cited by Wesley, involves Matthew II, 23 - "And he came and dwelt in a city called Nazareth: that it might be fulfilled which was spoken by the prophets, He shall be called a Nazarene." Wesley quickly claimed that none of the Old Testament prophets "expressly" spoke this prophecy. However, he argued, there are numerous prophetic passages which might suggest Nazareth as the home of the Christ.[48] But, Wesley did not identify such passages. Clearly the gospel author quoted without exactness, and Wesley recognized it.

An interesting passage of similar status, oft debated by the major Protestant reformers, is Matthew XXVII, 9 - "Then was fulfilled that which was spoken by Jeremie the prophet, saying, And they took the thirty pieces of silver, the price of him that was valued, whom they of the children of Israel did value." John Calvin in his *COMMENTARY ON MATTHEW*, simply stated that the writer of Scripture was in error, that Zechariah had prophesied this and not Jeremiah.[49] Wesley, however, argued that the name "Jeremiah" was not in the original copy of the gospel. It was added later by some copyist "and thus received into many translations." Its place in Matthew is "evidently a mistake."[50] Wesley joined Calvin by saying, "For he who spoke what St. Matthew here cites, or rather paraphrases, was not Jeremy, but Zechariah."[51] Wesley cut across the grain of all previous editions of the English Bible, when in the biblical text of his *EXPLANATORY NOTES UPON THE NEW TESTAMENT* he deliberately deleted "Jeremy" from the verse, so that it read, "Then was fulfilled what was spoken by the prophet, saying, And they took. . ."[52] The previous English translations - the Tyndale Bible of 1525, the Great Bible of 1539, the Geneva Bible of 1560, the Bishops' Bible of 1568, the Rheims Bible of 1582, and the King James Bible of 1611 - all identified Jeremiah as the prophet of this passage.[53] As a result, the Methodists were scandalized by Wesley's deletion of Jeremiah from the gospel. Suddenly, with the appearance of his *EXPLANATORY NOTES UPON THE NEW TESTAMENT* in 1754, Wesley was accused by the general public of being a "tamperer" of Scripture.

Before leaving the subject of human agency in the writing of the Bible, an allied concern for Wesley should be examined, that is, the transmission of the Scriptures from one century to the next. As observed earlier, Wesley regarded all mistakes and most contradictions in the Bible to be the result of corruptions by copyists and translators. He was thoroughly familiar with the intricacies of textual glosses and interpolations. He often hypothesized about what must have been contained in the original texts of Moses, of Paul, and of John. He was well-versed in the Hebrew and Greek manuscripts behind the English translations. He studied this textual material while a student at Oxford and later in Georgia where he passionately devoured the *APPARATUS BIBLICUS*.[54] He was not a radical, a destroyer of Scripture. He stood in a long line of

Christian scholars who studied the Bible critically - right back to Clement of Alexandria in the second century. Moreover, textual criticism was being taught at Oxford University long before Gunkel and the German critics ever came upon the scene in the nineteenth century. In studying the Scriptures, Wesley always took the textual considerations into account. Still the Bible remained the word of God for Wesley, clearly showing the way of salvation. It was his "touchstone" whereby he and other Christians might examine all things, real or supposed.[55] God inspired special persons and eternal truth was communicated through the earthen vessels of thought and language. By divine providence, the incarnate truth survives and now those who read it, with prayerful expectation, experience its on-going inspiration.

Wesley's power to summarize concisely and effectively is best demonstrated by his description of the structure and contents of the Old Testament -

> "The Bible or Book, is so called by way of eminency, as it is the best book that ever was written. . . The part of the Bible which we call the Old Testament, contains the acts and monuments of the Church from the creation, almost to the coming of Christ in the flesh, which was about four thousand years; the truths then revealed, the laws enacted, the prophecies given, and the chief events that concerned the Church. This is called a testament or covenant, because it was a declaration of the will of God concerning man in a federal way, and had its force from the designed death of the great testator, the Lamb slain from the foundation of the world. . . 'tis called the Old Testament with relation to the New, which doth not cancel, but crown and perfect it, by bringing in that better hope which was typified and foretold in it."[56]

Wesley was frequently plagued by ignorant zealots who rejected the Old Testament, denying it a place in Scripture. His favorite response to this ill-conceived position recounted Paul's advice to young Timothy to continue living according to the Scriptures that he had known from childhood - "The Scriptures Timothy had known from a child...must have been those of the Old Testament, for the New was not then wrote."[57]

As for the structure and content of the New Testament, Wesley divided it into two sections: (1) The writings of the evangelists and apostles, describing the history of Jesus Christ and the history of the Church; and (2) The book of Revelation - The Apocalypse of Jesus Christ - treating "what will be" with "regard to Christ, the Church, and the universe, till the consummation of all things."[58]

Wesley believed the gospels were written in the same order as they appear in the New Testament - Matthew, Mark, Luke, and John. Mark "presupposes" the gospel of Matthew, and "supplies" what is omitted therein. Luke supplies what is omitted by both the former, and John, what is omitted by all three.[59] More specifically -

> "Matthew particularly points out the fulfilling of the prophecies, for the con-
> viction of the Jews. St. Mark wrote a short compendium and yet added many
> remarkable circumstances omitted by St. Matthew, particularly with regard to
> the apostles, immediately after they were called. St. Luke treated principally
> of the office of Christ, and mostly in the historical manner. St. John refuted
> those who had denied His Godhead; each choosing to treat more largely on
> those things which most suited the time when, and the persons to who he
> wrote."[60]

Most troublesome to serious students are the verse and chapter divisions of the Bible. Wesley often lamented them. Imposed on the biblical books during the Middle Ages, they generally work against effective communication, Wesley argued, "separating things that are closely joined, and joining those that are entirely distinct from each other."[61] Unfortunately, Wesley realized, there is no remedy for this condition. The Christian world has come to think of the chapter and verse divisions as divinely inspired, and no one dares "tamper" with them. Why, some simple souls believe that God himself thinks of the Scriptures only in numerical terms of III, 16 and XIV, 54. Nevertheless, in his *EXPLANATORY NOTES*, Wesley attempted to overcome the inadequacies of the divisions.

Wishing to rescue the minds of his Methodist followers from the simplistic biblicism that was so rampant in England, Wesley published two sets of commentaries, *EXPLANATORY NOTES UPON THE OLD TESTAMENT* and *EXPLANATORY NOTES UPON*

THE NEW TESTAMENT. The latter was published first, and its Preface is dated January 4, 1754.[62] The results were amazing, although corrections were needed immediately. In a short time, Wesley responded to the demand for a commentary on the Old Testament. This was a gargantuan undertaking, consuming vast amounts of time and energy. At long last, he published his *EXPLANATORY NOTES UPON THE OLD TESTAMENT* on April 25, 1765.[63]

Actually, Wesley did not write these commentaries. Knowing his limitations, he wisely chose to abridge the works of pious Bible scholars, incorporating some of his own material into theirs. For the Old Testament, he began by using the famous commentary of Matthew Henry, a seventeenth century Puritan divine. Wesley, however, made considerable modifications, making Henry's work "shorter and plainer" and stripping it of its theological emphasis on "unconditional predestination." He also purged it of "particular redemption" and its "too learned" terminology.[64] He even altered key words and expressions used by Henry. While Henry had said, "God feeds His birds," Wesley changed that to "God feeds His babes." In another place, Wesley changed "Pharaoh's princes" to Pharaoh's "pimps."[65]

After Wesley got well into the Old Testament, he forsook Matthew Henry's commentary and turned to Pool's *ANNOTATIONS.*[66] He still found it necessary to add his own material to the abridgement of Pool as he had done with Henry - "I...found it needful to add to both such farther observations, as from time to time have occurred to my own mind in reading or thinking on the Scriptures, together with facts I have occasionally extracted from other authors."[67]

Wesley's purpose in offering the *EXPLANATORY NOTES UPON THE OLD TESTAMENT* to his Methodist followers is clearly stated in the Preface -

"Every thinking man will now easily discern my design in the following sheets. It is not, to write sermons, essays, or set discourses, upon any part of the Scripture. It is not to draw inferences from the text, or to show what doctrines may be proved thereby. It is this: To give the direct, literal meaning of every verse, of every sentence, and as far as I am able, of every word in the oracles of God. I design only, like the hands of a dial, to point every man to this: not to take up his mind with something else, how excellent soever: but to keep his eye fixt upon the naked Bible, that he may read and hear it with understanding."[68]

The "*direct, literal meaning*" of the Bible was Wesley's highest goal and greatest challenge. His concept of "taking the Bible literally" meant a number of things: Is the passage historical in nature? If so, treat it as such and do not make it allegorical. Is the passage poetical? If so, do not force a dogmatic cast upon it. Is the passage wisdom literature? If so, do not erect a systematic theology from it. Is the passage apocalyptical? If so, do not neglect other such passages, and, above all, avoid a private interpretation.

But, there are other steps to Wesley's "literal" meaning of Scripture. In addition to those above, one must consider the authorship of the passage - identity, personality traits and tempers, gifts and talents, intention in writing, literary skill, and whatever else may be known about him from the Bible. What was the time and occasion for writing the passage? Who were the recipients? What historical and cultural phenomena affect the passage? What is the general context surrounding the passage? What language was it written in, and what semantical and syntactical features exist? How does this passage compare with others that treat the same subject? What is the history of the "received text" of this passage? How did Christian scholars of antiquity treat this passage? This is the method Wesley employed to find the "literal" meaning of the Bible. The Church needs more "literalism" of this sort.

For his *EXPLANATORY NOTES UPON THE NEW TESTAMENT*, Wesley relied heavily upon the *GNOMON NOVI TESTAMENTI* of Bengelius,[69] or Johann Albrecht Bengel as he was known in Germany. Of this scholar Wesley said, "(He is) the most pious, the most judicious and the most laborious, of all the modern commentators on the New Testament,"[70] and more pious than the fabled Bishop Newton.[71] In the planning stage for the *EXPLANATORY NOTES UPON THE NEW TESTAMENT*, Wesley considered using only his own knowledge of the biblical text, then he read Bengelius. From then onward, he was convinced that the better course would be an abridgement of the *GNOMON NOVI TESTAMENTI*, with a few of his comments added here and there.[72] But, Wesley found value in the commentaries of two other writers, John Heylyn and Philip Doddridge, and blended in material from the *THEOLOGICAL LECTURES* and *THE FAMILY EXPOSITOR* of these two men respectively.[73]

The purpose for Wesley's commentary on the New Testament was clearly practical -

> "I have endeavoured to make the notes as short as possible, that the comment may not obscure or swallow up the text; and as plain as possible, in pursuance of my main design, to assist the unlearned reader. For this reason I have studiously avoided, not only all curious and critical inquiries, and all use of the learned languages, but all such methods of reasoning and modes of expression as people in common life are unacquainted with. For the same reason as I rather endeavour to obviate than propose and answer objections, so I purposely decline going deep into many difficulties, lest I should leave the ordinary reader behind me."[74]

That Wesley should choose this course for these NOTES is significant. Rather than stressing his own erudition, he desired to impart the "basics" or "first principles" of the Bible message for the spiritual benefit of common folk. *The EXPLANATORY NOTES UPON THE NEW TESTAMENT*, then, is not a means for discovering the deep, scholarly biblicism of John Wesley. At best, the work is like a Tillichian sign that points to the reality without actually participating in it. And yet, there are some passages which rise above the level of "common people." For instance, Wesley's treatment of the Apocalypse, as we shall see in detail in a later chapter, certainly needs the preparation of a scholar to understand.

In summarizing the importance of these two Wesleyan commentaries, Ole Borgen rightly observes - "As Wesley constantly claims Scripture as his basic authority, these Notes on the two testaments must be considered central and of importance for any evaluation of Wesley's theology as well as of his practice."[75]

The biblicism of Wesley featured a strong emphasis upon the original languages of Scripture, Hebrew and Greek. Wesley held that these languages are "the very languages of God" -

> "Is it (Hebrew) not the language which God Himself used? And is not Greek too the language God Himself used? And did He not use it in delivering to man a far more perfect dispensation than that he delivered in Hebrew? Who can deny it? And does not even this consideration give us reason at least to suspect that the Greek language is as far superior to the Hebrew as the New Testament is to the Old?" [76]

Old Testament Hebrew was always fascinating to Wesley. He began its study as a ten year old student at Charterhouse, continued it at Oxford University, and used it systematically until his vision failed him late in life. On January 20, 1747, he was visited by a scholar named Bland, who wished Wesley's opinion concerning the vowel points of Hebrew. Bland held that the points "are absolutely essential" to the language, and that they are older than Ezra the Scribe, and that they were probably given to Moses by God at Mount Sinai. [77] Bland's argument was a reaction to one advanced by John Hutchinson. In a scholarly article, Hutchinson theorized that the Hebrew vowel points were not as ancient as generally supposed, only thirteen or fourteen centuries old at best. He concluded that biblical Hebrew was written only with consonants. [78] A furor arose immediately because of Hutchinson's views. Bland was not the only dissenter - there were many. The controversy lasted for years. Wesley was noncommittal at first, but, as time advanced, he finally agreed with Bland in 1785. His conversion to this position came in stages. In the autumn of 1756, he read Leusden's *DISSERTATION IN DEFENCE OF THE HEBREW POINTS*, and he realized that both sides in the controversy had strong arguments. However, the problem for Wesley was that historical evidence was scanty and theoretical reasoning should never settle such an important issue. So, he kept the arguments in suspension, not closing his mind to the one side or the other. [79] The next May, Wesley read Whitefield's *DISSERTATION IN DEFENCE OF THE HEBREW POINTS*. Whitefield offered more than theory, and Wesley responded positively - "(It) is far more satisfactory than anything which I have ever heard or read upon the subject."[80] By 1785, Wesley announced to the world that he agreed with Bland, Leusden, and Whitefield, and that he disagreed with Hutchinson and his followers - "I believe Ezra if not Moses (wrote) with points."[81]

There were other controversies involving the Old Testament Hebrew that caught Wesley's attention. One treated the origin and development of the language. Was the Hebrew originally a tribal language, with its own evolutionary development? To the traditionalists, and perhaps Wesley, such a question was horrid and bordered on blasphemy. As noted above, Wesley was convinced that Hebrew was a divine language, being used by the eternal God. It was the tongue used by God in the Garden of Eden when he first addressed Adam. Indeed, Wesley thought, it was the *lingua franca* of mankind until the Tower of Babel brought other languages. How then could it start with a small Semite tribe and evolve into a sophisticated literary language? The traditionalists held that Hebrew was a sophisticated, literary language at the very beginning of creation and needed no evolution. As time passed, Wesley became more convinced of this. In September 1781, Parson's book, *REMAINS OF JAPHETH*, came into Wesley's hands. He read it with great enthusiasm because it examined this problem in great detail. The book traced Hebrew from creation to Babel, as the only language. After the dispersion of mankind at Babel, only the sons of Shem retained the original language, while the sons of Ham and Japheth spoke new and inferior languages. Whatever changes took place in the original Hebrew since then accounts for the many dialects of the Semitic family.[82] Wesley accepted this explanation by Parsons, whom he regarded as "very ingenious" and one who had "struck light into some of the darkest parts of ancient history."[83]

Another dimension of Old Testament linguistics, important to Wesley, was the Septuagint, a Greek translation, the earliest parts of which were made in B.C. 282 in Alexandria, Egypt. The term "septuagint" means "seventy" and refers to the number of translators who worked on it. The Roman numerals LXX are often used as an abbreviation. The translation presented Wesley with a problem. He was convinced that it was a poor translation, but "it should be remembered that the apostles constantly cited the Septuagint ...very frequently without any variation."[84]

As early as 1730, Wesley was critical of the Septuagint's integrity. He imbibed the skepticism of his father at this point, as shown in the text of this letter to his parents -

"December 11, 1730 ...I breakfasted today with a great admirer of the Septuagint, who was much surprised to hear that anyone should charge them with want of integrity, and seemed to think that the charge could not be made out. Nay, he went so far as even to assert that he took this Greek to be more faultless than our present Hebrew copy. I wish I had had one or two of the places you mention at hand, and I would have given him them to chew upon."[85]

The "great admirer" was Emanuel Langford of Christ Church College, an associate two years younger than Wesley.[86]

In the writing of his *EXPLANATORY NOTES UPON THE OLD THE TESTAMENT*, John Wesley treated Psalm VIII, 5 in an interesting fashion. The biblical text above the commentary was from the King James Version of 1611, which relied on the LXX, causing the verse to read, "For Thou has made him a little lower than the angels." In his commentary, however, Wesley hastened to correct an inaccuracy - "the words more literally rendered are, 'Thou madest him a little less than God.'" The source of Wesley's authority for this correction was the Hebrew text wherein man is made lower than "Elohim" (God).[87] In his NOTES on the New Testament, where the author of the Epistle to the Hebrews quoted this verse from Psalms in chapter II, Wesley corrected the apostolic author for following the Septuagint instead of the Hebrew.[88] Whatever Old Testament passage is under consideration, he argued, it is best understood from the Hebrew text and not the Greek translation. While it is true that he once stated, "The Greek language is as far superior to the Hebrew as the New Testament is to the Old," he did not mean that the Hebrew of the Old Testament should be replaced by the Greek Septuagint. For Wesley the message of the Old Testament is best given in Hebrew, and the message of the New Testament is best given in Greek. He never turned from this conviction.

On August 29, 1787, he read Archbishop Usher's LETTERS, and he learned that the LXX "continually adds to, takes from, and changes the Hebrew text at pleasure."[89] He became convinced by Usher that the numerous alterations of the Septuagint were made deliberately by its translators, and, consequently, they were not simple "mistakes." Other alterations were made by copyists. What now passes as the LXX, Wesley maintained, is "a spurious copy, abounding with omissions, additions, and alterations of the Hebrew text."[90] Providentially, however, these are "not such as anyway destroy the foundation."[91] For this reason - providence protecting the foundation of Scripture in translations - the apostles were able to quote from the Septuagint.

The Greek New Testament, as Wesley knew and loved it, deserves some attention here. It was his favorite book during his stay in Georgia.[92] His energetic preaching campaign, after Aldersgate, featured frequent citations of Hebrew and Greek -"the original Scripture."[93] While he scaled down erudition in these evangelical sermons, he did not give up mentioning the meaning of Hebrew and Greek words and phrases. A serious study of his sermons reveals the importance he placed upon Greek in particular. For instance, he quoted from the Greek New Testament in the following sermons: *The Almost Christian*;[94] *Scriptural Christianity*;[95] *Justification by Faith*;[96] *The Way to the Kingdom*;[97] *The First Fruits of the Spirit*;[98] *The Spirit of Bondage and Adoption*;[99] *The Witness of the Spirit* (Discourse I);[100] *The Witness of Spirit* (Discourse II);[101] *The Witness of Our Own Spirit*;[102] *Sin in Believers*;[103] *The Great Assize*;[104] *The Means of Grace*;[105] *Marks of the New Birth*;[106] *The Privilege of Those Who are Born of God*;[107] *The Lord Our Righteousness*;[108] *Sermon on the Mount* (Discourse I);[109] *Sermon on the Mount* (Discourse II);[110] *Sermon on the Mount* (Discourse III);[111] *Sermon on the Mount* (Discourse IV);[112] *Sermon on the Mount* (Discourse V);[113] *Sermon on the Mount* (Discourse VI);[114] *Sermon on the Mount* (Discourse VII);[115] *Sermon on the Mount* (Discourse VIII);[116] *Sermon on the Mount* (Discourse X);[117] *Sermon on the*

Mount (Discourse XI);[118] *Caution Against Bigotry;*[119] and *The Catholic Spirit.*[120] This list does not, however, exhaust the subject for there are many other sermons that could be cited.

The commentary part of the *EXPLANATORY NOTES UPON THE NEW TESTAMENT* is heavily laced with material from the Greek New Testament. While the biblical text above the commentary is essentially that of the King James translation, Wesley frequently altered it to bring it into closer agreement with the original Greek. One such alteration involved the word "charity" in I Corinthians XIII. "Charity" was chosen by the translators of 1611 because it reflected St. Augustine's *charitas*, which meant "rightly ordered love." But, Wesley held, no reader of the English Bible understands charity to mean that. Consequently, he changed "charity" in Corinthians to "love" because the Greek used *agape*, or "self-sacrificing love."[121] Curiously, Wesley seldom quoted the original Greek in the New Testament NOTES, as he did in his sermons. Instead, he usual noted that "the Greek for this means..." In his commentary on St. John I, 42, where Jesus gives Simon a new name, Wesley said, "Cephas, which is Peter - meaning the same in Syriac which Peter does in Greek, namely, a rock."[122] His definitions of terms in the commentary, and the arguments, were generally straight from the Greek.

John and Charles Wesley compiled their own Greek text, working through great numbers of ancient manuscripts of the various New Testament books. While the Erasmus compilation was the standard among biblical scholars, the Wesleys were not satisfied with it. It had been good enough for Martin Luther, but not for John Wesley. The Wesley Greek text was completed in 1759 and immediately incorporated into a new edition of the *EXPLANATORY NOTES UPON THE NEW TESTAMENT.*[123]

How could John Wesley, with this biblical background, ever be content with any translation of the Bible? The answer is simple - He was not satisfied with any of them. However, he admitted, some are better than others, but none is perfect. In the Preface to the New Testament NOTES, he stated emphatically -

"I design first, to set down the text itself, for the most part, to the common English translation, which is, in general, so far as I can judge, abundantly the best that I have seen. Yet I do not say it is incapable of being brought, in several places, nearer to the original. Neither will I affirm that the Greek copies from which this translation was made are always the most correct; and therefore I shall take the liberty, as occasion may require, to make here and there a small alteration."[124]

The "common English translation" was the King James version of 1611. By Wesley's day it had become generally accepted after a controversial beginning. As for alterations, Wesley employed three rules: (1) They should never be made for alterings sake; (2) They should only be made where the sense is made better, stronger, clearer, or more consistent with the context; and (3) They should only be made when the sense, being equally good, the new phrase is better or nearer the original.[125]

A persistent theme throughout Wesley's writings is a somber criticism of the King James translation, although generally it was the best translation of the Bible he had ever seen. One particular passage of it which vexed him was Psalm LXXIV, 12. While preaching on this text, on September 14, 1785, he attacked the translators for issuing such a poor rendition -

"In the *Old* translation it runs, 'The help that is done on earth, God doeth it himself.' A glorious and important truth! In the *New*, 'Working salvation in the midst of the earth.' What a wonderful emendation! Many such emendations there are in this translation: One would think that King James had made them himself!"[126]

Other translations are faulty too, propagating mistakes which mislead even "men of education and learning. Thousands are misled thereby."[127] Wesleyan congregations, therefore, need to be instructed so no Methodist is ever victimized by Bible translations. Wesley was committed to this ministry.

When Anthony Purvis, a close friend of Wesley, published his *A NEW AND LITERAL TRANSLATION OF ALL THE BOOKS OF THE OLD AND NEW TESTAMENT, WITH CRITICAL AND*

EXPLANATORY (in two volumes), in 1764, Wesley was not elated. He had read the work years earlier in 1745 and thought it was "dead" then. The years of polishing the translation for publication were not enough to bring it to life. Purvis did more than "think" his way through the work. He spent many days fasting and praying before translating difficult passages.[128] When pressed by Purvis for a critique, Wesley wrote - "I found the text flat and dead; much altered indeed, but commonly for the worst; and the notes merely critical, dull, and dry, without any unction, or spirit, or life,"[129] Such is the fate of any translation of the entire Bible that is the work of one person.

Translations may be tested for effective communication of God's message. One of Wesley's methods of testing was linguistic in nature. An illustration of this involved the use of I Corinthian XIII.[130] A good translation will render the Greek *agape* as "love" and a poor one as "charity." Cataloging the English translations accordingly, omitting the Roman Catholic Rheims version, Wesley noted that the Tyndale Bible (the first English translation), and those under the reigns of Edward VI, Queen Elizabeth, King James I, and King Charles I, all originally translated *agape* as "love." However, "those printed by Roger Daniel and John Field, printers to the Parliament, in the year 1649," changed it to "charity."[131] Despite this, however, Wesley habitually used the Field translation for his out-of-doors preaching. He referred to it as the "Small Field's Bible." This was not a King James Bible. It was published to honor Oliver Cromwell, who received one copy bound in heavily chased silver as the nation's gift to its Protector. Consequently, the translation became very popular, but, alas, popularity brings poor imitations! By Wesley's day many volumes of the bible were printed under the title *THE FIELDS BIBLE* (Small Edition), but they were not. Preaching to an "uncommon congregation" near Bristol in 1782, Wesley offered this help in identifying a real FIELDS BIBLE - "Permit me to observe here how you may distinguish a genuine Small Fields Bible from a spurious one: The genuine one reads here, 'Ye *can* serve God and Mammon.' In the spurious one 'not' is supplied."[132] But (*alla* in Greek, meaning a radical "but"), Wesley was wrong, dead wrong, at this point. Nehemiah Curnock rightly observed, "Wesley is in error. Quoting from memory, he forgets that in a genuine Small Fields Bible it is the word 'God' that is omitted."[133]

What place, if any, did the Apocrypha have in Wesley's biblicism? A mixed one. The young Wesley in Georgia identified his favorite apocryphal passage as *THE SONG OF THE THREE CHILDREN*. It had been so since his first days at Oxford.[134] It is hard to believe that he ever discarded this affection since the the-ology of the song was consistent with his mature thought. However, Wesley regarded the Apocrypha to be less than Scripture, mainly because the Jewish Church had earlier judged it so.[135] Esdras, To-bit, Judith, Ecclesiasticus, Baruch, I and II Maccabees, and a new part of Esther and Daniel were written "after prophecy and divine inspiration ceased, and so were not received by the Jewish Church... nor by the Christian Church as the sixtieth canon of the Council of Laodicea shows, where there is a catalog of the canonical books, without any mention of these."[136] While Wesley quoted from the Apocrypha, from time to time,[137] he gave it no authority in matters of faith and practice. It may show minor principles of truth, such as "honor the physician," but that is all. By maintaining this position, Wesley continued in the Reformed Tradition of *sola scriptura*.

Comparative study of the Bible was an important tool for discovering all the connections of truth a passage might yield. It was one of Wesley's indispensible tools. After applying the guidelines for finding the "literal meaning" of a passage, the Christian pilgrim must be certain that his understanding "be not contrary to some other text." Hence, comparing Scripture with Scripture. If other passages parallel the studied one, the obscure one must "be interpreted by those which speak more plainly."[138] The basis for this principle is quite simple -"Scripture is the best expounder of it-self."[139] Wesley linked "reason" with this comparative tool. The use of reason, he argued, brings analysis, discovery of relationships, and, most importantly, synthesis. Wesley took as his chief mission with his Methodist disciples "to make them think, and assist them in thinking.   This is the way to understanding the things of God: 'Meditate thereon day and night.'"[140]

"To make them think." Immortal words! Reason - redeemed reason - is to be an integral part of scriptural interpretation. Wesley saw a universal gift of "reason" being imparted to all mankind by virtue of Christ's atonement. Hence, he concluded, "We are reasonable creatures, and undoubtedly reason is the Candle of the Lord. By enlightening our reason to see the meaning of Scripture, the Holy Spirit makes our way plain before us."[141]   Moreover, he continued, "to renounce reason is to renounce religion."[142] "Reason" is not the same as "proof-texting." Wesley was never a proof-texter.[143]   Reason finds the setting of texts in their proper contexts. It finds the proper place of contexts in the whole Bible. It explores the linguistic dimensions of semantics and syntactics. It discovers the historical environment of text and passage. It roots out the facts of authorship, time and occasion for having been written, the author's intention, and the history of its interpretation within the Church. Rhetorically Wesley asked, "Is it not reason (assisted by the Holy Ghost) which enables us to understand what the Holy Scriptures declare concerning the being and attributes of God? - concerning his eternity and immensity; his power, wisdom, and holiness?" His query continued, "Is it not by reason that God enables us by some measure to comprehend his method of dealing with the children of men; the nature of his various dispensations, of the old and new covenant, of the law and gospel?"[144]

Wesley added another interpretive tool to his exegetical method - the primary meaning of Scripture should be confirmed in experience.[145]   He came to embrace this principle late in the Spring of 1738, after numerous interviews with the Moravian Peter Bohler.[146]   At first confused by Bohler's insistence that religious experience confirms Scripture, Wesley turned to reading the Bible as he always had, comparing passage with passage -"endeavouring to illustrate the obscure by the plainer" - but he seemed denied any comprehension or satisfaction.[147]   Bohler, Wesley concluded, was apparently right. Bohler then produced three Moravian witnesses who testified to Wesley how Scripture comes alive in the experience of grace. Wesley began to seek this confirming experience, but with what he termed "a strange indifference." May 24 came as a day of scriptural confirmations. In the early morning, Wesley threw open his Bible and his eyes fell upon the words of St. Peter - "There are given to us exceeding great and precious promises. . ." Later, the words of Jesus came from the opened book. "Thou art not far from the kingdom. . ." Then, at St. Paul's Cathedral in London, he heard a Psalm sung, "Out of the deep have I called unto Thee, O Lord." In the evening he went to the Bible Society in Aldersgate Street. It was during the reading of Luther's preface to Romans that Wesley came to believe that the message of Scripture was now confirmed in his life.[148] From then onward, he was sympathetic to confirming religious experience in regard to the Bible's theme of salvation. Such confirmation, he affirmed, is God's work of grace - "We know there is no power in the words that are spoken in prayer, in the letter of Scripture read, the sound thereof heard. . . but that it is God alone who is the Giver of every good gift, the author of all grace; that the whole power is of Him, whereby. . . there is any blessing conveyed to our souls."[149]

While John Wesley insisted upon the confirming experience of Scripture, he was realistic enough to recognize that not every passage of Scripture needs a confirming experience by the Holy Spirit to bring understanding. One does not have to enter the belly of Jonah's fish to appreciate his prayer. One does not have to ascend to the highest heaven to understand that God is there, nor into Sheol to exclaim, "Thou art there!" Historical passages speak quite clearly of understandable events which present no crisis for soul or mind. The Scripture that lends itself to confirming experience is that which is primary, relating to salvation and progressive revelation for the ethical living of holiness. In this sense, Wesley was a cautious existentialist, reminding his Methodists that "we are no more to expect any living man to be infallible, than to be omniscient."[150]

The eighteenth century, however, had many religious personalities who regarded themselves as infallible by virtue of religious experiences they had enjoyed. Some related their full and flawless knowledge of the Bible. Others, like Robert Barclay, claimed infallibility through religious experiences without the Bible. His visions and mystical revelations transcended the Scriptures. In writing to Barclay (February 10, 1748), Wesley struck the difference between Barclay's Quaker faith and the Christian faith - "Here there is a difference. The Scriptures are the touchstone whereby Christians examine all, real or supposed, and try every spirit thereby."[151] Wesley argued that there can be no experience of grace, wrought by the divine Spirit, which transcends the Scriptures. In our day, Bishop Stokes has aptly phrased this same point - "Christian experience is not the final basis for Christian doctrine. Only the Bible is that basis. But experience confirms what Scripture teaches."[152]

The principle that "the Scriptures are the touchstone whereby Christians examine all," captures the whole spirit and letter of Wesley's being *homo unius libri.* Reason and confirming experience enable one to understand the basic meaning of the Bible, but they are not substitutes for Scripture, nor are they on an equal footing with the Bible. It is only in conjunction with Scripture that they have an authority, and that authority is granted by the divine author of the Bible.

Another interpretive tool for understanding the Scriptures, for Wesley, was the Ante-Nicene Fathers of the Church. In addition to the Scripture itself, reason, and confirming experience, Wesley said, "I regard no authorities but those of the Ante-Nicene Fathers; nor any of them in opposition to Scripture."[153] These spiritual leaders of the primitive Church were important to Wesley because of their closeness to the times of Jesus and his apostles. Moreover, their knowledge of the original faith and life of the early Church is invaluable to the Church of later generations.[154] In the preface to his EPISTLES OF THE APOSTOLIC FATHERS, Wesley stated -

"The authors of the following collection were contemporaries of the holy apostles, one of them bred under our Lord Himself, and the others well instructed by those great men whom he commissioned to go forth and teach all nations. We cannot therefore doubt, but what they delivered to us is the pure doctrine of the Gospel; what Christ and His apostles taught, and what these holy men had themselves received from their own mouths. . . having here the writings of men who had attained to so perfect a knowledge of the mystery of godliness, as to be judged worthy by the Apostles themselves to be overseers of the great churches of Rome, Antioch, and Smyrna; we cannot with any reason doubt of what they deliver to us as the Gospel of Christ; but ought to receive it, though not with equal veneration, yet with only little less regard than we do the sacred writings of those who were their masters and instructors."[155]

Wesley insisted that the writings of these men "ought" to be received, "though not with equal veneration" to Scripture. These works add much to our understanding of the Bible, making explicit what may be only implicit in many scriptural passages. Wesley's list of Ante-Nicene Fathers included Clement of Rome, Ignatius, Polycarp, Justin Martyr, Irenaeus, Clement of Alexandria, Origen, Cyprian, Macarius, and Ephraim Syrus.[156] Wesley maintained that these authors were "endued with the extraordinary assistance of the Holy Spirit."[157] Nevertheless, this assistance did not make their writings equal to the Scriptures. In fact, where they might be found in contradiction with the Bible, Wesley would quickly reject them.[158]

In 1771, Wesley completed the revision of his WORKS, and, in his brief address to the readers, he concluded - "So that in this edition I present to serious and candid men my last and maturest thoughts, agreeable, I hope, to Scripture, reason, and Christian antiquity."[159] It is extremely important that Wesley did not include "experience" as part of his "last and maturest thoughts." Bishop Borgen, however, argues that Wesley retained it in his four-fold practicum of authority.[160]

To the novice in theology such a system of authority must seem unnecessary and bewildering. However, as the history of the Church has proven, such systems come into being because of the occurrence of bewildering controversies. Some boundaries must be set, some authoritative standards struck or every thinker will be left adrift in a sea of subjectivity, and the Church must be something more than a boundless sea full of desperate and lonely sailors. Then too, the Church can only be the Church when some continuity of reality exists in faith, practice, and in the imitation of Christ in sacrificial mission. In the history of the Western Church, there are three basic systems of authority. Colin Williams identifies them accordingly: (1) The Catholic view which stresses not only Scripture but also the continual emergence of church tradition by way of decisions of councils, and additions of creedal and liturgical forms - the Church being the final authority in matters of faith and orders: (2) In Classical Protestantism the view of authority emphasizes the Living Word of God as recorded in the Scripture as the final authority; and (3) While in the "Free Church" tradition the "tendency is to shift the ultimate seat of authority to the living voice of the Holy Spirit spoken to true believers."[161] Williams argues correctly that Wesley stood in the Classical Protestant position by continually subjecting tradition and experience to the "written Word of God" as any casual reader of Wesley can attest.[162] Bishop Borgen, states the case another way - "It has been said that the principles of the Lutheran Reformation were the Bible and private judgement; and of the English Reformation the Bible and the Primitive Church. . . Wesley's principles actually include all three."[163] The result is Wesley's clear embracing of the Reformation doctrine of *sola scriptura*, with the final authority in Scripture in matters of faith and practice. For this reason, Williams concludes -

> "Wesley must be placed with the Reformers in this principle of *sola scriptura*, in the sense that Scripture is the final authority in matters of faith and practice; not in the sense that tradition and experience have no value, but in the sense that these further sources of insight must be congruous with the revelation recorded in the Scripture."[164]

Wesley's biblicism must be examined in one more area before we enter the main body of this work. In his view the Bible and the Church enjoy a special relationship. He was forever irritated by the Roman Church's subjugation of Scripture to the Church. He often treated this complaint in his writings. In one particular place he wrote -

"... it is a known principle of the Church of England, that nothing is to be received as an article of faith, which is not read in the Holy Scriptures, or to be inferred therefrom by just and plain consequences. Hence it follows, that every Christian has a right to read and know the Scripture, that he may be sure what he hears from his teachers agrees with the revealed word of God. On the contrary, at the very beginning of the Reformation, the Church of Rome began to oppose this principle, that all articles of faith must be provable from Scripture... and to add, if not prefer, to Holy Scripture, tradition, or the doctrine of the Fathers and Councils, with the decrees of popes. And soon after she determined in the Council of Trent, 'That the Old and New Testament, and the traditions of the Church, ought to be received pari pietatis affectu ac reverentia, 'with equal piety and reverence;' and that 'it suffices for laymen if they believe and practice what the Church believes and requires, whether they understand the ground of that doctrine or not.'"[165]

What were the specific doctrines of the Roman Church that Wesley believed were founded on an authority other than Scripture? He answered - "Transubstantiation... the seven sacraments. . . purgatory. . . half communion. . . worshipping of saints and images. . . and service in an unknown tongue."[166] Because of their extra-biblical origin, Wesley rejected them all, saying - "For as all faith is founded upon divine authority, so there is now no divine authority but the Scriptures; and, therefore, no one can make that to be of divine authority which is not contained in them."[167]

Wesley knew the full Roman argument - Since the Church produced the Scripture in the first place, it reserves the right to judge what is Scripture and how to interpret it, giving it whatever place within the life of the Church it deems best. By this control, the laity are kept from misunderstanding the Bible. So, Wesley summarized, "since the Scripture may be misunderstood. . . 'It belongs to the Church. . . to judge of the sense of Scripture, and no one may presume to interpret the Scripture contrary to the sense which Mother Church hath held and doth hold.'"[168] His Anglican viewpoint caused Wesley to turn the argument around - "As long as we have the Scripture, the Church is to be referred to the Scriptures, and not the Scripture to the Church."[169] Putting it more bluntly - The Scripture is to judge the Church and not *vice versa*.[170] In a surprising exhortation, Wesley admonished his readers - "Surely, it is high time now that we should be guided, not by custom, but by Scripture and reason."[171] What became of the Fathers? What of confirming experience?

The importance of the ecumenical councils of the Roman Church to that tradition is well known. Since Wesley believed that Scripture was often trampled on by various councils, he felt obliged to attack the credibility of many of these ecclesiastical gatherings. We have already noted his attack on the Council of Trent (A.D. 1545-1563) for its subjugation of the Bible to proliferating Church tradition. While a student at Oxford University, Wesley studied the history of the Church and continued the study while in Georgia. In September 1736, at Savannah, he read with seriousness Bishop Beveridge's *PANDECTAE CANONUM CONCILIORUM.* This work, more than any other, convinced him that church councils may err and indeed have erred, and that there is "an infinite difference" between "the decisions of the wisest men" at councils and "those of the Holy Ghost recorded in His word." Consequently, the things legislated at councils as necessary for salvation "have neither strength nor authority unless they be taken out of Holy Scripture."[172] Moreover, Wesley discovered, the history of the councils is scandalous. "How has one council been perpetually cursing another, and delivering all over to Satan, whether predecessors or contemporaries, who did not implicitly receive their determinations, though generally trifling, sometimes false, and frequently unintelligible or self-contradictory."[173] One needs only to remember the Great Schism and the Conciliar Movement in the early fifteenth century to appreciate Beveridge's evaluation and Wesley's subsequent lack of faith in the councils of the Church. To his dying day, Wesley believed that councils produce no valid authority *extra scriptura*.

Several quotations from Wesley on the Bible deserve the attention of every Methodist Christian -

"My ground is the Bible. . . I follow it in all things great and small."[174]

"The Bible is the whole and sole rule of Christian faith and practice."[175]

"Might it not be well. . . to spend at least two hours every day, in reading and meditating upon the Bible? . . .If you would. . . be assisted in thinking, add the 'Explanatory Notes.'"[176]

"I design only, like the hands of a dial, to point every man to this: not to take up his mind with something else, how excellent so ever; but to keep his eye fixed on the naked Bible, that he may read and hear it with understanding."[177]

In certain circles of eighteenth century England, Wesley's reputation was summarized by such terms as "enthusiast" - "Bible Moth" - "Bible Bigot" and worse. However distasteful these designations might have been to others, he seemed to enjoy them, especially the "Bible Bigot" label. He unequivocally embraced it - "My ground is the Bible. Yea, I am a Bible-bigot. I follow it in all things, both great and small."[178] Indeed, he did! He read the Bible, searched its passages, memorized large portions of it, studied it critically so he could distinguish the "glosses of men" from the "word of God," meditated upon its truths both day and night, preached only on its explicit themes, wrote commentaries and treatises upon it, lectured on its simplicities and its profundities, sang its sweet psalms and hymns, prayed its great prayers, related all recognized knowledge to its fundamental truths, and lived its highest revealed ethics as instituted by Christ. He did not keep the vibrant Bible to himself. He could not do that. He dared not do that. His destiny and mission were one - to spread Bible religion everywhere. He knew that Methodism had the same calling - "We are called to propagate Bible religion through the land; that is, faith working by love; holy tempers and holy lives. Let us do it with our might!"[179] This kind of bigotry might better be called "enlightened zeal."

John Wesley did not regard the Bible magically, as if it had a great inherent power all its own in each word.[180] His employing of bibliomancy - the sudden opening of the Bible and taking the first verse read as a special message from God - was not an habitual practice, in spite of the fact that he did it twice on May 24, 1738, under the temporary spell of the Moravians. Nowhere in sermons, treatises, or letters did Wesley teach or advise the use of bibliomancy. He saw no virtue in it. Instead, he urged the systematic study of Scripture and not the haphazard opening of it. He knew from his encounter with it that there are too many variables involved for it to be God's means of conveying guidance. For one thing, it makes a difference how the binding of a Bible naturally divides, or divides by the reader's habit of reading. The reader, who for years habitually reads Psalms, may expect his Bible to part in Psalms. Then too, where should the reader look on the page? To the right or left, high or low? The first column or the second? What divine message is imparted when one turns to the Preface dedicated to King James I? Or the title page of the New Testament - The maps or concordances of more modern Bibles? Wesley knew that bibliomancy is more mechanical in nature than revelatory, being subject mostly to chance rather than God's distinct guidance. Moreover, if bibliomancy has any validity, then scriptural meaning must be either by chance or magic, and then the "literal meaning" must be totally meaningless.

Wesley desired his followers to use the Bible as he used it. The Methodist pilgrim should accept it as "his rule of right and wrong, of whatever is really good or evil." The "good" is what is scripturally "enjoined" either "directly or by plain consequence."[182] The pilgrim must learn to "enjoin" what is "enjoined" and "condemn" what is "condemned." However, Wesley warned, "It is sinful to condemn anything which Scripture does not condemn."[183] By setting forth this last principle, he was determined to have a "progressive" Methodist movement, one that could accept the advances of modernity without condemning the new for being new. It was an age of enlightenment, and the new science was discovering truth that long had been obscured by false notions of truth. Electricity, for instance, as Wesley discovered by his experiments,[184] could be used in the medical treatment of heart patients - Let no one condemn such advances! However, not all the proclaimed "new" is really new. Wesley, the historian, knew this. Old vices have strange ways of being revived, then being termed "new." Methodists, he believed, should never condemn the truly new, but it must beware of an old wolf disguised as a new lamb. One may well ask, Would Wesley be satisfied with contemporary Methodism's commitment to modernity?

In order to assist Methodists in maintaining a balance between the Bible and on-rushing modernity, Wesley urged his followers to be proficient students of the Bible first and then other subject areas. He insisted that "a reading people will always be a knowing people." But, "a people who talk much will know little."[185] For this reason, he required every Methodist Society to have its own library.[186] Furthermore, he compiled a great number of books into a work he chose to call *THE CHRISTIAN LIBRARY*. He published it and distributed it throughout Methodism. He began his initial compilation while he was in Georgia.[187] The completion of it was demanding, the cost very great, and the financial losses overwhelming.[188] The *LIBRARY* featured the lives of illustrious Christians, Bible helps, basic theology, and devotional aids. It was just a small portion of literature Wesley floated out over Methodism. He wrote tirelessly on subjects from A to Z, emphasizing the harmony of all true knowledge and God revealed in the Bible. His followers had plenty to read, but, like today, many kept talking!

Much reading, leading to much knowledge, can have its dangers, however. Some become carried away with learning so that they soon forsake the biblical foundation of faith. Wesley warned against this, "Keep close to the Bible. Be not wise above what is written. Enjoin nothing that the Bible does not clearly enjoin. Forbid nothing that it does not clearly forbid."[189] The Christian pilgrim should keep in mind that success in maintaining the biblical foundation also depends on the reality of grace -grace channeled to those who sincerely search the Scriptures. Without this grace, successful biblicism, salvation and Christian holiness are not possible in the scriptural sense.[190]

Wesley held it essential for clergymen to possess a thorough knowledge of the Bible, from cover to cover. He was convinced that the majority of the English clergy were biblically illiterate. It has been a modern Methodist myth that Wesley was a low churchman, using the Bible against the majority of clergy who were High Churchmen. Actually, the reverse is the case. He was the High Churchman in regards to the Bible, the Articles of Religion, the Creeds, the Homilies, and the Liturgy.[191] The Anglican Church of Wesley's day had become low-church. Wesley was one of a vanishing breed. Biblicism was not part of the low tradition, and academic preparation for the profession had, for some time, neglected biblical studies in favor of subjects less demanding. Under strong compulsion to reverse this trend, Wesley sounded a strong call for better theological education -biblically oriented for a more effective clergy -

"The Scriptures teach us how to teach others. So that, whether it be true or not, that every good textuary is a good Divine, it is certain none can be a good Divine who is not a good textuary. But this requires a 'knowledge of the original tongues', without which he will 'frequently be at a stand, even as texts which regard practice only. . . He will be ill able to rescue these out of the hands of any man of learning that would pervert them: For whenever an appeal is made of the original, his mouth is stopped at once. The clergyman should know: The grammatical construction of the four Gospels, of Acts, of the Epistles; the spiritual (symbolic) sense as well as the literal; the scope of each book, and how each part fits into the whole; the various objections to the passages of Scripture raised by Jews, Deists, Papists, Arians, Socinians, and all sectaries that corrupt the word of God; Greek and Hebrew."[192]

Notes

1 John Wesley, *EXPLANATORY NOTES UPON THE NEW TESTAMENT* (London: The Epworth Press, 1976), 9.
2 Nehemiah Curnock (Ed), *THE JOURNAL OF THE REV. JOHN WESLEY* (London: The Epworth Press, 1960), III, 34.
3 *Ibid*, III, 37.
4 John Telford (Ed), *THE LETTERS OF THE REV. JOHN WESLEY* (London: The Epworth Press, 1931), VI, 161. Cf. Frank Baker (Ed), THE WORKS OF JOHN WESLEY (Oxford: The Clarendon Press, 1980), XXV, 133.
5 Baker, *op.cit.*, XXV, xxi.
6 Halford E. Luccock, Paul Hutchinson, and Robert W. Goodloe, *THE STORY OF METHODISM* (New York: Abingdon Press, 1949), 46-47.
7 Baker, *op.cit.*, XXV, xxi.
8 Abel Stevens, *THE HISTORY OF THE RELIGIOUS MOVEMENT OF THE EIGHTEENTH CENTURY CALLED METHODISM* (New York: The Methodist Book Concern), I, 65.
9 JOURNAL, *op.cit.*, I, 39.
10 *Ibid*, I, 47.
11 *Ibid*, I, 56.
12 *Ibid*, I, 55.
13 Baker, *op.cit.*, XXV, xxi.
14 JOURNAL, *op.cit.*, I, 65-66.
15 Baker, *op.cit.*, XXV, xxi.
16 JOURNAL, *op.cit.*, V, 117. Cf. *THE WORKS OF JOHN WESLEY* (Grand Rapids: Zondervan Publishing House), V, 3.
17 Mack B. Stokes, *THE BIBLE IN THE WESLEYAN HERITAGE* (Nashville: Abingdon Press, 1979), 20.
18 Colin W. Williams, *JOHN WESLEY'S THEOLOGY TODAY* (New York: Abingdon Press, 1960), 24.
19 *Ibid*, 24-25. Cf. JOURNAL, *op.cit.*, III, 391. In 1749 Wesley gave seventeen of his preachers an introductory course in logic.
20 *Ibid*, 25.
21 JOURNAL, *op.cit.*, I, 167, 170, 175, 180, 183, 184, 185, 187, 191, 209, 218, 248, 258, 278, 294, 295, 299, 302, and many more.
22 *Ibid*, I, 181, 183, 192, 217, 219, and others.
23 *Ibid*, I, 185.
24 *Ibid*, I, 476.
25 WORKS, *op.cit.*, XII, 65.
26 EXPLANATORY NOTES NEW TESTAMENT, *op.cit.*, 794.

27 *Ibid*, 9.
28 JOURNAL, *op.cit.*, VI, 117.
29 Williams, *op.cit.*, 26.
30 WORKS, *op.cit.*, VIII, 340.
31 *Ibid*, V, 192.
32 *Ibid*, VIII, 340.
33 Ole Borgen, *JOHN WESLEY ON THE SACRAMENTS* (Nashville: Abingdon Press, 1972), 277.
34 EXPLANATORY NOTES NEW TESTAMENT, *op.cit.*, 10.
35 *Ibid*, 546.
36 *Ibid*, 912.
37 *Ibid*, 670.
38 *Ibid*, 670-671.
39 *Ibid*, 81.
40 *Ibid*, 362-363.
41 *Ibid*, 856.
42 *Ibid*, 926. Cf. 14 - The evangelists deliberately added what others omitted.
43 Williams, *op.cit.*, 26.
44 EXPLANATORY NOTES NEW TESTAMENT, *op.cit.*, 814.
45 *Ibid*, 810.
46 *Ibid*, 929.
47 *Loc.cit.*
48 *Ibid*, 21.
49 John Calvin, *COMMENTARY ON A HARMONY OF THE EVANGELISTS, MATTHEW, MARK, AND LUKE* (Grand Rapids: Wm. B. Eerdmans Publishing Company, 1957), III, 272.
50 EXPLANATORY NOTES NEW TESTAMENT, *op.cit.*, 130-131.
51 *Ibid*, 131.
52 *Ibid*, 130.
53 Luther Weigle, *THE NEW TESTAMENT OCTAPLA* (New York: Thomas Nelson and Sons), 170-171.
54 JOURNAL, *op.cit.*, I, 355.
55 Stokes, *op.cit.*, 22-23.
56 John Wesley, *EXPLANATORY NOTES UPON THE OLD TESTAMENT* (Salem, Ohio: Schmul Publishers, 1975), I, 1.
57 WORKS, *op.cit.*, V, 193.
58 EXPLANATORY NOTES NEW TESTAMENT, *op.cit.*, 10.
59 *Ibid*, 11.
60 *Ibid*, 12.
61 *Ibid*, 9.
62 *Ibid*, 10.
63 EXPLANATORY NOTES OLD TESTAMENT, *op.cit.*, I, ix.
64 *Ibid*, I, iv, v. Cf. Borgen, *op.cit.*, 24-25.
65 *Ibid*, I, vii.
66 *Ibid*, I, viii.
67 *Loc.cit.*

68 *Loc.cit.*
69 EXPLANATORY NOTES NEW TESTAMENT, *op.cit.*, 7.
70 WORKS, *op.cit.*, VI, 201. Cf. Borgen, *op.cit.*, 24-25.
71 *Ibid*, XII, 427.
72 EXPLANATORY NOTES NEW TESTAMENT, *op.cit.*, 7.
73 *Ibid*, 8.
74 *Ibid*, 7.
75 Borgen, *op.cit.*, 25.
76 Telford, *op.cit.*, VII, 252. Cf. WORKS, *op.cit.*, XIV, 147-160 and 78-146. Wesley wrote a short Hebrew grammar and a short Greek grammar.
77 JOURNAL, *op.cit.*, III, 274.
78 Telford, *op.cit.*, VII, 252.
79 JOURNAL, *op.cit.*, IV, 191.
80 *Ibid*, IV, 204.
81 Telford, *op.cit.*, VII, 252.
82 JOURNAL, *op.cit.*, VI, 333-334. Parsons was an imminent physician who also studied the origin of languages.
83 *Loc.cit.*
84 EXPLANATORY NOTES NEW TESTAMENT, *op.cit.*, 814.
85 JOURNAL, *op.cit.*, VIII, 275.
86 Baker, *op.cit.*, XXV, 258.
87 EXPLANATORY NOTES OLD TESTAMENT, *op.cit.*, II, 1635.
88 EXPLANATORY NOTES NEW TESTAMENT, *op.cit.*, 814.
89 JOURNAL, *op.cit.*, VII, 322.
90 *Loc.cit.*
91 *Loc.cit.*
92 *Ibid*, I, 161, 166-192, 209, 222, 320, 338, 356, 364, 376, 388, to cite a few.
93 WORKS, *op.cit.*, V, 2 - from Wesley's 1747 Preface to his sermons.
94 *Ibid*, V, 18.
95 *Ibid*, V, 39.
96 *Ibid*, V, 60.
97 *Ibid*, V, 83.
98 *Ibid*, V, 88.
99 *Ibid*, V, 103.
100 *Ibid*, V, 112-113.
101 *Ibid*, V, 129.
102 *Ibid*, V, 139.
103 *Ibid*, V, 145.
104 *Ibid*, V, 172.
105 *Ibid*, V, 192.
106 *Ibid*, V, 213.
107 *Ibid*, V, 232.
108 *Ibid*, V, 236.
109 *Ibid*, V, 249.
110 *Ibid*, V, 273.
111 *Ibid*, V, 282.

112   *Ibid*, V, 295.
113   *Ibid*, V, 317.
114   *Ibid*, V, 331.
115   *Ibid*, V, 347.
116   *Ibid*, V, 369.
117   *Ibid*, V, 397.
118   *Ibid*, V, 411.
119   *Ibid*, V, 480.
120   *Ibid*, V, 497. 121.
121   EXPLANATORY NOTES NEW TESTAMENT, *op.cit.*, 6, 625.
122   *Ibid*, 307.
123   JOURNAL, *op.cit.*, IV, 361. The date was December 12, 1759.
124   EXPLANATORY NOTES NEW TESTAMENT, *op.cit.*, 6.
125   *Loc.cit.* Cf. JOURNAL, *op.cit.*, VI, 143. Wesley was greatly impressed by Dr. Gell's *ESSAY TOWARD AN AMENDMENT OF THE LAST TRANS-LATION OF THE BIBLE.*
126   JOURNAL, *op.cit.*, VII, 114.
127   WORKS, *op.cit.*, VII, 47.
128   JOURNAL, *op.cit.*, II, 188.
129   *Ibid*, III, 197.
130   WORKS, *op.cit.*, VII, 46-47.
131   *Ibid*, VII, 46.
132   JOURNAL, *op.cit.*, VI, 372.
133   *Loc.cit.*
134   *Ibid*, I, 359.
135   Stokes, *op.cit.*, 22.
136   WORKS, *op.cit.*, X, 92, 141. In the EXPLANATORY NOTES NEW TESTAMENT, Wesley failed to cite the closeness of Matthew XXIII, 37 with I Esdras I, 30 - "I gathered you together as a hen gathered her chickens under her wings."
137   JOURNAL, *op.cit.*, VII, 212.
138   Stokes, *op.cit.*, 24. Cf. Baker, op.cit., 158, 533.
139   WORKS, *op.cit.*, X, 94. Here Wesley quoted from Clement of Alexandria's *STROMATEIS* I, 7 - "The way for understanding the scriptures, is to demonstrate out of themselves concerning themselves."
140   *Ibid*, XIV, 252. Cf. EXPLANATORY NOTES OLD TESTAMENT, *op.cit.*, I, viii.
141   *Ibid*, XII, 284. Telford, *op.cit.*, V, 96.
142   *Ibid*, X, 511. Cf. Williams, *op.cit.*, 30.
143   Williams, *op.cit.*, 24.
144   WORKS, *op.cit.*, VI, 354: X, 511. Cf. EXPLANATORY NOTES NEW TESTAMENT, *op.cit.*, 9; JOURNAL, *op.cit.*, III, 197; Williams, *op.cit.*, 27-28.
145   Williams, *op.cit.*, 28.
146   JOURNAL, *op.cit.*, I, 471.
147   *Loc.cit.*

148   *Ibid*, I, 475-476.
149   WORKS, *op.cit.*, V, 188.
150   Umphrey Lee, *JOHN WESLEY AND MODERN RELIGION* (Nashville: Cokesbury Press, 1936), 131.
151   WORKS, *op.cit.*, X, 178. Cf. Stokes, *op.cit.*, 22-23.
152   Stokes, *op.cit.*, 23.
153   WORKS, *op.cit.*, XII, 430.
154   Williams, *op.cit.*, 29.
155   WORKS, *op.cit.*, XIV, 223-224.
156   Lee, *op.cit.*, 132. Cf. WORKS, *op.cit.*, XIV, 223.
157   WORKS, *op.cit.*, XIV, 224.
158   *Ibid*, XII, 430. Cf. Stokes, *op.cit.*, 21-22. Stokes quotes Wesley - "The esteeming of the writings of the first three centuries not equally but next to the Scriptures never carried any man yet into dangerous errors, nor probably never will. But it has brought many out of dangerous errors."
159   *Ibid*, I, iv. Cf. Lee, *op.cit.*, 97.
160   Borgen, *op.cit.*, 277.
161   Williams, *op.cit.*, 23.
162   *Loc.cit.*
163   Borgen, *op.cit.*, 276.
164   Williams, *op.cit.*, 26.
165   WORKS, *op.cit.*, X, 90-94, and 133-134.
166   *Ibid*, X, 90.
167   *Ibid*, X, 91.
168   *Ibid*, X, 93-94.
169   *Ibid*, X, 94.
170   *Ibid*, X, 142.
171   *Ibid*, X, 511.
172   JOURNAL, *op.cit.*, I, 275.
173   *Ibid*, IV, 97. Wesley had just read Baxter's *HISTORY OF THE COUNCILS*.
174   *Ibid*, V, 169. Cf. Stokes, *op.cit.*, 20.
175   WORKS, *op.cit.*, XIII, 258.
176   *Ibid*, XII, 260.
177   *Ibid*, XIV, 252.
178   JOURNAL, *op.cit.*, V, 169.
179   WORKS, *op.cit.*, XII, 428.
180   *Ibid*, V, 188.
181   JOURNAL, *op.cit.*, I, 472. Cf. Lee, *op.cit.*, 89.
182   WORKS, *op.cit.*, V, 136.
183   Telford, *op.cit.*, VIII, 125.
184   JOURNAL, *op.cit.*, VI, 16.
185   Telford, *op.cit.*, VIII, 247.
186   WORKS, *op.cit.*, VIII, 315.
187   JOURNAL, *op.cit.*, I, 425.

188   *Ibid*, III, 391; IV, 48, 91, 94; VIII, 160. Cf. Williams, *op.cit.*, 25; Lee, *op.cit.*, 228.

189   Telford, *op.cit.*, VIII, 192.

190   WORKS, *op.cit.*, V, 192.

191   JOURNAL, *op.cit.*, II, 274-275

192   WORKS, *op.cit.*, X, 482-483. Wesley's statement, "that every good textuary is a good Divine," had its genesis in Martin Luther's famous statement: *"Denn ein guter Textkenner ist auch ein guter Theologe."* See, Martin Luther, *TISCHREDEN* (Stuttgart: Ehrenfried Klotz, 1956), 16. Also, WORKS, X, 491. Wesley asked the English clergy -

"Do I understand Greek and Hebrew? Otherwise, how do I undertake . . . not only to explain books which are written therein, but to defend them against all opponents? Am I not at the mercy of everyone who does understand, or even pretends to understand, the original? For which way can I confute his pretense? Do I understand the language of the Old Testament? Critically? At all? Can I read into English one of David's Psalms; or even the first chapter of Genesis? Do I understand the language of the New Testament? Am I a critical master of it? Have I enough of it even to read into English the first chapter of St. Luke? If not, how many years did I spend at school? How many at the University? And what was I doing all those years? Ought not shame to cover my face?"

PART ONE

ETERNITY: A PARTE ANTE
(Before Time)

Chapter One

God's Eternal Existence

PSALM XC.

"Probably Moses wrote this psalm, on the occasion on the sentence passed on the Israelites, that their carcasses should fall in the wilderness. Herein he considers the eternity of God, ver. 1-3. And the frailty of man, ver. 4-6. He submits to the righteous sentence of God, ver. 7-11. And prays for the return of his favour, ver. 12-17.

Lord, thou hast been our dwelling place in all generations. Before the mountains were brought forth, or ever thou hadst formed the earth, and the world, even from everlasting to everlasting, thou art God. Thou turnedst man to destruction, and saidest return ye children of men. For a thousand years in thy sight are but as yesterday when they are past, and as a watch in the night. Thou carriest them away as with a flood; they are as a sleep: in the morning they are like grass which groweth up. In the morning it flourisheth, and groweth up; in the evening it is cut down, and whithereth. For we are consumed by thine anger, and by thy wrath are we troubled. Thou hast set our iniquities before thee; our secret sins in the light of thy countenance. For all our days are passed away through thy wrath; we spend our years as a tale that is told. The days of our years are threescore years and ten; and if by reason of strength they be fourscore years, yet is their strength then labour and sorrow; for it is soon cut off, and we flee away. Who knoweth the power of thine anger? Even according to thy fear, so is thy wrath. So teach us to number our days, that we may apply our hearts unto wisdom. Return, O Lord, how long? And let it repent thee concerning thy servants. O satisfy us early with thy mercy, that we may rejoice, and be glad all our days. Make us glad according to the days

wherein thou hast afflicted us, and the years wherein we have seen
evil. Let thy work appear unto thy servants, and thy glory unto
their children. And let the beauty of the Lord our God be upon us,
and establish thou the work of our hands in us; yea, the work of our
hands establish thou it."[1]

The foregoing passage from Scripture, important to Wesley for
many reasons, introduces us to a veritable treasure of historical
theology. The word "theology" has its origin in the Greek language, meaning "the science of God." The Angelic Doctor,
Thomas Aquinas, began his famous book *NATURE AND GRACE*
with arguments defending "Sacred Doctrine" as a true science.[2]
While John Wesley never argued this position, he did theologize
considerably, bringing the Bible, the Ante-Nicene Fathers, select
theologians and philosophers, and the new science of the eighteenth century together into a rational and spiritual synthesis.
However, that did not make him a systematic theologian because
much of his theological perspective was inherited from the previous century. He was both a traditionalist and an eclectic in theological matters. While he was not a systematic theologian, he nevertheless possessed a systematic theology of eternity and time, to
which he was always adding new insights to the traditional ones.
Some of these new insights came from Galileo, Copernicus, Har-
vey, Gilbert, Bacon, Newton, and others. Hence Wesley's theology
was extremely dynamic. Psalm XC - one of his favorites - best pre-
pares us for this dynamic theology. God is from everlasting to everlasting!

THE KNOWLEDGE OF GOD

Wesley's understanding of how we know anything about God,
and what we know about him, is the proper starting place for our
study of eternity and time. The epistemological issue must be faced
and settled early, or else everything that follows will have no secure
place. Wesley was optimistic about knowing God, in terms of both
his existence and nature. Such knowledge is not possible without
intense search and perpetual patience. There are constant chal-

lenges and obstacles for anyone who would attempt to know God. In his optimism, Wesley presents a number of surprises as to how and what may be known of deity.

The greatest obstacle to the knowledge of God, according to Wesley, is the perennial gulf fixed between the infinite and the finite. It did not take the nineteenth century's Kierkegaard to teach anyone that there is "a qualitative difference between the finite and the infinite." That truth was early discovered and attested to in the Bible itself, and Wesley took it into consideration. For a theological definition of "infinite," Wesley turned to St. Augustine. In refuting the Manichaeans, Augustine argued that their dualism violated logic -

> ". . . two supreme, independent principles, is next door to a contradiction in terms. . . if there can be two essentially distinct, absolute infinities, there may be an infinity of such absolute infinities. . . none of them would be an absolute infinity. For real infinity is strict and absolute infinity, and only that."[3]

Wesley, quoting Augustine, understood that whatever is qualified or limited by another entity of the same essential kind can never be infinite, that is, "not limited." Wesley, although he would never admit it publicly, knew and alluded to Benedict Spinoza's famous distinction - "Finite after its kind - a thing that can be limited to another thing of the same nature. For instance, a body can be called finite because we always conceive another greater body. So, also a thought is limited by another thought, but a body is not limited by a thought, nor a thought by a body."[4] Wesley would quickly agree that this is the logical definition to be given the finite side of the coin. Furthermore, Wesley employed the arguments on the infinite and the finite of St. Anselm of Canterbury. The reading of Anselm was required of beginning students at Christ Church College. One of these Anselmic arguments reads - ". . .everything that is in someway enclosed by place or time is less than that which no law of place or time confines."[5] Wesley's eclecticism, at this point, combined Augustine, Spinoza, and Anselm, and he concluded that the finite consists of entities of the same essential

kinds, and limited by place and time, while the infinite is one essential reality that resides unconfined by place and time, that is, God
alone. The infinite is qualitatively superior to the finite - The One
is above the many, as Plato had clearly taught and the Church had
consistently held for centuries. In fact, Anselm concluded -
"Therefore, since there is nothing greater than Thou, no place or
time holds Thee, but Thou art everywhere and always. And since
this can be said of Thee alone, Thou alone art uncircumscribed and
eternal."[6] Wesley accepted this concept of the infinite pervading
the finite without the finite limiting the infinite. He quoted Sir
Isaac Newton, that God is in every place, filling the immensity of
space - space which is "the Sensorium of the Deity."[7] In addition,
Wesley claimed that even the heathen "did not scruple to say, 'All
things are full of God.'"[8] Such a concept was, for Wesley, an indu-
bitable truth.

As for man's finitude, Wesley recognized a two-fold dimension -
(1) from Creation and (2) from the Fall. (1) Wesley made the classical distinction between the Creator and the creature, the maker
being infinitely superior to the thing created. In his sermon on
GOD'S APPROBATION OF HIS WORKS, Wesley stated the case
as follows -

> "There was a 'golden chain' (to use the expression of Plato) 'let down from
> the throne of God; an exactly connected series of beings, from the highest to
> the lowest; from dead earth, through fossils, vegetables, animals, to man, cre-
> ated in the image of God, and designed to know, to love, and enjoy his Cre-
> ator to all eternity.'"[9]

In addition to blending Plato and Scripture for the "golden
chain," and its successive stages of descent from God, Wesley
treated Psalm VIII, in his unique soteriological way - The Psalmist
exclaimed to God, "Thou hast in Christ mercifully restored man to
his primitive estate, wherein he was but one remove below the angels...But the words more literally rendered are, *Thou madest him a
little less than God.*"[10] Moreover, Wesley employed various titles
of honor for God which imply the greater/lesser motif: "The Author of our being" - authors being greater than their works; "The

Father of angels and men" -fathers being greater than their sons; "Our Governor" - governors being greater than those governed; and "Preserver" - the preserving agent being greater than the thing preserved.[11]

In being made a little less than God, but in the image of God, man was given a corporeal body, subject to place and time. The *imago Dei*, as a "spirit," was "mingled together" with the corporeal body.[12] This was the condition of created finitude -"For an embodied spirit cannot form one thought but only the mediation of its bodily organs. For thinking is not, as many suppose, the act of a pure spirit; but the act of a pure spirit connected with a body, and playing upon a set of material keys."[13]

While man was initially without corruption, he was still finite because his material body, being subject to place and time, gave residence to a spirit that could not think by itself. The spirit was a created spirit, made by the Father of spirits, and thus less than its progenitor. But, in man's creation, body and spirit were made interdependent and one personality came into being. The body was subject to place and time, and the spirit was subject to the body. This description of created finitude reminds one of an hypostatic union, two whole and distinct natures - one physical and the other spiritual - being united without discord as one personality.

(2) Fallen finitude. The Fall of first man from created goodness greatly complicated his finite condition. Wesley believed that while God created man to attain the glory of his Maker, God made him finite "to keep him humble."[14] But, as every reader of the Bible knows, Adam became proud. His created finitude had also been designed by God to teach him faith,[15] but, alas, Adam became a rebel. Original finitude was further intended to increase resignation,[16] but instead Adam exercised self-will. By his pride, rebellion, and self-will, Adam reduced first and good finitude to what Wesley called "mortal finitude." His sermon on THE FALL OF MAN describes this tragic reduction -

"But since he sinned, he is not only dust, but mortal, corruptible dust. And by sad experience we find, that this 'corruptible body presses down the soul.'

It very frequently hinders the soul in its operation; and, at best, serves it very imperfectly. . . . Hence every disorder of the body, especially of the parts more immediately subservient to thinking, lay an almost insuperable bar to the way of its thinking justly. Hence the maxim received in all ages, *Humanum est errare et nescire*, - 'Not ignorance alone,' (that belongs, more or less, to every creature in heaven and earth; seeing none is omniscient, none knoweth all things, save the Creator,) 'but error, is entailed on every child of man.' ...every child of man is in a thousand mistakes, and is liable to fresh mistakes every moment."[17]

Since the Fall, Wesley maintained, this "mortal finitude" has been "our infant state of existence."[18] The result is that we only "know in part." "The wisest men have here but short, narrow, imperfect conceptions, even of the things round about them, and much more of the things of God."[19] Indeed, since the Fall, Wesley reasoned, man's finitude means a greater limitation of human knowledge. Man can only know a little, although his appetite to know is insatiable. His mind is locked into an infantile state, and it will never grasp the whole of reality until "there will be some future state of being, wherein that now insatiable desire will be satisfied, and there will be no longer so immense a distance between the appetite and the object of it."[20] However, the natural man - Wesley's sinner - does not aspire to this future state "because so thick a veil is interposed as he knows not how to penetrate."[21] But, blessed is the man whom God brings to spiritual sight -

"We see, when God opens our eyes, that we were before. . . *without God*, or, rather, *Atheists, in the world.* We had, by nature, no knowledge of God, no acquaintance with him. It is true, as soon as we came to the use of reason, we learned 'the invisible things of God, even his eternal power and Godhead, from the things that are made.' From the things that are seen we inferred the existence of an eternal, powerful Being, that is not seen."[22]

It should be observed here that Wesley placed faith prior to coming "to the use of reason" by which believers learn "the invisible things of God." The eyes of the soul are not opened by reason, but by faith. As in the *SHEPHERD OF HERMAS*, where faith is depicted as "the Mother of all virtues," so in Wesley's epistemological understanding faith is the progenitor of reason. Reason is born of faith, and the believer, by employing it, may acquire knowledge of the God in whom he has believed. Wesley was much in debt to St. Anselm for this emphasis. The prayer of Anselm is one of the most profound in Christian tradition -

"I acknowledge, O Lord, with thanksgiving, that thou hast created this thy image in me, so that, remembering thee, I may think of thee. But this image is so effaced and worn away by my faults, it is so obscured by the smoke of my sins, that it cannot do what it was made to do, unless thou renew and reform it. I am not trying, O Lord, to penetrate thy loftiness, for I cannot begin to match my understanding with it, but I desire in some measure to understand thy truth, which my heart believes and loves. For I do not seek to understand in order to believe, but I believe in order to understand. For this too, I believe, that unless I believe, I shall not understand."[23]

However, to "believe in order to understand" does not necessarily guarantee knowledge of God. There will always remain, for the Christian believer, an incomprehensible mystery about the reality of God. Writing to Elizabeth Dennis (1771), Wesley treated this fact -

"It is no wonder that finite cannot measure infinite; that man cannot comprehend the ways of God. There always will be something incomprehensible, something like Himself, in all his dispensations. We must therefore be content to be ignorant, until eternity opens our understanding; particularly with regard to the reasons of His acting thus or thus. These we shall be acquainted with when in Abraham's bosom."[24]

Wesley's reference to being "ignorant" should not be universalized to cover all aspects of divine life and activity. He simply meant that the "incomprehensible" things of God should be accepted as such, while the "comprehensible" things of God should be spiritually and rationally enjoyed. There are plenty of both. Redeemed reason, building upon faith and enabled by the Holy Spirit, may consistently encounter the "comprehensible."[25] The work of the Holy Spirit in this epistemological process is essential, bringing the believer from the atheism of birth to the knowledge of God.[26] By asserting this, Wesley denied a very ancient tradition in theology - that man begins this earthly life with an innate idea of God. Augustine had Christianized this Platonic tenet, and John Calvin, in the sixteenth century, made it part of Reformed Theology. In his *INSTITUTES OF THE CHRISTIAN RELIGION* (Book One - The Knowledge of God), Calvin stated this idea with great authority - "There is within the human mind, and indeed by natural instinct, an awareness of divinity. This we take to be beyond controversy... God himself has implanted in all men a certain understanding of his divine majesty."[27] Bishop Stillingfleet, a century before Wesley, wrote extensively about the reality of innate ideas of God's existence, engaging in a polemic against the philosopher John Locke, who had denied the reality of any innate ideas, regardless of their referents. The human mind at birth, Locke held, is a *tabula rasa* - a blank or fair sheet, devoid of any ideas, even that of God.[28] John Wesley was a complete Lockean on this subject. This is why he could claim that man at birth is a "natural atheist."[29] Wesley, following Locke, held that knowledge must be acquired through the empirical process of creating ideas. Consequently, he wrote -

> "God has not 'stamped an idea of himself on every human soul' - no man every did, nor does now, find any such idea stamped upon his soul. The little which we know of God (except what we receive by the inspiration of the Holy One,) we do not gather from any inward impression, but gradually acquire from without. 'The invisible things of God,' if they are known at all, are known from the things that are made; not from what God hath written in our hearts, but what he hath written in all his works."[30]

By no means did Wesley wish to imply that acquiring knowledge of God by studying his works is easy. Far from it. Moreover, when we have pursued the path of reasonable analysis and synthesis, we may still be viewing reality as a shadow -

> "Although we have faith's abiding impression, realizing things to come; yet as long as we are in the body we have but an imperfect, shadowy knowledge of the things of eternity. For now we only see them in a glass, a mirror, which

gives us no more than a shadow of them; therefore, we see them darkly, or in a riddle, as St. Paul speaks. The whole invisible world is as yet a riddle to us."[31]

Continuing his theme further, Wesley in his *EXPLANATORY NOTES UPON THE NEW TESTAMENT*, added -

". . .*a glass* - Or mirror, which reflects only their imperfect forms, in a dim, faint, obscure manner; so that our thoughts about them are puzzling and intricate, and everything is a kind of riddle to us."[32]

It is certain that Wesley agreed with Augustine's assessment of how much knowledge of God is possible for a believer to have. Augustine cautioned that God is more true in our thoughts than in our words, and that he is greater and truer in reality than in our thoughts.[33] Christians need to remember this relationship of human minds and words to divine reality. In a sense, there is room for reverent agnosticism, but not a total agnosticism.

The Wesleyan principle of acquiring some degree of knowledge about God from the study of his works, since there are no innate ideas, needs more consideration. This kind of study requires more than mere human reason. Reason must be redeemed by Christ's atonement. Also, it must be a faith-subsumed reason. Above all, it must be enabled by the Holy Spirit to perform its proper function of "inferring" from things seen to things that are eternal.[34]

But, Wesley insisted, the Scriptures also have an important place in this study of God's nature - "Is it not reason (assisted by the Holy Ghost) which enables us to understand what the Holy Scriptures declare concerning the being and attributes of God? -Concerning his eternity and immensity; his power, wisdom, and holiness?"[35] The Bible is descriptive of God's person and his works in nature and salvation. Thus, the Scripture is a valid touchstone for every aspect of reason's search and discovery.

The questing believer's soul, Wesley maintained, being born of God's Spirit, is made "sensible" to God.[36] As a result, the Christian can "discern" the things of God as the Spirit, Scripture, and reason combine dynamically, each fulfilling the God-given role. When this happens, Wesley claimed, "it does not require a large share of natural wisdom to see God in all things; in all his works of creation as well as providence. This is rather a branch of spiritual wisdom, and is given to believers more and more, as they advance in purity of heart."[37] "Natural wisdom," Wesley argued, produces only an "atheist," but the "spiritual wisdom" of holy questing - the Spirit, Scripture, and reason - produces a Christian.[38] The challenge to this process is treated in his sermon on *THE IMPERFECTION OF HUMAN KNOWLEDGE* -

"Hence, then, from his works, particularly his works of creation, we are to learn the knowledge of God. But it is not easy to conceive how little we know even of these. To begin with those that are at a distance: Who knows how far the universe extends? What are the limits of it? The morning stars can tell, who sang together when the lines of it were stretched out, when God said, 'This be thy just circumference, O world!' But all beyond the fixed stars is utterly hid from the children of men. And what do we know of the fixed stars? Who telleth the numbers of them? Even that small portion of them that, by their mingled light, form what we call 'the Milky Way?' And who knows the use of them? Are they so many suns that illuminate their respective planets? Or do they only minister to this. . . and contribute, in some unknown way, to the perpetual circulation of light and spirit? Who knows what the comets are? Are they planets not fully formed? or planets destroyed by a conflagration?. . . Who knows what is the precise distance of the sun from the earth? Many astronomers are persuaded it is a hundred millions of miles; others, that it is only eighty-six millions, though generally accounted ninety. . . So little do we know even of this glorious luminary, the eye and soul of the lower world! . . .of the planets which surround him? . . .Of our own planet, the moon? . . .Of light? How is it communicated to us? . . .Is it subject to the general laws which obtain in all other matter? Who can explain the phenomena of electricity? . . .But surely we understand the air we breathe, and which encompasses us on every side. . . Is elasticity essential to air, and inseparable from it? Let us now descend to the earth which we tread upon, and which God has peculiarly given to the children of men. Do the children of men understand this? . . .But who can inform us, what lies beneath the region of stones, metals, minerals, and other fossils? This is only a thin crust, which bears an exceedingly small portion of the whole. Who can acquaint us with the inner parts of the globe? . . .Is there a central fire, a grand reservoir, which not only supplies the burning mountains, but also ministers (though we know not how) to the ripening of gems and metals; yea, and perhaps to the production of vegetables, and the well-being of animals too? . . .How little we know of the polar regions, either north or south, either in Europe or Asia! . . .Much less do we know what is contained in the broad sea, the great abyss, which covers so large a part of the globe. . . Proceed we to the vegetable kingdom. Who can demonstrate that the sap, in any vegetable, performs a regular circulation through its vessels, or that it does not? . . .With regard to animals: Are microscopic animals so called, real animals or no? . . .With regard to insects, many are the discoveries which have been lately made. But how little is all that is discovered yet, in comparison to what is undiscovered! . . .With birds we are a little better acquainted: And, indeed, it is but a little. . . How little do we know of beasts! . . .Are they mere machines? . . .Well; but if we know nothing else, do not we know ourselves? Our bodies and our souls? What is our soul? It is a spirit, we know. But what is a spirit? Here we are at a full stop. . . How is the soul united to the body? A spirit to a clod? What is the secret, imperceptible chain that couples them together? . . .And as to our body itself, how little do we know! . . .What is flesh? . . .Are the fibers that compose it of a determinate size, so that they can be divided only so far? Or are they resolvable *in infinitum*? O how little do we know even concerning ourselves! What then can we expect to know concerning the whole creation of God?"[39]

Wesley, with his faith-subsumed reason, the Holy Spirit, and the Bible, set about to answer these questions and many more. The discoveries of the new science provided him with more data to analyze and synthesize in order to move from knowledge of God's works to knowing something of God's existence and nature. He realized that whatever knowledge he acquired would be small compared to the remaining mystery of the Infinite God, but he could wait for complete knowledge in Abraham's bosom (Consult Chapter VIII).

GOD'S EXISTENCE

The two main sources for Wesley's understanding of God's existence were the Bible and what he called "nature philosophy." He claimed that faith, reason, and the Holy Spirit aided him in harmonizing these sources, bringing him to a basic knowledge of God. He instructed his Methodist disciples to make the same pilgrimage

- to believe in order that they might understand, and understanding something of God, love and serve him better.

Wesley's knowledge of Scripture was phenomenal and also enviable. He observed that the Bible never argues the existence of God, but simply affirms it as the foundation of faith. Like Augustine, Anselm, and many others before him, Wesley accepted the definition of faith stated in the *EPISTLE TO THE HEBREWS* XI, 1 - "Now faith is the subsistence of things hoped for, the evidence of things not seen"(Wesley's translation). Augustine referred to this as the "standard" definition of the Catholic faith,[40] and claimed it was prerequisite to understanding.[41] The commentary on this text, in the *EXPLANATORY NOTES UPON THE NEW TESTAMENT*, reads -

> *"Now faith is the subsistence of things hoped for, the evidence* or conviction *of things not seen* - Things hoped for are not so extensive as things not seen. The former are only things future and joyful to us; the latter are either future, past, or present, and those either good or evil, whether to us or others. . . the divine supernatural *evidence* exhibited to, the conviction hereby produced in a believer *of things not seen*, whether past, future or spiritual, particularly of God and the things of God."[42]

According to Wesley, every person has the capacity for faith by virtue of his soul's sense perceptions. These perceptions are parallel to the physical senses of the body - sight, smelling, hearing, tasting and touching.[43] Faith is bestowed as a gift when the Holy Spirit excites the spiritual senses of the soul to see, hear, taste, and feel God's love and presence.[44] Consequently, Wesley argued, faith is "the demonstrative evidence of things unseen, the supernatural evidence of things invisible, not perceivable by eyes of flesh, or by any of our natural senses or faculties." Moreover, faith is that divine "evidence whereby the spiritual man discerneth God, and the things of God."[45] So, he continued, it is impossible to please God without faith, "for he that cometh to God must believe that he *is*, and *that* he is a rewarder of them that diligently seek him."[46] The first great act of faith, then, is the coming to the firm conviction that God exists, and that he has a special providence for those who have such faith.

The believer has an increase of faith through the grace of Christ, which grace is channeled by the Holy Spirit through the ministry of the Church. The preaching and teaching of the Scripture, and the duly administered sacraments, combine to bring about favorable conditions for this growth. While Wesley was concerned about effective preaching and "constant communion," his most vital concern was the teaching ministry. For this reason he gave his movement its own set of Bible commentaries - *THE EXPLANATORY NOTES UPON THE OLD TESTAMENT*, and *THE EXPLANATORY NOTES UPON THE NEW TESTAMENT*. In both volumes he employed linguistic arguments from Hebrew and Greek to biblically demonstrate the existence of God. A notable instance is found in his Old Testament NOTES, treating Exodus III, 14 - "And God said unto Moses, I AM THAT I AM: And he said, Thus shalt thou say unto the children of Israel, I AM hath sent me unto you." Wesley's commentary on this verse reads -

"*I AM* - ...God would now be known by . . .a name that speaks what he is in himself. *I AM THAT I AM* - this explains his name *Jehovah*, and signifies, 1st, that he is self-existent; he has his being of himself, and *has* no dependence upon any other, and being self-sufficient, and the inexhaustible fountain of being and bliss. 2dly, that he is eternal and unchangeable, always the same, *yesterday, today* and *forever;* he *will be* what *he will be*, and what he is. 3dly, that he is faithful and true to all his promises, unchangeable in his word as well as in his nature, and not a man that he should lie."[48]

A parallel passage from the New Testament NOTES treats St. John VIII, 58 - "Jesus said to them, Verily, verily, I say unto you, before Abraham was, I AM." Wesley not only recognized the link of Jehovah (Exodus III) with Jesus, but, in his commentary on this Johannine verse, he linked Jesus with the God of Psalm XC - making Jesus the "I AM" who is "from everlasting to everlasting."

"*Before Abraham was*, I AM - even from everlasting to everlasting. This is a direct answer to the objection of the Jews, and shows how much greater He

was than Abraham... *Then took they up stones* - To stone Him as a blasphe-
mer. *But Jesus concealed himself* - Probably by becoming invisible."[49]

Wesley was so intent on illustrating the link between Jehovah
and Jesus, that, by suggesting Jesus became invisible, he nearly denied the traditional doctrine of the Incarnation for Docetism. This
is something he would never consciously do.

The Lord's Prayer also offered Wesley a strong biblical witness
to the existence of God, again from a linguistic perspective. In
THE EXPLANATORY NOTES UPON THE NEW TESTAMENT,
he treated the prayer as it first occurs, in St. Matthew VI, 9-13.
Verse 9, especially concerned him - "Hallowed be thy name." Behind his commentary on this phrase, within his mind, laid the Hebrew *Yahweh* and the Greek *ego eimi*. The commentary says -

"*Hallowed be thy name* - the name of God is God himself; the nature of God,
so far as it can be discovered to man. It means. . . together with his existence,
all his attributes or perfections; - His eternity, particularly signified by his
great and incommunicable name, JEHOVAH, as the Apostle John translated it. . .'the Alpha and Omega, the beginning and the end; He which is, and
which was, and which is to come;' -His fullness of Being, denoted by his other
great name, I AM THAT I AM; - His omnipresence; His omnipotence; who
is indeed the only Agent in the material world; all matter being essentially dull
and inactive, and *moved* only as it is moved by the finger of God; and he is
the spring of action in every creature, visible and invisible, which could neither act nor exist, without the continual influx and agency of his almighty
power; - His wisdom, clearly *deduced* from the things that are seen, from the
goodly order of the universe; - His Trinity in Unity, and Unity in Trinity, discovered to us in the first time of his written Word. . . The Gods created, a
plural noun joined with a verb of the singular number. . . - His essential purity
and holiness; -and above all, his love, which is the very brightness of his
glory."[50]

Wesley concluded this commentary with a fitting prayer -"Mayest
Thou, O Father, be truly known by all intelligent beings, and with
affections suitable to that knowledge! Mayest Thou be duly hon-
oured, loved, feared, by all in heaven and earth, by all angels and all
men!"[51]

Of all the scriptural passages treating God's existence, examined by Wesley, none is as powerful as Acts XVII, 22-31, in which St. Paul preached in Athens. Wesley's exegesis of this passage is worthy of a complete citation -

"22. *Then Paul standing in the midst of the-Areopagus* - An ample theatre! *Said* - Giving them a lecture of natural divinity, with admirable wisdom, acuteness, fullness, and divinely philosophical discourse, begins with the first and goes on to the last things, both which are new things to them. He points out the origin and end of all things, concerning which they had so many disputes, and equally refutes both the Epicurean and Stoic. *I perceive* - With what clearness and freedom does he speak! Paul against Athens.

23. *I found an altar* - Some suppose that this was set up by Socrates, to express in a covert way his devotion to the only true God, while he derided the plurality of the heathen gods, for which he was condemned to death; and others, that whosoever erected this altar, did it in honour of the God of Israel, of whom there was no image, and whose name, JEHOVAH, was never made known to the idolatrous Gentiles. *Him proclaim I unto you* - Thus he fixes the wandering attention of these blind philosophers; proclaiming to them an unknown, and yet not a new, God.

24. *God who made the world* - Thus is demonstrated, even to reason, the one, true, good God; Absolutely different from the creatures, from every part of the visible creation.

25. *Neither is he served as though he needed anything* - Or person, the Greek word equally takes in both. *To all* - That live and breathe. *Life* - in Him we live. *And breathe* - In Him we move. By breathing, life is continued. I breathe this moment; the next is not in my power. *And all things* - For in Him we are. So exactly do the parts of this discourse answer each other.

26. *He hath made of one blood the whole nation of men* - By this expression the Apostle showed them, in the most unaffected manner, that, though he was a Jew, he was not enslaved to any narrow views, but looked on all mankind as his brethren. *Having determined the times* - That it is God who gave men the earth to inhabit, Paul proves from the order of time and places, showing the highest wisdom of the disposer, superior to all human counsels. *And the bound of their habitations* - By mountains, seas, rivers, and the like.

27. *If haply* - The way is open; God is ready to be found; but he will lay no force upon man. *They might feel after him* - this is in the midst between seeking and finding. Feeling, being the lowest and grossest of all our senses, is fitly applied to that low knowledge of God. *Though he be not far from everyone of us* - We need not go far to seek or find Him. He is very near us; in us. It is only perverse reason which thinks He is afar off.

28. *In him* - Not in ourselves. *We live, and move, and have our being* - This denotes His necessary, intimate, and most efficacious presence. No words can better express the continual and necessary dependence of all created beings, in their existence and all their operations, on the first and almighty Cause, which the truest philosophy as well as divinity teaches. *As certain also of your own poets have said* - Aratus, whose words these are, was an Athenian, who lived almost three hundred years before this time. They are likewise to be found, with the alteration of one letter only, in the hymn of Cleantes to Jupiter, or the Supreme Being, one of the purest and finest pieces of natural religion in the whole world of pagan antiquity.

29. *We ought not to think* - A tender expression; especially in the first person plural. As if he had said, Can God Himself be a less noble being than we who are His offspring? Nor does he only here deny, that these are like God, but that they have any analogy to Him at all, so as to be capable of representing Him.

30. *The times of ignorance* - What, does he object ignorance to the knowing Athenians? Yes; and they acknowledge it by this very altar. *God overlooked* - As one paraphrases it, 'The beams of His eye did in a manner shoot over it.' He did not appear to take notice of them, by sending express messages to them, as he did to the Jews. *But now* - This day, this hour, saith Paul, puts an end to the divine forbearance, and brings either greater mercy or punishment, now *he commandeth all men everywhere to repent* - There is a dignity and grandeur in this expression, becoming an ambassador from the King of heaven. And this universal command of repentance declared universal guilt in the strongest manner, and admirably confronted the pride of the haughtiest Stoic of them all. At the same time it bore down the idle plea of fatality. For how could anyone repent of doing what he could not but have done?

31. *He hath appointed a day, in which he will judge the world* - How fitly does he speak this in their supreme court of justice! *By the man* - So he speaks, suiting himself to the capacity of his hearers. *Whereof he hath given assur-*

ance to all men, in that he raised him from the dead - God raising Jesus demonstrated hereby, that He was to be the glorious Judge of all. We are by no means to imagine that this was all which the Apostle intended to have said. But the indolence of some of his hearers, and the petulance of others, cut him short."[52]

Using the scriptural witnesses to God's existence as his "touchstone," Wesley sorted through theology and philosophy, borrowing rational arguments for supportive and confirming evidence. His knowledge of philosophy was extraordinary, a fact often overlooked in some studies of Wesley. Therefore, before examining his usage of philosophical reasoning for God's existence, a brief survey of his philosophical credentials will prove helpful.

His treatises, sermons, letters, journals, and diaries abound with references and allusions to, and quotations from, the most important thinkers of western philosophy. One treatise was completely given over to the survey of philosophy, being entitled *THE GRADUAL IMPROVEMENT OF NATURAL PHILOSOPHY*. Its opening paragraph states -

"Natural philosophy treats both of God himself, and of his creatures, visible and invisible. Of these I purpose to speak, in such a manner as to ascend from the consideration of man through all the orders of things, as they are farther and farther removed from us, to God the centre of all knowledge (I mean, of visible things: Of the invisible world we cannot know much, while we dwell in houses of clay.) Thus speculative philosophy ascends from man to God; practical descends from God to man."[53]

According to Wesley's definition "natural philosophy" and "speculative philosophy" are one and the same discipline. He not only traced its gradual development over the centuries, but he also used the best from it. He began his philosophical studies under his mother, Susanna. He learned more at Charterhouse, but Wesley became fully immersed in the discipline at Christ Church College, Oxford. There he delved into the Pre-Socratic thinkers and developed a great appreciation for them.[54] Years later, he included the study of the Pre-Socratic philosophers in the curriculum of his

Kingswood School for boys.[55]   He knew well the concepts and principles of Hesiod, Thales, Anaximander, Anaximenes, Heraclitus, Cratylus, Xenophanes, Parmenides, Zeno, Melissus, Empedocles, Anaxagoras, Leucippus, Democritus, Pythagoras, and finally, Socrates. Socrates was one of his favorite thinkers,[56] as was Plato, Socrates' student.[57] The impact of Plato on Wesley's thought was phenomenal, especially in reference to the metaphysical problem of the One and the many -Ultimate Being and particular beings, and the qualitative difference between the Infinite and the finite, the latter being a sort of "shadow" of the Real Infinite Being.

Moreover, Wesley knew the system of Aristotle equally well, with its emphasis upon potentiality, whereby the finite, under certain conditions, may "become" other than what it was created - the unreal becoming real, the finite becoming infinite. Wesley accepted this part of Aristotle but not his science. He often demonstrated an indebtedness to this philosopher, and he often criticized him.[58]

The Stoic philosophers, Zeno and Emperor Marcus Aurelius, were frequently mentioned by Wesley, sometimes sympathetically and sometimes critically.[59] Furthermore, he knew and used Jewish philosophy as well as the Classical and Hellenistic types.   He quoted and cited Philo Judaeus, the first century Alexandrian thinker who blended Moses and Plato into a system of thought.[60] In addition, he was familiar with the works of Saadia, Gabirol, Halevi, and Maimonides. On the Latin side, Wesley knew the writings and thoughts of Virgil and Cicero.[61] Masterfully versed in the Scholastic thinkers of the Middle Ages, Wesley constantly cited them as authorities on many issues.[62] Roger Bacon and Albertus Magnus[63] were favorites, as were Anselm and Duns Scotus.[64] Wesley embraced the Christianizing of Aristotle's metaphysics by Thomas Aquinas, and it became his chief philosophical tool to aid theology. In fact, he urged all clergymen to study Aquinas for their betterment.[65]

In modern philosophy, he knew and detested the political philosophy of Machiavelli, and like Erasmus, Wesley unleashed sharp criticism against it.[66] Of the materialism of Thomas Hobbes, with its mechanistic phantasms and atheism, Wesley noted the hopelessness of Hobbes upon his death-bed.[67] In the case of Francis Bacon, Wesley was much kinder.[68] John Locke was Wesley's favorite modern thinker. Wesley quickly followed his mother's prompting and accepted Locke's epistemology, never departing from it.[69] But when David Hume carried Locke's empiricism to its logical conclusion - skepticism - Wesley rejected Hume.[70] The philosophical conclusion of Bishop Berkeley, that material substance does not exist, was known by Wesley but not appreciated (Wesley arguing that material substance does exist as a created substance).[71] The German mystic and theosophist, Jakob Behmen, did not escape Wesley's philosophical notice, either.[72] The monadology of Leibniz presented Wesley with numerous philosophical challenges.[73] Pascal, with his rational arguments for God's existence, was read and greatly esteemed by Wesley.[74]

Of the French philosophers, with the notable exception of Descartes, Wesley was quite negative, primarily of Voltaire and Rousseau.[75] As we shall see later in this study, Rene Descartes was a special source of rational truth for Wesley.

On one occasion, Wesley praised the Islamic philosophers of Arabia for their intellectual progressiveness during the Middle Ages. They had embraced Aristotelianism.[76]

These are but a few of the philosophers cited by Wesley. A thorough and systematic study of this area is sorely needed.

On February 6, 1756, John Wesley published his famous *ADDRESS TO THE CLERGY*, in which he treated the subject of sound education for those taking holy orders. After placing the Bible as the foundation, with intense study in Hebrew and Greek, Wesley argued that logic is the next necessary subject to be mastered. The popular and mistaken notion that "logic is good for nothing" was strongly rejected by Wesley. It has numerous benefits, among which are - it makes people talk less, showing them what is and what is not, "and how extremely hard it is to prove anything."[77] Furthermore, logic is the key to understanding metaphysics, and metaphysics has long been used by the Church to clarify theology. The Scholastic Age of the Church was the zenith of this application. Unlike Luther, Wesley did not see the Scholasticism of the Middle Ages as the "whore of Babylon." Instead, he told the clergy that a proficiency in the metaphysics of the Schoolmen is essential to the understanding of the best thought of the Christian faith -

> "Do I understand metaphysics; if not the depths of the Schoolmen, the subtleties of Scotus or Aquinas, yet the first rudiments, the general principles, of that useful science? Have I conquered so much of it, as to clear my apprehension and range my ideas under proper heads; so much as enables me to read with ease and pleasure, as well as profit, Dr. Henry More's Works, Malebranche's 'Search after Truth,' and Dr. Clarke's 'Demonstration of the Being and Attributes of God?"[78]

Wesley's return to the Schoolmen involved the ontological argument of St. Anselm, as a rational device for establishing the existence of God. The argument was also termed a "proof" by many. The word "ontological" has its origin in the Greek word *ontos*, or "being." Reduced to its most basic form, the argument affirms -

> "Now we believe that Thou art a being than which none greater can be thought. Or can it be that there is no such being, since 'the fool hath said in his heart, There is no God'? But when this same fool hears what I am saying - 'A being than which none greater can be thought' - he understands what he hears, and what he understands is in his understanding, even if he does not understand that it exists. For it is one thing for an object to be in the understanding, and another thing to understand that it exists... Even the fool, then, must be convinced that a being than which none greater can be thought exists at least in his understanding, since when he hears this he understands it, and whatever is understood is in the understanding. But clearly that than which a greater cannot be thought cannot exist in the understanding alone, it can be thought of as existing also in reality, and this is greater. Therefore, if that than which a greater cannot be thought is in the understanding alone, this same thing than which a greater cannot be thought is that than which a greater can be thought. But obviously, this is impossible. Without doubt, therefore, there exists, both in the understanding and in reality, something than which a greater cannot be thought... So, then, there truly is a being than which a greater cannot be thought - so truly that it cannot be thought of as not existing. And Thou art this being, O Lord our God."[79]

Wesley, no doubt, recognized what any student of philosophy sees behind and underneath Anselm's argument - the ancient ontology of Parmenides (circa 515 B.C.). Parmenides concluded that "only Being is." What led to this conclusion? This line of reasoning - Substantial change is impossible, for if being has originated, it must have come from Being or non-being. In the latter case being would have come from nothing, which is impossible. In the former case, however, it would have come from itself, which means that it always was. Another logical tack by Parmenides ran - Either being exists or it does not. If it originated, it is not being, and it will not ever be if it comes into existence. If it exists, however, it exists without beginning or end, unmoved.[80] Moreover, Parmenides asserted, Being is not capable of being divided, since it is all of the same substance (*homoousios*). Hence, there is no more or less of it in one place which might keep it from holding together. It abides fixed everywhere, and all is full of what is - a *plenum* of Being.[81] This means that there is *no* nothing, that is, the word "nothing" does not name anything. What is (Being) is indestructible. Destruction means change into nothing, and there is no nothing. Hence, Being is eternal in its existence.[82] Being is motionless, because in order to move it must have a place to which it can move, but all is full of what is - and Being is.[83]

Little wonder that Anselm exclaimed to God - "What art Thou, save the highest of all beings, alone self-existent. . ."[84] From his *PROSLOGION*, Anselm's conclusion from Parmenides has the ring of finality -

"Thou art through thyself, and not through another. Thus Thou art the very life Thou livest, and the wisdom by which Thou art wise, and the very goodness by which Thou art good. . . and so with all Thine attributes."[85]

"There are no parts in Thee, O Lord, and Thou art not many; rather, Thou art so truly one being, and identical with Thyself, that Thou art unlike Thyself in nothing, but art unity itself, divisible by no understanding. . . There are no parts in Thee or in Thy eternity which Thou art, there is no part of Thee or of Thy eternity anywhere or ever, but Thou art everywhere whole, and Thy eternity is always whole."[86]

Finality indeed! The existence of God is understood by the mind
when faith has directed reason through precise avenues of logic.
However, Anselm was embattled by an anti-intellectual element
within the Church, a movement that claimed reason destroys true
faith and leads to skepticism.[87] History has vindicated Anselm, to a
degree, in that the Church of England incorporated his essential
theology into its *HOMILIES*,[88] and Wesley incorporated his chief
arguments into treatises and sermons, directly quoting him but often without naming him.[89]

   In addition to the ontological argument, Anselm offered other
logical proofs for the existence of God, which Wesley used in describing divine eminence and causality to his Methodist followers.
"The Way of Eminence" was one of two Medieval ways of arguing
for God's existence. It was a deductive argument that had its origin
with Parmenides, then Plato refined it, St. Augustine Christianized
it, and Anselm sharpened it.[90] The second Medieval argument was
termed "The Way of Causality," which will be treated later in this
chapter.

   Anselm's version of the Way of Eminence emphasized God's
existence from "Goodness." Its logical progression moved along
this line of reasoning - Wherever there is a better, there must be a
best; where an attribute admits of degree, since some attributes are
comparative (for one thing may be as good as, better than, or less
good than), there is some element common throughout its variation; that which causes something to be good must itself be good,
supremely good; a thing is better if it exists through itself, than if it
exists through something else; moreover, it is identical with the
supreme Good; Goodness is supremely good and must, therefore,
exist through itself, but what exists through itself is existence; Existence and Goodness are one, and God is that One. Anselm further
reasoned that God (as Supreme Being), therefore, is living, wise,
powerful, true, just and blessed, since he (as Supreme Good) must
be whatever he is - it is absolutely better to be than not to be. His
divine nature does not have these characteristics because that
would imply something higher than himself - the divine nature *is*
these characteristics.[91]

The "Way of Causality" originated in the philosophy of Aristotle,[92] was used by the Arabian thinkers of Islam in the early Middle Ages, by Jewish philosophers like Maimonides, and finally by Christian Scholastic teachers, especially Duns Scotus and Aquinas. Scotus refined it into an elaborate piece of logic, then Aquinas popularized it.[93] Wesley relied on this argument, and he liked the no-nonsense spirit of Scotus who once said, "If you hold that nothing is self-evident, I will not argue with you for it is clear you are a quibbler and are not to be convinced."[94]

Before surveying the causality-proof of God's existence, several observations about Aristotle are needed, or else the argument as it came to Wesley will lack precision. Behind this Scholastic line of reasoning was Aristotle's definitions of substance, being/becoming, change, motion, causality, and God. John Wesley was well-schooled in Aristotelian thought, and he was both an admirer and a critic of the great thinker. When he read John Locke's broadside attack on Aristotle's syllogisms, Wesley charged Locke with gross ignorance of logic.[95] Moreover, in his praise of Aristotle, against Locke's claim that logic has perverted language, Wesley wrote -

"The abuse of logic has; but the true use of it is the noblest means under heaven to prevent or cure the obscurity of language. To divide simple terms according to the logical rules of division, and then to define each member of the division according to the three rules of definition does all that human art can do, in order to our having a clear and distinct idea of every word we use."[96]

However, on the subject of Aristotelian science, Wesley was the persistent critic. He generally agreed with the devasting evaluations of Francis Bacon, which had been institutionalized against Aristotelian science at Oxford and Cambridge universities. Like Bacon, Wesley went to the Greek's jugular by ridiculing his abstracting of natural philosophy by the use of mathematics and symbolic representations.[97] Wesley detested all forms of "mathematical reasoning" in relation to religion.[98] He would be horrified by contemporary attempts to quantify empirical experiences of a spiritual nature.

Nevertheless, Wesley remained a conscious Aristotelian in reference to logic, causality, and related subjects, as long as they were not contrary to Scripture.

Aristotle rearranged Plato's two separate worlds - the upper (Real World) being completely transcendent from the lower (Unreal world). He removed the gulf that Plato argued existed between the two worlds, making but one world of actual things.[99] However, Aristotle recognized a division within the visible and sensible aspect of the world order - the celestial and the terrestrial. The celestial is characterized by perfect circular motions of heavenly bodies, while the terrestrial possesses bodies of compounded elements (earth, air, fire, and water) that move in rectilinear fashion.[100] For instance, Aristotle believed, earth tends to move toward the center of the universe, and fire toward the orb of the universe. The pre-Socratic doctrine of opposites was involved in the creation of the four elements that compose matter: the hot and cold, the dry and moist. The hot and dry combined to make fire. The hot and moist formed air. The cold and moist created water; and the cold and dry made earth. Once existent, the four elements combined in various proportions (Pythagoras) to form composite bodies, subject to the transformation of qualitative changes. Knowledge, therefore, consists of the analysis of physics and metaphysics, the two being inseparable.[101] Aristotelian metaphysics is the study of matter taking on form - the potential becoming actual.[102]

In physics, Aristotle held, Plato's "particulars" are really "substances." But, they are "individual substances," having two dimensions: (1) an universal character, sharing common properties with other objects like themselves; and (2) a character of individuality that may be shared with other objects, but it generally belongs to this object alone. This latter characteristic Aristotle called "primary substance."[103] "Matter" is the physical stuff from which an object is made, and "form" is the physical shape the thing has. When considering matter, we are concerned with "thisness," while with form it is "whatness." The material question, "What is this?" refers to a particular property somehow unique to this object, such as being made of this "particular" bit of stuff. On the other hand, the formal question, "To what class does this object belong?" treats the concern with a property shared in common with other similar objects.[104] But, form also involves the function or purpose of an object, and this factor means the form has a functional structure that enables the object to fulfill its purpose. Such a functional principle was essential for Aristotle's teleological system of metaphysics (And Wesley's too!). Form is naturally imposed upon matter, organizing it into specific arrangements. Hence matter possesses the "possibility" of serving a purpose.[105] Form without matter (Plato) is a mere abstraction, as matter without form would be. Each individual thing (object), then, is comprised of matter and form together, with the possibility of serving a purpose. In fact, the whole universe, for Aristotle, is an hierarchy of individual objects of this composition. Each individual object of nature is on some particular level in this hierarchical structure, being subject to a process of development, called "potentiality." The purpose of each object is to finally complete itself (actuality). Aristotle's acorn (potentiality) finally, at long last, becomes altogether an oak tree (actuality). Aristotle called the driving force within this developmental process "entelechy."[106] Within the term, the Greek word *telos* (end, goal) can be detected. If the goal/end of actuality is ever attained, a great number of changes will have to be made. Some Aristotelian changes are simple, involving only form, and others are complex, involving form and matter. There are four kinds of change: (1) qualitative change - in which a transformation of one thing into another occurs, moving toward actuality; (2) quantitative change - in which a thing increases or decreases; (3) locomotive change - in which something changes place; and (4) substantival change - when things come into being and then pass out of being.[107] All changes are wrought by causes within the teleological process of potentiality. There are four kinds of causes: (1) Material cause - by which the operational behavior of matter determines changes under certain conditions; (2) Efficient cause - begun by a motion or action; (3) Final cause - related to the purpose for which a thing exists; and (4) Formal cause - by which a thing actualizes

and fulfills its purpose.[108]   Aristotle affirmed that we can know
things only in terms of their causes.[109] But, there can never be an
infinite series of causes.[110]   Causes effect changes, and every
change is caused by an antecedent change, and this by another, and
so on, but not to infinity. Each cause is a "mover" and eventually
there must be a mover who "himself is unmoved." The "Unmoved
Mover" - as Aristotle called God - must transmit motion, by which
change is effected, while being free from it Himself. Eternal motion has an eternal cause which causes circular locomotion within
the universe. Since the four elements have already combined to
make matter, losing their rectilinear tendencies, all material objects
move in the vortex of eternal circular motion (spheres), because
every particular thing desires and loves the Unmoved Mover. The
universe turns in its spheres in emulation of his goodness, and represents the nearest approximation of his perfection that sense objects can achieve.[111]   But while God is the Unmoved Mover, he is
not a providential deity who looks after his creatures. Aristotle's
God was not like the God of Judaism and Christianity. He is not
worshipped, nor does he move the world in love, but rather the
world is moved by love of him.[112]

   John Wesley learned the logic and metaphysics of Aristotle while
a young student at Oxford.[113]   Later in life, he incorporated vast
amounts of Aristotelian material into his writings, but this material
was usually the Christianized version of Thomas Aquinas (A.D.
1225-1274). The intellectual work of reconciling Aristotelian philosophy and Christian theology, however, began with Albertus
Magnus (A.D. 1200-1280), the teacher of Aquinas at Cologne.[114]
Thomas completed the reconciliation.[115]   Wesley recommended
the study of Albertus Magnus[116] and Thomas Aquinas[117] for their
valuable contributions to Christian knowledge. Young ministers,
Wesley argued, should especially master "the first rudiments, (and)
the general principles of the useful science (metaphysics)" of
Aquinas.[118]

   Until the thirteenth century, the theology of St. Augustine
dominated the Church. He had reconciled Christian faith and Platonic thought, but without the pantheistic implications of Ploti-

nus.[119] In the thirteenth century, however, Albertus and Thomas replaced Plato with Aristotle, making a sanitized Aristotelianism the new "Handmaid of Theology." Like Augustine, the two Schoolmen had to avoid pantheism in such a reconciliation.[120] Aquinas recognized that Platonism's view of two radically different worlds - one sensible and material and the other non-sensible and spiritual, the one created and the other eternal - comes very close to Christian belief. Nevertheless, because of the dangers inherent in Platonic mysticism, the whole tradition should be scrapped in favor of a new synthesis. Moreover, he believed, Platonism hinders a valid doctrine of revelation by insisting on the reality of innate ideas. Aquinas, like Aristotle, rejected the notion of innate ideas. Knowledge must be acquired empirically, both of these pre-Lockean thinkers asserted. As a result, Aquinas rejected Augustine's ontological argument for God's existence because it was dependent upon a doctrine of innate ideas.[121] Thomas claimed that all created things reflect the being of God who is the first cause. Also, in order to discover his Being we must use our reason as far as it will go - aided by both grace and revelation. Reason must analyze the creation and its creatures, for there is no knowledge of God which does not depend on this knowledge of his works in creation. Thomas Aquinas erected an hierarchy similar to Aristotle's sensible order of things, complete with its own doctrine of potentiality, entelechy, and actuality. His featured nature and supernature, with man beginning in the natural and, by divine grace as a driving force of entelechy, finally actualizing himself in the supernatural. God, for St. Thomas, unlike Aristotle's deity, is the gracious Mover who steers man through his pilgrimage.[122] Using Aristotle's reasoning, Aquinas offered some logical demonstrations of God's existence. He prefaced them with a caution about the short-coming of the linguistic proof -

". . .This proposition that 'God exists' is self-evident in itself, since its predicate is the same with its subject. For God is his existence. . . But since we do not know what God is, it is not self-evident to us, but must be proved...by means of the effects of God."[123]

Consequently, proof must be found by the rational analysis of "the effects of God." In Aristotelian fashion, Aquinas began with a demonstration from cause and effect -

"...When an effect is more apparent to us than its cause, we reach a knowledge of the cause through its effect... Even though the effect should be better known to us, we can demonstrate from any effect that its cause exists, because effects always depend on some cause, and a cause must exist if its effect exists. We can demonstrate God's existence in this way, from his effects which are known to us, even though we do not know his essence."[124]

The next Thomistic demonstration, from efficient cause, proved to be Susanna Wesley's favorite argument on divine existence. Its classical statement reads -

"There is a sequence of efficient causes in sensible things. But we do not find that anything is the efficient cause of itself. Nor is this possible. But neither can the sequence of efficient causes be infinite, for in every sequence the first efficient cause is the cause of an intermediate cause, and an intermediate cause is the cause of the ultimate cause, whether the intermediate causes be many, or only one. Now, if a cause is removed, its effect is removed. Hence if there were no first efficient cause, there would be no ultimate cause, and no intermediate cause. But if the regress of efficient causes were infinite, there would be no first efficient cause. There would consequently be no ultimate effect, and no intermediate cause. But this is plainly false. We are therefore bound to suppose that there is a first efficient cause. And all men call this God."[125]

Susanna Wesley's affection for this Thomistic demonstration from efficient causes deserves a brief notice here. In a letter to her son Jacky (John's nickname), dated December 7, 1725 she wrote -

"Who but an atheist will deny that God, and God alone is the supreme efficient cause of all things, the only uncreated good! But can it be inferred from hence that he hath imparted no degree of goodness to his creatures? ...We may full as well argue that because they are not self-existent, therefore they have no being at all."[126]

Susanna was responding to a sermon by Reverend Norris, heard earlier in the day at Wroote. In that sermon, Norris implied that God's creatures were devoid of goodness. Following Thomism, Susanna rejected such depravity, as the logic of the efficient cause demonstration requires. Furthermore, as her children's school-marm, she fed their young minds with other Thomistic arguments for God's existence.[127] Jacky, for one, never forgot this maternal influence.

Another demonstration from reason for God's existence, offered by Aquinas, and known by Wesley, involved the Aristotelian principle of motion -

"We see that all things that are moved are moved by others, lower things by higher ones. The elements, for instance, are moved by the celestial bodies, and among the elements, the stronger move the weaker. Even among the celestial bodies, the lower ones are moved by the higher ones. Now this procedure cannot go on to infinity. Since everything that is moved functions as a sort of instrument of the first mover, if there were no first mover, then whatever things are in motion would be simply instruments. Of course, if an infinite series of movers and things moved were possible, with no first mover, then the whole infinity of movers and things moved would be instruments. Now it is ridiculous, even to unlearned people, to suppose that instruments are moved but not by any principal agent. For, this would be like supposing that the construction of a box or bed could be accomplished by putting a saw or a hatchet to work without any carpenter to use them. Therefore, there must be a first mover existing above all - and this we call God."[128]

John Wesley knew this particular demonstration well, and used it in his sermon on *GOD'S APPROBATION OF HIS WORKS*. It was the foundation for his argument that God infused the "principle of motion" in the Creation.[129]

In addition to Thomistic influence, Wesley was indebted to the ontological and existential arguments of John Duns Scotus. In his advice to clergymen, Wesley singled out Duns Scotus as the best of the School philosophers, worthy to be mastered.[130] Wesley rightly referred to the "subtleties of Scotus" because historically he is known as the "Subtle Doctor."

Born in A.D. 1266 in Scotland, Scotus lived a short life of forty-two years. He was educated at Oxford and later taught there and at Cambridge. Like Magnus and Aquinas, Scotus attempted a synthesis of Aristotle and Christian theology.[131] In his approach, however, he emphasized the *univocity of being*. There are two modes of being - the infinite and the finite - and yet but one being. The task of the Christian thinker is to prove that the *prime mover* is the *First Being*. The Scot set about to do just that, conducting an analysis of *being as being* and its several kinds of attributes. This analysis had four basic ideas: (1) The idea of Being - defined as a subject whose existence implies no contradiction; (2) The idea of Existence - defined as the Real or Extramental World; (3) The idea of two types of attributes - those coextensive with Being (One, True, and Good -in unity with Being), and the disjunctive attributes of which there are an unlimited number (infinite-or-finite, neces-sary-or-contingent, and cause-or-caused); and (4) Other predicates whose definitions contain no hint of imperfection or limitation.[132]

Surprisingly, it was from the "disjunctive attributes" that Scotus erected his rational demonstration for God's existence. The argu-ment unfolds accordingly - If some being is finite, then some being must be infinite; If some being is contingent, then some being must be necessary, for it is not possible for the more imperfect extreme of the disjunction to be existentially predicated of being particu-larly taken *unless* the more perfect extreme be existentially verified by some other being upon which it depends. The conclusion is clear - There is one, and only one, being in which pure perfection coexists. Such an infinite being we call God.[133]

To our knowledge, Wesley's first recognition of this demonstra-tion came in January 1731, in a letter to his father concerning this argument and how Archbishop King had lately used it.[134] Years later, still under the spell of its rational power, Wesley affirmed, "I am assured that there is an infinite and independent Being, and that it is impossible there should be more than one... that this One God is the Father of all things, especially of angels and men."[135] Furthermore, he added, this one God is rightly called "The Father of the spirits of all flesh,"[136] and "The Father of the Universe."[137]

Wesley's conclusion arose from a Scotian question - "What is the proportion between finite and infinite?" Reason necessitated that the "existence of the creatures demonstratively shows the existence of their Creator."[138] This Scholastic approach became one of Wesley's favorite tools for treating the subject of God's existence, appearing in treatises, sermons, and even prayers -"Ask. . .in some manner resembling this - 'O Thou Being of beings, Thou cause of all!'"[139]

Behind this philosophical nomenclature lies traditional metaphysics. Aristotle had said that "Being is what a thing is." Being is also a thing of a certain quality. *Substance* is the primary sense of Being.[140] During the Scholastic Age, thinkers spoke of "finite substances" as well as "infinite substance." St. Thomas Aquinas, the Angelic Doctor, made such a distinction. In the Modern Period, the seventeenth century French thinker, Rene Descartes, the Father of Continental Rationalism, made the same distinction. Both Aquinas and Descartes held that finite substances were created by the Infinite Substance (God) and were consequently made dependent upon him for their being. Infinite Substance, however, is not dependent on anything outside itself. John Wesley would later argue this distinction as his own, and he would reject Bishop Berkeley's position that finite substance (material substance) does not exist. But, a further distinction is necessary, involving *substance* and *attribute*. An attribute cannot stand alone. It depends for its being and existence on something else, on a substance.[141] Descartes asserted that everything that exists is either a substance or an attribute of substance (from Scotus). A thing which so exists that it needs no other thing in order to exist can only be God. All other things are attributes and can only exist "by the help of the concourse of God."[142] In this metaphysical context, Descartes modified the finite/infinite argument of Scotus for the existence of God. His version proceeds along this line - Finite things, such as the self, not only lack the power to produce themselves, but also the power to maintain themselves in existence, unless they are continually recreated by God. Nothing could prevent the world from suddenly ceasing to be, at this moment, if God did not at this very moment, create the next moment.[143]

Descartes' philosophy was no mystery to John Wesley. He knew and understood it well. He often employed it in his sermons and treatises, without mentioning the name of this controversial French thinker.[144] He never gave Descartes blanket approval, however, and frequently took him to task. On the finite/infinite argument for God's existence, Wesley was in complete agreement with the Frenchman. As did Descartes, Wesley often spoke of God as Creator, Preserver, and Governor of all things.[145] In an elaboration of Descartes' rational demonstration, Wesley claimed that the true God is also -

> ". . .the Supporter of all things he hath made. He beareth, upholdeth, sustaineth, all created things by the word of his power, by the same powerful word which brought them out of nothing. As this was absolutely necessary for the beginning of their existence, it is equally so for the continuance of it; Were his almighty influence withdrawn, they could not subsist a moment longer. Hold up a stone in the air; the moment you withdraw your hand, it naturally falls to the ground. In like manner, were he to withdraw his hand for a moment, the creation would fall into nothing."[146]

In his sermon *ON DIVINE PROVIDENCE*, Wesley further explained this Cartesian version of the demonstration from the finite to the infinite -

> "And as this all-wise, all-gracious Being created all things, so he sustains all things. He is the Preserver as well as the Creator of everything that exists... Now it must be that he knows everything he has made, and everything he preserves, from moment to moment; otherwise, he could not preserve it, he could not continue to it the being which he has given it."[147]

Hidden beneath the words of this quotation lays a controversy involving Sir Isaac Newton and Wilhelm Gottfried Leibniz. Newton, oft cited by Wesley, maintained that God knows everything because of his universal presence in created space. Leibniz, on the other hand, argued that God knows everything because, in addition to his omnipresence, his "operation" in preserving what he has created is involved.[148] Wesley sided with Leibniz on this issue - "Now it must be that he (God) knows everything he has made, and everything he preserves."

One should not suppose that Wesley was appreciative of every modification of the argument of Scotus from finitude. Descartes offered another version, synthesized with Anselm's ontological proof. Its logic runs - I have an idea of God. I myself cannot be the cause of it. It is a necessary consequence that I am not alone in the world, but that there is besides myself some other being who exists as the cause of that idea. That other Being is God.[149] Wesley warned against such "clear ideas" -

"For thinking is not, as many (Descartes) suppose, the act of a pure spirit; but the act of a spirit connected with a body, and playing upon a set of natural keys. It cannot possibly, therefore, make any better music than the nature and state of its instruments allow it."[150]

The radical conclusion of Descartes, that "minds are distinct from bodies," was much too radical for Wesley. The Methodist founder saw thinking as a psychosomatic process in which there is no guarantee that any idea may be adequate in representing reality. While Henry More publicly referred to Descartes as "that pleasant wit,"[151] Wesley chose never to credit Descartes when he used his arguments.

In his *ADDRESS TO THE CLERGY*, Wesley advised ministers to study the metaphysics of Aquinas and Scotus so that they could then read and appreciate the works of Henry More, Nicolas Malebranche, and Samuel Clarke, "with ease and pleasure, as well as profit."[152] These thinkers were recognized for their arguments concerning the existence of God. Henry More and Nicolas Malebranche had something in common - Cartesian philosophy. As for Samuel Clarke, he was both a disciple and advocate of Sir Isaac Newton.

Henry More (A.D. 1614-1687) was commonly known as the "Cambridge Platonist." While a student at Christ Church College

(Cambridge), he studied Aristotle and the Scholastic thinkers, but he rejected them all for Neoplatonism.[153] Despite his mysticism, he began a correspondence with Descartes in 1648. As a result, his views changed somewhat. In one letter to Descartes, More pledged his admiration and marveled that their views were almost identical - "So entirely have my own thoughts run along the channels in which your fertile mind has anticipated me."[154]

More's book, AN ANTIDOTE AGAINST ATHEISM (1653), represents a reformulation of Anselm's ontological argument and Aquinas's teleological argument for God's existence. Interspersed throughout are anecdotes about witches and ghosts, introduced into the argument to verify that spiritual forces are at work in the world.[155] Such forces point beyond themselves and their existences to the reality of God's existence. Disembodied souls (spirits), as well as souls within bodies, demonstrate the metaphysical need to be grounded in infinite existence. More's argument was not unique in the seventeenth century. Richard Baxter, a Puritan divine of the same era, had also written on this subject, and Wesley was an admiring reader of Baxter.[156] In fact, Wesley equally admired More's ANTIDOTE. More convinced Wesley that rightly understanding witchcraft and apparitions undergirds Christian Theism. In his JOURNAL, Wesley stated this thesis -

> ". . .Most of the men of learning. . .have given up all accounts of witches and apparitions, as mere old wives' fables. I am sorry for it. . . the giving up (of) witchcraft is, in effect, giving up the Bible; and they know. . . that if but one account of the intercourse of men with separate spirits be admitted, their whole castle in the air (Deism, Atheism, Materialism) falls to the ground."[157]

The thought of Nicolas Malebranche elicited great admiration from John Wesley. His book, THE SEARCH AFTER TRUTH, was one of Wesley's favorite resources in natural philosophy.[158] In fact, Wesley placed this work on his suggested bibliography for ministerial preparation. Malebranche wrote with a preaching style, and Wesley liked this approach. His ideas carried the biblical ring as well as Descartes' philosophical arguments.

The life of Malebranche spanned from 1638 to 1715. He was French, and the mantle of Descartes fell upon him, making him the second most important Cartesian thinker.[159] Ordained in the Roman Catholic Congregation of the Oratory, Malebranche sought to synthesize St. Paul and Descartes. His intellectual conversion to Descartes came after reading his famous TREATISE ON MAN, which describes the mechanics of human physiology, drawing a sharp distinction between the soul and the body. From St. Paul's sermon in Athens (Acts XVII), Malebranche emphasized that "in God we live, and move, and have our being." Leibniz summarized his synthesis as "the natural theology of the Chinese."[160] Obviously this characterization did not please Malebranche, and Leibniz continued to be his constant critic. Malebranche, however, pursued his inquiry by treating the problem of causality -created things being dependent upon God who is the "true cause" of change in the universe. Like Descartes, he affirmed that "it is God who creates and conserves us from moment to moment and who alone acts on and for us."[161]

Malebranche was also interested in demonstrating the existence of God, and he used the finite/infinite argument noted above, but with some modifications -

"One must remember that when we see a creature, we see it neither in itself nor of itself, for we see it only through the perception of certain perfections in God that represent it. Thus, we can see the essence of this creature, without seeing its existence, i.e., we can see its idea without seeing it; we can see that necessary existence is not included in the idea that represents it, since it is not necessary for it actually to exist in order for us to see it, unless we claim that created objects are immediately visible, intelligible in themselves and capable of illuminating, affecting, and modifying intelligences. But it is not the same with infinitely perfect being; one can see it only in itself, for nothing finite can represent the infinite. Therefore, one cannot see God without his existing; one cannot see the essence of an infinitely perfect being without seeing its existence; one cannot conceive it simply as a possible being; nothing limits it; nothing can represent it. Therefore, if one thinks of it, it must exist."[162]

Wesley was correct - one should master Aquinas and Scotus before moving on to Malebranche! A good understanding of Descartes is essential also. Wesley, of course, knew and appreciated them all, but only when they somehow squared with the Bible rightly understood.

Wesley's philosophical eclecticism was selective and not without its tensions. A case in point involved his recommendation that ministers read and understand the works of Dr. Samuel Clarke, especially his *A DEMONSTRATION OF THE BEING AND ATTRIBUTES OF GOD.*[163] Wesley offered this advice in 1756, at the height of his evangelical ministry. The Wesley of 1731, however, was extremely critical of Clarke because of his views concerning the Church - the Church is not of God![164] Dr. Frank Baker claims Clarke's writings were both Deistic and Unitarian in implication.[165] Nevertheless, over the years, Wesley found some redeeming virtues in the DEMONSTRATION.

Samuel Clarke (A.D. 1675-1729) was educated at Cambridge, being subjected to a rigid study of Cartesian physics. While there, he became friends with Isaac Newton and converted to the ways of Newtonian physics. Thereafter, he set about to refute Cartesianism. He took holy orders in the Church of England and gained the reputation of being a great pulpiteer. His sermons were collected and published.[166] He also delivered a series of sermons at St. Paul's Cathedral in London, as the Boyle Lectures, the year being 1705.[167] These sermons were drawn from his *DEMONSTRATION OF THE BEING AND ATTRIBUTES OF GOD.* Paul Edwards notes that these sermon-lectures offered a new argument for God's existence and attributes. The argument was a chain of eight propositions: (1) It is absolutely and undeniably certain that something has existed from all eternity. There is something now, and since something cannot come from nothing, there must have always been something (reminiscent of Parmenides?). (2) There has existed from eternity some one, unchangeable and independent being - a single, persistent being. (3) This unchangeable and persistent being, who has existed from eternity without any external cause of its existence, must, therefore, be self-existent. "Self-existent" means

"Necessarily-existent." (Is this an acceptable transition, from self-existence to necessary-existence?).[168] (4-8) In these propositions, Clarke treated the attributes of this self-existent, necessarily-existent being -infinite, omnipresent, intelligent, free, omnipotent, wise, good, and just.[169] This book, together with his other entitled DISCOURSE, proved helpful to all embattled theists of that day. Clarke's writings were so very quotable. They became an Enlightenment version of Peter Lombard's SENTENCES. The following sentences of Clarke find their way into Wesley's numerous writings - (1) The self-existent Being, of necessity must be infinite and omnipresent.[170] (2) Whatever exists therefore by an Absolute Necessity in its nature, must needs be infinite as well as eternal.[171] (3) The infinity of the self-existent Being must be an infinity of fullness as well as of immensity; that is, it must not only be without limits, but also without diversity, defect, or interruption.[172] (4) The self-existent Being must be a most simple, unchangeable, incorruptible Being, without parts, figure, motion, divisibility, or any other properties we find in matter.[173] (5) The self-existent Being must of necessity be but One.[174] (6) The unity of God is a unity of Nature or Essence.[175] (7) It is impossible there should be two different self-existent independent principles, as some thinkers have imagined; such as God and matter.[176] (8) From an infinite cause effects must necessarily follow.[177] (9) The self-existent and original cause of all things, must be an intelligent Being.[178] (10) The Supreme Cause and Author of all things must of necessity be infinitely wise.[179] (11) The Supreme Cause and Author of all things must of necessity be a Being of infinite goodness.[180] (12) If God be an all-powerful, omnipresent, intelligent, wise, and free Being, he cannot possibly but know at all times and in all places everything that is, and foreknow all things.[181]

These propositions find their way into many of Wesley's discussions, without him citing their origins. A thorough reading of Clarke and then Wesley is profitable, illuminating this entire area of God's existence and attributes.[182]

GOD'S ETERNITY

It was New Years Day, 1733. Susanna Wesley took pen in hand and began a lengthy letter to one of her sons, John. She found it difficult to write, being troubled with family matters, but, after a while, she was overwhelmed with the memory of William Law. His mind, it has been said, was always "full of the sense of that Blessed Being." Now she became inspired and began to imitate Law's literary style -

> "Who can think, much less speak on that vast subject - his greatness, his dignity, astonishes us! The purity of his goodness, his redeeming love, confounds and overwhelms us! At the perception of his glory our feeble powers are suspended, and nature faints before the God of nature.
>
> For my part, after many years' search and inquiry, I still continue to pay my devotions to an unknown God. I cannot know him. I dare not say I love him - only this, I have chose him for my only happiness, my all, my only God, in a word, for my God. And when I sound my will, I feel it adheres to its choice, though not so faithfully as it ought. Therefore, I desire your prayers, which I need much more than you do mine.
>
> That God is everywhere present, and we always present to him, is certain, but that he should always be present to us is scarce consistent with our mortal state. Some choice souls, 'tis true, have attained such a habitual sense of his presence as admits of few interruptions. But what my dear - Consider, he is so infinitely blessed! So altogether lovely! That every perception of him, every approach (in contemplation) to his supreme glory and blessedness imparts such a vital joy and gladness to the heart as banishes all pain and sense of misery - And were eternity added to this happiness it would be heaven."[183]

Susanna's reverent agnosticism, and its accompanying deep piety, recognized the existing gulf between the mind of the Christian and the eternal reality of God. Who can speak a word concerning God's greatness? His dignity? Or even his eternity? Seven years after the Aldersgate experience, Wesley echoed his mother's reverent agnosticism, while more than matching her piety -

"What is the proportion between finite and infinite? I grant, the existence of the creatures demonstratively shows the existence of their Creator. The whole creation speaks that there is a God. Thus far is clear. But who will show me what God is? The more I reflect the more convinced I am that it is not possible for any or all creatures to take off the veil which is on my heart, that I might discern this unknown God; to draw the curtain back which now hangs between, that I may see him which is invisible. This veil of flesh now hides him from my sight; and who is able to make it transparent? so that I may perceive, through this glass, God always before me, till I see him face to face! I want to know this great God who filleth heaven and earth, who is above, beneath, and on every side, in all places of his dominion; who just now besets me behind and before, and lays his hand upon me; and yet I am no more acquainted with him, than one of the inhabitants of Jupiter or Saturn."[184]

This public confession and aspiration was concluded by Wesley with an Anselmic-type prayer - "O Thou Being of beings, Thou cause of all, Thou seest my heart: Thou understandest all my thoughts: But how small a part of Thy ways do I understand! I know not what is above, beneath, on every side; I know not my own soul."[185] He did not pretend to understand divine mysteries, especially that of eternity. Insights into mysteries are one thing, understanding is quite another. Understanding of all mysteries awaits the Christian only in Abraham's bosom or in the Resurrection, which ever comes first. Until then, however, the believer's power of reason is assisted by the Spirit to apprehend in some basic way the Scriptures that treat God's being and attributes, his eternity and immensity, his power, wisdom and holiness.[186] Then too, the historic Christian community with its great scholars, persons of faith and rational integrity, had long addressed these biblical themes. Wesley was convinced that the contributions of these persons should be taken into consideration, but only when subjected to the authority of Scripture.

The biblical theme of eternity runs the whole length of Holy Writ. Wesley chose to exegete three main Old Testament passages on the subject - Exodus III, IV, and Psalm XC.

His commentary on Exodus III, 14 - from the *EXPLANATORY NOTES UPON THE OLD TESTAMENT* - treats the holy name Jehovah given by God to Moses at the burning bush. Wesley argued that this name signifies several things: (1) that God's true nature is revealed linguistically in the name - *I AM THAT I AM* - It is God's nature to be self-existent, having his being of himself, without dependency upon any other. Also, it is his nature to be self-sufficient, and thus all-sufficient, as "the inexhaustible fountain of being and bliss." (2) that he is eternal and unchangeable, always the same, yesterday, today and forever.[187]

The *EXPLANATORY NOTES* on Exodus IV, 2, show Wesley's ability to elaborate on a theme previously treated with only a minimum of repetition. "*I am Jehovah* - The same with *I am that I am*, the fountain of being and blessedness, and infinite perfection... A God performing what he had promised, and so giving being to his promises... A God perfecting what he had begun, and finishing his own work."[188] The reader should observe that Wesley, in these two passages from Exodus, combined both biblical and philosophical languages. The philosophical are reminiscent of Scotus, Descartes, and Malebranche - "self-existent," "being of himself," "without dependency," "self-sufficient," "all-sufficient," "inexhaustible," "unchangeable," and "infinite perfection." For Wesley the Bible and reason clearly unite to affirm the nature and eternity of God.

Before leaving the Yahwist theme of the divine name, going on to a consideration of Psalm XC, a brief adventure into the New Testament version of the divine nature and eternity, as depicted by Wesley, is appropriate. In his sermon *UPON OUR LORD'S SERMON ON THE MOUNT - DISCOURSE VI*, Wesley treated the phrase "Hallowed be thy name." The "name" was "Jehovah," which, he argued, "implies God's existence and all his attributes and perfections." It also signifies God's eternity, as the Apostle John later translated the name as "The Alpha and the Omega, the beginning and the end; He which is, and which was, and which is to come."[189] Behind these Wesleyan comments, one can detect the thought of Anselm - that God and eternity are actually one, inseparable reality

- "Thy eternity which Thou art!"[190] In the same spirit, Wesley spoke of "the Divine Eternity" as the "*vitae interminabilis tota simul et perfecta possessio*" (The at once entire and perfect possession of never-ending life).[191] This *vitae* is synonymous with the *zoa* of the Johannine Tradition - *zoa* being the very life of God imparted to mankind through the new birth, and generally translated as *everlasting life*. With eternity interpreted by Wesley as "never-ending life" - the very life of God - the reality of eternity becomes *awful* indeed! Eternity, then, is not super-time strung out for millions of years or aeons. Eternity, according to Wesley, meant the very life of God, without beginning and end, always self-existent, self-sufficient, unchangeable, inexhaustible, and of infinite perfection.

Psalm XC now takes on a specific meaning in Wesley's encounter with eternity. Using verse two for his text, Wesley developed his famous sermon entitled ON ETERNITY - "From everlasting to everlasting Thou art God." His opening words were serious - "I fain would speak of that awful subject, - eternity." "Awful" indeed! The term means "to be filled with awe." Such sermons often fall upon little and narrow minds which never catch the spirit of awe! A "good sermon" for these minds is that which is light, humorous, and entertaining - one that leads simple emotions around the cow pasture of earthy pleasures. Wesley was never one to entertain a congregation with humorous anecdotes. He took his calling and message to be above that sort of thing. He viewed his preaching commission as demanding the turning of each congregation's attention towards the qualities of the real and invisible world. His sermon *ON ETERNITY* is such a sermon, depending on the assistance of the Holy Spirit to press its message home in every hearing soul, and to compensate for the weakness of the preacher.

The sermon begins with a consideration of how one can appreciate the principle of eternity. Wesley's solution is the "use of analogy," a common philosophical device of logic. He selected a difficult pair of concepts for his analogies -immensity and duration. For many contemporary sermon-tasters, these concepts might be incomprehensible. Wesley's basic analogy runs as follows -

"Does it (eternity) not bear some affinity. . . to. . . immensity? May not space, though an unsubstantial thing, be compared with another unsubstantial thing, - duration? But what is immensity? It is boundless space. And what is eternity? It is boundless duration."[192]

Philosophically, Wesley was over-simplifying the eternity side of the analogy. He surely knew better than this, but seeing his hearers might not be able to grasp the orthodox semantics and syntactics of a philosopher, he settled for the simpler approach. Why did he turn to "duration" as the meaning of eternity after he had earlier rooted its meaning in the *zoa* of God? Because he thought the latter would explain the former. But, the life of God is a qualitative concept and duration is a quantitative concept. In what sense can the one be an analogy for the other? Yet, throughout this sermon the Johannine and the quantitative mix, with the latter being Wesley's chief argument.

With eternity being defined as "boundless duration," Wesley used the popular idea of seventeenth century English theology -dividing eternity into two parts: (1) eternity a *parte ante*; and (2) eternity a *parte post*.[193] A *parte ante* signifies eternity that is already past - that is, eternity prior to the creation of time, and eternity and time until this present moment. A *parte post* is eternity yet to come when time ceases to be.[194] Wesley's argument for this distinction was essentially a Puritan one, implied in the text of Psalm XC - "And does there not seem to be an intimation in the text? 'Thou art God from everlasting;' -Here is an expression of that eternity which is past: 'To everlasting:' Here is an expression of that eternity which is to come."[195] Anticipating criticism, Wesley defended this point -

"Perhaps, indeed, some may think it is not strictly proper to say, there is an eternity that is past. But the meaning is easily understood: We mean thereby duration which has no beginning; as by eternity to come, we mean that duration which will have no end. It is God alone (to use the exalted language of Scripture) who 'inhabiteth eternity,' in both these senses. The great Creator alone (not any of his creatures) is from everlasting to everlasting: His duration alone, as it had no beginning, so it cannot have any end."[196]

Wesley's comprehension of time needs a brief treatment at this point. He followed Aquinas who argued that time is a succession of motions according to before and after, a succession of motions that can be numbered. In time, everything is moved, therefore having a beginning and an end.[197] And yet, Wesley went beyond Aquinas to press that time is also a "fragment of eternity, broken off at both ends."[198] As such, it is sandwiched between the two eternities, but it will come to an end when the great judgment takes place.[199]

The sermon *ON ETERNITY* contains another quantitative analogy, offered in an attempt to illustrate the principle of eternity. This analogy originated in the third century with St. Cyprian, Bishop of Carthage. Wesley used it repeatedly.[200] It proceeds as follows -

"Suppose there were a ball of sand as large as the globe of earth; suppose a grain of this sand were to be annihilated, reduced to nothing, in a thousand years; yet that whole space of duration, wherein this ball would be annihilating, at the rate of one grain in a thousand years, would bear infinitely less proportion to eternity, duration without end, than a single grain of sand would bear to all the mass."[201]

Wesley, the preacher, offered another comparison for the purpose of clarifying eternity as duration -

"Suppose the ocean to be so enlarged, as to include all the space between the earth and the starry heavens. Suppose a drop of this water to be annihilated once in a thousand years; yet that whole space of duration, wherein this ocean would be annihilating, at the rate of one drop in a thousand years, would be infinitely less in proportion to eternity, than one drop of water to that whole ocean."[202]

The remainder of the sermon *ON ETERNITY* treats the future aspect of boundless duration - "There is another division of eternity, which is of unspeakable importance: That which is to come, as it relates to immortal spirits, is either a happy or a miserable eternity."[203] Our study of this division must await a later chapter.

The God of John Wesley exists in the punctilear dimension of eternity, which eternity is also the very life of God, the Being of beings. However, for the ease of communicating effectively to common people, he repeatedly used quantitative and linear successions to teach the first Methodists something about the nature of God.

Notes

1   EXPLANATORY NOTES OLD TESTAMENT, *op cit.*, III, 1758-1759.
2   A.M. Fairweather (Ed), *THE LIBRARY OF CHRISTIAN CLASSICS*, "Thomas Aquinas: Nature and Grace." (Philadelphia: The Westminster Press, 1954), XI, 35ff.
3   WORKS, *op.cit.*, XII, 1-2. Cf. Baker, op.cit., XXV, 24.
4   Walter Kaufmann, *PHILOSOPHIC CLASSICS* (Englewood Cliffs: Prentice Hall, 1960), II, 110.
5   E.R. Fairweather (Ed), *THE LIBRARY OF CHRISTIAN CLASSICS*, "A Scholastic Miscellany: Anselm to Ockham." (Philadelphia: The Westminster Press, 1956), X, 82. Cf. WORKS, op.cit., VII, 169.
6   *Loc.cit.*
7   WORKS, *op.cit.*, VI, 338.
8   *Loc.cit.* Cf. WORKS, VII, 169.
9   *Ibid*, VI, 213.
10   EXPLANATORY NOTES OLD TESTAMENT, *op.cit.*, II, 1635. Cf. EXPLANATORY NOTES NEW TESTAMENT, *op.cit.*, 465.
11   WORKS, *op.cit.*, VI, 234.
12   *Ibid*, VI, 219.
13   *Loc.cit.* - Wesley here took exception to Descartes - i.e., that minds are distinct from bodies.
14   *Ibid*, VI, 349.
15   *Ibid*, VI, 349-350.
16   *Ibid*, VI, 350.
17   *Ibid*, VI, 219. Wesley quoted directly from Augustine's treatise, "On the Trinity." Cf. Philip Schaff (Ed), *THE NICENE AND POST-NICENE FATHERS* (Buffalo: The Christian Literature Company, 1887), III, 223 - "The corruptible body... presses down the soul."
18   *Ibid*, VI, 337-338.
19   EXPLANATORY NOTES NEW TESTAMENT, *op.cit.*, 627.
20   WORKS, *op.cit.*, VI, 337.
21   *Ibid*, V, 226.
22   *Ibid*, VI, 58. See also VI, 355 - Wesley flatly asserted that reason cannot produce faith. He challenged his readers to "try whether your reason will give you a clear satisfactory evidence of the invisible world." He concluded that the experiment will end in doubt rather than faith.
23   E.R. Fairweather, *op.cit.*, X, 73. Cf. WORKS, *op.cit.*, VII, 232-233.
24   WORKS, *op.cit.*, XII, 392.
25   *Ibid*, VI, 354.
26   *Ibid*, VI, 58.

27 John T. McNeill (Ed), *THE LIBRARY OF CHRISTIAN CLASSICS*, "Calvin: The Institutes of the Christian Religion." (Philadelphia: The Westminster Press, 1960), XX, 43.
28 John W. Yolton, *JOHN LOCKE AND THE WAY OF IDEAS* (London: Oxford University Press, 1956), 36.
29 JOURNAL, *op.cit.*, V, 89. Cf. WORKS, *op.cit.*, VI, 352; XIII, 39, 455.
30 WORKS, *op.cit.*, VI, 339; VII, 231.
31 *Ibid*, XII, 290.
32 EXPLANATORY NOTES NEW TESTAMENT, *op.cit.*, 627.
33 NICENE FATHERS, *op.cit.*, III, 227-228.
34 WORKS, *op.cit.*, VI, 58.
35 *Ibid*, VI, 354.
36 *Ibid*, V, 226; VI, 354 - "Is it not reason (assisted by the Holy Ghost) which enables us to understand what the Holy Scriptures declare concerning the being and attributes of God?"
37 *Ibid*, XII, 275; V, 227.
38 *Ibid*, VI, 58. Cf. McNeill, *op.cit.*, XX, 95. Earlier, Calvin insisted the Scripture and the Holy Spirit "belong inseparably together," and the Scripture "must be confirmed by the Witness of the Holy Spirit." See also XX, 74-75.
39 *Ibid*, VI, 339.
40 NICENE FATHERS, *op.cit.*, III, 239.
41 *Ibid*, III, 362, 370.
42 EXPLANATORY NOTES NEW TESTAMENT, *op.cit.*, 841. Cf. WORKS, *op.cit.*, VII, 232 - "Sense is the evidence of things that are seen." Faith, on the other hand, is the "evidence of things not seen." See also WORKS, VII, 256ff; and Mary W. Calkins, *BERKELEY: ESSAY, PRINCIPLES, DIALOGUES* (New York: Charles Scribner's Sons, 1957), 127. Berkeley is being quoted here by Wesley. He uses Berkeley's translation of "subsistence" instead of the Authorized text's "substance."
43 WORKS, *op.cit.*, VIII, 5, 13. Cf. Lycurgus M. Starkey, *THE WORK OF THE HOLY SPIRIT* (New York: Abingdon Press, 1962), 48.
44 *Loc.cit.* Cf. WORKS, *op.cit.*, XIII, 136; EXPLANATORY NOTES NEW TESTAMENT, *op.cit.*, 465 - "Feeling, being the lowest and grossest of all our senses, is fitly applied to that low knowledge of God."
45 *Ibid*, VIII, 4. Cf. E.H. Sugden (Ed), *THE STANDARD SERMONS OF JOHN WESLEY* (London: The Epworth Press, 1956), I, 94, 125, 269-270. Also, WORKS, XIII, 20 - To Miss Bishop, Wesley wrote, "Faith is sight; that is, spiritual sight."
46 EXPLANATORY NOTES NEW TESTAMENT, *op.cit.*, 842-843.
47 Telford, *op.cit.*, VII, 252.
48 EXPLANATORY NOTES OLD TESTAMENT, *op.cit.*, I, 204.
49 EXPLANATORY NOTES NEW TESTAMENT, *op.cit.*, 342.
50 WORKS, *op.cit.*, V, 334-345.
51 EXPLANATORY NOTES NEW TESTAMENT, *op.cit.*, 37.
52 *Ibid*, 464-467.
53 WORKS, *op.cit.*, XIII, 482.

54 *Ibid*, VI, 362; X, 483, 484, 492. Cf. Telford, op.cit., VI, 121.
55 *Ibid*, XIII, 287.
56 JOURNAL, *op.cit.*, VI, 112. Cf. EXPLANATORY NOTES NEW TES- TAMENT, *op.cit.*, 465.
57 WORKS, *op.cit.*, IV, 194; IX, 194; XIII, 288. Cf. JOURNAL, *op.cit.*, I, 302.
58 *Ibid*, IV, 404; XIII, 482-483. Cf. JOURNAL, *op.cit.*, VII, 340.
59 *Ibid*, X, 458, 462, 469. Cf. EXPLANATORY NOTES NEW TESTA- MENT, *op.cit.*, 465-466.
60 *Ibid*, XIII, 482; III, 28; X, 47.
61 JOURNAL, *op.cit.*, I, 412; II, 163, 422; Cf. WORKS, *op.cit.*, VI, 268.
62 WORKS, *op.cit.*, X, 491-492.
63 *Ibid*, XIII, 483.
64 *Ibid*, V, 254; X, 492.
65 *Ibid*, X, 492.
66 *Ibid*, I, 94; II, 361; XII, 42. Cf. JOURNAL, *op.cit.*, I, 312, 313, 320; IV, 157.
67 *Ibid*, VI, 356-357.
68 *Ibid*, XIII, 483. Cf. JOURNAL, *op.cit.*, VII, 162, 340.
69 *Ibid*, I, 496; II, 390; XIII, 288, 455-465.
70 *Ibid*, III, 485, 504, 354; VII, 271, 342; XIII, 288.
71 JOURNAL, *op.cit.*, V, 458. Cf. Baker, *op.cit.*, XXV, 186-188.
72 *Ibid*, III, 17, 382; IV, 411; V, 46, 521. Cf. WORKS, *op.cit.*, II, 46, 375-376; III, 18, 160, 502; IX, 509ff - Wesley wrote a scathing attack on Behman's perspective and style - "I totally object to his blending religion with philoso- phy; and as vain a philosophy as ever existed; supported neither by Scripture nor reason, nor anything but his own *ipso dixit*."
73 *Ibid*, VI, 63.
74 *Ibid*, IV, 45. Cf. WORKS, *op.cit.*, XIII, 29, 288.
75 *Ibid*, IV, 45, 157, 188, 211; V, 352.
76 WORKS, *op.cit.*, XIII, 483.
77 *Ibid*, X, 492.
78 *Loc.cit.*
79 E.R. Fairweather, *op.cit.*, X, 73-74 - Anselm of Canterbury, A.D. 1033-1109. Cf. EXPLANATORY NOTES NEW TESTAMENT, *op.cit.*, 466 - Wesley clearly had this argument in mind when, in his commentary on Acts XVII, 29, he affirmed, "Can God himself be a less than noble being than we which are his offspring?"
80. T.V. Smith, *FROM THALES TO PLATO* (Chicago: University of Chicago Press, 1956), 16.
81 John M. Robinson, *AN INTRODUCTION TO EARLY GREEK PHILOS- OPHY* (New York: Houghton-Mifflin Company, 1968), 114.
82 W.T. Jones, *THE CLASSICAL MIND* (New York: Harcourt, Brace, and World, Inc., 1964), 21-22.
83 Robinson, *op.cit.*, 114.
84 E.R. Fairweather, *op.cit.*, X, 75-76.
85 *Ibid*, X, 82. Cf. EXPLANATORY NOTES OLD TESTAMENT, *op.cit.*, I, 204. Wesley applied Anselm: "...He (God) is self-existent; he has his being

of himself and has no dependency upon any other, and being self-sufficient, and the inexhaustible fountain of being and bliss."

86 *Ibid*, X, 86.
87 Paul Edwards (Ed), *THE ENCYCLOPEDIA OF PHILOSOPHY* (New York: The MacMillan Company, 1967), I, 128.
88 *THE HOMILIES* (London: The Prayer Book and Homily Society, 1833), 13. Cf. E.R. Fairweather, *op.cit.*, X, 150-151; Harald Lindstrom, *WESLEY AND SANCTIFICATION* (London: The Epworth Press, 1946), 62.
89 WORKS, *op.cit.*, V, 254. Cf. Williams, op.cit., 83.
90 ENCYCLOPEDIA OF PHILOSOPHY, *op.cit.*, I, 429.
91 *Ibid*, I, 128-129. Cf. Baker, *op.cit.*, XXV, 445 - Susanna Wesley, in a letter to her son (John), dated November 27, 1735, applied this argument of Anselm: "God is being itself! The I AM, and therefore must be the supreme good! He is so infinitely blessed that every perception of his blissful presence imparts a vital gladness to the heart. Every degree or approach toward him is in the same proportion a degree of happiness."
92 *Ibid*, I, 429.
93 *Loc.cit.*
94 K. Codell Carter, *A CONTEMPORARY INTRODUCTION TO LOGIC* (London: Glencoe Press, 1977), 149.
95 WORKS, *op.cit.*, XIII, 463-464. Wesley charged Locke with criticizing the Schoolmen without having read them seriously. See WORKS, XIII, 461.
96 *Ibid*, XIII, 462; XIV, 164. This was the mature Wesley, not the young student at Oxford, nor the lost missionary in Georgia. The year was 1761. Wesley was interested in Aristotle's system of definition. Cf. W.D. Ross (Ed), *ARISTOTLE'S SELECTIONS* (New York: Charles Scribner's Sons, 1955), 75-77; Lee, *op.cit.*, 53-55.
97 *Ibid*, XIII, 482.
98 *Ibid*, XII, 211.
99 W.T. Jones, *op.cit.*, 219.
100 T.V. Smith, *ARISTOTLE TO PLOTINUS* (Chicago: University of Chicago Press, 1956), 39.
101 *Loc.cit.* Cf. WORKS, *op.cit.*, VII, 225, 227. Wesley believed that the matter of the human body is a "proportional mingling of the four elements, earth, air, fire, and water."
102 *Ibid*, 47.
103 Ross, *op.cit.*, 77. Cf. Jones, *op.cit.*, 219-220; Baker, *op.cit.*, XXV, 186-188. Bishop Berkeley's position, that material substance does not exist, brought a resounding criticism from Wesley. He rooted this criticism in Aristotle's physics -"Becoming is between being and not-being, so that which is becoming is always between that which is and that which is not."
104 Jones, *op.cit.*, 220.
105 *Ibid*, 221. Cf. Ross, *op.cit.*, 50.
106 *Ibid*, 222. Cf. WORKS, *op.cit.*, VI, 427. Wesley followed Aristotle in this, affirming that all matter is absolutely and totally inert, not being able to move itself, and when it does move it is moved by something other than itself. See

also, WORKS, VII, 227 - Here Wesley identified this "something other" as the Holy Spirit, "The Almighty Spirit, the source of all motion in the universe." The Holy Spirit, for Wesley in this argument, was analogous to Aristotle's "entelechy."

107 T.V. Smith, ARISTOTLE, *op.cit.*, 39. Cf. Jones, *op.cit.*, 228.
108 Ross, *op.cit.*, 51-57. Cf. Jones, *op.cit.*, 224.
109 Jones, *op.cit.*, 226.
110 Ross, *op.cit.*, 49.
111 Jones, *op.cit.*, 230-231. Cf. WORKS, *op.cit.*, VI, 427.
112 *Ibid*, 232.
113 Lee, *op.cit.*, 53, 55.
114 Paul K. Meagher (Ed), *ENCYCLOPEDIC DICTIONARY OF RELIGION* (Washington, D.C.: Corpus Publications, 1979), III, 3523.
115 A.M. Fairweather, *op.cit.*, XI, 22.
116 WORKS, *op.cit.*, XIII, 483.
117 *Ibid*, X, 492.
118 *Loc.cit.*
119 A.M. Fairweather, *op.cit.*, XI, 22.
120 *Ibid*, XI, 23.
121 *Ibid*, XI, 22. Wesley's embracing of Thomism at this point helps explain his rejection of the doctrine of innate ideas, and his enthusiastic endorsement of John Locke's empiricism.
122 *Loc.cit.* Cf. Vernon J. Bourke, *THE POCKET AQUINAS* (New York: The Washington Square Press, 1968), 26-27 - "Knowledge occurs by virtue of the fact that the thing known is present in the knower... the created intellect cannot see God in His essence unless God through His grace joins Himself to the created intellect as a thing to be understood by it."
123 A.M. Fairweather, *op.cit.*, XI, 51.
124 *Ibid*, XI, 52-53.
125 *Ibid*, XI, 54-55.
126 Baker, *op.cit.*, XXV, 189.
127 Maldwyn Edwards, *FAMILY CIRCLE* (London: The Epworth Press, 1949), 68.
128 Bourke, *op.cit.*, 158-159.
129 WORKS, *op.cit.*, VI, 207.
130 *Ibid*, X, 492.
131 Meagher, *op.cit.*, III, 3231.
132 ENCYCLOPEDIA OF PHILOSOPHY, *op.cit.*, I, 428. Cf. Richard McKeon (Ed), *SELECTIONS FROM MEDIEVAL PHILOSOPHERS* (New York: Charles Scribner's Sons, 1958), 340-348.
133 *Ibid*, I, 429. Cf. WORKS, *op.cit.*, X, 81.
134 Baker, *op.cit.*, XXV, 264.
135 WORKS, *op.cit.*, X, 81.
136 *Ibid*, VII, 266.
137 *Ibid*, V, 334.
138 *Ibid*, VIII, 197.

139 *Ibid*, VIII, 199.
140 Ross, *op.cit.*, 63.
141 Jones, *op.cit.*, 199. Cf. Ralph M. Eaton (Ed), *DESCARTES SELECTIONS* (New York: Charles Scribner's Sons, 1955), 275.
142 *Ibid*, 175. Cf. Eaton, *op.cit.*, 276. Descartes allowed two created substances: corporeal and thinking.
143 Eaton, *op.cit.*, xxxii, and 122.
144 WORKS, *op.cit.*, VI, 337ff; VII, 225. Wesley extracted directly from Descartes for sections of these two sermons -Primarily from Descartes' *MEDITATIONS ON FIRST PHILOSOPHY*, from *THE WORLD: OR ESSAY ON LIGHT*, from *THE TREATISE ON MAN*, and from *THE PASSIONS OF THE SOUL*. See also, WORKS, *op.cit.*, XIV, 176, where Wesley cites the dictum of Descartes that "Reason and nature are not often deceived, and seldom deceive their followers." See also, WORKS, VII, 226-228, 319; X, 475.
145 *Ibid*, VI, 224.
146 *Ibid*, VI, 426; V, 335-336.
147 *Ibid*, VI, 315.
148 Philip P. Wiener (Ed), *LEIBNIZ SELECTIONS* (New York: Charles Scribner's Sons, 1951), 219. Cf. WORKS, *op.cit.*, VII, 240.
149 Kaufmann, *op.cit.*, II, 39.
150 WORKS, *op.cit.*, VI, 219.
151 Eaton, *op.cit.*, xiii.
152 WORKS, *op.cit.*, X, 492.
153 ENCYCLOPEDIA OF PHILOSOPHY, *op.cit.*, V, 388.
154 *Loc.cit.*
155 *Ibid*, V, 389.
156 JOURNAL, *op.cit.*, V, 103.
157 *Ibid*, V, 265; IV, 148, 166; V, 32, 103, 178, 224, 267-275, 487; VI, 212-213; VII, 398. Cf. WORKS, *op.cit.*, VI, 306 - Wesley quoted the ancient Greek thinker Hesiod: "Millions of spiritual creatures walk the earth unseen."
158 WORKS, *op.cit.*, VII, 232. Cf. Nicolas Malebranche, *THE SEARCH AFTER TRUTH* (Columbus, Ohio: Ohio State University Press, 1980), 319. Compare: WORKS, *op.cit.*, VII, 351 with Malebranche pages 99, 230-231. Also, WORKS, VII, 264-273 with Malebranche pages 318ff. Also WORKS, VI, 337-350 with Malebranche pages 89, 91-92, 101. Also WORKS, VI, 424-435 with Malebranche pages 448ff. Also WORKS, VI, 206-215 with Malebranche pages 472ff. Also WORKS, VI, 189-198 with Malebranche pages 273, 469. In addition, Wesley relied on Malebranche in the following passages: WORKS, VI, 191, 207, 339, 340, 343, 427; VII, 170, 225-227, 230, 232, 265, 351, 477.
159 Meagher, *op.cit.*, II, 2221.
160 Wiener, *op.cit.*, 553.
161 ENCYCLOPEDIA OF PHILOSOPHY, *op.cit.*, V, 140.
162 Malebranche, *op.cit.*, 318. Cf. ENCYCLOPEDIA OF PHILOSOPHY, *op.cit.*, V, 442.

163 WORKS, *op.cit.*, X, 492.
164 Baker, *op.cit.*, XXV, 288.
165 *Loc.cit.* Cf. Footnote 4.
166 ENCYCLOPEDIA OF PHILOSOPHY, *op.cit.*, II, 118.
167 Samuel Clarke, *DISCOURSE CONCERNING THE UNCHANGEABLE OBLIGATIONS OF NATURAL RELIGION AND THE TRUTH OF CERTAINTY OF THE CHRISTIAN REVELATION* (London: W. Botham, 1706), iii.
168 ENCYCLOPEDIA OF PHILOSOPHY, *op.cit.*, II, 119; I, 429. Duns Scotus left an indelible mark upon the thinking of Samuel Clarke.
169 Samuel Clarke, *A DEMONSTRATION OF THE BEING AND AT-TRIBUTES OF GOD* (Stuttgart - Bad Cannstatt: Friedrich Frommann Verlag, 1964), 86ff.
170 *Ibid*, 86.
171 *Ibid*, 88.
172 *Ibid*, 89. Cf. WORKS, *op.cit.*, VI, 189.
173 *Ibid*, 89-90.
174 *Ibid*, 93.
175 *Ibid*, 95.
176 *Ibid*, 96. Cf. WORKS, *op.cit.*, XII, 1-2. Baker, *op.cit.*, XXV, 241.
177 *Ibid*, 100.
178 *Ibid*, 101.
179 *Ibid*, 221.
180 *Ibid*, 230.
181 Clarke, DISCOURSES, *op.cit.*, 23. Cf. WORKS, *op.cit.*, VI, 315-318.
182 WORKS, *op.cit.*, VI, 189, 190, 226, 315, 317, 318, 324, 326, 338; VII, 240, 241, 265, 271; X, 361.
183 Baker, *op.cit.*, XXV, 364.
184 WORKS, *op.cit.*, VIII, 197-198.
185 *Ibid*, VIII, 199.
186 *Ibid*, VI, 354.
187 EXPLANATORY NOTES OLD TESTAMENT, *op.cit.*, I, 204.
188 *Ibid*, I, 212-213.
189 WORKS, *op.cit.*, V, 335; VII, 272-273.
190 E.R. Fairweather, *op.cit.*, X, 86.
191 WORKS, *op.cit.*, VI, 339. Cf. Bourke, *op.cit.*, 83 - Wesley here quoted directly from Aquinas.
192 *Ibid*, VI, 189.
193 *Loc.cit.* Cf. E.R. Fairweather, *op.cit.*, X, 86-87. Anselm objected: "There are no parts in Thee or Thy eternity."
194 *Loc.cit.*
195 *Loc.cit.*
196 *Loc.cit.* Cf. WORKS, *op.cit.*, VII, 265.
197 Bourke, *op.cit.*, 82-83. Cf. WORKS, *op.cit.*, VI, 190 - Wesley argued that time is measured by the movement of the sun and planets.
198 WORKS, *op.cit.*, VI, 190.

199 *Loc.cit.*
200 JOURNAL, *op.cit.*, I, 416; II, 263; IV, 97. Cf. WORKS, *op.cit.*, VI, 193, 504.
201 WORKS, *op.cit.*, VI, 193; VII, 240.
202 *Loc.cit.*
203 *Loc.cit.* Cf. JOURNAL, *op.cit.*, VI, 16 - Concerning his preaching on "eternity," Wesley often said that he had "delivered" his soul, based on Ezekiel's watchman (III, 17).

Chapter Two

God's Attributes and the Trinity

"Who can search out this God to perfection? None of the creatures that he has made. Only some of his attributes he hath been pleased to reveal to us in his word. Hence we learn that God is an eternal Being."[1]

Nowhere in the thought of John Wesley is the marriage of Bible and reason as apparent as in his description of the divine attributes and the Trinity. He was not, however, the officiate at this marriage. The nuptials had taken place long before Wesley came upon the stage of history. In fact, he was a very late witness to this dynamic relationship. He agreed with the Christian thinkers before him who rooted the divine perfections - attributes - and the Trinity in the Bible but explained them by the rational tools of Christianized philosophy. Wesley followed their methodology, using the same scriptural passages and the same rational arguments. As noted in the previous chapter, Wesley employed this very method in his *EXPLANATORY NOTES UPON THE OLD TESTAMENT* in treating Exodus III, 14. The scriptural "I AM" was described by him as "self-existent," "self-sufficient," "inexhaustible fountain of Being," "eternal" and "unchangeable."[2] He was at home mixing the biblical and the philosophical.

His consistent usage of philosophical nomenclature makes it important for us to define basic terms, giving them the meaning he posited for them. The term *substance* is the proper starting place. Behind this English noun was the Latin *substantia*. However, the Greek preceded the Latin, giving several important meanings that would carry down into the Latin and English. The Greek *ousia* meant "property" or "that which is owned." As such, it was closely linked with the Greek word *physis* which had four particular meanings: (1) the origin of a thing; (2) the natural constitution of a thing; (3) the natural species of a thing; and (4) the stuff of which a thing is made.[3] *Ousia*, with several shades of these meanings, was incorporated into the theological controversy of *homoousios* at the Council of Nicea in A.D. 325. Yet, another Greek word, later translated into the Latin *substantia* and the English *substance*, was *hypostasis*. The conceptual meaning of this term is "standing under" as a supporting reality.

Aristotle's description of substance, both *ousia* and *hypostasis*, set a course for substantial thinking which in time would influence Christian theology in a positive way. He affirmed that an existing substance possesses qualities. It is no more possible for a substance to exist without qualities than for qualities to exist without a substance. The qualities of a substance form a set that conjointly embody the nature of the substance they qualify. Aristotle called this "set of qualities" the *essence* of the substance.[4] Much later, St. Augustine argued that substance and essence are inextricably linked in God and thus may be considered synonymous.[5] In the thirteenth century, Thomas Aquinas made the same analysis, stressing, however, the "extension of essence" as God's existence. Aquinas added that God does not belong to a genus as a species. This is necessarily true because God is the one ground of all existence.[6]

THE ATTRIBUTES OF GOD

The term *attribute* traditionally refers to the extended qualities of the divine substance - the full set of qualities being identified as the divine essence. Baruch Spinoza, the seventeenth century Dutch thinker - whose writings Wesley knew well - defined the term as follows: "By attribute, I understand that which the intellect perceives as substance, as if constituting its essence."[7] In this sense, Wesley spoke of God's "essential attributes."[8] In his sermon on THE IMPERFECTION OF HUMAN KNOWLEDGE, Wesley exclaimed, "How astonishingly little do we know of God! How small a part of his nature do we know of his essential attributes."[9] Wesley often referred to these essential attributes of God as divine "perfections."[10] In DISCOURSE VI of his Sermon on the Mount series, Wesley equated these attributes with God's perfections.[11] This equation was common in English theology. Susanna Wesley used it in a letter to son Jacky in 1725.[12] Samuel Clarke, in his *DEMONSTRATION OF THE BEING AND ATTRIBUTES OF GOD*, used the equation repeatedly.[13] Wesley used both terms interchangeably and frequently modified *attributes* with the adjective "glorious."[14]

While believing that an infinite God must have an infinite number of qualities/attributes/perfections, Wesley found it reverently discreet to list only the few mentioned in the Bible. After all, he repeated, "How small a part of his nature do we know of his essential attributes?"[15] His list included the following - eternity, omnipresence, omnipotence, omniscience, holiness, Spirit, glory, wisdom, love, truth, and justice. We shall treat this finite list accordingly.

God's Eternity - "God is an eternal Being," Wesley affirmed in his sermon entitled THE UNITY OF THE DIVINE BEING.[16] Eternity is the very life of God. It is his existence that he wills to extend as a "self-caused" reality, being "self-sufficient" as well.[17] In this sense, God is "the Father of eternity," its progenitor because of his self-causing will.[18] Since eternity is his quality of willing existence, God imparts (in philosophical terminology - "extends" from "extension") eternity to all creatures that he has made.[19] The Hebrew name for God, *Jehovah*, signifies this meaning, as does the New Testament affirmation that he is the "Alpha and the Omega."[20] While this is all true, Wesley argued, eternity itself is "an unsubstantial thing" - it is a quality of substance and not substance.[21] It is an attribute and not God himself. It is an extension, an emanation of God's *ousia*, extending in "boundless duration." This boundless duration, however, is coextensive with God's substance, or else eternity would not be eternity - God's substantial being means continuous extension. Hence, eternity is without beginning and end.[22]

Nevertheless, Wesley - speculating as men often do when trying to describe a divine mystery - divided eternity into two parts, as noted earlier - *a parte ante* (eternity before time) and *a parte post* (eternity after time and yet to come).[23] He would have done well to remember St. Anselm's position on this subject: Nothing of God's eternity passes away -

> "Thou simply art, outside all time...yesterday and today and tomorrow belong solely to time, but, though nothing exists without Thee, Thou art not in place or time, but all things are in Thee. For nothing contains Thee, but Thou containest all things."[24]

Samuel Clarke's treatment of the "infinity of the self-existent Being" was the sure foundation of Wesley's view of "boundless duration." In presenting his case, Clarke argued that such an infinity must be "an infinity of *Fullness* as well as *immensity*. . .without Limits. . .Boundless."[25] Wesley's reasoning followed Clarke's rather closely: Boundless duration is synonymous with eternity. But eternity depends for its extension upon immensity, which is synonymous with "boundless space." God, the eternal Being, fills both eternity as duration and all space (Parmenides, again?) as immensity, making the doctrine of God's omnipresence logically possible.[26]

God's Omnipresence - Intimately allied with the attribute of eternity, Wesley taught, is the tenet of God's omnipresence.[27] As stated earlier, Wesley's premise was that since God exists through infinite duration, he cannot but exist through infinite space as well. Wesley learned this from both the Bible and Samuel Clarke. The Bible stated the case spiritually and Clarke stated it philosophically.

Citing the biblical book of Jeremiah, Wesley observed, "Do not I fill heaven and earth, saith the Lord? - Yea, not only the utmost regions of creation, but all the expanse of boundless space."[28] But before exploring this in detail, a brief review of popular notions about space in Wesley's day will help to clarify our treatment of omnipresence. Space had been a controversial subject since the pre-Socratic philosophers of ancient Greece. For instance, Parmenides (B.C. 510) argued that since Being is one, all space is full of Being - hence there is no such thing as motion. Democritus, in the next century, argued that space is empty, making it possible for atoms to actually move through space and form aggregations or bodies in space. By the seventeenth century the space controversy had entered another phase. Leibniz attacked the space theories of the Cartesians (Descartes, Malebranche, and Spinoza) and Sir Isaace Newton. The German maintained that bodies are aggregations of units of force called *monads*. Space, then for Leibniz, is nothing but a receptacle for these aggregated bodies. In particular, he attacked the Cartesians for believing that space is *extension* of the essence of divine substance, or God. It must be noted that Wesley's view of space was quite Cartesian. Leibniz also attacked Newton's cherished belief that space is "an organ, which God makes use of to perceive things by."[29] He quoted Newton -"Space is the *sensorium* of God," and he pointed out that the term *sensorium* "hath always signified the *organ* or sensation."[30] Samuel Clarke sought to rescue Newton from Leibniz, but became the next victim of an intellectual attack. Accusing Newton and Clarke of equating God with space, Leibniz said - "Such a being must needs be eternal and infinite. Hence some have believed it (space) to be God *himself*, or, one of his attributes, his *immensity*. But since space consists of parts, it is not a thing which can belong to God."[31] In this controversy, Wesley stood on the side of the Cartesians with Newton and Clarke. In a sermon, he quoted Newton's statement concerning space as God's *sensorium*, illustrating the reality of God filling all space with his presence.[32] Furthermore, Wesley greatly disliked Leibniz, accusing him of being "so poor a writer" who has false ideas.[33]

Wesley, the eclectic, pieced together his own conception of space in which Scripture, Cartesian and Newtonian elements combine. Wesley's space exists in two dimensions - (1) within the material universe, being finite by virtue of the time limitation placed upon it as a created thing. Material bodies, as aggregations of atoms,[34] fill portions of this finite space according to their size, but they do not fill all of this space.[35] The space such bodies occupy, however, does not block out God from occupying the same space because the substance of material bodies is created substance and

God's substance is of another sort - a purely spiritual *ousia*. By virtue of his superior spiritual substance, God fills all space within the created order.[36] (2) outside the created universe space has the infinite dimension called by Clarke and Wesley *Immensity*. Since God is infinite, immensity as infinite space must be one of his qualities or attributes. In creating time and the material cosmos, God immediately inhabited them too.[37] Whether space be without or within the created order, Wesley believed, God is there." ... where no creature is, still God is there. The presence or absence of any or all creatures makes no difference with regard to him. He is equally in all, or without all."[38]

Lest anyone suppose that Wesley's interest in the attributes of God was entirely speculative, devoid of any practical application, attention should be given to a sermon by Wesley, delivered at Portsmouth on August 12, 1788 - just three years before his death - entitled *ON THE OMNIPRESENCE OF GOD*. His biblical text was Jeremiah XXIII, 24 - "Do not I fill heaven and earth? Saith the Lord." The words of this text, he claimed, are "strong and beautiful" on a "sublime subject."[39] Every rational creature may profit by a serious consideration of it. Christians especially benefit from its deep instruction. It is a "useful" subject and yet, so little has been written upon it.[40] Consequently, Wesley argued, this sermon is perpetually appropriate. His conceptual starting point was the equation of divine omnipresence and the "Ubiquity of God." The ubiquitous God "is in this and every place."[41] Wesley took this last quotation from Psalm CXXXIX. He continued to cite this psalm, verse by verse. Verse 3 - "God is in every place... Thou art about my bed, and about my path, and spiest out all my ways." Verse 5 - "Thou hast fashioned me behind and before, and laid thine hand upon me." Verse 6 - "Such knowledge is too wonderful for me: I cannot attain unto it." Verses 7 and 8 - "Whither shall I go from thy Spirit, or whither shall I go from thy presence? If I climb up into heaven, thou art there: If I go down into hell, thou art there also." Continuing to quote still more, Wesley blended commentary with it -

"If I could ascend, speaking after the manner of men, to the highest part of the universe, or could I descend to the lowest point, thou art alike present both in one and the other. 'If I should take the wings of the morning, and remain in the uttermost parts of the sea, even there thy hand would lead me,' - thy power and thy presence would be before me, - 'and thy right hand hold me;' seeing thou art equally in the length and breadth, and in the height and depth, of the universe. Indeed, thy presence and knowledge not only reach the utmost bounds of creation; but

> Thine omnipresent sight,
> Even to the pathless realms extends
> Of uncreated night."[42]

The primary conclusion of the sermon, to this point, is that there is no segment of space "within or without the bounds of creation" where God is not. "The great God, the eternal, the almighty Spirit, is as unbounded in his presence, as in his duration and power."[43] Wesley also noted that while God is said to dwell in heaven, "the heaven of heavens cannot contain him...The universal God dwelleth in universal space. So that we may say,

> Hail, Father! whose creating call
> Unnumber'd worlds attend!
> JEHOVAH, comprehending all,
> Whom none can comprehend!"[44]

The remainder of this sermon contains some important considerations. Surprisingly, Wesley used an argument of Leibniz that emphasized that God acts everywhere, and therefore "is everywhere" - for it is an utter impossibility that "any being, created or uncreated, should work where it is not."[45] Moreover, he reasoned, even the heathen bear witness to this truth, saying, *Jovis omnia plena* - "All things are full of God!" Wesley added, "Yea, and whatever space exists beyond the bounds of creation, (for creation must have bounds, seeing nothing is boundless, nothing can be, but the great Creator), even that space cannot exclude Him who fills the heaven and the earth."[46] Joining Leibniz again, Wesley condemned as blasphemous the idea that space outside the material, created universe is "extra-mundane space" in which God is not present, and where he cannot work.[47]

The practical application of this "deep instruction" involves the Christian acknowledging God's presence everywhere, at all times, and living accordingly - "inspecting your heart, your tongue, your hand, every moment."[48] This application of God's omnipresence was frequently made in other Wesleyan writings.

God's Omnipotence - Wesley's biblical foundation for this property of God was Job XXXVI, 22 - "Behold, God is exalted by his power." His commentary on this verse was short but pungent - "God is omnipotent."[49] Brevity does not necessarily mean insignificance. For Wesley, brevity in reference to God's omnipotence signified the overwhelming evidence of divine power so that long rational arguments are unnecessary. In a sense, the Bible is a catalog of the mightly works of God, attested to by people of earlier times. In connection with some of these works, those of the Old Testament, two divine names from the Hebrew text were important to Wesley. The first name was *El Shaddai* -systematically translated in English Bibles of Wesley's day as "God Almighty." In his EXPLANATORY NOTES UPON THE OLD TESTAMENT, Wesley gave this commentary on this name, found in Genesis XVII, 1 - "I am God Almighty - I am God All-sufficient...he hath everything and needs not any thing."[50] God's power is so very great, Wesley's argument went, that he is all-sufficient, without any needs. We have met the other divine name before - *Jehovah*. Wesley acknowledged that its root meaning in Hebrew is "he will be what he will be."[51] To this he added, "A God performing what he has promised."[52] Wesley saw Jehovah as a God of action - not Aristotle's Unmoved Mover - but the Almighty Creator and Sustainer.[53] Such an omnipotent God was the God revealed upon every page of Wesley's Bible. Consequently, he insisted, to deny the omnipotence of God is to deny the Bible and sound reason.

The reality of God's omnipotence, Wesley held, is metaphysically guaranteed by the reality of God's omnipresence. "To deny the omnipresence of God implies, likewise, the denial of his omnipotence... If there were any space where God was not present, he would not be able to do anything there."[54] In his sermon on *THE UNITY OF THE DIVINE BEING*, Wesley linked these two attributes superbly -

". . .he is omnipotent, as well as omnipresent; there can be no more bounds to his power, than to his presence. He 'hath a mighty arm; strong in his hand, and high in his righthand.' He doeth whatsoever pleaseth him, in the heavens, the earth, the sea, and in all deep places. With men we know many things are impossible, but not with God: With him 'all things are possible.' Whensoever he willeth, to do is present with him."[55]

On the rational side of Wesley's understanding of divine omnipotence, he relied heavily upon Samuel Clarke's *DISCOURSE CONCERNING THE UNCHANGEABLE OBLIGATIONS OF NATURAL RELIGION AND THE TRUTH AND CERTAINTY OF THE CHRISTIAN REVELATION*. In particular, proposition seven of this work treats God's almighty power in three dimensions: (1) as a creative power; (2) as a power of beginning motion; and (3) as a power of free will.[56]

Wesley borrowed Clarke's three dimensions: (1) God's creative power - The eternal, almighty God called out of nothing, by his "all-powerful word," the whole universe of heaven and earth, "and the hosts of them."[57] He created all forms of life, with man alone being made with the *imago Dei*. And "when the Lord saw that every distinct part of the universe was good... behold, it was very good."[58] The Creative power of God is also the same power that sustains the entire creation.[59] God the Creator is also God the Preserver. In beginning his creation, God determined when to begin - "Had it pleased him, it might have been millions of years sooner, or millions of ages later."[60] He also determined "the place of the universe, in the immensity of space" where he would place it.[61] From determining the number of bodies in the heavens, to determining their size, the Almighty God determined the "magnitude of every atom" in creation.[62] This creative power, let it be said again, now sustains his universe. (2) God's power of beginning motion - The omnipotence of the great, I AM THAT I AM, Wesley affirmed, is to be seen in this universe of motion. Unlike Parmenides, who denied any reality to motion, Wesley maintained that all motion within the material world is initiated by "the finger of God."[63] Unexpectedly, Wesley argued this view in his sermon *ON THE LORD'S PRAYER*, not in one of his treatises on natural philosophy. When God first created matter, it was "essentially dull and inactive."[64] God's finger - the Holy Spirit[65] - "is the spring of action" in every creature, visible and invisible, "which could neither act nor exist, without the continual influx and agency of his almighty power."[66] In another sermon, *WHAT IS MAN?*, Wesley pursued this subject further, "The almighty Spirit, the source of all motion in the universe," governs every motion in the body; that is, the involuntary motions of the body. The all-wise Creator has given to men the motions of the will - "By a single act of my will, I put my head, eyes, hands, or any part of my body into motion: Although I no more comprehend how I do this."[67] In a very real sense, Wesley claimed, "We live, and move, and have our being" in God.[68] And (3) God's power of free will - Wesley stoutly defended the doctrine of free will, as originally imparted to man at creation, lost through the first or original sin, but reinstated as a benefit of Christ's atonement as the "preventing grace" of the Holy Spirit. In linking free will with omnipotence, Wesley observed -

"For he (God) created man in his own image; A spirit like himself; a spirit endued with understanding, with will or affections, and liberty; without which, neither his understanding nor his affections could have been of any use, neither would he have been capable either of vice or virtue."[69]

God's omnipotent power was given to man in a small degree to allow him to be a moral agent, without which "he could not be a moral agent, any more than a tree or a stone."[70] But, this divine gift to man makes for a dilemma -

"If, therefore, God were thus to exert his power, there would certainly be no more vice; but it is equally certain, neither could there be any virtue in the world. Were human liberty taken away, men would be incapable of virtue as stones. Therefore, ...the Almighty himself cannot do this thing. He cannot contradict himself, or undo what he has done. He cannot destroy out of the soul of man that image of himself wherein he made him; And without doing this, he cannot abolish sin and pain out of the world."[71]

To summarize this last point, Wesley believed that divine omnipotence was placed under a principle of self-restriction by God in reference to the extension of his power to man, making man a free moral agent. This self-restriction, on the part of God, was necessary because without it man is not in the image of God but is only an inanimate object, such as a tree or a stone. Nonetheless, God's almighty power, having created all things, now operates to sustain all things, including man, even reconciling him when he had wilfully alienated himself from God by sin, cleansing him from evil's pollutions and propensities, imparting new life and hope, and finally, in a moment, in the twinkling of an eye, raising man to full participation in eternity *a parte post*, for ever and ever! Such a possibility was risky for God, but his omnipotence ultimately will be vindicated with "the revelation of the Sons of God" (Romans VIII, 19).[72]

God's Omniscience - The most concise statement of God's omniscience, made by Wesley, is found in his sermon entitled *THE UNITY OF THE DIVINE BEING* -

"The omniscience of God is a clear and necessary consequence of his omnipresence. If he is present in every part of the universe, he cannot but know whatever it is, or is done there; according to the work of St. James, 'Known unto God are all his works,' and the works of every creature, 'from the beginning' of the world; or rather, as the phrase literally implies, 'from eternity.' His eyes are not only 'over all the earth, beholding the evil and the good; 'but likewise over the whole creation, yea, and the paths of uncreated night."[73]

In another sermon, *ON DIVINE PROVIDENCE*, Wesley continued his articulation of omniscience -

"And as this all-wise, all-gracious Being created all things, so he sustains all things. He is the Preserver as well as the Creator of everything that exists.

'He upholdeth all things by the word of his power;' that is, by his powerful word. Now it must be that he knows everything he has made, and everything he preserves, from moment to moment; otherwise, he could not preserve it, he could not continue to it the being which he has given it. And it is nothing strange that he who is omnipresent, who 'filleth heaven and earth,' who is in every place, should see what is in every place, where he is intimately present. If the eye of man discerns things at a small distance; the eye of an eagle, what is at a greater; the eye of an angel, what is at a thousand times greater distance; . . .How shall not the eye of God see everything, through the whole extent of creation? Especially considering, that nothing is distant from him in whom we all 'live, and move, and have our being.' . . .He is above, beneath; . . .He besets us behind and before, and as it were, 'lays his hand upon us.' We allow, 'such knowledge is too high' and wonderful for us; we cannot 'attain unto it.' . . .he (God) is not only 'All in the whole,' but 'All in every part.' . . .it cannot be doubted but he sees every atom of his creation, and that a thousand times more clearly than we see the things that are close to us; Even of those we see only the surface, while he sees the inmost essence of everything."[74]

Wesley's sermon continued by cataloging the ways in which God knows his created order. He knows all the properties of his creatures, all the "connexions," all dependencies, all relationships, all influential stimulations, and all the inanimate parts of the universe. He knows how all heavenly bodies influence people on earth - a Wesleyan astrology! God also knows the influence the lower heavens, "with magazines of fire, hail, snow, and vapours, winds, and storms, have on our planet." Furthermore, he knows what effects are produced in the bowels of the earth by fire, air and water. "All these lie naked and open to the eye of the Creator and Preserver of the universe."[75] Moreover, he knows all the animals of the earth, "whether beasts, birds, fishes, reptiles, or insects: He knows all the qualities and powers he hath given them, from the highest to the lowest." He knows all the angels, good and evil, and every man. He knows what every angel and man thinks, feels, suffers and speaks or does.[76] Wesley's God was not lazy nor Epicurean![77] Involved in all the motions of his creation, God is "loving to every man, and his mercy is over all his works."[78] He exhibits a constant concern for all his creatures, especially for the sons of

Adam caught in the web of complicated wickedness and misery.[79] Consequently, many men have cried out, with wonder and amazement, "O the depth! The depth of the riches, both of the wisdom and of the knowledge of God."[80]

While the subject of divine foreknowledge is reserved for more complete treatment later in this work, a brief statement concerning it is appropriate here because Wesley's understanding of omniscience rests upon God's inhabiting of eternity and all space. The eternity of God is a constant *NOW* - a never-ending present, without beginning, past, future, or end. As for time, it is a segment of eternity marked with a beginning, a middle, and an end - a past, present, and future - completely surrounded by the eternal NOW of God. As God looks at time, he sees it all at once, Wesley believed.[81] Our finite dimensions of past, present, and future, do not exist for God. He views our time as a single and whole unit of his present. Hence God knows all time-bound things from an infinite, eternal perspective. Wesley argued that "foreknowledge" is not a correct term for this divine knowledge, since God "does not know one thing before another, or one thing after another."[82] "God sees all things in one point of view from everlasting to everlasting. As all time, with everything that exists therein, is present with him at once, so he sees at once, whatever was, is, or will be, to the end of time."[83] But, Wesley warned, one should not conclude that "these things are because he knows them. No: he knows them because they are."[84] The practical aspect of this position is reducible to this - "God, looking on all ages, from the creation to the consummation, as a moment, and seeing at once whatever is in the hearts of all the children of men, knows everyone that does or does not believe, in every age or nation. Yet what he knows, whether faith or unbelief, is in nowise caused by his knowledge. Men are as free in believing or not believing as if he did not know it at all."[85] Hence, to speak of the "foreknowledge of God" is to speak "after the manner of men," that is, foolishly. It is equally improper, Wesley held, to speak of God's "afterknowledge."[86]

God's Holiness - There are two dimensions to Wesley's view of the *sanctitatis Dei*. (1) Holiness is relational, a separation from evil. As such, it is another perfection of the almighty, all-wise God. "He is infinitely distant from every touch of evil."[87] Wesley made the Old Testament idea of divine transcendence a moral idea rather than a cosmological one. The God who is omnipresent in the created order cannot, at the same time, be transcendent from the cosmos. While there is a sense in which God inhabits the "heaven of heavens," Wesley reasoned, God dwells "not there alone; for (he) fillest heaven and earth, the whole expanse of space."[88] Evil is a condition peculiar only to the created order, and God inhabits and fills that order, sharing occupancy with evil. However, his being is distinctly separate from evil. This holiness is symbolized as "light" and evil is symbolized as "darkness."[89] And (2) Holiness is a quality or essence of God's *ousia*, in extension as an attribute. In his *EXPLANATORY NOTES UPON THE NEW TESTAMENT*, Wesley defined this dimension of God's holiness as "purity of intention."[90] This quality of Being, in extension, creates acts of mercy and grace, longsuffering, abundant goodness and truth.[91]

These two aspects of divine holiness, Wesley taught, were imparted in some degree to man at creation. Created holiness was, however, not perfect, only good with a potential to increase to a consummated perfection. Leviticus XIX, 2 - "Be ye holy, for I am holy" - was an important divine imperative for Wesley. His commentary on it, in the *EXPLANATORY NOTES UPON THE OLD TESTAMENT*, reads - "*Be ye holy* - Separated from all the forementioned defilements, and entirely consecrated to God and obedient to all his laws. *I am holy* - Both in my essence, and in all my laws, which are holy and good."[92] The man of God must approximate the essence of God's holiness and separation from evil.

Wesley's comnmentary on St. Matthew V, 48 - "Ye shall be perfect, as your Father in heaven is perfect" - emphasized - "So the original runs, referring to all that holiness which is described in the foregoing verses...purity of intention."[93] The man of God must, therefore, strive after holiness as "purity of intention" in matters of alms-giving, prayer, fasting, and in all other things.[94] While Wesley

treated many biblical passages on the subject of holiness, he repeated some more than others in his sermons, commentaries, and
treatises. In addition to those cited above, Wesley also favored St.
Matthew V, 8 - "Happy are the pure of heart, for they shall see
God"[95] - and Hebrews XII, 14 -"Follow peace with all men, and
holiness, without which no man shall see the Lord."[96] Noticeably
absent from Wesley's movement today is any imperative for
Methodist pilgrims to strive after holiness!

God is Spirit - Following the popular theological tradition of the
western Church, Wesley spoke of "Spirit" as the "substance of
God," and he also spoke of it as the divine essence in extension (an
attribute). He blended these two into one description -

> "This God is a Spirit; not having such a body, such parts or passions as men
> have. It was the opinion both of the ancient Jews and the ancient Christians,
> that he alone is a pure Spirit, totally separate from all matter, whereas they
> supposed all other spirits, even the highest angels, even cherubim and
> seraphim, to dwell in material vehicles, though of an exceeding light and sub-
> tile substance. At that point of duration which the infinite wisdom of God
> saw to be most proper, for reasons which lie hid in the abyss of his own un-
> derstanding, not to be fathomed by any finite mind, God 'called into being all
> that is;' created the heavens and the earth, together with all that they contain.
> 'All things were created by him, and without him was not anything made that
> was made." He created man, in particular, after his own image, to be 'a pic-
> ture of his own eternity.' When he had raised man from the dust of the
> earth, he breathed into him an immortal spirit. Hence he is peculiarly called,
> 'The Father of our Spirits;' yea, 'The Father of the spirits of all flesh.'"[97]

An additional description was given by Wesley in his sermon *ON
DIVINE PROVIDENCE*. In stressing that God made man in the
divine image, the argument ran, man was made "a spirit like himself
(God)," endued with understanding, will, affections, and liberty.[98]
Understanding, will, affections, and liberty are the essential properties of God's Spirit, extended now, in a lesser degree, to man at
creation.

Another quality of the divine Spirit, for Wesley, was its 'sensible'
nature. Without doubt, Wesley adhered to St. Anselm's dictum -

"God is sensible, not as a body, but as the 'Supreme Spirit' - our knowledge of him is a spiritual sensation."[99] Wesley incorporated this idea into his sermon entitled *THE IMPERFECTION OF HUMAN KNOWLEDGE*, adding to it Isaac Newton's doctrine of the "Sensorium of the Deity."[100] God, as Supreme Spirit, fills all space as a sensible being, feeling and being felt by other spirits made by him. This creaturely feeling of God is clearly mystical, although Wesley generally rejected all mystical systems. His numerous references in his writings to "feeling" God have a solid foundation in the *HOMILIES* and the ARTICLES of the Church of England, where frequent mention of "feeling" abound. For instance, ARTICLE XVII, speaks of true Christians as those who "feel the workings of the Spirit."[101]

God's Glory - The glory of God is one of the grandest themes in the Bible. Wesley's two EXPLANATORY NOTES contain many commentaries on this subject, and he seldom had to turn to philosophy to undergird the biblical material. Only a few passages betray philosophical descriptions. Wesley saw two specific dimensions to the divine glory: (1) in reference to God's own Being; and (2) in reference to God's plans being accomplished in the created order. Into one or the other of these categories, Wesley placed the many scriptural passages on the subject.

(1) Glory was related to God's Being - "The glory of God, strictly speaking, is his glorious essence and his attributes, which have been ever of old. And this glory admits of no increase, being the same yesterday, today, and for ever."[102] His "glorious essence" meant, for Wesley, the biblical tradition of super, effulgent light. The *EXPLANATORY NOTES UPON THE NEW TESTAMENT* - the Epistle to the Hebrews I, 2 - best demonstrates this principle - "*The brightness of his glory* - Glory is the nature of God revealed in its brightness."[103] But, the EXPLANATORY NOTES UPON THE OLD TESTAMENT has more than its share of similar passages. The luminous cloud of Exodus XXIX, 16 led Wesley to exegete - "*A cloud covering the mountain for six days* - A visible token of God's special presence there, for he so shows himself to us, as at

the same time to conceal himself from us, he lets us know so much as to assure us of his power and grace, but intimates to us that we cannot find him out to perfection."[104] The source of this great brightness is the "eternal power" of the "Godhead."[105] In another place, Wesley added wisdom and mercy to the power of the Godhead.[106] In 1758, John Wesley investigated a vision of a reported theophany at Spitalfields. The young daughter of Joseph West claimed to have seen God. Wesley immediately interviewed her, asking many pertinent questions, and taking notes. He was greatly impressed by her sincerity, and he observed that her experience did not contradict Christian propriety. She exclaimed to him, "I saw God. I did not see him as a man, but as a glorious brightness."[107] Wesley took this vision as being authentically valid. It was, for him, a modern confirmation of an ancient biblical phenomenon.

(2) Glory as related to God's plans being accomplished in the created order - God's manifestation of his goodness, justice, mercy, and truth, for the benefit of man, constitutes this sense of divine glory.[108] To illustrate this point, Wesley exegeted the story of Moses pleading with God to show him the bright glory of the divine essence. Moses had seen it before, and now his soul craved another look - Exodus XXXIII, 18 - "*Shew me thy glory* - This was sufficient answer to his request: *Shew me thy glory*, saith Moses; *I will shew thee my goodness*, saith God. God's goodness is his glory, and he will have us to know him by the glory of his mercy, more than by the glory of his majesty."[109] In his sermon THE UNITY OF THE DIVINE BEING, Wesley elaborated on this dimension of glory and the well-being of man -

"He 'made all things,' as the wise man observes, 'for himself;' 'for his glory they were created.' Not 'as if he needed anything;' seeing 'he giveth to all life, and breath, and all things.' He made all things to be happy. He made man to be happy in Himself. He is the proper centre of spirits; for whom every created spirit was made. So true is that well-known saying of the ancient Fathers. . . 'Thou hast made us for thyself; and our heart cannot rest, till it resteth in thee.' This observation gives us a clear answer to that question in the Assembly's Catechism: 'For what end did God create man?' The answer is, 'To glorify and enjoy him for ever.'"[110]

God's Wisdom - In addition to preaching about the various attributes of the Eternal God, John Wesley also composed hymns for his Methodist followers, hymns extolling the essential qualities or perfections of God. One such hymn, cited now, incorporated many of the attributes treated thus far -

> "O God, thou bottomless abyss!
> Thee to perfection who can know?
> O height immense! what words suffice
> Thy countless attributes to show?
>
> Greatness unspeakable is thine:
> Greatness, whose undiminished ray,
> When short-lived worlds are lost, shall shine,
> When earth and heaven are fled away.
>
> Unchangeable, all-perfect Lord,
> Essential life's unbounded sea,
> What lives and moves, lives by thy word;
> It lives, and moves, and is, from thee.
>
> High is thy power above all height;
> Whate'er thy will decrees is done;
> Thy wisdom, equal to thy might,
> Only to thee, O God, is known!"[111]

God's wisdom is "equal" to his might! While this was a faith affirmation, it did not exclude a place for reason. Faith, for Wesley, enabled him to intuitively recognize rational truth which breathes the air of Scripture. Furthermore, he enjoyed reading the works of outstanding Christian authors who offered penetrating insights into these deeper truths of the faith. The metaphysical reasoning of Samuel Clarke,[112] especially on the subject of divine wisdom, held considerable power over Wesley's understanding of that attribute. Clarke's passage, from his *A DEMONSTRATION OF THE BEING AND ATTRIBUTES OF GOD*, reads -

"Every effect of the Supreme Cause, must be the product of Infinite Wisdom. More particularly: The Supreme Being, because he is infinite, must be everywhere present: And because he is an Infinite Mind or Intelligence; therefore wherever he is, his Knowledge Is, which is inseparable from his Being, and therefore must be infinite likewise: And where ever his Infinite Knowledge is, it must necessarily have a full and perfect Prospect of all things, and nothing can be concealed from its Inspection: He includes and surrounds everything with his boundless Presence; and penetrates every part of their Substance with his all-seeing eye: So that the inmost Nature and Essence of all things, are perfectly Naked and Open to his View; and even the deepest Thoughs of Intelligent Beings themselves, are manifest in his sight. Further, all things being not only present to him, but also entirely Depending upon him; and having received both their Being in itself, and all their Powers from Him; 'tis manifest that, as he knows all things that are, so he must likewise know all Possibilities of Things, that is, All effects that Can be. For, being himself only Self-Existent, and having Alone given to all Things all the Powers and Faculties they are indued with; 'tis evident He must of necessity know perfectly, what All and Each of those Powers and Faculties, which are derived wholly from himself; can possibly produce: And seeing at one boundless View, all the Possible Compositions and Divisions, Variations and Changes, Circumstances and Dependencies of Things; all their possible relations one to another, and Dispositions or Fitness to certain and respective Ends; He must without Possibility of Error, know exactly what is Best and Prperst in every one of the Infinite Possible Cases or Methods of Disposing Things; and understand perfectly how to Order and Direct the Respective Means, to bring about what he so knows to be in its Kind or in the Whole the Best and Fittest in the End. This is what we mean by *Infinite Wisdom*. And having before shown, that the Supreme Cause is moreover *All Powerful*, so that He can no more be Prevented by Force or Opposition, than he can be hindered by Error or Mistake, from Effecting always what is absolutely Fittest and Wisest to be done; It follows undeniably that he is actually and effectively, in the Highest and most complete Sense, *Infinitely Wise*; and that the World, and all Things therein, must be and are Effects of Infinite Wisdom."[113]

Wesley scattered Clarke's demonstration of divine wisdom throughout his many sermons and his EXPLANATORY NOTES. His sermon *ON DIVINE PROVIDENCE*, for instance, restates Clarke's conclusions but with homiletic simplicity - "He is infinite in wisdom as well as power."[114]   All his wisdom is continually employed in managing the affairs of his creation for the good of all his creatures."[115] "His wisdom and goodness go hand in hand."[116] "They are inseparably united, and continually act in concert with Almighty power."[117] "His power being equal to his wisdom and goodness, continually cooperates with them."[118] "To him all things are possible: He doeth whatsoever pleaseth him, in heaven and earth, and in the sea, and all deep places."[119]

Wesley's sermon, *THE UNITY OF THE DIVINE BEING*, explained the creation of the universe in terms of God's wisdom. "At that point of duration which the infinite wisdom of God saw to be most proper, for reasons which lie hid in the abyss of his own understanding, not to be fathomed by any finite mind, God 'called into being all that is;' created the heavens and the earth, together with all that they contain."[120] In particular, God made man, in the divine image, breathing the wisdom of God into him.[121]

Sermon LXVIII, *THE WISDOM OF GOD'S COUNSELS*, further treated Wesley's view of divine wisdom. His text was from Romans XI, 33 - "O the depth of the riches both of the wisdom and knowledge of God." Wesley's beginning premise is that wisdom and knowledge of God are actually one - "The wisdom of God, in its most extensive meaning, must include the one as well as the other, the means as well as the ends."[122] This one intelligent quality of the divine mind expressed itself in creation by establishing the "formation and arrangement" of all God's works, "in heaven above and earth beneath; and in adapting them all to the several ends for which they were designed."[123] Wisdom's product - each created thing - was, "apart from the rest," good in itself. Moreover, all things "together" were "very good."[124] The creation, then, was not made a universe of isolated, separate things, each possessing goodness *in abstracto*, but it was made a vast system of connected parts *in concreto* that made for a greater goodness - the goodness of the whole work of God.[125] It is incredible, Wesley preached, that men should generally be prone to shortsightedness and not recognize God's wisdom in creation.[126] Look at the various parts of the cosmos -

"How admirably does his wisdom direct the motions of the heavenly bodies! of all the stars in the firmament, whether those that are fixed, or those that wander, though never out of their several orbits! of the sun in the midst of heaven! of those amazing bodies, the comets, that shoot in every direction through the immeasurable fields of ether! How does he superintend all the parts of this lower world, this 'speck of creation,' the earth! So that all things are still, as they were at the beginning, 'beautiful in their seasons;' and summer and winter, seed-time and harvest, regularly follow each other. Yea, all things serve their Creator; 'Fire and hail, snow and vapour, wind and storm, are fulfilling his word; 'so that we may well say, O Lord, our Governor, How excellent is thy name in all the earth!'"[127]

Wesley, in the same sermon, spoke of the divine wisdom being explicit in the realm of "inanimate Creation." Aristotle once taught that inanimate matter consists of secondary, finite substances. Wesley, through Medieval Thomism, embraced such a definition and added that in its original condition remains "totally passive and inert." As such, it cannot oppose its Creator's will. Hence, all inanimate bodies, being moved by the First Unmoved Mover, continue on "in an even, uninterrupted course."[128] The same is not true, however, of animate creatures, endowed by their Creator with free will, capable of rebellion as well as obedience. "Evil men and evil spirits continually oppose the divine will, and create numberless irregularities." These irregularities are "contingencies" which, Wesley believed, give occasion for the "riches both of the wisdom and knowledge of God" to counteract all the "wickedness and folly" of men and devils.[129] Wisdom's response to the subtlety of Satan is "the salvation of lost mankind."[130] Moreover, the wisdom of God is also evidence in the fact of "his Church." Planted as a grain of mustard-seed, the least of all seeds, divine wisdom preserves and continually increases the Church, until it has grown into a great tree, "notwithstanding the uninterrupted opposition of all the powers of darkness." Like St. Augustine, Wesley thought of the Church in two dispensations - the Old Testament Church and the New Testament Church - two church ages but only one Church! In the fulness of time, Wesley preached, the wisdom of God brought the "first begotten" into the world to be the Incarnate Son and foundation of the Church.[131]

Later in this study, we will return to the subjects of creation, providence, sin and grace, fall and restoration, the Church, and many other related issues. But before departing this theme of divine wisdom, let it be noted that Wesley's preoccupation with it is found throughout his extant writings. It is similar to God's omnipresence and omnipotence, in that his wisdom is found everywhere and in all things, always working, always confirming created goodness, and always redeeming from moral and spiritual chaos those creatures needing restoration to original being and holiness.

God's Love - Of the revealed attributes of God, none was as important and vital to Wesley as divine love. He no doubt envied the superior ability of his brother Charles who penned that immortal line - "Love divine, all loves excelling!" At least he approximated his grandeur, however, with his own description of God's love as his "Darling, His reigning attribute!"[132] Wesley was obsessed with the workings and evidences of divine love. His sermons especially abound with instances and assurances of that love. The most striking feature of these references is the lack of analytical description for them. Perhaps Wesley's position was akin to that of a Welsh Calvinistic Methodist I once knew who explained that the love of God is "better felt than tellt!" What Wesley knew of this attribute came by revelation from the Bible, from the phenomenology of God's created world, and from the learned scholars of the Church, especially Aquinas and Clarke.

In his study - treatise for Methodists - *PREDESTINATION CALMLY CONSIDERED* - John Wesley combined "love and goodness" into one attribute which God "peculiarly claims...(and) glorifies above all the rest."[133] Love and goodness are inextricably linked, love being the essence of God's nature, "for God is love," and goodness being the effect or "love in action." This explanation was not original with Wesley. Thomas Aquinas, in the thirteenth centruy, had combined the separate views of Augustine and Anselm on love and goodness to provide future generations with a dynamic synthesis. Aquinas argued - God is love. Love refers to the good universally and is, therefore, naturally the first action of the will and of the appetite.[134] Divine love wills the good!

Wesley's treatment of the Johannine affirmation - "God is love" (I John IV, 16) - built upon this Thomistic synthesis -

"It is not written, 'God is justice' or 'God is truth:' (Although he is just and true in all his ways:) But it is written, 'God is love,' love in the abstract, without bounds; and 'there is no end of his goodness.' His love extends even to those who neither love nor fear him. He is good, even to the evil and the unthankful; yea, without any exception or limitation, to all the children of men. For 'the Lord is loving' (or good) 'to every man, and his mercy is over all his works.'"135

Furthermore, Wesley depicted divine love as "the very brightness of his (God's) glory."[136] Hence, as noted earlier in this chapter, the "effulgent brightness of his glory" was, for Wesley, "the effulgent brightness of his love." The bright glory that led Israel as a luminous cloud by day and a pillar of fire by night was God's love guiding his people through a trackless wilderness. The glory that enshrouded the holy mount in Sinai was also God's love revealed to Israel. The overwhelming brightness of God's *shekinah* in the Tent of Meeting, and later in the Solomonic Temple, again represented God's love in the midst of his people. Wesley anticipated the coming of the New Jersualem, where there will be no need of sun nor moon, "for the Lord God shall give them light," representing the ultimate and perfect encounter with the love that *IS* God.

Treating love in action as goodness, Wesley further linked love/goodness with God's eternal wisdom and power, seeing they all go hand in hand.[137] The ways of divine love are infinitely wise and inexhaustible, being enacted through his almighty power. Wesley illustrated this in his *EXPLANATORY NOTES UPON THE OLD TESTAMENT*, in exegeting Exodus XXXIV, 6-8. The verses read -

"And the Lord passed by before him, and proclaimed, The Lord, the Lord God, merciful and gracious, longsuffering, and abundant in goodness and truth. Keeping mercy for thousands, forgiving iniquity, transgression and sin, and will by no means clear the guilty, visiting the iniquity of the fathers upon the children, and upon the childrens' children, unto the third and unto the fourth generation."

The commentary may be summarized by the following points: (1) God is not only the God of Israel, but of all - his goodness is "extended" universally as "mercy." (2) He is a great God -the cause of his own being, and "the fountain of all being," whose name is *Jehovah*, "the Lord." He also calls himself *Jehovah-El - The Strong God*, the "originator of all power." This affirmation prefixes God's mercy "to teach us to think and to speak even of God's goodness with a holy awe, and to encourage us to depend upon these mercies." (3) God's goodness and his greatness cooperate - "That his greatness may not make us afraid, we are told how good he is; and that we may not presume upon his goodness, we are told how great he is." (4) There are specific expressions of God's loving goodness - *mercy*, as a fatherly pity and compassion for his children; *grace*, as "freeness and kindness;" and *longsuffering*, "a branch of God's goodness which our wickedness gives occasion for," being slow to anger, and slow to execute his justice - God waits to be gracious.[138] Moreover, Wesley claimed, God's love is extravagant in supplying "abundant goodness." It abounds "above our defects, above our conception. The springs of mercy are always full, the streams of mercy always flowing; there is mercy enough in God, enough for all, enough for each, enough for ever."[139] This goodness is, as Wesley termed it, "promised goodness." God gives to some, and keeps for others, and it is never exhausted.[140] He promises to continue his loving goodness to thousands of generations, many yet to come - the "line of it (loving goodness) is drawn parallel with that of eternity itself."[141]

God's Truth and Justice - These two properties of the divine nature are consistently mentioned in conjunction with one another by Wesley. While distinctly different, neverthless, they shade into the other in both essential meaning and extension.[142]

The most common approach in defining truth, in pre-Wesleyan thought, was to settle for Plato's doctrine of Forms (Ideas, Patterns, or Universals). Accordingly, truth is an eternal Idea - essentially good, permanent, spiritual, and the basic, perfect pattern from which each individual good is copied. However, not every thinker followed Plato. Many used the modification of his Forms by Aristotle, emphasizing the participation of those Forms in their particulars, creating the condition of potentiality within the copy or particular. Whether Plato or Aristotle, truth is an Idea, or, in more vulgar terms, a "blueprint."

However Wesley may have regarded the doctrine of eternal Forms, it is quite obvious that he never applied it to his understanding of God's truth. The foundation of truth's meaning for Wesley is to be found exclusively in the scriptures. At no point of discussion of this attribute did he go outside the Bible for definitive material. He treated two important passages from the Old Testament, affirming a moral dimension as the basic meaning of truth. In fact, viewing the truth of God in a moral light is consistent with the best biblicism of Judaism and Christianity. (1) Genesis I, 1 - In his commentary on this passage, Wesley identified the Hebrew name "Elohim" as meaning "the Covenant God, being derived from a word that signifies to *swear*."[143] The Covenant God swears by his very nature that he will certainly keep the promises he has made. What he foreswears, that he will surely do - "He is faithful and true to his promises, unchangeable in his word, and not a man that he should lie."[144] And (2) Exodus VI, 2 - Wesley's commentary indicates the divine name as being *Jehovah* - "A God performing what he had promised, and so giving being to his promise."[145] Wesley used these two etymological passages to clarify all subsequent biblical texts touching truth. For instance, his commentary on Deuteronomy XXXII, 4, reads - "A God of truth -constant to his promises: you cannot accuse him of any unfaithfulness to this day."[146] And again, on Psalm CXLVI, 6, Wesley claimed - "He liveth for ever to fulfill his promises, and because he is eternally faithful."[147] Bluntly stated, it is God's essential nature and habit to be faithful to his sworn promises. Truth is God's *moris* and *ethika* -

it is his customary behavior, stemming from his essential being. And, as Wesley suggested, God gives "being" to his promises. That is, God's essential being (which is truth) emanates his word of love and wisdom to become a "promise" - His promise then is guaranteed to us by his very nature and extension. He will not, he cannot, retract his promise. Nor can he, nor will he, cut it short! It has the status of eternity. It is good. It is right. His faithfulness is perpetuity, from everlasting to everlasting! God's truth, for Wesley, was clearly a moral attribute.

Divine justice was likewise a moral attribute, as Wesley understood it. Basically, God's justice is all his action and reaction to the responses of moral agents to the divine promises. When moral agents believe, trust, or obey God's promises, God acts in accordance with what he has sworn - this is the justice moral agents may expect from God. However, when moral agents disregard his promises, either by indifference or actual rebellion, God reacts by withdrawing the benefits of those promises - this is God's justice too.

Justice, Wesley acknowledged, is a legal concept. Acts and motivations are both judged. The All-wise, All-loving God, Creator of all things, and Governor of all things, is the Judge.[148] Moreover, this Judge is All-knowing by virtue of his omnipresence. He is likewise the "Perfect Judge" by virtue of his omnipotence - no one escapes his court! His sense of what is just is a reflection of his pure nature as the "Supreme Eternal Moral Being."

In a letter to one who openly denied the doctrine of divine justice, Wesley advised his reader to consider what "God says" on the matter -

"(1.) 'The just Lord is in the midst of you.' (Zeph. III, 5.) 'Justice and judgment are the habitation of thy throne.' (Psalm LXXXIX, 14.) 'Wilt thou condemn him that is not just?' (Job XXXIV, 17.) 'He is excellent in power, and in plenty of justice.' (Job XXXVII, 23.) 'Just and true are thy ways, O King of saints.' (Rev. XV, 3.) 'Thou art just in all that is brought upon us.' (Neh. IX, 33.) 'There is no God beside me, a just god and a Saviour.' (Isaiah XLV, 21.) 'Whom God hath set forth, that he might be just, and the justifier of him that believeth in Jesus.' (Rom. III, 25, 26.)

"(2.) 'The Lord heard their words, and was wroth.' (Deut. I, 34.) 'The Lord was wroth with me for your sakes.' (Deut. III, 26.) 'I was wroth with my people.' (Isaiah XLVII, 6.) 'For his covetousness I was wroth.' (Isaiah LVII, 17.) 'And the anger of the Lord was kindled against Israel.' (Num. XXV, 3.) 'His wrath is against them that forsake him.' (Ezra VIII, 22.)"149

God the Judge judges every person. No one is exempt. Just men are not locked into obedience to God's word, nor are unjust men hopelessly destined to remain injust. Consequently, all men must ultimately stand before the bar of God. Wesley was extremely fond of a passage from Ezekiel XVIII. While citing its key verses, he interspersed his commentary -

"The soul that sinneth, it shall die,' for its own sin, and not another's. 'But if a man be just, and do that which is lawful and right, he shall surely live, saith the Lord God. If he beget a son which is a robber, shall he then live? He shall not live, - he shall surely die. Yet ye say, Why? Doth not the son bear the iniquity of the father? (Temporally he doth, as in the case of Achan, Korah, and a thousand others; but not eternally.) 'When the son hath done that which is lawful and right, he shall surely live. The soul that sinneth, it shall die;' shall die the second death. 'The son shall not bear the iniquity of the father, neither shall the father bear the iniquity of the son. The righteousness of the righteous shall be upon him, and the wickedness of the wicked shall be upon him. Yet ye say, The way of the Lord is not equal. Hear now, O Israel, Is not my way equal?' (equitable, just?) 'Are not your ways unequal? When a righteous man turneth away from his righteousness, and committeth iniquity, and dieth in them, for his iniquity that he hath done shall he die. Again, when the wicked man turneth away from his wickedness that he hath committed, and doeth that which is lawful and right, he shall save his soul alive.'"150

While a more complete study of divine justice will follow in a subsequent chapter, it is appropriate to examine one more aspect of this attribute. In his treatise THOUGHTS UPON GOD'S SOVEREIGNTY, Wesley argued that God is not capricious nor arbitrary in granting salvation, so that some are irresistibly saved and others not. True justice must exclude arbitrariness -

"The general rule stands firm as the pillars of heaven: 'The Judge of all the earth will do right. He will judge the world in righteousness,' and every man therein, according to the strictest justice. He will punish no man for doing anything which he could not possibly do. Every punishment supposes the offender might have avoided the offense for which he is punished: Otherwise, to punish him would be palably unjust, and inconsistent with the character of God our Governor."[151]

THE TRINITY

John Wesley's younger brother, Charles, wrote numerous hymns extolling the Trinity, and Methodists still know and sing some of them. It is not generally known by contemporary Methodists that John wrote a trinitarian hymn in which he linked certain attributes with the personages of the Trinity. The reader would benefit, at this juncture, to pause from the present study, instruct an organist or pianist to play the tune known as "Duke Street, L.M." and then sing with vim and vitality this magnificent hymn -

"Father of all, whose powerful voice
Called forth this universal frame!
Whose mercies over all rejoice,
Through endless ages still the same.

Thou by thy word upholdest all;
Thy bounteous love to all is showed;
Thou hear'st thy every creature's call,
And fillest every mouth with good.

In heav'n thou reign'st enthroned in light,
Nature's expanse before thee spread;
Earth, air, sea, before thy sight,
And hell's deep gloom, are open laid.

Wisdom, and might, and love are thine;
Prostate before thy face we fall,
Confess thine attributes divine,
And hail thee sovereign Lord of All.

Blessing and honor, praise and love,
Co-equal, co-eternal Three,

In earth below, and heaven above,
By all thy works be paid to thee.

Let all who owe to thee their birth,
In praises every hour employ;
Jehovah reigns! be glad, O earth
And shout, ye morning stars, for joy!"[152]

It is appropriate to observe that Wesley's blending of the divine attributes and the Trinity in hymn-form represents a significant liturgical development. The hymn linked theological faith with worshipping Society. The Methodists had something for the head, as well as the heart, as they offered themselves up to God in worship. But Wesley gave more than a single hymn for this purpose. In 1784, he sent an unbound liturgy called *THE SUNDAY SERVICE OF THE METHODISTS* to America for his people there. It was his editorial reduction of the Anglican *BOOK OF COMMON PRAYER OF 1662*. In the *SUNDAY SERVICE* Wesley even retained the "signing of the cross."[153] The idea of giving American Methodism its own liturgy came from Wesley's closest friend, John Fletcher. In a letter to Wesley, dated August 1, 1775, Fletcher suggested that "the most spiritual part of the Common Prayer. . . be extracted and published with the 39 rectified articles, and the minutes of the conferences (or the Methodist canons) which. . . shall be, next to the Bible, the *vade mecum* of the Methodist preachers."[154]

Wesley's SUNDAY SERVICE perpetuated throughout its offices the highly Trinitarian emphasis of the *BOOK OF COMMON PRAYER* from whence it was taken. He had earlier "rectified" the Thirty-nine Articles of Religion of the Church of England for the American Methodists by reducing them to twenty-five articles.[155] The first article, as edited by Wesley into a more concise statement than found in the original form, treated the subject of the divine Trinity -

"There is but one living and true God, everlasting, without body or parts, of infinite power, wisdom, and goodness; the maker and preserver of all things,

visible and invisible, and in unity of this Godhead there are three persons, of
one substance, power, and eternity - the Father, the Son, and the Holy
Ghost."[156]

Wesley accepted this article as essential to the Christian faith,
and he wished it to be essential to the faith of every Methodist believer. Behind its written form, Wesley saw an implicit biblical witness to its reality, made explicit by the developing Catholic tradition within the Church, especially at the Council of Nicea (A.D.
325). Wesley noted that Antitrinitarian groups, like the Arians and
the Socinians, are inevitably reduced to "Christless" religions and
die.[157] Wesley refused to allow Methodism to become Arian or
Socinian. So, he wrote his Trinity hymn, rectified the first article of
the *SUNDAY SERVICE*, and preached many sermons upon the
doctrine's centrality to the Christian faith. His most important
sermon on the subject was entitled *ON THE TRINITY*, preached at
Cork on May 7, 1775. Its text was I John V, 8 - "There are three
that bear record in heaven, the Father, the Word, and the Holy
Ghost: And these three are one." The congregational response
was overwhelmingly positive and he was asked to write it down and
publish it.[158] However, this was not the first time he had preached
upon this text, and this was probably the same sermon he had
preached in 1760 at the Market-house of Athlone.[159] It became
one of his favorite sermons, and when he preached it in April of
1788, John Fletcher's widow was deeply moved by it, and she exclaimed, "I could not but discern a great change. His soul seems far
more sunk into God."[160]

The opening argument of this sermon treats the nature of religious truth -

"There are some truths more important than others. It seems there are some
which are of deep importance. I do not term them *fundamental* truths; because that is an ambiguous word: And hence there have been so many warm
disputes about the number of *fundamentals*. But surely there are some
which it nearly concerns us to know, as having a close connexion with vital religion. And doubtless we may rank among these that are contained in the

words above cited: 'There are three that bear record in heaven, the Father, the Word, and the Holy Ghost: And these three are one."[161]

The simple reality stated in the text - the three in heaven (Father, Word and Spirit) who are one - was the focus of the preacher's personal faith. It was not an explication or logical deduction drawn from an obscure text.[162] Citing the famous sermon on the Trinity by Dean Swift, Wesley rejected philosophical explications of scriptures on this special subject - "He shows, that all who endeavoured to explain it at all, have utterly lost their way; have, above all other persons, hurt the cause which they intended to promote; having as Job speaks, 'darkened counsel by words without knowledge.'"[163] So, Wesley refused to give a philosophical explication - "I insist upon no explication at all; no, not even on the best I ever saw; I mean, that which is given us in the creed commonly ascribed to Athanasius."[164]

Wesley thought it unnecessary to explain the Athanasian Creed because most Methodist people were quite familiar with it. But times and Methodism have both changed. Has one in a thousand contemporary Methodists in America ever heard of Athanasius, let alone know that he composed a trinitarian creed more explicit than that of Nicea? Can one Methodist minister in a hundred speak knowledgeably for ten minutes on Athanasius and the formation of the orthodox definition of the Trinity, unless given the luxury of several days to first research the matter?

It is imperative that we engage briefly in considering the Athanasian Creed to understand why Wesley regarded it to be the *best* statement ever given to the reality known as the Trinity.

Athanasius of Alexandria (A.D. 296-373), Bishop, Confessor and Doctor of the Church, argued effectively at the Council of Nicea (A.D. 325) against the Arians who held that God the Father and God the Son possess similar metaphysical substances (homoiousios), making Christ less than the Father, though like him, but not equal to him. In debate Athanasius contended for "the same substance" being the metaphyusical link between God the Father and God the Son (*homoousios*), making them separate but equal beings. The arguments of Athanasius were later reduced to written form as a creed which also bore his name. Although the creed is lengthy, it deserves a full citation because of Wesley's devotion to it -

"Whosoever will be saved, before all things it is necessary that he hold the Catholic Faith. Which Faith except everyone do keep whole and undefiled, without doubt he shall perish everlastingly. And the Catholic Faith is this, that we worship one God in Trinity and Trinity in Unity. Neither confounding the Persons, nor dividing the Substance. For there is one Person of the Father, another of the Son, and another of the Holy Ghost. But the Godhead of the Father, of the Son and of the Holy Ghost is all One, the Glory Equal, the Majesty Co-Eternal. Such as the Father is, such is the Son, and such is the Holy Ghost. The Father Uncreate, the Son Uncreate, and the Holy Ghost Uncreate. The Father Incomprehensible, the Son Incomprehensible, and the Holy Ghost Incomprehensible. The Father Eternal, the Son Eternal, and the Holy Ghost Eternal and yet they are not three Eternals but One Eternal. As also there are not three Uncreated, nor three Incomprehensibles. So likewise the Father is Almighty, the Son Almighty, and the Holy Ghost Almighty. And yet they are not three Almighties but One Almighty.

So the Father is God, the Son is God, and the Holy Ghost is God. and yet, they are not three Gods, but One God. So likewise the Father is Lord, the Son Lord, and the Holy Ghost Lord. And yet not three Lords but One Lord. For, like we are compelled by the Christian verity to acknowledge every Person by Himself to be God and Lord, so are we forbidden by the Catholic Religion to say, there be three Gods or three Lords. The Father is made of none, neither created, nor begotten. The Son is of the Father alone; not made, nor created, but begotten. The Holy Ghost is of the Father, and of the Son; neither made, nor created, nor begotten, but proceeding. So there is One Father, not three Fathers; One Son, not three Sons, One Holy Ghost, not three Holy Ghosts. And in this Trinity none is afore or after the Other. None is greater or less than Another, but the whole three Persons are Co-Eternal together, and Co-Equal. So that in all things as is aforesaid, the Unity in Trinity, and the Trinity in Unity is to be worshipped. He therefore that will be saved, must think of the Trinity.

Furthermore, it is necessary to everlasting Salvation that he also believe rightly the Incarnation of our Lord Jesus Christ. For the right Faith is, that we believe and confess, that our Lord Jesus Christ, the Son of God, is God and Man.

God, of the Substance of the Father, begotten before the worlds; and Man, of the Substance of His Mother, born into the world. Perfect God and Perfect Man, of a reasonable Soul and human Flesh subsisting. Equal to the Father as touching his Godhead, and inferior to the Father as touching His Manhood. Who, although He be God and Man, yet He is not two, but One Christ. One, not by conversion of the Godhead into Flesh, but by taking of the Manhood into God. One altogether, not by confusion of substance, but by Unity of Person. For as the reasonable Soul and Flesh is One Man, so God and Man is One Christ. Who suffered for our Salvation, descended into Hell, rose again the third day from the dead. He ascended into Heaven, He sitteth on the right hand of the Father, God Almighty, from whence He shall come to judge the quick and the dead. At whose coming all men shall rise again with their bodies, and shall give account for their own works. And they that have done good shall go into life everlasting, and they that have done evil into everlasting fire. This is the Catholic Faith, which except a man believe faithfully and firmly, he cannot be saved."[165]

Let us now return to Wesley's sermon on the Trinity. While claiming the theological description of the doctrine in the Creed to be the best he ever saw, Wesley rejected the curse of the Creed, pronounced on anyone "who does not assent to this." The founder of Methodism disliked curses in general, and Athanasius's in particular - "He who does not assent to this 'shall without doubt perish everlastingly."[166] The uncharitableness of Catholic Orthodoxy, Wesley said, kept him for some years from "subscribing" to the Athanasian Creed.[167] Then he came to realize that the curse was intended only for *willfull* unbelievers, rather than for *involuntary* unbelievers. Willfull unbelievers possess all the means of knowing the truth, and yet obstinately reject it. Involuntary unbelievers are deprived of the means of knowing the truth, so that unbelief is more a matter of spiritual ignorance than obstinacy. Moreover, Wesley argued, the curse pertains to the theological "substance of the doctrine" and not to the "philosophical illustrations" of it.[168] Wesley was convinced that the heart of the Creed (the theological affirmation of the Trinity) was normative, not just for the Catholic

Tradition (Roman and Anglican), but for himself and his beloved Methodism. As for the philosophical side of the Creed, he would not insist that it be received as normative also. But, one must ask Wesley, How can the theological dimension of this Creed be separated from its philosophical dimension? How can the theological principle of Godhead be justified without the philosophical undergirding of *homoousios*? If one answers, "The Godhead does not need a rational undergirding - it needs only faith!" - then, why include philosophical substance into the faith affirmation? Take it out! Curse the name of Novatian who was one of the first to have introduced it. And curse everyone, including Augustine, Luther, and Calvin who later used it. But that approach is absurd! The Church, consistently from the second century onward, accepted the synthesis of theology and philosophy, even when the issue turned to the consideration of the Trinity. Wesley's approach to this synthesis is most unusual since he readily favored it in other areas of theologizing.

In continuing his sermon on the Trinity, Wesley defended his usage of the terms *Trinity* and *Person*. That he felt it necessary to give an apology for these terms indicates that an anti-Trinitarian, or an anti-Catholic, movement was permeating Methodist congregations. He mentioned that some persons are offended by these terms, but that his conscience gave no offence as he used them. Moreover, he reasoned, there are no better terms anywhere to express the truths to which these words point.[169] But, on the other hand, he could never "burn a man alive. . .with moist, green wood, for saying, 'Though I believe the Father is God, the Son is God, and the Holy Ghost is God; yet I scruple using the words *Trinity* and *Persons*, because I do not find those terms in the Bible.'"[170] Here Wesley was making reference to the death of Michael Servetus in Calvinistic Geneva (A.D. 1553) for rejecting these two terms. By including this sad episode in the sermon, Wesley seemed to be calling Methodists to accept as a Christian anyone who believes in the reality of the Trinity while having objections to some of its special terminology. Belief in the reality is the heart of religion, while linguistic terms are relative, ambiguous, and peripheral. Linguistic

Orthodoxy - he would warn Methodists - should never be normative so that burning a man in reference to linguistic correctness seems justifiable! Wesley's argument here reminds the historian of the evaluation to the Servetus affair by Sebastian Castellio, who said - "To burn a man is not to defend a doctrine; it is to burn a man."[171] Wesley claimed that orthodox linguistics got Servetus burned at the stake.[172]

Wesley also used the story of Servetus in this sermon to show how Orthodoxy can become so linguistically rigid that true religion is altogether lost. Specifically, he argued, Orthodox Calvinism is a classic example, from Geneva in 1553 to London in the eighteenth century. To avoid such dogmatism in linguistics, Wesley would prefer the words of his sermon text - "There are three that bear record in heaven, the Father, the Word, and the Holy Ghost: And these three are one."[173] And his conscience would also allow him to use *Trinity* and *Person*. He would not, however, use his linguistics to judge another who believed in the reality of the triune Godhead and preferred other terms.

Following his homiletical treatment of linguistics, Wesley turned to being the textual critic. The sermon's text was historically a controversial one. It was a long standing question whether I John V, 7-8 was included in the original version of the epistle or whether it was an insertion added by trinitarians of a later age to give the doctrine a scriptural validation. Wesley stated the case in a no-nonsense manner -

"Is that text genuine? Was it originally written by the Apostle, or inserted in later ages? Many have doubted of this; and, in particular, that great light of the Christian Church, lately removed to the Church above, Bengelius, - the most pious, the most judicious, the most laborious, of all the modern Commentators on the New Testament. For some time he stood in doubt of its authenticity, because it is wanting in many of the ancient copies. But his doubts were removed by three considerations: (1.) That though it is wanting in many copies, yet it is found in more; and those copies of the greatest authority; - (2.) That it is cited by a whole train of ancient writers, from the time of St. John to that of Constantine. This argument is conclusive: For they could not have cited it, had it not then been in the sacred canon; - (3.) That we can easily account for its being, after that time, wanting in many copies, when we remember that Constantine's successor was a zealous Arian, who used every means to promote his bad cause, to spread Arianism throughout the empire; in particular in erasing this text out of as many copies as fell into his hands. And he so far prevailed, that the age in which he lived is commonly styled, *Seculum Arianum*, - 'The Arian Age;' there being then only one imminent man who opposed him at the peril of his life. So that it was a proverb, Athanasius contra mondum: *'Athanasius against the world.'*"[174]

Wesley's position on the authenticity of I John V, 7-8, is clear - The Apostle John wrote it, the early Church quoted it frequently, and later Arians deleted it from certain copies of the epistle. The end result is that the text is apostolic support for the doctrine of the Trinity. The sermon is based on a valid, apostolic truth - "There are three that bear record in heaven, the Father, the Word, and the Holy Ghost: And these three are one."

Wesley's sermon on *THE TRINITY*, after establishing the textual veracity of I John V, 7-8, becomes extremely apologetical in nature, if not polemical. He set about to answer once and for all an historical objection to the doctrine - "Whatever becomes of the text (I John V, 7-8), we cannot believe what we cannot comprehend, therefore, you require us to believe mysteries, we pray you to have us excused." Wesley attacked the objection, claiming it rests upon two mistakes: (1) The objectors wrongly conclude that they are required to believe mysteries; and (2) they wrongly assume they can believe only what they can comprehend. Concerning their first mistake, no one requires them to believe mysteries. Concerning the second, he assured them that they already believe "many things" which they cannot comprehend. For instance, he argued, "the sun above your head -You believe there is a sun...But whether he stands still in the midst of his system, or not only revolves on his own axis, but 'rejoiceth as a giant to run his course;' you cannot comprehend the one or the other."[175] Another example of believing without comprehending is -

"You believe there is such a thing as light, whether flowing from the sun, or any other luminous body; but you cannot comprehend either its nature, or the manner wherein it flows. How does it move from Jupiter to the earth in eight minutes; two hundred thousand miles in a moment? How do the rays of the candle, brought into the room, instantly disperse into every corner? Again: Here are three candles, yet there is but one light. Explain this, and I will explain the Three-One God."[176]

Furthermore, he continued, "you believe there is such a thing as air. . .but can you give me a satisfactory account of its nature, or the cause of its properties? . . .You believe there is such a thing as earth...but do you comprehend what it is that supports the earth?"[177] The truth is, Wesley concluded, the objectors of the Trinity believe in the existence of the sun, light, air, and earth, although they cannot comprehend "how" these things exist. "Matter of fact sweeps away our cobweb hypothesis."[178] The objectors' position is a cobweb hypothesis. Lamentably, Wesley observed, there are always those who will not believe "anything but what they can comprehend." Such mistaken unbelief is unfortunate because a fact of reality is thereby neglected as an all-negating mystery. In reference to the Trinity, the fact of reality is that "there are three that bear record in heaven, the Father, the Word, and the Holy Ghost: and these three are one." The remainder of Wesley's argument is worthy of citation -

"(Therefore) you are not required to believe any mystery. Nay, that great and good man, Dr. Peter Browne, some time Bishop of Cork, has proved at large that the Bible does not require you to believe any mystery at all. The Bible barely requires you to believe such facts; not the manner of them. Now the mystery does not lie in the fact, but altogether in the manner...There are many things 'which eye hath not seen, nor ear heard, neither hath it entered into the heart of man to conceive.' Part of these God hath 'revealed to us by his Spirit: - 'Revealed;' that is, unveiled, uncovered: That part he requires of us to believe. Part of them he has not revealed: That we need not, and indeed cannot, believe: It is far above, out of our sight."[179]

The sermon on *THE TRINITY* was concluded with an empirical argument by Wesley. The reality of the Trinity has provided many Christians, from the first century onward, with spiritual experiences summarily described by the Marquis de Renty - "I bear about with me continually an experimental verity, and a plenitude of the presence of the ever-blessed Trinity."[180] Wesley noted that such an experience, "is not the experience of babes...but of fathers in Christ."[181] Moreover, he continued, "I do not see how it is possible for any to have vital religion who denies that these Three are One. And all my hope for them is, not that they will be saved during their unbelief, but that God, before they go hence, will 'bring them to the knowledge of the truth.'"[182] Here ended the sermon!

Behind Wesley's historical understanding of the doctrine of the Trinity laid a biblical tradition that reached back beyond the First Epistle of John into the Old Testament. The Old Testament yields evidence of the reality of the Trinity, being part of the divine revelation which every Christian is required to believe. For instance, Genesis I, 1 - "In the beginning God created the heavens and the earth" - must be appreciated in Trinitarian terms. Wesley explained this in his *EXPLANATORY NOTES UPON THE OLD TESTAMENT* -

> "The author and cause of this great work, *God*. The Hebrew word is *Elohim*; which (1.) seems to mean *the Covenant God*, being derived from a word that signifies to *swear*. (2.) The plurality of persons in the Godhead, Father, Son, and Holy Ghost. The plural name of God in Hebrew, which speaks of him as many, tho' he be but one, was to the Gentiles perhaps a *savour of death unto death*, hardening them in their idolatry; but it is to us a *savour of life unto life*, confirming our faith in the doctrine of the Trinity, which tho' darkly *intimated* in the Old Testament, is clearly revealed in the New."[183]

In all subsequent passages of the Old Testament, employing *Elohim*, Wesley's *NOTES* consistently contain the Trinitarian interpretation. One of the most important of these is Genesis I, 26 - "And God (Elohim) said, Let us make man in our own image, after our likeness." Wesley's exegesis reads -

> "Now, the word of command is turned into a word of consultation, *Let us make man* - For whose sake the rest of the creatures were made. Man was to be a creature different from all that had been hitherto made. Flesh and spirit, heaven and earth must be put together in him, and he must be allied to

both worlds. And therefore God himself not only undertakes to make, but is pleased to express himself as if he called a council to consider of the making of him; *Let us make man* - The three persons of the Trinity, Father, Son, and Holy Ghost, consult about it and concur in it; because man, when he was made, was to be dedicated and devoted to the Father, Son and Holy Ghost."[184]

Linking *Elohim* and the Trinity was not original with Wesley. It was a Christian tradition from the second century, but Augustine systematized and popularized it in his treatise ON THE TRINITY.[185]

Another Old Testament passage, of similar antiquity, emphasizing the plural name of deity, was Genesis XI, 7 - "Let us go down, and there confound their language." Again, Wesley linked plurality with the Trinity in his NOTES - "This was not spoken to the angels, as if God needed either their advice or assistance, but God speaks it to himself, or the Father to the Son and Holy Ghost."[186] Another passage, Isaiah VI, 3 - "And one cried to another, and said, Holy, Holy, Holy, is the Lord of hosts, the whole earth is full of his glory" - was especially important to Wesley and the entire Trinitarian tradition. The "Holy, Holy, Holy" affirmation was known in early Christian theology and liturgy as the *Trisagon*. Wesley's commentary describes the chanting of the seraphim - "Singing in consort, *Holy* - this is repeated thrice, to intimate the Trinity of persons united in the divine essence."[187] And verse 8 of the same chapter - "and who shall go for us?" - was also part of the Trinitarian revelation for Wesley. The "us" refers to the divine plurality of the Godhead, and uncontestably means the Trinity.[188]

While Wesley discovered many other Old Testament passages in which the Trinity is "intimated," those cited here are the major ones. Perhaps one day some enterprising graduate student will contribute significantly to Wesleyan studies by offering a dissertation on *WESLEY'S BIBLICAL UNDERSTANDING OF THE TRINITY*. Such a work must isolate all Wesley's biblical references, explicit and implicit, employing linguistic and patristic approaches.

Wesley's use of New Testament material treated Scripture more easily linked to the Trinity. These passages were essentially christological but yielded trinitarian meaning. A survey of six of these New Testament passages, as Wesley used them, will be helpful to this study.

(1) John I, lff - "In the beginning was the Word (*logos*)" -Wesley viewed the prologue to the Fourth Gospel as an explicit revelation of God and the Godhead. While Genesis was revelatory in an implicit way, the prologue was revelatory in an explicit way. It shows us the Word as God, eternal life, light (spiritual and moral), and God Incarnate who perfectly reveals the Father. Nevertheless, for Wesley, the Word as God is not "a second God," so that the unity of the Godhead is divided. Wesley's commentary on this prologue's opening verses is lengthy because he did not want any antitrinitarian sentiments to hatch from his exegesis -

> "In the beginning existed the Word, and the Word was with God, and the Word was God. - *In the beginning* - Referring to Gen. I, l, and Prov. VIII, 23, when all things began to be made by the Word. In the beginning of heaven and earth, and this whole frame of created beings, *the Word existed* without any beginning. He *was* when all things began to be, whatsoever had a beginning.

> *The Word* - so termed, Ps. XXXIII, 6; and frequently by the Seventy, and in the Chaldee Paraphrase. So that St. John did not borrow this expression from Philo, or any heathen writer. He was not yet named Jesus, or Christ. He is *the Word* whom the Father begot or spoke from eternity; by whom the Father speaking maketh all things; who speaketh the Father to us. We have, in the eighteenth verse, both a real description of the Word, and the reason why He is so called. 'He is the only begotten Son of the Father, who is in the bosom of the Father, and hath declared Him.'

> *And the Word was with God* - Therefore distinct from God the Father. The word rendered *with* denotes a perpetual tendency, as it were, of the Son to the Father, in unity of essence. He was with God alone; because nothing beside God had then any being. *And the Word was God* - Supreme, eternal, independent. There was no creature, in respect of which He could be styled God in a relative sense. Therefore he is styled so in the Old Testament (Jer. XXIII, 6; Hos. I, 7; Ps. XXIII, l); the other evangelists aim at this - to prove that Jesus, a true man, was the Messiah. But when at length some from hence began to doubt of His Godhead, then St. John expressly asserted it,

and wrote in his book as it were a supplement to the Gospels, as in the Revelation to the prophets.

In him was life - He was the foundation of life to every living thing, as well as of being to all that is.

And the life was the light of men - He who is essential life to all that liveth, was also the light of men, the fountain of wisdom, holiness, and happiness to man in his original state."[189]

(2) Philippians II, 5ff - "Let this mind be in you, which was also in Christ Jesus." Commonly known as the *kenosis* passage, this powerful section of Scripture was one of Wesley's favorites, setting forth "Christ...your common head... (and) God, your common Father."[190] Wesley's *EXPLANATORY NOTES UPON THE NEW TESTAMENT* gives this interpretation -

"*Who being in the essential form* - The incommunicable nature. *Of God* - From eternity, as He was afterward in the form of man; real God, as real man. *Counted it no act of robbery* - That is the precise meaning of the words: no invasion of another's prerogative, but His own strict and unquestionable right. *To be equal with God* - The word here translated *equal* occurs in the adjective form five or six times in the New Testament...In all which places it expresses not a bare resemblance, but a real and proper *equality*. It here implies both the fullness and the supreme height of the Godhead; to which are opposed, *He emptied* and *He humbled Himself. . .Yet* - He was so far from tenaciously insisting upon, that He willingly relinquished His claim. He was content to forego the glories of the Creator, and to appear in the form of a creature; nay, to be made in the likeness of the fallen creatures; and not only to share the disgrace, but to suffer the punishment, due to the meanest and vilest among them all. *He emptied himself* - Of that divine fullness, which He received again at His exaltation. Though he remained full (John I, 14.), yet He appeared as if He had been *empty*; for He veiled His fullness from the sight of men and angels. Yea, He not only veiled, but in some sense, renounced, the glory he had before the world began. *Taking* - And by that very act emptying Himself. *The form of a servant* - The *form*, the *likeness*, the *fashion*, though not exactly the same, are yet nearly related to each other. The *form* expresses something absolute; the *likeness* refers to other things of the same kind."[191]

(3) Colossians I, 15ff - "(Jesus Christ) who is the image of the invisible God, the first begotten of every creature." For Wesley this key passage testifies to the pre-eminence of Christ above angels and to his exclusive right to represent God as the "very image" of God. The *EXPLANATORY NOTES* treats this passage accordingly -

> "*Who is* - By describing the glory of Christ, and His preeminence over the highest angels, the apostle here lays a foundation for the reproof of all worshippers of angels. *The image of the invisible God* - Whom none can represent, but His only begotten Son; in His divine nature the invisible image, in His human the visible image, of the Father. *The first begotten of every creature* - subsisting before all worlds, before all time, from all eternity."[192]

(4) Hebrews I, 2ff - "God...hath in these last days spoken to us by his Son, whom he hath appointed heir of all things, by whom he also made the worlds; Who, being the brightness of his glory, and the express image of his person, and sustaining all things by the word of his power, when he had by himself purged our sins, sat down on the right hand of the Majesty on high." The significance of this passage for Wesley is readily detectible by the great length of his commentary on it. Being much too long to cite here in its entirety, an analysis of key phrases is appropriate. Wesley explained the phrase, *the heir of all things*, in these words - "God appointed him the heir long before He made the worlds (Eph. III, ll; Prov. VIII, 22; etc.). The Son is the firstborn, born before all things; the *heir* is a term relating to the Creation which followed." Therefore, the Son was before all worlds, from eternity.[193] Furthermore, the Son is "the brightness of his glory" -

> "Glory is the nature of God revealed in its brightness. *The express image* - Or stamp. Whatever the Father is, is exhibited in the Son, as a seal in the stamp on wax. *Of his person* - Or substance. The word denotes the unchangeable perpetuity of divine life and power. *And sustaining all things* - Visible and invisible, in being. *By the word of his power* - describes his glory chiefly as He is the Son of God; afterwards, Heb. II, 6 etc., the glory of the man Christ Jesus. He speaks, indeed, briefly of the former before His humiliation, but copiously

after His exaltation; as from hence the glory He had from eternity began to be evidently seen."[194]

(5) Revelation IV, 8ff - "Holy, holy, holy is the Lord God, the Almighty, who was, and who is, and who cometh." Even the casual reader of the Bible recognizes this text as having its origin in Isaiah, at least the *Trisagon* portion. John, the Presbyter, added to the thrice holy the thesis that God is everything past, everything present, and everything yet to come. Wesley's commentary on Isaiah VI, 3, treated earlier in this chapter, was recapitulated in his treatment of John's passage -

"Holy, holy, holy - Is the Three-One God. There are two words in the original very different from each other, both which are translated *holy*. The one means properly *merciful*; but the other, which occurs here, implies much more. This holiness is the sum of a praise, which is given to the Almighty Creator, for all that He does and reveals concerning Himself, till the new song brings with it new matter of glory. This word properly signifies *separated*, both in Hebrew and other languages. And when God is termed *holy* it denotes that excellence which is altogether peculiar to Himself; and the glory flowing from all His attributes conjoined, shining forth from all His works, and darkening all things besides itself, whereby He is, and eternity remains in an incomprehensible manner separate and at a distance not only from all that is impure, but likewise from all that is created. God is separate from all things. He is, and works from himself, out of Himself, in Himself, through Himself, for Himself. Therefore, He is the first and the last, the only One and the Eternal, living and happy, endless and unchangeable, almighty, omniscient, wise and true, just and faithful, gracious and merciful. Hence it is that *holy* and *holiness* mean the same as *God* and *Godhead*; and as we say of a king, his majesty; so the Scripture says of God, his holiness, Heb. XII, 10. The Holy Spirit is the Spirit of God. When God is spoken of, he is often named The Holy One. And as God swears by his name, so he does also by his holiness, that is by himself. This holiness is often styled glory; often his holiness and glory are celebrated together, Lev. X, 3; Isa. VI, 3; for holiness is covered glory and glory is uncovered holiness. The Scripture speaks abundantly of the holiness and glory of the Father, the Son, and the Holy Ghost. And hereby is the mystery of the Holy Trinity eminently confirmed."[195]

(6) Hebrews IX, 14 - "How much more shall the blood of Christ, who through the eternal Spirit offered himself without spot to God, purge our conscience from dead works to serve the living God?" In this passage Wesley found the foundation for salvation - the Trinity! His exegesis from the *EXPLANATORY NOTES* states the case as follows -

> "*How much more shall the blood of Christ* - The merit of all His sufferings. *Who through the eternal Spirit* - The work of redemption being the work of the whole Trinity. Neither is the Second Person alone concerned even in the amazing condescension that was needful to complete it. The Father delivers up the kingdom to the Son; and the Holy Ghost becomes the gift of the Messiah, being, as it were, sent according to his good pleasure. *Offered himself* -Infinitely more precious than any created victim, and that *without spot to God. Purge our conscience* - our inmost soul. *From dead works* - From all the inward and outward works of the devil, which spring from spiritual death in the soul, and lead to death everlasting. *To serve the living God* - In the life of faith, in perfect love and spotless holiness."[196]

We have already given attention to the First Article of Wesley's *TWENTY-FIVE ARTICLES* - Of Faith in the Holy Trinity. It is now appropriate to consider Articles II and IV (Of the Word or Son of God, and Of the Holy Ghost). Such an inclusion will complete our review of authoritative sources for Methodist doctrine, as Wesley designed - the Fifty-two Sermons, the Explanatory Notes, and the Articles of Religion. Of the ARTICLES, II and IV treat the second and third persons of the Trinity.

ARTICLE II - THE WORD OR SON OF GOD

"The Son, who is the Word of the Father, the very and eternal God, of one substance with the Father, took man's nature in the womb of the blessed virgin; so that two whole and perfect natures, that is to say, the Godhead and manhood, were joined together in one person, never to be divided; whereof is one Christ, very God and very man, who truly suffered, was crucified, dead, and buried, to reconcile his Father to us, and to be a sacrifice, not only for original guilt, but also for the actual sins of men."[197]

ARTICLE IV - OF THE HOLY GHOST

"The Holy Ghost, proceeding from the Father and the Son, is of one substance, majesty and glory with the Father and the Son, very and eternal God."[198]

The Word and second person of the Trinity, Wesley held, was directly involved in the many Old Testament theophanies as the pre-existent Christ. Contemporary Christians, upon hearing of this idea, demand evidence that this was so. The tradition emerged in the patristic theology of the second century, became part of Catholic orthodoxy, and in the seventeenth century was popularized in Anglican theology by Bishop George Bull's book *DEFENSIO FIDEI NICAENAE.* In Volume One, entitled "Pre-existence of the Son of God," Bishop Bull began by asserting that the fathers of the first three centuries were in general agreement that the "Son of God frequently appeared to holy men" in the Old Testament. Moreover, these same fathers believed that every visible appearance of *Jehovah* was actually an appearance of the Son of God, properly receiving all the honors due *Jehovah.* When the Old Testament speaks of an "angel" who visits, again it was the Son of God *incognito.* Bull exclaimed, "One who is ignorant of this is a stranger to the writings of the Fathers."[199]

Examples of church fathers cited by Bishop Bull, at some length, are - (1) Justin Martyr (A.D. 165), author of *DIALOGUE WITH TRYPHO THE JEW* - "It was Christ who appeared to Abraham at the Oak in Namre" - "sent fire and brimstone down on Sodom" -"appeared in dreams to Jacob... (and) wrestled with him as a man, and comforted him in exile" - "Christ appeared to Moses in the burning bush."[200] (2) Irenaeus (A.D. 180), the author of *FIVE BOOKS AGAINST HERESIES* - Christ appeared to both Abraham and Moses on occasions.[201] (3) Theophilus of Antioch (circa A.D. 160) - Christ appeared to Adam shortly after the Fall, "assuming the person of the Father and Lord of all, he came into paradise in the person of the Father and conversed with him."[202] (4) Clement of Alexandria (A.D. 150-215) - The pre-existent Christ appeared to Abraham and Jacob (with whom he wrestled), and he gave the Law to Moses.[203] (5) Tertullian (A.D. 160-240) - Christ was at the Tower of Babel, causing it to fall, and also confounding the languages of the people - He also held conversations with Adam, the patriarchs, Moses, and the prophets - Christ also appeared in dreams, visions, mirrors, and in dark sayings.[204] Bull also cited many other ancient authorities -Origen, Novatian, Cyprian, Athanasius, Hilary, Philastrius, Chrysostom, Ambrose, and Augustine.[205]

While John Wesley disagreed strongly with Bishop Bull's views of good works being prerequisite for justification, he openly embraced the Bishop's understanding of Christ in the Old Testament. Wesley was well read in the writings of Bull.[206] He also knew the writings of the Fathers of the Ante-Nicene period, having mastered them while a student at Oxford. From this background, Wesley attempted some remarkable interpretations of his own - Genesis XXII, ll and 15, is a classic example. The story involves Abraham's test and his attempt to offer up Isaac as a human sacrifice. Verse ll mentions "The angel of the Lord" and Wesley exclaimed, "That is, God himself, the eternal Word, the Angel of the Convenant, who was to be the great Redeemer and Comforter."[207] And his explanation of verse 15 reads - "*And the Angel* - Christ, *called* unto Abraham." Another similar passage, treated by Wesley in his NOTES, was Genesis XXXII, 24 - wrestling Jacob, a popular theme for Wesleyan preaching and singing! The text spoke of the stranger as a "man" but Wesley argued it should read "an angel." However, it was not a created angel who wrestled with Jacob, but "rather the angel of the Covenant, who often appeared in a human shape, before he assumed the human nature (as the Christ).[209]

God is no Aristotelian Unmoved mover, according to Wesley. He is One and yet Three, Unity in Trinity and Trinity in Unity.[210] The Trinitarian Godhead is active - planning, creating, moving, governing, filling heaven and earth and the immensity of all space, visiting in human form, allowing the second person to become incarnate, to hunger, to thirst, to grow tired, to be mocked and rejected, to suffer, to die, to be buried, to be resurrected, and finally to be returned to the heaven of heavens as the Lord of eternal life.

Notes

1   WORKS, *op.cit.*, VII, 265.
2   EXPLANATORY NOTES OLD TESTAMENT, *op.cit.*, I, 204. Cf. WORKS, *op.cit.*, VI, 354 - Wesley argued that reason enables us to "understand what the Holy Scriptures declare concerning the Being and Attributes of God... concerning His eternity and immensity; his power, wisdom, and holiness." See also, Clarke, DEMONSTRATION, op.cit, 89-90; NICENE FATHERS, *op.cit.*, II, 210.
3   ENCYCLOPEDIA OF PHILOSOPHY, *op.cit.*, VIII, 36-37.
4   *Ibid*, VIII, 39. Cf. McKeon, *op.cit.*, 458.
5   *Ibid*, I, 59.
6   A.M. Fairweather, *op.cit.*, XI, 65.
7   John Wild (Ed), *SPINOZA SELECTIONS* (New York: Charles Scribner's Sons, 1930), 94. Wesley knew the writings of Spinoza both directly and through the criticism of Samuel Clarke.
8   WORKS, *op.cit.*, VI, 339.
9   *Ibid.*, VI, 338. Cf. Malebranche, *op.cit.*, 231.
10 EXPLANATORY NOTES OLD TESTAMENT, *op.cit.*, I, 59 - In commenting on Genesis XIV, 19, Wesley said "*Most High God* - speaks of this absolute perfections in himself." Cf. WORKS, *op.cit.*, VII, 265 - "These perfections we usually term, the attributes of God."
11 WORKS, *op.cit.*, V, 335. Cf. EXPLANATORY NOTES OLD TESTAMENT, *op.cit.*, I, 59.
12 Baker, *op.cit.*, XXV, 178.
13 Clarke, DEMONSTRATION, *op.cit.*, 232.
14 WORKS, *op.cit.*, X, 231 - Wesley also referred to the "glorious essence" of God. See also VII, 239, 264.
15 *Ibid*, VI, 338.
16 *Ibid*, VII, 265.
17 EXPLANATORY NOTES OLD TESTAMENT, *op.cit.*, I, 204. Cf. Clarke, DISCOURSE, *op.cit.*, 2. Also, WORKS, *op.cit.*, VI, 339 - "The divine eternity" is the *vitae interminabilis tota simul et perfecta possessio*.
18 WORKS *op.cit.*, VI, 190.
19 *Ibid*, VI, 190-191.
20 *Ibid*, V, 335; VII, 265.
21 *Ibid*, VI, 189.
22 *Loc.cit.*
23 *Ibid*, VI, 191.
24 E.R. Fairweather, *op.cit.*, X, 86-87.
25 Clarke, *op.cit.*, 89.

26 WORKS, *op.cit.*, V, 335; VI, 189f.
27 *Ibid*, VII, 265.
28 *Ibid*, VI, 190; VII, 265.
29 Wiener, *op.cit.*, 216. Cf. ENCYCLOPEDIA OF PHILOSOPHY, *op.cit.*, II, 120.
30 *Ibid*, 219, 232, 234.
31 *Ibid*, 223.
32 WORKS, *op.cit.*, VI, 338.
33 JOURNAL, *op.cit.*, VI, 63.
34 WORKS, *op.cit.*, VI, 316, 340.
35 *Ibid*, VII, 241. Cf. Wiener, *op.cit.*, 218 - Newton held that matter fills up only a small part of space.
36 *Ibid*, VI, 338.
37 EXPLANATORY NOTES OLD TESTAMENT, *op.cit.*, III, 1758. Cf. WORKS, *op.cit.*, VII, 239, 241, 242. Also, Clarke, DEMONSTRATION, *op.cit.*, 89.
38 *Ibid*, VII, 241.
39 *Ibid*, VII, 238.
40 *Loc.cit.* Cf. Baker, *op.cit.*, XXV, 364 - Susanna Wesley once wrote to son John on the subject of God's omnipresence: "God is everywhere present, and we (are) always present to Him."
41 *Ibid*, VII, 239. Wesley borrowed here from Bishop Beveridge's famous sermon on the being and attributes of God - *in omnibus extra omnia, ubique totus* - "In all things, beyond all things, everywhere wholly the same God." Beveridge was quoting from Augustine.
42 *Loc.cit.*
43 *Ibid*, VII, 240. Cf. Clarke, *op.cit.*, DEMONSTRATION, *op.cit.*, 79.
44 *Loc.cit.* Cf. EXPLANATORY NOTES NEW TESTAMENT, *op.cit.*, 37. Also, WORKS, *op.cit.*, V, 334 - "*In heaven* - Eminently there. Heaven is thy throne, 'the place where honour particularly dwelleth.' But not there alone, for thou fillest heaven and earth, the whole expanse of space." Also, Clarke, DISCOURSE, *op.cit.*, 23; and WORKS, *op.cit.*, VI, 226, 315, 317, 318.
45 *Loc.cit.* Cf. Wiener, *op.cit.*, 219.
46 *Ibid*, VII, 241.
47 *Ibid*, VII, 242. Cf. Wiener, *op.cit.*, 229.
49 EXPLANATORY NOTES OLD TESTAMENT, *op.cit.*, II, 1606.
50 *Ibid*, I, 68.
51 *Ibid*, I, 204.
52 *Ibid*, I, 213.
53 *Ibid*, I, 10.
54 WORKS, *op.cit.*, VII, 242.
55 *Ibid*, VII, 265.
56 Clarke, DISCOURSE, *op.cit.*, 3.
57 WORKS, *op.cit.*, VI, 315.
58 *Loc.cit.*
59 *Ibid*, VI, 315-326.

60   *Ibid*, X, 361. Cf. Wiener, *op.cit.*, 230 - Leibniz attacked the Cartesians at this point, saying, "It is like fiction... to suppose that God might have created the world some million of years sooner."

61   *Loc.cit.*

62   *Loc.cit.*

63   *Ibid*, V, 335.

64   *Loc.cit.* Cf. WORKS, *op.cit.*, VI, 427-428. The matter of the universe is inert in itself, but the "first material mover" (the "Main-spring") is employed by the Creator to "move the universe." The moving parts of the creation are moved every moment by the divine "main-spring." Clearly, this argument, popular in the seventeenth and eighteenth centuries, was a late modification of Aristotle's doctrine of motion.

65   *Ibid*, VII, 227.

66   *Ibid*, V, 335.

67   *Ibid*, VII, 228.

68   EXPLANATORY NOTES NEW TESTAMENT, *op.cit.*, 466.

69   WORKS, *op.cit.*, VI, 222, 318; X, 229, 232, 362.

70   *Loc.cit.*

71   *Loc.cit.*

72   EXPLANATORY NOTES NEW TESTAMENT, *op.cit.*, 549.

73   WORKS, *op.cit.*, VII, 265.

74   *Ibid*, VI, 315-316. Cf. Clarke, DISCOURSE, *op.cit.*, 23 - Clarke wrote: "For if God be an All-powerful, Omnipresent, Intelligent, Wise, and Free-Being. . . *He cannot possibly but know* at all times and in all places everything that is, and foreknow what at all times and in all places it is fittest and wisest should be, and have perfect power without the least labour, difficulty or opposition, to order and bring to pass, what He so judges fit to be accomplished; And consequently it is impossible but He must actually direct and appoint every particular thing and circumstance that is in the World or ever shall be, excepting only what by His own good pleasure He puts under the power of choice of subordinate Free Agents." See, WORKS, *op.cit.*, VI, 226, 315, 317, 318.

75   *Ibid*, VI, 316. Cf. Clarke, DEMONSTRATION, *op.cit.*, 222.

76   *Ibid*, VI, 316-317.

77   *Ibid*, VI, 317.

78   *Loc.cit.*

79   *Loc.cit.*

80   *Ibid*, V, 334.

81   *Ibid*, VI, 226.

82   *Loc.cit.*

83   *Ibid*, VI, 226-227.

84   *Ibid*, VI, 227.

85   *Loc.cit.* Cf. EXPLANATORY NOTES NEW TESTAMENT, *op.cit.*, 454 -Wesley here claims that God knows our future contingencies. See also WORKS, *op.cit.*, VI, 232.

86   EXPLANATORY NOTES NEW TESTAMENT, *op.cit.*, 872.

87   WORKS, *op.cit.*, VII, 266.   Cf. EXPLANATORY NOTES NEW
      TESTAMENT, *op.cit.*, 957-958.
88   *Ibid*, V, 334.
89   EXPLANATORY NOTES NEW TESTAMENT, *op.cit.*, 303, 904.
90   *Ibid*, 35. Cf. EXPLANATORY NOTES NEW TESTAMENT, *op.cit.*, II,
      1697.
91   WORKS, *op.cit.*, VII, 266.
92   EXPLANATORY NOTES OLD TESTAMENT, *op.cit.*, I, 408.
93   EXPLANATORY NOTES NEW TESTAMENT, *op.cit.*, 35.
94   Loc.cit.
95   Ibid, 29.
96   Ibid, 849.
97   WORKS, *op.cit.*, VII, 266, 239, 240; VI, 242; VIII, 189, 198. Also,
      EXPLANATORY NOTES NEW TESTAMENT, *op.cit.*, 318 - Spirit
      possesses power, wisdom, love and holiness.
98   *Ibid*, VI, 318.
99   E.R. Fairweather, *op.cit.*, X, 76.
100 WORKS, *op.cit.*, VI, 338. Cf. Wiener, *op.cit.*, 232. Also E.R. Fairweather,
      op.cit., X, 76 - Anselm spoke of God being "sensible" but without a body.
101 *BOOK OF COMMON PRAYER* (Oxford: 1897), 561.
102 WORKS, *op.cit.*, X, 231.
103 EXPLANATORY NOTES NEW TESTAMENT, *op.cit.*, 811, 955. Cf.
      EXPLANATORY NOTES OLD TESTAMENT, *op.cit.*, I, 240.
104 EXPLANATORY NOTES OLD TESTAMENT, *op.cit.*, I, 283, 318.
105 Ibid, II, 1651.
106 EXPLANATORY NOTES NEW TESTAMENT, *op.cit.*, 711.
107 JOURNAL, *op.cit.*, IV, 251.
108 WORKS, *op.cit.*, X, 231.
109 EXPLANATORY NOTES OLD TESTAMENT, *op.cit.*, I, 320.
110 WORKS, *op.cit.*, VII, 266-267.
111 *HYMNAL OF THE METHODIST EPISCOPAL CHURCH* (New York:
      Phillips and Hunt, 1884), 126. Wesley translated this hymn by Ernest Lange,
      one of many from German Pietism. See WORKS, *op.cit.*, VII, 239f -
      Concerning Moravian hymns, Wesley said - "I translated many of their
      hymns, for the use of our own congregations."
112 WORKS, *op.cit.*, X, 492.
113 Clarke, DEMONSTRATION, *op.cit.*, 222-225.
114 WORKS, *op.cit.*, VI, 317.   Cf. EXPLANATORY NOTES NEW
      TESTAMENT, *op.cit.*, 318 - God, as Spirit, "is full of wisdom."
115 *Loc.cit.* Cf. EXPLANATORY NOTES OLD TESTAMENT, *op.cit.*, II,
      1605 - Wesley argued that the wisdom of God involves the use of his power
      so as not to "do anything unbecoming God, or unjust to his creatures."
116 *Loc.cit.*
117 *Loc.cit.*
118 *Loc.cit.*
119 *Loc.cit.*

120 *Ibid*, VII, 266. Cf. EXPLANATORY NOTES OLD TESTAMENT, *op.cit.*, III, 1878 - Commenting on Proverbs XXV, 2 - "It is the glory of God to conceal a thing." It is "a testimony of his infinite wisdom."

121 *Ibid*, VIII, 266. Cf. EXPLANATORY NOTES OLD TESTAMENT, *op.cit.*, III, 1835 - Wesley held that the "Divine Perfection of wisdom... is the fountain of wisdom in man."

122 *Ibid*, VI, 325.

123 *Ibid*, VI, 325-326; V, 335 - "His wisdom (is) clearly deduced from things that are seen, from the goodly order of the universe."

124 *Ibid*, VI, 326.

125 *Loc.cit.*

126 *Loc.cit.*

127 *Loc.cit.* Cf. Wiener, *op.cit.*, 220 - Leibniz argued, "God's excellence arises from another cause, viz., *wisdom*, whereby his machine lasts longer, and moves more regularly than those of any other artist whatsoever."

128 *Loc.cit.* - If this were not so, Wesley would have to deny all grounds for science. He was too much a man of the Enlightenment to do this.

129 *Loc.cit.* Wesley relied on Augustine's optimistic view that God uses every occasion of evil for a higher good. See, WORKS, VII, 464.

130 *Loc.cit.* Cf. EXPLANATORY NOTES OLD TESTAMENT, *op.cit.*, II, 1606 - Wesley's argument runs, God is infinitely wise, so much so that he needs "no help governing his creation."

131 *Ibid*, VI, 327. Cf. EXPLANATORY NOTES OLD TESTAMENT, *op.cit.*, 711 - "The Church is the theatre of God's wisdom." Also, page 590 - Christ is portrayed as the "wisdom of God hidden from the world for ages, then revealed."

132 EXPLANATORY NOTES NEW TESTAMENT, *op.cit.*, 914.

133 WORKS, *op.cit.*, X, 227.

134 A.M. Fairweather, *op.cit.*, XI, 78-79.

135 WORKS, *op.cit.*, X, 227; VI, 241.

136 *Ibid*, V, 335.

137 *Ibid*, VI, 317. Cf. Clarke, DISCOURSE, *op.cit.*, 3.

138 EXPLANATORY NOTES OLD TESTAMENT, *op.cit.*, I, 321-322. Wesley's commentary on divine graciousness and justice stressed the incarnation, passion and death, and resurrection of Christ as evidence of God's love. See, II, 1015; and WORKS, *op.cit.*, VI, 232-233.

139 *Ibid*, I, 322.

140 *Loc.cit.*

141 *Loc.cit.*

142 WORKS, *op.cit.*, VII, 269; X, 231.

143 EXPLANATORY NOTES OLD TESTAMENT, *op.cit.*, I, 2.

144 *Ibid*, I, 204.

145 *Ibid*, I, 213.

146 *Ibid*, I, 684.

147 *Ibid*, III, 1826; II, 1668, 1689, 1710, 1715; III, 1751.

148 WORKS, *op.cit.*, X, 361.

149 *Ibid*, IX, 486.
150 *Ibid*, X, 216. Cf. EXPLANATORY NOTES OLD TESTAMENT, *op.cit.*, III, 2328-2331.
151 *Ibid*, X, 363, 220-221.
152 HYMNAL, *op.cit.*, 139.
153 *PROCEEDINGS OF THE WESLEY HISTORICAL SOCIETY* (London), XXIX, 14.
154 JOURNAL, *op.cit.*, VIII, 333.
155 Henry Wheeler, *HISTORY AND EXPOSITION OF THE TWENTY-FIVE ARTICLES OF RELIGION OF THE METHODIST EPISCOPAL CHURCH* (New York: Eaton and Mains, 1908), 9 - Wesley set the standard of theological authority upon the foundation of the EXPLANATORY NOTES (both Old and New), THE TWENTY-FIVE ARTICLES OF RELIGION, and the FIFTY-TWO SERMONS. As for the history of the ARTICLES in the Church of England: in 1536 there were but ten; in 1538 there were thirteen; in 1555 there were forty-two; and in 1571 there were thirty-nine.
156 *Ibid*, 15. Wesley was in solid agreement with the theology of the THIRTY-NINE ARTICLES and the HOMILIES of the Church of England. See, JOURNAL, *op.cit.*, III, 28, and WORKS, *op.cit.*, VII, 461.
157 WORKS, *op.cit.*, VI, 205.
158 *Ibid*, VI, 199 - Wesley had several sermons on the subject of the Trinity. Cf. JOURNAL, *op.cit.*, IV, 391, VI, 61 and note; VII, 367, 368, 375.
159 JOURNAL, *op.cit.*, IV, 391.
160 *Ibid*, VII, 367.
161 WORKS, *op.cit.*, VI, 200. Cf. Williams, *op.cit.*, 16-17. Wesley's essential doctrines were: original sin, the deity of Christ, the atonement, justification by faith, the works of the Holy Spirit, and the Trinity. Also, Borgen, *op.cit.*, 41 - Wesley was quite orthodox in his understanding of the Trinity, distinguishing between the "substance" of the doctrine and the philosophical "illustrations" of it. He always appreciated the philosophical.
162 *Loc.cit.*
163 *Loc.cit.* Cf. NICENE FATHERS, *op.cit.*, III, 222. Wesley could have quoted Augustine at this point - "The Trinity is now seen through a glass by the help of faith, that it may hereafter be more clearly seen in the promised sight, face to face."
164 *Loc.cit.*
165 Charles Herbermann (Ed), *THE CATHOLIC ENCYCLOPEDIA* (New York: Robert Appleton Company, 1907), II, 33-34. Cf. JOURNAL, *op.cit.*, I, 363. Wesley recited this creed while in Georgia.
166 WORKS, *op.cit.*, VI, 200.
167 *Loc.cit.* Cf. Williams, *op.cit.*, 96. Williams maintains that creeds represent "recital theology." Wesley rarely used the creeds as such.
168 *Loc.cit.* Cf. Williams, *op.cit.*, 93, 95. Also, Borgen, *op.cit.*, 41. Further, WORKS, *op.cit.*, X, III - Wesley rejected all pictorial presentations of the Trinity, such as the three interlocking rings, marked Father, Son, and Holy

Spirit. Another was a picture of God as a reclining old man, with the Son leaning on his bosom, and the Holy Spirit, in the form of a dove, hovering above them. Quoting Cassander, Wesley stated that such representations are "a deformation of it (Trinity)."

169 *Loc.cit.*
170 *Ibid*, VI, 201.
171 Rufus M. Jones, *THE CHURCH'S DEBT TO HERETICS* (New York: George H. Doran Company, 1924), 240. Cf. WORKS, *op.cit.*, VI, 201. Also, Lee, *op.cit.*, 113 - Wesley was convinced that Servetus was not a real antitrinitarian.
172 *Loc.cit.*
173 *Loc.cit.* Cf. WORKS, *op.cit.*, V, 335 - "His Trinity in Unity, and Unity in Trinity," is a quotation from Augustine. See NICENE FATHERS, *op.cit.*, I, 201.
174 *Loc.cit.*
175 *Ibid*, VI, 202.
176 *Loc.cit.*
177 *Loc.cit.*
178 *Ibid*, VI, 203.
179 *Ibid*, VI, 204-205; XII, 293; XIII, 30.
180 *Ibid*, VI, 205.
181 *Loc.cit.*
182 *Ibid*, VI, 206.
183 EXPLANATORY NOTES OLD TESTAMENT, *op.cit.*, I, 2. Cf. Arthur W. Wainwright, *THE TRINITY IN THE NEW TESTAMENT* (London: S.P.C.K., 1962), 21ff.
184 *Ibid*, I, 7.
185 NICENE FATHERS, *op.cit.*, III, 24, 111, 157.
186 EXPLANATORY NOTES OLD TESTAMENT, *op.cit.*, I, 48.
187 *Ibid*, III, 1961; I, 790 - Treating Joshua XXIV, 19, Wesley translated the Hebrew text as, "*He is the holy Gods*," then he identified the Trinity with this translation.
188 *Ibid*, III, 1962. Cf. Wainwright, *op.cit.*, 23.
189 EXPLANATORY NOTES NEW TESTAMENT, *op.cit.*, 302-303.
190 *Ibid*, 730.
191 *Loc.cit.* Cf. JOURNAL, *op.cit.*, IV, 146; WORKS, *op.cit.*, VII, 292 - Wesley rejected all ideas of the Son being a "second God."
192 *Ibid*, 742. Cf. John H.S. Burleigh (Ed), *THE LIBRARY OF CHRISTIAN CLASSICS* (Philadelphia: Westminster Press, 1953), VI, 239.
193 *Ibid*, 810.
194 *Ibid*, 811.
195 *Ibid*, 957-958.
196 *Ibid*, 835. Cf. Williams, *op.cit.*, 96; Borgen, *op.cit.*, 83.
197 Wheeler, *op.cit.*, 15-16.
198 *Ibid*, 18-19.

199 George Bull, *DEFENSIO FIDEI NICAENAE* (Oxford: John Henry Parker, 1851), 16.
200 *Loc.cit.* Cf. Cyril C. Richardson (Ed), *LIBRARY OF CHRISTIAN CLASSICS* (Philadelphia: Westminster Press, 1953), I, 284-285.
201 *Ibid*, 16-17.
202 *Ibid*, 17.
203 *Loc.cit.*
204 *Ibid*, 18.
205 *Ibid*, 19.
206 JOURNAL, *op.cit.*, II, 144, 470, 473, 477. Cf. WORKS, *op.cit.*, I, 316-317.
207 EXPLANATORY NOTES OLD TESTAMENT, *op.cit.*, I, 87; VII, 455; XIII, 67.
208 *Loc.cit.*
209 *Ibid*, I, 130.
210 WORKS, *op.cit.*, V, 335.

PART TWO

TIME: TEMPUS FUGIT
(Time Flies)

Chapter Three

The Creation

"From Creation we come to know about God!"[1]

The beginning of time was also the beginning of God's creation of the heavens and the earth and all that is contained within them - that is, the material universe. Apart from this activity, John Wesley reasoned, God generally cannot be known by his creatures. Creation furnishes the universal context for all succeeding revelations of God, including the Christ event. It is especially the context of the Incarnation. The Word (*Logos*) of the Fourth Gospel, who was with God and was God, created all things, and without him was nothing created that was created. Then he took flesh and "dwelt" among us, coming into his own things (*ta idia*), and "we beheld his glory, the glory as of the only begotten of the Father, full of grace and truth."[2] For the Christian who enjoys the spiritual realities bestowed by virtue of the Incarnation, the story of Creation is vitally important, pulling back the curtains from mystery, revealing God's infinite power and wisdom at work in the macrocosm containing a thousand or more worlds, and unveiling his activity in the microcosm with myriads of atoms whirling in vortex motion as the "finger of God" moves them, since they are in themselves inert and passive.[3]

While we have the apostles and evangelists to thank for the written accounts of Christ's Incarnation, we have Moses to thank for the written account of Creation. Wesley was convinced of the Mosaic authorship of Genesis, as well as the remainder of the Pentateuch. He entitled Genesis "First Moses" as did Luther. Exodus was "Second Moses," for Wesley, and so on.[4] According to Wesley, Moses wrote Genesis in the wilderness, after "he had been on the mount with God." Much later in history, the Greek title *Genesis* was given it, signifying the "original" or "generation."[5] It is a book of origins - not only the original creation, but the original sin, the first death, the invention of the arts, the rise of nations, the planting of the Church (an Augustinian idea), and the passage of human generations.[6] Little wonder Wesley so boldly asserted in conclusion - "Creation is the ground for all the works of God."[7] Moreover, Wesley argued, God's reasons for creating the universe must be clearly understood and appreciated. Wesley recognized two main reasons - (1) God created all things for himself, not that he needed anything since he is all-sufficient, but because he wished to express his great power and wisdom in a world which could live and move and have its created being in himself;[8] and (2) God created all things with himself as the *telos* or "end" or "goal" to be attained, so that eventually everything created would fulfill his great plan and participate fully in him.[9] These reasons were not original with Wesley. They came from St. Anselm, who reasoned in the eleventh century - "The universe is entirely dependent on the creative power of God, and its nature and purpose are determined by his nature and reason."[10] The Genesis account of Creation, therefore, involves a "Being of indefinite wisdom and power, who was himself before all time."[11]

THE PRE-HISTORY BEFORE TIME AND THE CREATION

The story of Creation had its settling before time actually began. God planned the entire project in eternity and executed it in the duration of time. Time only began when God willed it from eternity, time being a measurement of duration in relation to created beings. Wesley asserted, "Before the beginning of time, there was none but that Infinite Being that inhabits eternity."[12] Time and created beings did not exist in eternity, but they were willed by God in eternity and God immediately created them. To ask why God did not make time and the universe sooner is a foolish question. Wesley reasoned that there is no "sooner" or "later" in eternity.[13] He was much indebted to Augustine and Leibniz for this argument.[14]

Consequently, when Moses said, "In the beginning God created," he meant, "In the beginning of time." Wesley's exegesis of Genesis I, lff, in the *EXPLANATORY NOTES UPON THE OLD TESTA-MENT*, treated the causes and effects of creation when time first began. This commentary is the most complete given the subject by John Wesley in any of his extant writings. *"In the beginning God created the heavens and the earth"* (Genesis I, 1) -God (*Elohim*) was the cause and the effects were the heavens and the earth, or both together, the "world." Wesley viewed the world or universe as consisting of both heavens and earth in the cosmological sense of the Greeks. In its beginning, God gave the world a particular "frame" - a basic structure into which the "furniture of the universe" could be placed.[15] The idea of the world being a framed house full of furniture was an old idea, not original with Wesley. It was very popular in the Creationism of the century before, Bishop George Berkeley especially teaching it in sermon and treatise.[16] In addition, Wesley argued, such a world consists of two other dimensions - the visible and the invisible. There are visible and invisible aspects to the world's frame, as there are visible and invisible aspects to the world's furniture. Moses, he believed, described only "the visible part of the created order," but he did not exhaust the subject so there are still many "secrets in the visible that are not explained."[17]

Using some Aristotelian logic of the deductive type, Wesley continued his exegesis - From the visible premises of "heaven and earth" we "may infer (deduce) the eternal power and Godhead of the Great Creator."[18] The name of the Creator, in the Hebrew text, is *Elohim*, the Covenant God who "swears" or "promises." The name is plural, signifying plurality in his nature, which, as cited earlier in Chapter Two, Wesley saw as a sign of the Trinity. The name *Elohim* "speaks of him as many, tho' he be but one."[19] In the exegesis of Exodus VI, 2, Wesley linked the name *Elohim* and the name *Jehovah*, arguing that one name signifies the God who promises and begins his plan, and the other name signifies the God who performs and completes his work. "In the history of creation, God is never called *Jehovah*, till the heavens and earth were finished. Gen. II, 4. When the salvation of the saints is completed in eternal life, then he will be known by his name *Jehovah* (Rev. XXII, 13)."[20]

The Great Creator (*Elohim*) is more than the "cause" of the world. Wesley also called him the "cement of the universe."[21] He "compacts into one system" all things that he has made, preserving, supporting, and cementing together "the whole universe."[22] Wesley would have nothing to do with the Deistic concept of God as the Great Architect who designs, builds, and then forsakes his creation to build elsewhere - "He beareth, upholdeth, sustaineth all created things by the word of his power, by the same powerful word which brought them out of nothing. . . Were his almighty influence withdrawn, they could not subsist a moment longer."[23]

The Hebrew term *bara*, meaning "created," came under Wesley's rather traditional analysis - "Created - made out of nothing."[24] Since God alone as Spirit inhabits eternity *a parte ante*, and matter is some sort of created stuff, it must have been created out of nothing. Wesley simply ignored the problem this position poses in philosophical terms. While matter in particular had its beginning in time and space, nevertheless, it surely had an ontological existence in the eternal Idea of the creation within the mind of the Creator. It may be that he saw no problem here, quietly assuming tradition right, or possibly he simply wanted to allow that "matter" as a finite stuff of time and space could not have existed until the conditions for time and space were actualized by the Creator in the first act of creation. If this were the case, Wesley would have made a better Aristotelian than a Platonist. His commentary on Genesis I, 1, boldly asserts, "There was not any pre-existent matter out of which the world was produced."[25] Yet in his sermon *ON ETERNITY*, Wesley explicitly affirmed that in "a sense" matter is eternal. The reader should remember Wesley's two dimensions of eternity - *a parte ante* and *a parte post*. For Wesley, matter is not eternal *a parte ante*, although it had an existence as a reality within the eternal mind of God. God had to create matter for it to have an existence in time and space. Creation of matter was an objectification of an eternal idea in time and space. The idea was eternal *a parte ante* but not the objectification. That became eternal *a parte post* -

"But although nothing beside the great God can have existed from everlasting, - none else can be eternal *a parte ante*; yet there is no absurdity in supposing that all creatures are eternal *a parte post*. All matter indeed is continually changing, and that into ten thousand forms; but that it is changeable, does in nowise imply that it is perishable. The substance may remain one and the same, though under innumerable different forms. It is very possible any portion of matter may be resolved into the atoms of which it was originally composed: But what reason have we to believe that one of these atoms ever was, or ever will be, annihilated? It never can, unless by the uncontrollable power of its almighty Creator. And is it probable that ever He will exert this power in unmaking any of the things that he hath made? In this also, God is not 'a son of man that he should repent.' Indeed, every creature under heaven does, and must, continually change its form, which we can now easily account for; as it clearly appears, from late discoveries."[26]

Wesley's Aristotelian doctrine of change is quite evident here. He subscribed to Aristotle's belief that eternal ideas are *a priori* to their particulars, but nonetheless participate in those particulars once they appear in time and space. The participation causes numerous and various changes in the forms of the particulars while the substance remains constant. Particular entities (created matter), while being subjected to the flow of formal change, are nevertheless substantially eternal *a parte post* since they remain indestructible by the plan of their Creator. Wesley's soteriology also depends upon this principle. For instance, the present material universe, he believed, will not be destroyed. Its form will be radically changed for the better, uniting perfect form with perfect substance in what Wesley called "the New Creation."[27]

Meanwhile, let us return to the Old Creation of Genesis I. In his *OLD TESTAMENT NOTES*, he does not treat matter in the broad philosophical manner employed in his other works. Here he made no mention of material substance as being created, nor of its being linked in some way with the divine substance which is its only cause. He also declined from criticizing Bishop George Berkeley for his outlandish doctrine that material substance does not exist - one of Wesley's pet criticisms of Berkeley. It is obvious that in his

NOTES on Genesis I Wesley was borrowing another's work and modifying it for the general level of early Methodist mentality.

Before Wesley began an exegesis of the creation story, he felt obliged to comment that the fish and fowl were "produced out of water," and that the beasts and man were "produced out of the earth."[29] He used these startling pronouncements to capture the attention of his readers, although any serious reader of the first chapter of the Bible would know this. But, as today, not all Bible readers of that day were serious readers, reading with a high degree of reason.

CHAOS: THE FIRST MATTER.

The earth was made on the third day. But on the first day, God created out of nothing the first matter, which Wesley termed "Chaos." It "was a heavy unwieldly mass."[30] In the Hebrew text of Genesis I, the chaos was called the *tehom* or in English "the deep," signifying "vastness" and "waters" - the earth's particles were scattered throughout this watery vastness. The earth then existed only potentially and not actually until the third day. "This mighty bulk of matter was it, out of which all bodies were afterwards produced." In time the watery part of the chaos produced fish and fowl, and the earthy particles came together to make the earth and produce beasts and man, on different days of creation, however.[31] But at first, the chaos was characterized by two Hebrew words: *Tohu* (confusion) and *Bohu* (emptiness). Isaiah, as well as Moses, used these terms in the exact manner (Isaiah XXXIV, 11), Wesley noted.[32] The chaos "'twas shapeless, 'twas useless, 'twas without inhabitants, without ornaments; the *shadow* or rough draft of *things to come*."[33] Moreover, "darkness was upon the face of the deep" - darkness as "want of light" and not a created thing of God.[34] It must be noted that Wesley's description of the primeval chaos was the orthodox interpretation of both Catholic and Protestant traditions. Yet, there were some modern interpreters in Wesley's century that tried to argue it away. The most popular modernistic view argued: (1) The almighty God, perfect in wisdom and goodness, could not and would not make a chaos; (2) Originally, God made a perfect universe that later fell into such wickedness that it was destroyed - the chaos of Genesis I was the result of that earlier catastrophy; (3) There was a great gap of time between Genesis I, 1 and I, 2, during which this fall and catastrophy took place; and (4) the creation story of Genesis I, 2ff is actually a "recreation" story.

Wesley saw no glimmer of truth in this hypothetical argument. In September 1753, he wrote a scathing denouncement of this view advanced by Mr. Ramsey. Wesley regarded Ramsey's book - *PRINCIPLES OF RELIGION* - to be filled with spurious ideas, especially the anti-chaos motif. Specifically, Wesley charged Ramsey with lacking "a very clear apprehension" of Genesis and other issues.[35] After treating each of Ramsey's arguments *reductio ad absurdum*, Wesley quoted from page 324 of Ramsey's book - "Hence it is that the chaos mentioned in the first chapter of Genesis cannot be understood of the primitive state of nature." Wesley sharply retorted, "Why not, if God created the world gradually, as we are assured he did?"[36] His assurance was based upon the scriptural account of Genesis, not upon a completely hypothetical theory forced into a context which overwhelmingly treats the gradual unfolding of that creation. As Wesley expressed it, "The Creator could have made his work perfect at first, but by this gradual proceeding he would show what is ordinarily the method of his providence and grace."[37] The Wesleyan understanding of the gradual development of creation, providence, and grace is a vital clue to apprehending all of Wesley's thought - things created good going on to perfection. In a divinely ordained and managed process, the created order is moving towards God. It is not things created perfect from the beginning that find completion in God, it is things created "good" in the beginning that finally arrive at perfection when God consummates all things in himself -

"Lastly, being the true God, he is the End of all things; according to that solemn declaration of the Apostle; (Romans XI, 36:) 'Of him, and through him, and to him, are all things:' *Of him* as the Creator, - *through him*, as the Sustainer and Preserver, - and *to him*, as the ultimate End of all."[38]

Before leaving this subject of first matter, Wesley's Aristotelian commitment to the four elements should be noted. Aristotle had taught that the four elements (air, earth, fire, and water) are the building blocks of matter. In the creation of the cosmos these elements got mixed in various proportions by vortex motion. Wesley held the same view and saw it implied in the Genesis I account -

> "In the beginning God created the matter of the heavens and the earth... He first created the four elements, out of which the whole universe was composed; earth, water, air, and fire, all mingled together in one common mass (chaos). The grossest part of this, the earth and water, were utterly without form, till God infused a principle of motion, commanding the air to move 'upon the face of the waters.'"[39]

THE HOLY SPIRIT: THE FIRST MOVER.

Instead of claiming vortex motion to be the cause of matter in motion, Wesley affirmed the phenomenon of motion to be the direct activity of the Holy Spirit, the third person of the Trinity.[40] It was a logical necessity that the Holy Spirit "moved upon the face of the deep," for Wesley's knowledge of eighteenth century physics told him that matter is in itself inert.[41] Yet, he was convinced, all matter moves, but only by the Holy Spirit, who is "the first material mover, the main spring whereby the Creator and Preserver of all things is pleased to move the universe."[42] Only man has the power of self-motion, and that is because he alone was created in the image of God.[43] It is interesting that Wesley could not follow Aristotle at this point. Aristotle's God was the Unmoved Mover. Wesley's God was the God of the Bible, always moving with providence and grace toward his creation, struggling on its path to perfection. The self-motion of God, Wesley held, was transmitted to man in his creation as part of the *imago Dei*. As it will be shown later, however, sinful man, while being able to move physically, cannot move spiritually towards God without the enablement of the Holy Spirit.

In the creation account of Genesis I, 2, Wesley found a rich metaphor for the moving of the Spirit upon the face of the primeval chaos: "He moved upon the face of the deep, as *the hen gathers her chicks under her wings,* and hovers over them, to warm and cherish them." And another metaphor reads, "as the eagle stirs up her nest, and *fluttereth* over the young."[44] The motion of the Holy Spirit, the First Mover, over the chaos began the process of separation. As the Spirit moved, the chaos was transformed by degrees into an order.

THE DAYS OF CREATION:
The First Day of the Week of Creation.

The creation of first matter (chaos) in total darkness, with the First Mover hovering upon it, was accomplished by *Elohim* on the first day. It was immediately followed by the creation of light. Wesley referred to light as the "first of all visible beings which God created."[45] Light, he continued, is also "the first-born. . .of all visible beings" resembling its "great parent in purity and power."[46] The effulgent brightness of God's glory, his very essence, became a visible being in the midst of created matter, and, as such, it became an immediate thing of beauty and blessing. The word of God brought this light into being - "Let there be light!"[47] Wesley added, "He willed it, and it was done; there was light - such a copy as exactly answered the original idea in the eternal mind."[48] The Platonic strain used by Wesley at this point is fascinating. Light, as a part of the created process, is treated as a particularized copy taken from an eternal idea/form/pattern/universal within the divine mind. Wesley enjoyed the happy freedom to flit back and forth between Plato and Aristotle, according to what the issues were, without ever giving justification for why he followed Plato here but Aristotle there. One philosophical difficulty in following Plato here is, of course, that Plato insisted that each particular is but a shadowy, imperfect copy of the real idea to which it relates for its origin and existence. If created light is a "copy" of the divine idea of light, it cannot "resemble its great parent in purity," as Wesley earlier asserted. Wesley should have known that you cannot have your Plato and purity too! But, it should be remembered, Wesley wrote his *EXPLANATORY NOTES UPON THE OLD TESTAMENT* for laymen and not scholars. Nevertheless, he should have found another way to express a great truth - that God does reveal his very essence in his creation.

In creating light, God saw that it was good, that is, that it was exactly as he designed it to be, and that it would accomplish every purpose for which he created it. Here Wesley followed Aristotle's arguments on efficient and final causes. From Plato to Aristotle, from shadowy copy to efficient and final causes, Wesley moved with haste in his exegesis of Scripture.[49] Then he returned to the Genesis text, treating *Elohim's* separation of light from darkness, "as they could never be joined together."[50] Moreover, God divided time between them, "the day for light, and the night for darkness, in a constant succession." The darkness, Wesley asserted, was "now scattered by the light, yet it has *its place*, because it has *its use*." As for the light, its place and use is obvious. Together, darkness and light reveal the wisdom of God at work in a "world of mixtures and changes." In the eternity to come, light and darkness will be forever separated - in "heaven there is perpetual light, and no darkness; in hell utter darkness, and no light; but in this world they are counter-changed, and we pass daily from one to another."[51]

Following the Genesis text further, Wesley noted that "God divided them from each other by distinguishing names. *He called the light Day*, and *the darkness he called Night* - He gave them names as Lord of both. He is the *Lord of time*, and will be so 'till *day and night shall come to an end*, and the stream of time be swallowed up in the ocean of eternity."[52] And so it was, Wesley concluded, that the first day of creation ended - "The evening and the morning were the first day."[53]

The Second Day of the Week of Creation.

Genesis I, 6-8 describes the second day of creation. Wesley's *EXPLANATORY NOTES UPON THE OLD TESTAMENT* and his sermon entitled *GOD'S APPROBATION OF HIS WORKS*, give lucid interpretation to the Mosaic scenario. In his NOTES, Wesley stated the Genesis passage first - "And God said, Let there be a firmament in the midst of the waters, and let it divide the waters from the waters. And God made the firmament, and divided the waters which were under the firmament from the waters which were above the firmament: and it was so. And God called the firmament Heaven: and the evening and the morning were the second day." After citing the passage, Wesley began his exegesis, which is worthy of quotation *in toto* -

"We have here an account of the second day's work, the creation of the firmament. In which *observe.* 1. The *command* of God: *Let there be a firmament* - An *expansion*; so the Hebrew word signifies, like a sheet spread, or a curtain drawn out. This includes all that is visible above the earth, between it and the third heavens, the air, its higher, middle, and lower region, the celestial globe, and all the orbs of light above; it reaches as high as the place where the stars are fixed, for that is called here the *firmament of heaven* ver. 14. 15. and as low as the place where the birds fly, for that also is called the *firmament of heaven*, ver. 20. 2. The *creation* of it: *and God made the firmament.* 3. The design of it: *to divide the waters from the waters* - That is, to distinguish between the waters that are wrapt. . .in the clouds, and those that cover the sea; the waters in the air, and those in the earth. 4. The naming it: *He called the firmament heaven* - 'Tis the visible heaven, the pavement of the holy city. The height of the heavens should mind us of God's supremacy, and the infinite distance that is between us and him; the brightness of the heavens, and their purity, should mind us of his majesty, and perfect holiness; the vastness of the heavens, and their encompassing the earth, and influence upon it, should mind us of his immensity and universal providence."[54]

The sermon on *GOD'S APPROBATION OF HIS WORKS* gives more commentary on the nature of the firmament. It specifically treats the "air" mentioned in the foregoing quotation, expanding the theme into the atmosphere above the earth. This oft neglected passage reads -

"On the second day God encompassed the terraqueous globe with that noble appendage, the atmosphere, consisting chiefly of air; but replete with earthly particles of various kinds, and with huge volumes of water, sometimes invisible, sometimes visible, buoyed up by that ethereal fire, a particle of which cleaves to every particle of air. By this water was divided into innumerable drops, which, descending, watered the earth, and made it very plenteous, without incommodating any of its inhabitants. For there were then no im-

petuous currents of air; no tempestuous winds; no furious hail; no torrents of
rain; no rolling thunders, or forky lightnings. One perennial spring was perpetually over the whole surface of the earth."[55]

The student of philosophy will quickly recognize Aristotle's
"particles" of the four elements which cling to one another in
Wesley's description. So, with the creation of the firmament, the
primeval chaos was stretched out into a vast expanse - the process
being somewhat like that rarefaction process of the Milesian
philosopher Thales. The more expansion (rarefaction), the more
division of water from water, upper from lower, and in the lower
region a growing division between water and particles of earth dif-
fused throughout the water. Particles of air and fire were so joined
as to create an atmosphere of balmy, spring-like breeze, without
extreme wind or heat. This process began on the second day, but it
continued into the third day, making then a complete division of
water and earth, the "sea and the dry land."

The Third Day of the Week of Creation.

"Genesis I, 9 - 13 - And God said, Let the waters under the heaven be gathered together unto one place, and let the dry land appear; and it was so. And
God called the dry land Earth, and the gathering together of the waters called
he Seas: and God saw that it was good. And God said, Let the earth bring
forth grass, the herb yielding seed, and the fruit-tree yielding fruit after his
kind, whose seed is in itself, upon the earth: and it was so. And the earth
brought forth grass, and herb yielding seed after his kind, and the tree yielding fruit, whose seed was in itself, after his kind: and God saw that it was
good. And the evening and the morning were the third day."

A very busy day for *Elohim*, this third day! He not only finished
separating the waters and earth particles in the lower region of the
chaos, but he also made the separate earth fruitful.[56] Included under the heading of herbs and fruit-trees, Wesley placed vegetables,
flowers, shrubs, "together with tall and stately trees, whether for
shade, or for fruit, in endless variety."[57] Trees were adapted "to
particular climates, or particular exposures; while vegetables of

more general use...were not confined to one country, but would flourish almost in every climate."[58] Excluded from the third day creation were weeds and useless plants. There were no poisonous plants to hurt any creature, "but everything was salutary in its kind, suitable to the gracious design of its great Creator."[59] God's creation of a fruitful earth fitted his purpose of preparing the lower world to be a suitable house for the children of men he would make on a subsequent day.[60] God made the house in which to dwell, and he spread the table for earth's inhabitants.

Wesley briefly treated the developing of the seas in relation to the earth -

> "The waters which covered the earth were ordered to retire, and to *gather into one place*, viz. those hollows which were fitted for their reception. The waters thus lodged in their proper place, he called *Seas*; for though they are many, in distant regions, yet either above ground or under ground, they have communication with each other, and so they are *one*, and the common receptacle of waters, into which all the rivers run."[61]

Wesley's paradisiacal earth, it must be noted, did not have the seas surrounding it at first. The seas were kept distinctly apart from the earth, until the time of Noah, when "the great deep burst the barriers which were originally appointed for it."[62]

God's providential furnishing of the earth with fruitful vegetation on the third day received further explanation by Wesley - "Present provision was made, by the immediate products of the earth, which, in obedience to God's command, was no sooner made but it became fruitful."[63] Wesley called this kind of immediate creation "spontaneous generation."[64] For Wesley, all instances of spontaneous generation are caused by God, and there are many instances of the phenomenon. In his *REMARKS ON THE LIMITS OF HUMAN KNOWLEDGE*, Wesley attacked the growing notion of "equivocal generation" that was spreading in the intellectual circles of his day, which notion was later to become biological evolution - all life forms created themselves and their evolutionary changes. Wesley angrily asked -

"But is there any such thing as equivocal generation, whether of plants or animals? It is impossible anything can appear more absurd to the eye of reason! Was there ever an instance, since the world began, that a house grew of itself? Nay, so much as a bed, a table, a chair, or the smallest piece of household furniture? And yet how trifling and inartificial is the construction of these to that of the meanest plant or animal! What is the workmanship of Whitehall or Westminister Abbey, to that of a tree or a fly? And yet, on the other hand, if we deny spontaneous generation, what difficulty surrounds us! If we can give a plausible account of the propagation of mistletoe on trees, and a few of the plants growing on the tops of houses, or on the walls of churches and towers, yet how many more confound all our sagacity! And how many animals are discovered in such places as no animal of that kind ever frequented!"[65]

The creation of all vegetation on the third day of creation was, for Wesley, the first great instance of spontaneous generation. Since that time, God has employed the method frequently to accomplish his will in given situations.[66] Spontaneous generation may or may not allow a shifting of a created thing into something else. Some advocates of spontaneous generation have accepted a divinely managed evolution of created things to other things, especially those thinkers with an Aristotelian prejudice. The debate concerning Wesley's Aristotelian commitment to divine evolution is not over. In one passage of his *A SURVEY OF THE WISDOM OF GOD IN THE CREATION: OR A COMPENDIUM OF NATURAL PHILOSOPHY*, Wesley seems to distance himself from the evolution of one thing to another *via* spontaneous generation -

"Ever since that week of creative wonders, God has ordered all these creatures to fill the world with inhabitants of their own kind; and they have obeyed him in a long succession of almost six thousand years. He has granted...a divine patent to each creature for the sole production of its own likeness, with an utter prohibition to all the rest; but still under the everlasting influence of his own supreme agency upon the moving atoms that form these plants or animals. God himself is the Creator still."[67]

However, as will be shown later, Wesley argued in the same work for a spontaneous generation in which one creature does change into another, and that in an orderly fashion.

The Fourth Day of the Week of Creation.

"Genesis I, 14 - 19 - And God said, Let there be lights in the firmament of heaven, to divide the day from the night; and let them be for signs, and for seasons, and for days, and years: And let them be for lights in the firmament of the heaven, to give light upon the earth: and it was so. And God made two great lights; the greater light to rule the day, and the lesser light to rule the night: he made the stars also. And God set them in the firmament of the heaven, to give light upon the earth. And to rule over the day and over the night, and to divide the light from the darkness: and God saw that it was good. And the evening and the morning were the fourth day."

The fourth day of creation featured the making and establishing of the heavenly bodies in their appointed places. Wesley especially enjoyed this subject. Since his Oxford days he was a lay astronomer. His sermons, treatises, and letters abound with references to the heavenly bodies. He often cited the astronomical writings of Claudius Ptolemy, Tycho, Brahe, and Copernicus.[68] However, he was not convinced that eighteenth century (modern) astronomy was infallible. On the contrary, he was suspicious of some of its methods and conclusions.[69] He occasionally chided his contemporary astronomers for their pride concerning telescopic technology, claiming that the ancients possessed telescopes too.[70] Moreover, he read every published work on astronomy, and he knew the meaning of every biblical passage touching the subject. When a wide difference existed between the astronomy of the Bible and modern astronomical interpretation, Wesley preferred the biblical over the modern. His exposition of Revelation VI, 13, illustrates this preference - "*And the stars fell to the earth* - Yea, and so they surely will, let astronomers fix their magnitude as they please."[71] But Wesley's greatest authority for astronomical understanding was Genesis I, 14 - 19. Where Scripture is not explicit

enough, he held, modern astronomy may be consulted as a possible
source of better understanding the heavenly bodies.

The *EXPLANATORY NOTES UPON THE OLD TESTAMENT*
treats this Genesis passage accordingly -

> This is the history of the fourth day's work, the creating the sun, moon, and
> stars. Of this we have an account, 1. In general, verse 14, 15, where we have -
> (1.) The command concerning them. *Let there be lights in the firmament of*
> *the heaven* - God had said, verse 3, *Let there be light, and there was light*, but
> that was, as it were, a chaos of light, scattered and confused; now it was col-
> lected and made into several luminaries, and so rendered both more glorious
> and more serviceable.

> (2.) The use they were intended to be of to this earth. . . They must be for
> the distinction of times, of day and night, summer and winter. . . They must
> be for the direction of actions: they are for the signs of the change of
> weather, that the husbandman may *order his affairs with discretion*. They do
> also *give light upon the earth* - That we may walk (John XI, 9) and work (John
> IX, 4) *according as the duty of every day requires*. The lights of heaven do not
> shine for themselves, nor for the world of spirits above, they need them not;
> but they shine *for us*, and for our pleasure and advantage. . . The sun is the
> greatest light of all, and the most glorious and useful of all the lamps of
> heaven; a noble instance of the Creator's wisdom, power and goodness, and
> an invaluable blessing to the creatures of this lower world. . . The moon is a
> lesser light, and yet is here reckoned one of the greater lights, because,
> though in regard of its magnitude, it is inferior to many of the stars, yet in re-
> spect of its usefulness to the earth, it is more excellent than they. . . *He made*
> *the stars also* - Which are here spoken of only in general; for the scriptures
> were written not to gratify our curiosity, but to lead us to God. Now these
> lights are said to *rule*. . . Here the *lesser light*, the moon, is said *to rule the*
> *night*; but Psal. CXXXVI, 9, the stars are mentioned as sharers in that gov-
> ernment, the moon and stars to rule by night. No more is meant, but that
> they *give light*."[72]

The Genesis account of the sun, moon, and stars had carried the
day for centuries without any serious challenge.   The medieval
Church had even blended into it the *ALMAGEST* of Claudius
Ptolemy, giving the account some scientific respectability. However, in the sixteenth century Galileo and Copernicus threatened it

with a doctrine of the solar system. In the next century, Johann Kepler telescoptically documented the fact of the solar system, proving that the sun's satellites make revolutions in elliptical orbits. By Wesley's time, most educated persons accepted the fact of the solar system, the founder of Methodism included. Many churchmen set about to prove in some textual or logical way that the solar system was latently present in Genesis. Wesley was not among them. He claimed to have no certainty that Moses knew about the solar system when he wrote Genesis.[73] He did not think it a sacrilege to add the system to his interpretation of Genesis I.

In his sermon on *WHAT IS MAN*, Wesley asked an interesting question - "What is the magnitude of the earth itself, compared to that of the solar system?" He enlarged the question to include "the vast body, the sun, so immensely larger than the earth" together with "the whole train of primary and secondary planets."[74] The "primary planets" revolve about the sun, while the "secondary planets revolve about the primary planets. Our moon is a secondary planet, as are the "moons of Jupiter and Saturn" - some of these moons being actually larger than the earth.[75] This was not a conclusion from biblical sources.

Wesley made another distinction between heavenly bodies -those that are fixed and those that move. This was an ancient distinction, going back beyond the time of Plato. The stars are fixed, many of them possessing their own smaller satellites or planets.[76] Planets, both primary and secondary, together with comets, move in fixed orbits.[77] "Who but the Creator himself can tell the number of these, and call them all by their names?"[78] The sun of our solar system, Wesley believed, is a fixed star, surrounded with its primary planets, some having secondary planets or moons. Comets often and regularly follow their orbits through the solar system. A survey of Wesley's specific views relating to the sun, moon, planets, and comets is worthwhile at this point in the study.

The sun, Wesley said, is "the fountain of fire." It is situated "at the most exact distance from the earth, so as to yield a sufficient quantity of heat (neither too little nor too much) to every part of it (earth)."[79] When the sun was first made by *Elohim* "there was no violent winter, or sultry summer; no extreme, either of heat or cold. No soil was burned up by the solar heat."[80] Moreover, the sun was both an "eye" and a "soul" for the created world. As the eye, it made "all things visible" by distributing light to very part of the system." As the soul, or principle of life, it brought life to both vegetable and animal.[81] The substance of the sun remains a mystery - "We are not yet able to determine, whether it be fluid or solid."[82] The exact distance between the sun and the earth is not precisely known either - "Many astronomers are persuaded it is a hundred millions of miles; others, that it is only eighty-six millions, though generally accounted ninety. But equally great men say, it is no more than fifty; some of them, that it is but twelve; Last comes Dr. Rogers, and demonstrates that it is just two millions nine hundred thousand miles."[83]

According to Genesis I, the earth was made on the third day and the sun on the fourth. The sun was made for the well-being of the earth which preceded it. In the eighteenth century astronomical understanding of the solar system, however, the sun must be considered the parent of the earth. The earth is but one of the planets which moves in elliptical fashion around the sun. How can Genesis I and modern astronomy be harmonized at this juncture? Wesley held that the sun is the largest of all the stars and is of great distance from the earth.[84] Moreover, the earth is part of the solar system.[85] Consequently, he realized, the earth cannot have been prior to the sun. The sun must be the parent of the earth, because the sun must have existed first in order for gravitation to fix an orbit for the earth. Wesley did not agonize over this discrepancy between Genesis I and modern astronomy. He did not try to defend Genesis by claiming it a "poetic description" of creation, not to be taken seriously. Nor did he claim that Moses was "pre-scientific" and should be excused from modern accountability. He gave lip-service to the Genesis account of the sun, but accepted the Copernican version of the solar system as an explicit insight into what the Bible had earlier mentioned with some degree of unreality. After all, the Bible must be understood by redeemed reason which can recognize truth as truth, regardless of when it is discovered and validated.

Concerning the moon, planets, and comets, Wesley was prone to treat them collectively rather than separately. The moon's utility, he argued, involved ruling the night, setting the seasons for agriculture,[86] and effecting the tides on earth.[87] As for the use of planets and comets, however, he could offer no reason for their existence, other than showing "God's handiwork" in the heavens. Beyond this, who can know what usefulness they have?

It was a growing and popular idea in Wesley's day to suppose that the moon and planets were inhabited like the earth with some type of intelligent life. Each heavenly body was thought to have its own atmosphere, water, vegetation, animals, fish, fowl, insects, and humans. If so, the usefulness of the moon and planets can be explained - God is duplicating elsewhere, for his own pleasure, what he is doing on the earth. In January 1765, Wesley wrote a description of this notion and his earlier embracing of it -

"It is now almost universally supposed that the moon is just like the Earth, having mountains and valleys, seas and islands, peninsulas and promontories, with a changeable atmosphere, where vapours and exhalations rise and fall; and hence it is generally inferred that she is inhabitable like the Earth, and, by parity of reason, that all the other planets, as well as the Earth and moon, have their respective inhabitants. . . It was this consideration chiefly which induced me to think for many years that all the planets were inhabited."[88]

What made Wesley abandon this intriguing idea? Just prior to 1759, Wesley read Huygens' *CONJECTURES ON THE PLANETARY WORLD*, which advanced the theory. Just before the death of Dr. Huygens, he recanted his position and withdrew his book from circulation. Wesley was always inclined to accept the word of a dying man above that of a healthy one. In his sermon on *WHAT IS MAN?* Wesley related the story of Huygens' recantation -

"Says the philosopher, 'If God so loved the world, did he not love a thousand other worlds, as well as he did this? It is now allowed that there are thousands, if not millions, of worlds, besides this in which we live. And can any reasonable man believe that the Creator of all these, many of which are probably as large, yea, far larger than ours, would show astonishingly greater regard to one than to all the rest?'

I answer, Suppose there were millions of worlds, yet God may see, in the abyss of his infinite wisdom, reasons that do not appear to us, why he saw good to show this mercy to ours, in preference to thousands or millions of other worlds. I speak this even upon the common supposition of the plurality of worlds, - a very favourable notion with all those who deny the Christian Revelation; and for this reason, because it affords them a foundation for so plausible an objection to it. But the more I consider that supposition, the more I doubt of it; Insomuch that, if it were allowed by all the philosophers in Europe, still I could not allow it without stronger proof than any I have met with yet.

'Nay, but is not the argument of the great Huygens sufficient to put it beyond all doubt? When we view, says that able astronomer, the moon through a good telescope, we clearly discover rivers and mountains on her spotted globe. Now, where rivers are, there are doubtless plants and vegetables of various kinds: And where vegetables are, there are undoubtedly animals; yea, rational ones, as on earth. It follows, then, that the moon has its inhabitants, and probably near akin to ours. But if our moon is inhabited, we may easily suppose, so are all the secondary planets; and in particular, all the satellites or moons of Jupiter and Saturn. And if the secondary planets are inhabited, why not the primary? Why should we doubt it of Jupiter and Saturn themselves, as well as Mars, Venus and Mercury?'

But do not you know, that Mr. Huygens himself, before he died, doubted of this whole hypothesis? For upon further observation he found reason to believe that the moon has no atmosphere. He observed, that in a total eclipse of the sun, on the removal of the shade from any part of the earth, the sun immediately shines bright upon it; whereas if the moon had an atmosphere, the solar light, while it shone through that atmosphere, would appear dim and dusky. Thus, after an eclipse of the moon, first a dusky light appears on that part of it from which the shadow of the earth removes, while that light passes through the atmosphere of the earth. Hence it appears that the moon has no atmosphere. Consequently, it has no clouds, no rain, no springs, no rivers; and therefore no plants or animals. But there is no proof or probability that the moon is inhabited: neither have we any proof that the other planets are. Consequently, the foundation being removed, the whole fabric falls to the ground."[89]

In another place, Wesley claimed that Huygens completely surprised him with this last argument. He summarized the astronomer's argument - "He clearly proves that the moon is not habitable; that there are neither rivers nor mountains on her spotty globe; that there is no sea, no water on her surface, nor any atmosphere, and hence he very rationally infers that neither are any of the secondary planets inhabited." Wesley hastened to ask - "And who can prove that the primary are? I know the earth is. Of the rest I know nothing."[90] So, Wesley, after 1759, came to reject the notion of a plurality of inhabited planets, primary and secondary. Therefore, God's wisdom extends to the earth alone a special providence.

The eighteenth century had a strong fascination with comets. Wesley asked a popular question - "Who knows what comets are?" Are they planets not fully formed? Are they the ruins of planets destroyed by some mysterious conflagration?[91] Should comets be classed among stars or planets? Were they part of the original creation?[92] If so, why was Moses silent about them? If not, when did God add them to the starry heavens? Immediately after the Fall of Adam, or after the Great Flood of Noah's time? Wesley reported that some astronomers conjecture that comets are ruined worlds, or that they are "immense reservoirs of fluids, appointed to resolve at certain seasons, and to supply the still decreasing moisture of the earth."[93] Wesley utterly rejected the connection of impending evil and comets, in spite of numerous old wives' tales. Pestilence and war seldom follow the appearance of comets. They are, like all the heavenly bodies of God's creation, quite benign. Although their use, in divine wisdom, is surely hidden from man's understanding, yet they fill man with awe and reverence when they appear. If they do nothing more than this, they have performed a noble task by enabling man to see himself as a small, dependent creature who is not "the measure of all things" after all!

The Fifth Day of the Week of Creation.

The account of the fifth day, as Wesley understood it, introduced living creatures to the world order. Citing Genesis I, 20 - 23, he proceeded to explain the events of that day -

> "And God said, Let the waters bring forth abundantly the moving creatures that hath life, and fowl that may fly above the earth, in the open firmament of heaven. And God created great whales, and every living creature that moveth, which the waters brought forth abundantly after their kind, and every winged fowl after his kind; and God saw that it was good. And God blessed them, saying, Be fruitful and multiply, and fill the waters in the seas, and let fowl multiply in the earth. And the evening and the morning were the fifth day."

It must be noted that the creatures of the fifth day were brought forth out of the waters, and not out of the earth. The earth creatures were created on the sixth day. The fifth day creatures were fish and fowl.[94] Two important considerations are involved here - (1) God commanded the fish and fowl to be produced abundantly - "The fish in the waters, and the fowl out of the waters."[95] God executed his own command, and great whales and birds came into being. Insects were also among these creatures as part of the fifth day's creation - "Insects which are as various as any species of animals, and their structure as curious, were part of this day's work, some of them being allied to the fish, and others to the fowl."[96] God made the insects "one degree above the inhabitants of the waters," Wesley declared in his sermon ON GOD'S APPROBATION OF HIS WORKS. He also reasoned that originally the insects did not feed on each other, "but lived in peace, "eating the sufficient food of Paradise."[97] Fish, insects, and fowl came forth abundantly when ordered by God. In his *A SURVEY OF THE WISDOM OF GOD IN THE CREATION: OR A COMPENDIUM OF NATURAL PHILOSOPHY*, Wesley claimed that in response to the divine command "the waters grew pregnant."[98] Fish came forth: The whale, as the "king of the waters," had sight, taste, and feeling, but lacked understanding proportionate to his size;[99] the trout and dolphin broke forth into life;[100] and bivalved shell-fish came into being with only the sense of feeling, if not a very low sense of taste, existing "but one degree above vegetables."[101] The many species of fish had one thing in common - "a more stupid nature. . . endowed with fewer senses and less understanding than other animals."[102] There are many million species of insects, Wesley explained, and most of them so minute that human comprehension of them is clearly impossible.[103] The birds came from the waters at the sound of God's voice - "The goose and the sparrow" arose and shook their wings.[104] All the birds were superior to the fish, insects, and reptiles, but they were inferior to the beasts created on the sixth day.[105] And (2) God blessed them all, "in order to their continuance" -

"Life is a wasting thing, its strength is not the strength of stones; therefore the wise Creator not only made the individuals, but provided for the several species, ver. 22. *God blessed them, saying Be fruitful and multiply* -Fruitfulness is the effect of God's blessing, and must be ascribed to it; the multiplying of the fish and fowl from year to year, is still the fruit of this blessing."[106]

And the "evening and the morning were the fifth day," but it ended only after "God saw that it was good."[107]

The Sixth Day of the Week of Creation.

This most important day in Genesis I featured the making of creatures out of the earth - cattle, creeping things, and man. God made "the earth teem with beasts and plants: and the earth like a common mother brought forth the lion, the fox, and the dog, as well as the cedar and the tulip."[108] The earth, for Wesley, was a mother as the waters had been the day before for fish and fowl.[109] By the gradual process of these two "common parents" the Creator exhibited his power and skills just as much as "if he had made them immediately with his own hands."[110] As we shall observe later in this treatment of the creation of man, God is said to have fashioned man's body from the earth, rather than having it, like the beasts and creeping things, spring forth from the earth. But, we must start where Wesley started for the creative activities of the sixth day - Genesis I, 24 - 25 -

> "And God said, Let the earth bring forth the living creature after its kind, cattle and creeping thing, and beast of the earth after its kind, and it was so. And God made the beast of the earth after its kind, and cattle after their kind, and every thing that creepeth upon the earth after its kind: and God saw that it was good."

The *EXPLANATORY NOTES UPON THE OLD TESTAMENT* treats these verses with a minimum of exposition. The only significant observation offered by Wesley concerns the phrase *after their kind*. He claimed that the phrase infers more than "divers shapes." It also infers "divers natures, manners, food and fashions: In all which appears the *manifold wisdom* of the Creator."[111] The creatures made from the earth were superior to all forms of life previously made.[112]

The most notable act of creation on the sixth day involved human kind, male and female. Genesis I, 26 - 28 was Wesley's touchstone for such a creation -

> "And God said, Let us make man in our image, after our likeness; and let them have dominion over the fish of the sea, and over the fowl of the air, and over the cattle, and over all the earth, and over every creeping thing that creepeth upon the earth. So God created man in his own image, in the image of God created he him; male and female created he them. And God blessed them, and God said to them, Be fruitful, and multiply, and replenish the earth, and subdue it: and have dominion over the fish of the sea, and over the fowl of the air, and over every living thing that moveth upon the earth."

In his *EXPLANATORY NOTES* on this passage, Wesley made a number of important observations - (1) That man was made last of all the creatures, "which was both an honour and a favour to him: an *honour*, for the creation was to advance from that which was less perfect, to that which was more so: and a *favour*, for it was not fit he should be lodged in the palace designed for him, till it was completely fitted and furnished for his reception."[113] At the time of man's making, his palace (the world) was already richly embellished with inanimate things of beauty (stars, planets, sun, moon, cedar trees, and even tulips), and it was inhabited with inferior subjects (fish, fowl, insects, beasts, and creeping things). As the Psalmist exclaimed concerning first man, "Thou hast crowned him with glory and honour."[114] (2) That man's creation involved a greater degree of divine wisdom and power than the creation of the other creatures. All previously created things followed the words of God, "Let there be. . ." In the instance of making man, however, God said something unique - *Let us make man* - no word of command here, but rather, the word of consultation! Furthermore, all things created before man were actually made for his sake. Then too, of all creatures, man alone is a composite of heaven and earth, of spirit and flesh, making him "allied to both worlds."[115] For this reason, a divine council "to consider of the making of him" was necessary. The council consisted of the three persons of the Trinity, Father, Son, and Holy Spirit, as noted earlier. They "consult about it, and concur in it: because man, when he was made, was to be dedicated and devoted to Father, Son, and Holy Ghost."[116] (3) That man was made in God's image, and after his likeness. The terms *image* and *likeness* were synonymous for Wesley. The image of God signified three particular aspects - (a) The image of God is essentially spirit, an "intelligent, immortal spirit," making God "the Father of spirits, and the soul of the world."[117] Hence man received the vital spirit or soul of God when he was created. He was flesh endowed with the image of God's spirit. Therefore, his spirit or soul was like God's -intelligent, immortal, active, capable of knowing God in the truest spiritual sense. (b) The *imago Dei* also relates to divine authority being transferred to first man, so that he might have dominion over the creatures of the earth. Wesley often called this the "political" image of God. He expressed it accordingly - "As he has the government of the inferior creatures, he is as it were God's representative on earth. Yet his government of himself by the *freedom of the will*, has in it more of God's image, than his government of the creatures."[118] (c) The image of God consists of

God's *purity* and *rectitude*. In first man, this aspect of God's nature produced knowledge, righteousness, and true holiness. Consequently, first man "had an habitual conformity of all his natural powers to the whole will of God. His understanding saw divine things clearly, and there were no errors in his knowledge."[119] Man's initial will was "readily and universally" at one with God's will. As for his affections, they were regular, without inordinate passions or desires. All of man's thoughts were noble and pure, being fixed always on the "best subjects."[120] The purity of God's image was so possessive, without coercing man's free will, that no vanity or "ungovernableness" could be found in him. The forces of his flesh (inferior powers) were constantly subject to the "dictates" of the soul (superior power). Wesley hurriedly turned this first state of man around -

> "Thus holy, thus happy, were our first parents, in having the image of God upon them. But how art thou fallen, O son of the morning? How is this image of God upon man defaced! How small are the remains of it, and how great the ruins of it! The Lord renew it upon our souls by his sanctifying grace!"[121]

(4) That man was made both *male* and *female*, being blessed by God with fruitfulness. Wesley was familiar with Rabbinic Judaism's interpretation of "male and female" as an hermaphroditic creature until Eve was separated out of Adam. Rabbi Eleazar had said, centuries before Wesley - "When the Holy One, blessed be He, created Adam, He created him an hermaphrodite. . . for it is said, 'Male and female created He them and called their name Adam.'"[122] However, Wesley would not use the term "hermaphrodite." Nevertheless, it is strongly implied in his exegesis of the passage - "God created him male and female, *Adam* and *Eve*: *Adam* first out of the earth, and *Eve* out of his side."[123] Eve was not taken immediately out of Adam. Until she was, Adam was one person, both male and female, referred to by Moses as "him" and "them."[124] Wesley also believed that Adam and Eve were the first male and first female respectively, thus, after their separation becoming the parents of all their kind.[125] All nations of mankind

have Adam and Eve as their first parents, making all humanity of one blood.[126] The overwhelming inference is, deductively, that all men are brothers who should "be induced to love one another."[127] God gave to our first parents, Wesley argued, a large inheritance - the whole earth to populate and govern. In his exposition of this passage, Wesley did not elaborate upon the English word "replenish" - a word important to those speculators who try to prove a gap of time existed between Genesis I, 1 and I, 2, erroneously concluding that the original world was destroyed into chaos and the present world was recreated from its ruins. Wesley, as noted earlier, totally rejected this "crack-brained theory." In his brief treatment of God's command to Adam and Eve, Wesley made "populate" to be synonymous with "replenish."[128] (5) That man has a divinely ordained dominion over all the creatures of the earth, seas, and air. "God designed hereby to put an honour upon man, that he might find himself the more strongly obliged to bring honour to his Maker."[129]

John Wesley recognized a third part to the divine activities of the sixth day in Genesis I, consisting of verses 29 and 30. However, he observed, what God graciously extended to the first parents for their sustentation was not a creation of that day.[130] "Food for all flesh" had been made on the third day. On the sixth day God announced to man that herbs and fruit were his appropriation, that "they must be his meat, including corn, and all the products of the earth."[131] Man, Wesley concluded, was originally designed to be a vegetarian in diet, as were all the inferior forms of life. But, Wesley frequently argued, the first sin changed the eating habits of all created beings. At first, all birds and animals were not "creatures of prey."[132] Then too, even insects were vegetarians and "did not feed on one another, but lived in peace, eating the sufficient food of Paradise."[133] More will be said of this theme in a subsequent section of our study.

Moses concluded his description of the sixth day with these words - "And God saw everything that he had made, and behold it was very good. And the evening and the morning were the sixth day."[134] Wesley's understanding of God's approbation of his creative works is truly Aristotelian in spirit! The meaning of the term *good* was defined by Wesley exactly as Aristotle defined it - a thing is good when it is answerable to the end (telos) for which it was created. Every thing created by God, then, was made to fulfill itself in an end or teleological goal designed by God the Creator. From creation of a thing onward there is movement or change toward the glorious end set by God for that thing. Wesley placed this evolutionary meaning of good into his commentary on God's approbation of his works - "Good, for it answers the end of its creation."[135] He had Aristotle's "final cause" as his basis for this application. But he also used Aristotle's "formal cause" principle. In that concept a created thing has at first a potential which must ultimately, with the passage of time, actualize its potential and fulfill its purpose which always implies some utilitarian benefit to the orderly universe. Wesley added this dimension to his understanding of *good*. He argued that the divine works of creation were *good* because they were "serviceable to man."[136] But Wesley quickly returned to the final cause concept of the term, arguing that every thing in the original creation was given its being "for God's glory." The progression of good things toward the glory of God is clearly discernible by perceptive man, revealing "God's being and perfections" which tend to spark in the human soul a deeply religious response to God.[137]

The approbation of God covered all the days of the week of creation, not just the sixth day. God saw that all of it, from the first day to the sixth, was "very good."[138] The best Wesleyan summary of this divine approval is found in the sermon *ON GOD'S APPROBATION OF HIS WORKS* -

"It was good in the highest degree whereof it was capable, and without any mixture of evil. . . There was a 'Golden Chain' (to use the expression of Plato) let down from the throne of God; an exactly connected series of beings, from the highest to the lowest; from dead earth, through fossils, vegetables, animals, to man, created in the image of God, and designed to know, to love, and enjoy his Creator to all eternity."[139]

Thus the creative activity of God was concluded on the sixth day - "So that in *six days* God made the world. We are not to think but that God could have made the world in an instant: but he did it in six days, that he might shew himself a free agent, doing his own work, both in his own way, and in his own time."[140] Through the process of six days, God's wisdom, power, and goodness appear to us, mediating those same essential qualities for the living of our days within the created order.[141]

The Seventh Day of the Week of Creation.

Wesley quoted Genesis II, 1 - 3, wherein Moses described the very first sabbath -

"Thus the heavens and the earth were finished, and all the host of them. And on the seventh day ended his work which he had made: and he rested on the seventh day from all his work which he had made. And God blessed the seventh day, and sanctified it: because that in it he had rested from all his work, which God created and made."

Treating this passage in his EXPLANATORY NOTES, Wesley noted that (1) the Mosaic reference to "host" referred to heavenly creatures as well as terrestrial ones. The heavenly host are numerous, marshalled, a disciplined army under the "command" of their Creator.[142] Furthermore, "God useth them as his hosts for the defence of his people, and the destruction of his enemies."[143] (2) The heavens and the earth are *finished pieces* as are all the creatures contained within them. *Finished* means an actualized perfection through the completion of a process. God's six days of work was finished so that nothing "can be added to it or taken from it."[144] (3) After the first six days God ceased from all work of creation. In ceasing, he ended the work of creation. The work that God now performs (St. John V, 17) is not the work of creating but of sustaining and preserving what he created the first six days. From the first week of time, God has not made any "new species of creatures."[145] (4) God did not rest because he was weary! Instead, he rested "as one well-pleased with the instances of his own goodness" - his was resting for reflection on his works. By sanctifying (setting apart from the other days) the seventh day for reflective rest, God began the "kingdom of grace" in which we are to labor six days and cease on the seventh. The Christian sabbath is to include the taking of satisfaction in our Creator - "holy work" as Wesley called it. As such, it is "the indispensible duty of all those to whom God has revealed his holy sabbaths." Sabbath observance is very ancient, Wesley affirmed, as old as the world itself. Christians are to honor the sabbath with strict observance, because it is divinely commanded, not simply because it is ancient. God instituted the first sabbath and kept it for an example to his creatures. On the eighth day, or the first day of the second week, God went to work sustaining and preserving his universe as a wise and just Governor.

THE SECOND GENESIS ACCOUNT OF MAN'S CREATION

With the commentary on Genesis II, 1 - 3, the seventh day as the sabbath, Wesley completed his treatment of the week of creation. From Genesis I, 1 to II, 3, Moses had told an orderly and progressive story of how *Elohim* created all things, and Wesley gave a faithful interpretation of that tradition in his *EXPLANATORY NOTES* and sermons on creation. But Genesis II, 4 - 7 presented Wesley with an exegetical nightmare.

This subsequent passage explicitly ignores the progressive nature and order of creation in the former seven day tradition of Genesis I, 1 - II, 3. For instance, the second account of creation begins with God making "every plant of the field, before it was in the earth," and making "every herb of the field before it grew." There was no rain, so that when God made man, he formed his body out of the dust of the earth. Only after the creation of man did God make "every beast of the field, and every fowl of the air, and brought them to Adam to see what he would call them."

Wesley, usually scrupulous in following the biblical text, glossed over these difficulties of two opposing creation sequences. He apparently favored the first account in Genesis, but the second, with *Yahweh* (Jehovah) as the divine name, had to be treated but not too completely.[147] If Wesley had only lived past 1791 to read the writing of the French physician, Jean Astruc (1793), on the significance of two different divine names in these passages, he might have written a strongly explicit commentary on the second creation account. Astruc's insight into this phenomenon led to further scholarly investigation in the nineteenth century, culminating in the famous Documentary Hypothesis, with the Graf-Wellhausen position becoming dominant. Simply stated, two radically different sources, completely opposite versions of creation, got edited into a single narrative by an unknown editor or editors, late in Old Testament times, so that Genesis I and II as a unit cannot be Mosaic. Whether Wesley would have accepted this hypothesis is itself quite hypothetical. Judging by his glossing over the differences that the second creation story present in reference to the first story, Wesley found the situation troublesome. He could not bring himself to try a rational harmonization of the two accounts. Nor could he treat the problem without confusing the ordinary reader. In the preface to his *EXPLANATORY NOTES UPON THE NEW TESTAMENT*, Wesley addressed such a dilemma - "I purposely decline going deep into many difficulties, lest I should leave the ordinary reader behind me."[148]

The Jehovah account of creation emphasizes the making of man as a composite creature - of heaven and earth, of spirit and flesh. So Wesley's *EXPLANATORY NOTES* treats Genesis II, 7 - "And the Lord God formed man of the dust of the ground, and breathed into his nostrils the breath of life; and man became a living soul" -

"Man is a little world, consisting of heaven and earth, soul and body. Here we have an account of the original of both, and the putting of both together: *The Lord God*, the great fountain of being and power, *formed man*. Of the other creatures it is said, they were *created* and *made*; but of man, that he was *formed*, which notes a gradual process in the work with great accuracy and exactness. To express the creation of this *new thing*, he takes a *new word*: a word (some think) borrowed from the potter's forming his vessel upon the wheel. The body of a man is *curiously wrought*. And the soul *takes its rise* from the breath of heaven. It came immediately from God; he *gave it* to be put into the body (Eccles. XII, 7.) as afterward he gave the *tables of stone* of his own writing to be put into the *ark*. 'Tis by it that man is a *living soul*, that is, a living man. The body would be a worthless, useless carcase, if the soul did not animate it."[149]

Usually exacting with biblical arguments, Wesley had instances of missing the main point too. This is the case here with his exegesis of Genesis II, 7. The simple argument of the verse is that God formed man's body from the dust, breathed into its nostrils the breath (*neshema*) of life and man "became" a living soul (*nephesh*). Wesley was correct in saying that man was "a living soul, that is, a living man," but he missed the point the author of the passage was trying to make - that man was not given a soul (as Wesley believed and argued) but "became" a living soul. The explicit teaching of the Genesis author was that a body formed from dust and possessing the breath of life becomes a living soul or living man. The Yahwist doctrine of man and the Wesleyan doctrine of man (as composed of body and soul) are not compatible. The reason for this difference is obvious. Wesley was a child of the Church, a church with a long tradition of harmonizing Scripture with practical needs. Such a tradition often moved beyond the simple affirmations of biblical chapters and verses for the sake of a systematic theological position. Such a position gave the thinkers of the tradition the benefits of a progressive Pharisaism - that is, finding in Scripture principles to be applied, rather than actual facts that must be preserved in historical isolation, never able to be repeated again. The Church, before Wesley, learned that the soul is more than the total personality of a living body. The Christianizing of Plato and Aristotle at this point meant that the Yahwist doctrine of Genesis II, 7 had to be opened up to a broader interpretation. The Yahwist doctrine could no longer be treated as the exhausted fact of soulness. For Christian thinkers, including Wesley, it was a "starting point" for exploration and discovery, but it was not the final word on the subject. For this reason, we must appreciate Wesley's attempt to lead his Methodists into systematic understanding with Scripture as the touchstone but not the complete account.

Before exploring Wesley's understanding of the soul, an analysis of his understanding of the human body is a necessity.

THE BODY OF MAN

In his exposition of Genesis II, 7, Wesley claimed that "the body would be a worthless, useless carcase, if the soul did not animate it." Nevertheless, the human body, considered by itself, is a remarkable and ingenious creation. It is a magnificent machine.[150] Wesley exclaimed -

"Here is a curious machine. . .fearfully and wonderfully made. It is a little portion of *earth*. The particles of which cohering, I know not how, lengthen into innumerable fibres, a thousand times finer than hairs. These crossing each other in all directions, are strangely wrought into membranes; and these membranes are strangely wrought into arteries, veins, nerves, and glands; all of which contain various fluids, constantly circulating through the whole machine. In order to the continuance of this circulation, a considerable quantity of air is necessary. And this is continually taken into the habit, by an engine fitted for that very purpose. But as a particle of ethereal *fire* is connected with every particle of air, (and a particle of water too), so both air, and fire are received into the lungs together; where the fire is separated from the air and water, both of which are continually thrown out; while the fire, extracted from them, is received into, and mingled with, the blood. Thus the human body is composed of all the four elements, duly proportioned and mixed together; the last of which constitutes the vital flame, whence flows the animal heat."[151]

Where did Wesley learn that the human body is like a machine? From the Bible? Hardly! Such a concept is foreign to biblical accounts of man's nature. Where then? From many thinkers of the modern era, with Rene Descartes definitely among them. The passage above is from Wesley's sermon entitled *WHAT IS MAN*? It is basically a paraphrase of Descartes' *TREATISE ON MAN*. Wesley did not borrow every idea or term in the Cartesian original, but the following he freely extracted with their Cartesian tones for his sermon - machine, nerves, veins, arteries, particles, blood, flame, animal spirits (which Wesley changed to animal heat), gland, and the heat of the heart (which Wesley paraphrased as "fire. . . mingled with. . .the blood").[152] In his sermon, Wesley described the mechanistic functioning of the human body, following the very descriptions of Descartes - blood pressure being "a force equal to the weight of a hundred thousand pounds to propel the blood from the heart through all the arteries."[153] Not only did he follow Descartes but also Malebranche.[154] As for Wesley's doctrine of the four elements (earth, air, fire, and water) being mixed proportionately together to constitute the body, the source of this idea was Aristotle as every beginning philosophy student knows.

In his *COMPENDIUM OF NATURAL PHILOSOPHY*, Wesley treated other mechanical aspects and functions of the human body -fibres, cellular membranes, bones, cartilage, lacteals, lymphatics, muscles and tendons, skin, pores and perspiration, the head, cerebrum, medulla oblongata, meninges (membrane of the brain), the origin of nerves, the Pineal gland, guards of the eye, eye muscles, Tunica adnata, eye structure, coats of the eye, external parts of the ear, internal ear parts, nostrils, tongue, teeth, palate, speech organs, circulation of blood, lungs, stomach, intestines, lacteal vessels, pancreas, liver, gall bladder, spleen, kidneys, ureters, bladder, hands and feet, fluid of the body, blood, animal heat, and more.[155] Quite a physical examination for Adam and his posterity! Wesley's sources for this study of human anatomy were John Francis Buddaeus (Professor of Philosophy at the University of Jena), Descartes, and Malebranche.

The trouble with a machine, however, is that it cannot operate itself. Being inert, it must be activated by an agent or energy not indigenous to itself. It needs help to pass through its stages before it can function as a machine or "engine" as Wesley often called it.[156] Descartes likened the human body to a clock.[157] Though Wesley never spoke of man as a clock-like machine, he alluded to the comparison when he spoke of the Holy Spirit as the "main-spring" which sets the physical machine in motion and keeps it going.[158] Hence, all the involuntary motions of the human body are performed in mechanical fashion, triggered by a divine force put into the machine.[159]

Wesley confused things at this point by making the Holy Spirit, the First Mover, part of the machine itself, as the main-spring is part of the watch or clock. It was a problem of not having a perfect illustration to show how the Holy Spirit sets man's inert body in motion. We must forgive him for this, remembering that all who would interpret lack perfect analogies. Nevertheless, he needs to be quoted more on this subject -

> "The Almighty Spirit, the source of all motion in the universe... governs every motion of the body; only with this exception, which is a marvelous instance of the wise and gracious providence of the great Creator: There are some motions of the body, which are absolutely needful for the continuance of life; such as the dilation and contractions of the lungs, the systole and diastole of the heart, the pulsation of the arteries, and the circulation of the blood. These are not governed by me at pleasure; They do not wait the direction of my will. And it is well they do not. It is highly proper that all the vital motions should be involuntary; going on, whether we advert them or not."[160]

Furthermore, the human body possesses organs of sense -sight, hearing, smelling, tasting, and touching.[161] Wesley was an avowed empiricist of the Lockean sort in epistemological matters. Moreover, his empiricism partially relies on the *bodies determinate* of Thomas Hobbes, the alleged Father of all atheists. Such bodies work upon the sensory organs, forming the first stage of knowledge. Yet these organs are simply parts of the machine, having no power of their own to see, to hear, to smell, to taste, or to feel. They are in place but cannot function until moved by a force from the Creator. For Wesley, this force is the soul, or the movement of the Holy Spirit within the body of earth, the machine of inert matter. It is only when the divine agent moves through the component parts of earth, air, fire, and water (blended with great wisdom to make the multitudinous cells, fibers, fluids, etc. of the human body) that man becomes more than a mere machine - he becomes a living man.[162] Such a being, Wesley held, possesses a body of clay and a spirit (soul) -

"The body is not the man. . . man is not only a house of clay, but an immortal spirit; a spirit made in the image of God; an incorruptible picture of the glory of God; a spirit that is of infinitely more value than the whole earth. . . sun, moon, stars. . . than the whole material creation."[163]

Wesley called the body "the earthly clod," and the soul "the heavenly flame." The two are "each dependent on the other."[164]

THE SOUL OF MAN

The Wesleyan understanding of the soul bears the marks of biblical and theological traditions. Our starting point, however, must be the Lockean empiricism which Wesley used to undergird the biblical and theological. His epistemological reasoning has these steps - (1) Every person discovers in himself certain bodily motions caused by outward objects or bodies determinate. These objects or bodies are seen, heard, smelled, tasted, or felt, causing motions within our bodies and perceptions within our minds. (2) We further discover that after the objects are removed, the perceptions of them remain, being "variously mixed and compounded together, which we term imagination." (3) A long time later, "when those objects are not only removed, but even cease to exist, those perceptions return to our minds. And this we call memory." (4) As we perceive these objects, "We know that we perceive them. The human mind is able to look into itself and "reflect upon its own perceptions." Reflection is a divine principle placed within us by a wise Creator. (5) We likewise discover within ourselves various appetites "for good things, and aversions to evil things." It is a general rule without exception that the involuntary motions of the body "tend to avoid the evil and attain the good." Another appetite exerts itself in our minds - a sublime appetite that "checks, controls, and exercises authority over the rest, convincing us that pleasant things are invariably harmful, and that we should find a desire to avoid them." (6) When our organs of sense are "struck by any of the bodies that surround us, and the motions caused thereby are continued through the nerves to the brain, the soul residing there, is suitably affected." The Creator has connected the soul and the body so closely "that on certain motions of the body, if conveyed to the brain by means of the nerves, certain perceptions of the mind always follow." It is also true that with certain perceptions of the mind, certain bodily motions follow. (7) This dynamic relationship of mind and body is caused by the soul that is within us, residing within our brains. The soul is immaterial, Wesley argued, because it is "a thinking substance." It possesses two faculties - (a) Understanding (passive) by which it perceives all the motions of the body, "and knows and reflects upon its own operations; and (b) Will (active) "by which we incline to good and are adverse to evil." Matter is incapable of thinking, hence the soul must be a spiritual substance.[165]

There is more to be said about the soul from Wesley's work in natural philosophy, and we will return to it immediately. But, other points of importance on this subject need to be gleaned from Wesley's commentaries and sermons.

Wesley maintained that Scripture teaches the soul to be "an immortal spirit, made in the image of God; together with all the powers and faculties thereof, understanding, imagination, memory, will, and a train of affections. . . love and hatred, joy and sorrow. . . desire and aversion, hope and fear."[166] Furthermore, the soul is endued with a "degree of liberty" and "self-moving, self-governing power."[167] This inward principle of motion governs every part of the body,[168] whether through voluntary motion or involuntary motion. The soul is, therefore, a microcosm of God's natural and moral self - "an immortal spirit, made in the image of God, in his natural and moral image; an incorruptible picture of God's glory."[169] While it is a scaled-down version of God's spiritual essence, it is "a spirit made equal to angels."[170] Since most angels have wings, souls also are winged, not literally but symbolically. Inspired by Plato's "wings of the soul," Wesley spoke of "simplicity of intention and purity of affection" as the "wings of the soul... without which *she* can never ascend to the mount of God."[171] In exegeting Proverbs XX, 27, Wesley equated the "Spirit of a man" with "the reasonable soul." The verse reads - "The spirit of a man is the candle of the Lord, searching all the inward parts of the belly." The

"candle" is a "clear and glorious light set up in man for his information and direction." The phrase *of the Lord* modifies *the candle*
(soul of man) which "comes from God in a more immediate manner
than the body. . . and because it is in God's stead, to observe and
judge all our actions." The word *belly* refers to the "heart."[172]
Wesley, with his commitment to the new science could not locate
the soul in the traditional heart of man. The heart, he knew, is but
a muscle used to pump blood through the vascular system of the
human machine.[173] Wesley preferred the brain as the lodging
place of the soul. Rene Descartes the century before argued it was
in the Pineal gland within the brain. Wesley was unsympathetic to
Descartes' theory. He thought the Pineal gland was an inappropriate place for the soul to dwell since it is only "a reservoir of
blood."[174]

Returning to Wesley's *A SURVEY OF THE WISDOM OF GOD
IN THE CREATION: OR A COMPENDIUM OF NATURAL
PHILOSOPHY*, the psychosomatic relationship was important to
Wesley's understanding of the soul. He recognized the elusiveness
of thorough understanding in this area of inquiry. He believed the
difficulty in comprehending the union of soul and body to be a matter of two radically different substances being involved. If soul and
body were "two bodily substances," they could "be implicated or
twisted together, but not two substances of so widely different natures, can be joined at all, we know not." This was the elusive psychosomatic problem for Wesley. However, he plunged onward
into a discussion of it -

"All we can tell is this: God has ordered that certain perceptions in the soul
should constantly follow certain motions of the body, and certain motions of
the body such perceptions in the soul. . . The scriptural account is this: God
made the body of man out of the earth, and breathed into him the breath of
life; not only an animal life, but a spiritual principle, created to live forever.
Even the body was then perfect in its kind; neither liable to death nor pain.
But what the difference was, between the original and the present body, we
cannot determine. But to form it even as it is now, no less than a divine
power was requisite. No less could mix the primary elements, in so exact a
proportion, and then frame so many different parts, of so various figure, tex-

ture, and magnitude. God alone was able to form the original fibres; to weave those fibres into hollow tubes; to dispose these tubes, filled with their several humours and variously interwoven with each other, into different organs: and of those organs connected together in a continued series and due situation, to finish so complicated and wonderful a machine as the human body. Nothing was wanting now, but that the immortal spirit should be sent into its habitation, to bear the image of its Creator and enjoy his glory. But the manner wherein this was done we cannot tell; this knowledge is too wonderful for us."[175]

Wesley believed that the human soul is both created and immortal, created in time to be eternal. But, what are the specific aspects of its origins? Wesley was constantly interested in determining this. In his day there were three popular ideas concerning the origin of the soul - Creationism, Traducianism, and Pre-existence. Creationism stresses the creation of the soul at the moment of conception, when the male sperm fertilizes the female egg. Aristotle was the great champion of this theory, treating the subject in Argument 60 - *SOUL IN THE SEMEN AND IN THE FERTILIZED GERM*.[176] Aquinas adapted it to the Christian usage, emphasizing that God "creates" the soul at the moment of conception.[177] Nehemiah Curnock claimed that Wesley leaned toward this theory at first.[178] The evidence for this assertion is a crucial passage from the *EXPLANATORY NOTES UPON THE NEW TESTAMENT* - from the commentary on Hebrews XII, 9, written circa 1754 -

"Now if we have had fathers of our flesh who corrected us, and we reverenced them: shall we not much rather be in subjection to the Father of spirits, and live? *And we reverenced them* - We neither despised nor fainted under their correction. *Shall we not much rather* - Submit with reverence and meekness. *To the Father of spirits* - That we may live with him forever. Perhaps these expressions, *fathers of our flesh* and *Father of spirits*, intimate that our earthly fathers are only the parents of our bodies, our souls not being originally derived from them, but all created by the immediate power of God; perhaps at the beginning of the world."[179]

Strictly speaking, Wesley's exposition is considerably removed from Aristotelian and Thomistic Creationism. It is closer to Traducianism, although it lacks the precision of that position. Curnock was in error in his identification. When he read Wesley's words - "all created by the power of God" - he mistook them for Creationism.

Traducianism, as a term, comes from the Latin *tradux*, meaning "an off-shoot." Pre-Christian Stoicism employed it in reference to a soul being an off-shoot of the substance of its parental soul. Wesley's exposition of Hebrews XII, 9 was more along the lines of Stoical Traducianism - our bodies, he argued, came from our earthly fathers, but our souls came from the Father of spirits at the beginning of the world. Since then, every child's soul is an off-shoot from his father's, right back to Adam. Tertullian introduced Traducianism into Christian theology in the late second century as a necessity for a consistent doctrine of original sin. His argument included the idea that all human souls were substantially in Adam at the time of the first sin.[180] Traducianism ruled in the Western Church until displaced by Thomistic Creationism in the thirteenth century. Wesley's explanation of original sin is completely compatible with Traducianism, whereas Creationism is not. Then too, it should be noted that in 1762 Wesley openly identified his views as being Traducianistic - "All the souls of his (Adam's) posterity, as well as their bodies, were in our first parents.[181] In 1763, he published a letter in his *JOURNAL* which defended Traducianism and took him to task for unclear reasoning in his commentary on Hebrews XII, 9.[182] Apparently he agreed with the author of this critical letter, choosing to publish it without a refutation. In another *JOURNAL* entry, in 1770, Wesley stated -

"I read and abridged an old treatise on the *Origin of the Soul*. . .I never before saw anything on the subject so satisfactory. I think he proves to a demonstration that God has enabled man, as all other creatures, to propagate his whole species, consisting of soul and body."[183]

Whatever he had been before 1762, it is certain that after that time Wesley was a Traducianist.

The theory of pre-existence of souls, implying some sort of heavenly stock-pile, found little sympathy with Wesley. He never advocated the Socratic/Platonic idea. Admittedly, once Wesley quoted Hippocrates, that "nothing is born but what had a prior existence."[184] But he never developed the saying into a Methodist axiom, nor did he ever quote it again. In fact, Wesley's multi-faceted attack on the errors of Chevalier Ramsay specifically treated Ramsay's belief in pre-existent souls.[185] In the *EXPLANATORY NOTES UPON THE NEW TESTAMENT*, Wesley argued against the suggestion in St. John IX, 2, that there is a pre-existent state for the soul - "Master, who sinned, this man, or his parents, that he was born blind?" Wesley's response came as a stake through the heart of all doctrines of pre-existent souls - "Who sinned. . .this man, or his parents. . .? - That is, Was it for his own sins, or for the sins of his parents? They supposed (as many of the Jews did, though without any grounds from Scripture) that he might have sinned in a pre-existent state, before he came into this world."[186] "Without. . .Scripture." Case closed!

What did Wesley believe concerning the destiny of the soul? He was very traditional on this subject. The soul is not eternal *a parte ante*, having been divinely created in time, but it is eternal *a parte post*. This immortal state is both its existence and its destiny. Hence, once souls come into being, they never die.[187] When the house of clay dissolves in death, the soul mysteriously leaves, no one knows precisely when.[188] Though it leaves the dead flesh, it retains understanding and memory, and the will and the affections remain "in full vigour."[189] The body returns through decomposition to the earth, but the soul returns to God who made it. God judges the departed soul with wisdom and love, and he ascribes it an appropriate place in eternity *a parte post*.

Souls from the beginning of their existence in time are on a pilgrimage - a pilgrimage through time, preparing for eternity to come. Woe unto that soul that neglects its Creator and Governor in this life of time, for in the next it will be cast into outer darkness for ever. Blessed, however, are all the souls who seek in the life of time to glorify God their Creator, Governor, and Redeemer, for in the life to come they shall for ever see God's face.

THE SOULS OF ANIMALS

The serious reader of Wesley knows that he often mentioned the souls of animals. Such an idea seems strange to contemporary minds. Actually, Wesley stood in a respectable tradition of theology in which animal souls were justified by scriptural reference and rational argument. Wesley, like many Christians before him, accepted Aristotle's types of souls as being realistic. He especially recognized two types of souls -sensible souls and reasonable souls. The human soul is of the latter type, and it has been described above. Of the earthly creatures, only humans possess reasonable souls. Immortality and salvation are extended only to reasonable souls.

The sensible soul, on the other hand, is a soul possessing empirical powers of sight, hearing, smelling, tasting, and feeling. It has a small degree of intellectual understanding and reflection. It is overwhelmingly a sense-oriented self instead of a rational self. It is the soul of animals and brutes, although, from time to time, some men have seemed to possess it. While the reasonable soul makes men free moral agents, the sensible soul lacks sufficient reason to make animals free moral agents. Free moral agency, according to Wesley, demands rational accountability in this life and the next. Sensible souls lack both free moral agency and immortality. Upon death of the animal body, the sensible soul returns back to an "original, elementary substance."[190] It is not subject to salvation, and there is no heaven for it. Nevertheless, Wesley felt a close kinship with animals because they are besouled. He worked throughout England to improve humane treatment of animals, and he often advised his Methodist followers to show care and compassion to God's lesser creatures.

MORE ON THE GOLDEN CHAIN

Earlier, Wesley's idea of a Golden Chain in creation was introduced. It is now appropriate to analyze the concept. His reference to the Golden Chain was in the famous sermon - *GOD'S APPROBATION OF HIS WORKS*. The passage states -

> "Such was the state of the creation, according to the scanty ideas which we can now form concerning it, when its great Author, surveying the whole system at one view, pronounced it 'very good.' It was good in the highest degree whereof it was capable, and without any mixture of evil. Every part was exactly suited to the others, and conducive to the good of the whole. There was 'a golden chain' (to use the expression of Plato) 'let down from the throne of God;' an exactly connected series of beings, from the highest to the lowest; from dead earth, through fossils, vegetables, animals, to man, created in the image of God, and designed to know, to love, and enjoy his Creator to all eternity."[191]

The "chain" signifies gradations of created things, animate and inanimate - "dead earth" up to "man." In his *A SURVEY OF THE WISDOM OF GOD IN THE CREATION: OR A COMPENDIUM OF NATURAL PHILOSOPHY*, Wesley made it clear that this chain of entities is not a static, abstract system of categories, useful only for classifying all forms of created things. On the contrary, he presented the chain as a dynamic process of Aristotelian change, moving upward, from one lower form to the next higher form, and yet, without adding "any new species of creatures" to the created order.[192] The SURVEY treats the passage from one species to another, up the chain. For instance, it shows the movement of insects upward to shell-fish, with the pipe-worm as the "link;"[193] from shell-fish to reptiles;[194] from reptiles to fish;[195] from fish to birds, flying fish being the link;[196] and birds to quadrupeds with bats and flying squirrels being links.[197] Needless to say, there are gradations within each species, from low to high. This, Wesley argued, is the case everywhere, even among the quadrupeds, with the ape being the highest form. Then too, in reference to the human species, there are gradations with a "prodigious number of continued links between the most perfect man and the ape."[198]

The most unusual statement by Wesley upon this subject is also the most surprising -

> "By what degrees does nature raise herself up to man? How will she rectify this head that is always inclined towards the earth? How change these paws into flexible arms? What method will she make use of (to) transform these crooked feet into supple and skilful hands? Or how will she widen and extend this contracted stomach? In what manner will she place the breasts, and give them a roundness suitable to them? The ape is this rough draft of man: this rude sketch, an imperfect representation, which nevertheless bears a resemblance to him, and is the last creature that serves to display the admirable progression of the works of God."[199]

It must be remembered that Wesley described this aspect of the created order in a work he entitled *A SURVEY OF THE WISDOM OF GOD IN THE CREATION. . .*, under the chapter heading, *A GENERAL VIEW OF THE GRADUAL PROGRESSION OF BEINGS.* Charles Darwin's book, *THE ORIGIN OF THE SPECIES*, was not published until 1859. Wesley, while pre-dating Darwin, was not the originator of this evolutionary idea. Aristotle had given a theory of physics that made such thinking philosophically possible and respectable. Centuries later, in Christian circles, Aristotle's theory evolved into the sort of thing Wesley published under his own name. However, behind his *SURVEY* was the significant work of Mr. Bonnet, of Calvinistic Geneva. The title of Bonnet's work was *THE CONTEMPLATION OF NATURE.* Wesley called it "a beautiful work" in his preface to the *SURVEY.*

THE CREATION OF ANGELS

It is a common mistake of Christian thinkers to end the story of creation with the making of man. According to Wesley, there is more to the story -

"But the scale of the creation does not terminate at man. Another universe commences there, whose extent, perhaps, compared to that of this, is as the space of the olar vortex to the capacity of a nut. There shine the Celestial Hierarchies, like glittering stars. There from all parts the angels, archangels, seraphim, cherubim, thrones, virtues, principalities, dominions, powers, cast forth their radiant beams."[200]

The idea of the *CELESTIAL HIERARCHY* is well known to church historians. Bonnet and Wesley made use of the famous book by that name, written, as was supposed before 1895, by Dionysius the Areopagite, one of St. Paul's converts at Athens (Acts XVII, 34). The work, prior to the Renaissance, enjoyed a place in the Western Church of nearly being Scripture. The influence of this book was significant, affecting popes, councils, synods, and doctors of the Church. Many commentaries were written upon it, elucidating the mystical, Neoplatonic lessons contained within it. Some of its more illustrious commentators were - Hugh of St. Victor, Albertus Magnus, Thomas Aquinas, Meister Eckhart, John Tauler, Jan van Ruysbroeck, and John of the Cross.[201] During the sixteenth century, however, questions concerning the Dionysian authorship began to surface. By 1895, Stiglmayt and Koch clearly demonstrated that its author was a Christian Neoplatonist who wrote it about A.D. 500. Since then, both Catholic and Protestant scholars have referred to it as PSEUDO-DIONYSIUS. However, in Wesley's day the *CELESTIAL HIERARCHY* was held in high esteem in London and Geneva.

Since Wesley used this Neoplatonic book in describing the creation of angels, a brief analysis of it is needful. In the work God's purpose is shown to be the bringing of man to deification (godlikeness) through sanctification, which involves various stages. Therefore, God has initiated two hierarchies, one celestial (angelic) and the other terrestrial (ecclesiastical).[202] Fifteen chapters are devoted to the celestial - the angels being divided into three separate hierarchies, each possessing three orders. The first hierarchy consists of seraphim, cherubim, and thrones. These three ranks receive purity, light, and perfection directly from God. They transmit these spiritual qualities down the ladder to the second hierarchy below them, which hierarchy consists of dominions, virtues, and powers. The second hierarchy then transmits these on to the third hierarchy below them. This hierarchy consists of principalities, archangels, and angels.

The second hierarchy watches over the entire creation for its good, and the third hierarchy helps humanity collectively and individually. According to the *CELESTIAL HIERARCHY*, all angels and archangels are spiritual beings, simple, intelligible, and intelligent.[203]

Wesley's list of spiritual realities in his celestial hierarchy is the same as in the work of Pseudo-Dionysius, but in a different order - angels, archangels, seraphim, cherubim, thrones, virtues, principalities, dominions, and powers.[204] Wesley's celestial beings also radiate "light" like "glittering stars" because they "borrow their light and splendour" from the "Sun of Righteousness."[205] They also have their being from God's Being, and their existence from his existence. Their perfection is from God's perfection, but cherubim (the highest of all for Wesley) cannot look into the perfection of God because a great gap exists between the Creator and created things.[206] When the celestial beings survey the works of God in creation, however, they experience great ecstasy.[207] These beings are "superior intelligencies," but they do not share the same degree of knowledge - "There may be some perhaps to whom is granted the knowledge of one world only; others may know several; others a much greater number."[208] In his *SURVEY* Wesley appealed to humanity to recognize the existence and activity of the celestial order -

"Ye inhabitants of the earth, who have received reason sufficient to convince you of these worlds, will you forever be denied entrance into them? Will the infinitely good being, who shows them to you at a distance, always refuse you admittance into them? No; since you are called to reside ere long among celestial hierarchies, you will like them fly from planet to planet; you will eternally advance from perfection to perfection, and every instant of your duration will be distinguished by the acquisition of farther degrees of knowledge. Whatever has been withheld from your terrestrial perfection, you will obtain under this economy of glory; 'You will know even as you are known.' 'Man is sown corruptible, he will rise incorruptible and glorious;' these are the words of the apostle and philosopher: the covering of the seed perishes; the germ subsists, and assures man of immortality."[209]

There are some remarkable ideas embedded in this passage -(1) The men of earth will one day join the ranks of the celestial beings. This does not mean, for Wesley, that after death men become angels. Angelic beings are spirits, lacking corporeal bodies. Men have both corporeal bodies and immortal souls, and in eternity *a parte post* man's soul will be united with his resurrected body. Then the righteous pilgrim, whose feet were habitually on the path of perfection on earth, will join the angelic hosts but with certain claims and experiences of God's love which angels will never appreciate. (2) "You will like them fly from planet to planet." What a strange idea, one never treated by Wesley in any other place. If Wesley's faith-subsumed view about the after-life is valid, why not visit Mars or Jupiter? And (3) eternal life, after this corruptible life, is a continuation of "going on to perfection," since, for Wesley, there are many degrees of perfection - the creatures move along a scale of relative perfection, while the Creator alone possesses absolute perfection from everlasting to everlasting. So, Wesley advised, "You will eternally advance from perfection to perfection." Whether one attains deification, as in Pseudo-Dionysius, is doubtful in Wesley's thought. He seemed incurably convinced that a gulf necessarily exists between the Creator and the creatures, even in eternity *a parte post.* That is why he continued to argue that throughout the remainder of eternity glorified man *will continue* to grow in knowledge. Acquisition of knowledge is the flow of relative perfection, while having complete knowledge is a necessary quality of absolute perfection. Man will continue to acquire knowledge in eternity, but God has enjoyed full and thorough knowledge of all things since before time and creation because he alone is absolutely perfect and does not need to learn anything.

In his sermon ON ETERNITY, Wesley struck the distinction between "duration without beginning" and "duration without end." While God uniquely enjoys both dimensions, his angelic creatures and human children enjoy only the second kind of eternity. It is a communicable "attribute of the great Creator" that "he has been graciously pleased to make innumerable multitudes of his creatures partakers of it."[210] The angels, archangels, and all the company of heaven participate in this attribute, and "are not intended to die, but to glorify him, and live in his presence for ever.[211] In Wesley's sermon OF EVIL ANGELS, he explicitly stated the angels are included in the Golden Chain of beings -

> "Accordingly, there is one chain of beings, from the lowest to the highest point, from an unorganized particle of earth or water, to Michael the archangel. And the scale of creatures does not advance *per saltum* (by leaps), but by smooth and gentle degrees; although it is true these are frequently imperceptible to our imperfect faculties. We cannot accurately trace many of the intermediate links of this amazing chain, which are abundantly too fine to be discerned either by our senses or understanding. . . We can only observe, in a gross and general manner, rising one above another, first, inorganic earth; then, minerals and vegetables, in their several orders; afterwards, insects, reptiles, fishes, beasts, men, and angels. Of angels, indeed, we know nothing with any certainty but by revelation."[212]

Natural philosophy cannot teach us anything about the angels, only the "Oracles of God" - the scriptures - can do that. But the confirming testimony of the Patristic Church may be trusted to interpret the biblical evidence.[213] One must approach the subject of angels in faith - one must believe in order to understand. In his sermon *THE DISCOVERIES OF FAITH*, Wesley made the existence and ministry of the angels one of the great discoveries of faith. He argued that unbelief never brings a discovery.[214] The contemporary Church often treats the subject of angels as peripheral at best. Not so with Wesley! Angels were for him an essential article of faith. His famous, and often misapplied affirmation, "We Methodists think and let think," applied only to peripheral doctrines and never to "essential" ones like angels. Whether such creatures actually exist and administer the will of God is not a matter of opinion or consensus. It is a matter of faith or unbelief! For this reason, Wesley included angels in his definitive sermon on the nature and contents of Christian faith.

Another sermon, entitled *ON GOOD ANGELS*, treats definitively the nature of angels from a scriptural perspective. Surprisingly, however, he began the sermon with a quotation from Hesiod, the first Greek philosopher and author of *THEOGONY* -"Millions of creatures walk the earth unseen." Wesley left out "whether we wake, or if we sleep" from Hesiod's poetic verse. He then turned to the biblical references to angels, making a series of points - (1) The essence or nature of angels is spiritual -"They are all spirits, not material beings; not clogged with flesh and blood like us." Nevertheless, they do have bodies, which differ from ours. Their bodies are "of a finer substance, resembling fire or flame," as suggested by Psalm CIV, 4 - "Who maketh his angels spirits, and his ministers a flame of fire."[215] Moreover, God endued these angelic spirits with understanding, will, and liberty, which qualities are "essential to, if not the essence of, a spirit."[216] (2) Angelic understanding is without defect in perception. Consequently, there is no error in their empirical understanding.[217] Their power to reason is not a slow, creeping movement from one truth to another, like human reasoning. It is instantaneous and complete, "at one glance." So, it seems, "that angels know not only words and actions, but also the thoughts, of those to whom they minister. And indeed without this knowledge, they would be very ill qualified to perform various parts of their ministry."[218] (3) In addition to the wisdom received in their creation, angels acquire more wisdom as they fulfill their ministries, as has been the case for nearly six thousand years. They, as humans, are on the path to greater perfection. (4) The angels possess holiness, derived directly from God himself. Wesley spoke of God's holiness as an "inexhaustible ocean - A boundless, fathomless abyss, without a bottom or a shore."[219] These "holy angels" practice goodness, philanthropy, and love to man "as we learn from his own oracles."[220] (5) The strength of angels is beyond human comprehension. Even fallen angels are termed by the Apostle "powers of the air." One angel alone "smote, in one hour, 'all the first-born of Egypt, both of man and beast.'" The strength of a good angel must be greater "than even an archangel ruined." The four angels of the Apocalypse are strong enough to hold back the four winds, Wesley argued. "Indeed we do not know how to set any bounds to the strength of these first-born children of God."[221] (6) Although God alone is omnipresent, yet he has given "an immense sphere of action (though not unbounded) to created spirits."[222] (7) The angels have great power over the human body, "power either to cause or remove pain and diseases, either to kill or heal." They understand how the human body is made, and "all the springs of this curious machine, and can, by God's permission, touch any of them, so as either to stop or restore its motion." Even evil angels possess such power as in the case of Job being "smote with sore boils."[223] (8) Some of the angels minister to the heirs of salvation. Wesley gave an interesting description of angels and backsliders -

> "I will not say, that they do not minister at all to those who, through their obstinate impenitence and unbelief, disinherit themselves of the kingdom. This world is a world of mercy, wherein God pours down many mercies, even on the evil and the unthankful. And many of these, it is probable, are conveyed even to them by the ministry of angels; especially, as long as they have any thought of God, or any fear of God before their eyes. But it is their favourite employ, their peculiar office, to minister to the heirs of salvation; to those who are now 'saved by faith,' or at least seeking God in sincerity."[224]

On December 9, 1781, Wesley wrote a letter to Hester Ann Roe, assuring her that the ministry of angels continues even while the Christian pilgrim sleeps -

> "How easy it is for them (the angels), who have at all times so ready an access to our souls, to impart to us whatever may be a means of increasing our holiness or our happiness! So that we may well say with pious Bishop Ken,
>   'O may Thy angels, while we sleep,
>   Around our beds their vigils keep,
>   Their love angelical instil,
>   Stop every avenue of ill.'"[225]

While Wesley was concerned with offering the Methodists an adequate description of the angels of the celestial hierarchy, he was equally concerned that they not reverence angels to the place of worship. His commentary on Colossians I, 14 - 17 (that Christ is the "first-begotten of every creature") indicates that Christ subsisted before all time, from all eternity, giving him preeminence over the highest angels who were created at the beginning of time. Hence the Apostle Paul laid a theological foundation for reproof of all angel worship.[226] Since Christ created "all things that are in heaven and that are on earth, visible and invisible, whether they be thrones, or dominions, or principalities, or powers, all things were created by him, and for him" (Colossians I, 16), then the Creator is prior to, and greater than, his creatures, the angels included.

But precisely when in the creative process did the Creator make the angels? Wesley treated this question in his *EXPLANATORY NOTES UPON THE OLD TESTAMENT* while exegeting Job XXXVIII, 6 - 7. The passage reads - "Or who hath stretched the line upon it? Whereupon are the foundations thereof fastened? Or who laid the cornerstone thereof? When the morning stars sang together, and all the sons of God shouted for joy." According to Wesley, the "morning stars" were "the angels because of their excellent lustre and glory." They were also called "the sons of God because they had their whole being from him, and because they were made partakers of his divine and glorious image." These angels also "shouted" at the beginning of God's creation. They did not "advise or any way assist him, nor dislike or censure any of his works," but rather they "rejoiced in and blessed God for his works."[227] So, Wesley concluded, the angels were witnesses to the creation. But, at what part of the creation were they made? Obviously, at the very outset.

Returning back to Wesley's NOTES on Genesis I, 1 - "In the beginning, God created the heavens and the earth" - he made a crucial observation- "When this work was produced: *In the beginning -* That is, in the beginning of time. Time began with the production of those beings that are measured by time. Before the beginning of time there was none but that Infinite Being that *inhabits eter-*

nity."[228]   His commentary on verse 3 gives more insight - "That the first of all visible beings which God created was *light*."[229]   On the surface, Wesley's argument seems thin. What has the creation of angels to do with the creation of light? Wesley did not have to answer that question because most Christians of his day knew its answer - the classical argument of Augustine on the subject was the answer -

> "Where Scripture speaks of the world's creation, it is not plainly said whether or when the angels were created; but if mention is made, it is implicitly under the name of 'heaven,' when it is said, 'In the beginning God created the heavens and the earth,' or perhaps rather under the name of 'light,' . . .But that they (angels) were wholly omitted, I am unable to believe, because it is written that God on the seventh day rested from all His works which He made; and this very book itself begins, 'In the beginning God created the heavens and the earth,' so that before heaven and earth God seems to have made nothing."[230]

> "The angels existed therefore before the stars; and the stars were made on the fourth day. Shall we then say they were made the third day? Far from it; for we know what was made that day. . . On the second day, then? Not even on this; for on it the firmament was made between the waters above and beneath. . . There is no question, then, that if the angels are included in the works of God during these six days, they are the light which was called 'Day,' and whose unity Scripture signalizes by calling that day not the 'first day,' but 'one day.'"[231]

Therefore, for both Augustine and Wesley, the angels were created on that "one day" when God made "light" as "the first of all visible beings." They were related to light in several ways - as "flaming spirits."[232] and as "fire. . . burning. . . brightness. . . glorious. . . subtile. . . pure."[233]   Furthermore, in his commentary on Isaiah XIV, 12, Wesley translated *Lucifer* from the Hebrew to mean "bright star" or "morning star,"[234] showing that even the fallen angel was originally essential light.

John Wesley's comparison of the creation of angels and the creation of man is an appropriate way of concluding this chapter. God first created the angels as his "first-born sons," and then later he "created a new order of intelligent beings" which he called "man."[235] What will happen to these two orders? Will the celestial hierarchy remain true to its created heritage? Will man retain the full *imago Dei*? Will the brutes, birds, reptiles, fish, insects, vegetables, and lower forms of the Golden Chain continue in their gradual progression toward dynamic perfection? Or, alas, will moral choices by angels and man bring catastrophic consequences until the whole creation groaneth together and travaileth together? Only time will tell!

Notes

1 WORKS, *op.cit.*, VI, 339.
2 EXPLANATORY NOTES NEW TESTAMENT, *op.cit.*, 302-304.
3 WORKS, *op.cit.*, VII, 172; VI, 242, 326, 427; XIV, 300ff.
4 EXPLANATORY NOTES OLD TESTAMENT, *op.cit.*, I, 1.
5 *Loc.cit.*
6 *Loc.cit.*
7 EXPLANATORY NOTES NEW TESTAMENT, *op.cit.*, 958.
8 WORKS, *op.cit.*, VI, 384, 445. Cf. EXPLANATORY NOTES NEW TESTAMENT, *op.cit.*, 466.
9 *Ibid*, VI, 429.
10 ENCYCLOPEDIA OF PHILOSOPHY, *op.cit.*, I, 129. Cf. WORKS, *op.cit.*, X, 220.
11 EXPLANATORY NOTES OLD TESTAMENT, *op.cit.*, I, 2.
12 *Loc.cit.* Cf. WORKS, *op.cit.*, VI, 139.
13 *Ibid*, X, 361 - God chose when to create the universe, as it seemed good to him.
14 NICENE FATHERS, *op.cit.*, II, 207-208. Cf. Wiener, *op.cit.*, 224. Also Baker, *op.cit.*, XXV, 264.
15 EXPLANATORY NOTES OLD TESTAMENT, *op.cit.*, I, 2. Cf. WORKS, *op.cit.*, VI, 325-326; X, 361-362 - Wesley argued that by God's sovereign will "he appointed the place of the universe, in the immensity of space."
16 Calkins, *op.cit.*, 127 - Bishop Berkeley (1685-1752), of the Church of England, was well read by Wesley who frequently cited him, especially using his idea of the "furniture" of the universe. See, WORKS, *op.cit.*, X, 361-362; XIII, 493.
17 EXPLANATORY NOTES OLD TESTAMENT, *op.cit.*, I, 2.
18 *Loc.cit.*
19 *Loc.cit.* Cf. NICENE FATHERS, *op.cit.*, III, 240 - Augustine held to the identification of *Elohim* and the Trinity.
20 *Ibid*, I, 213. Cf. INSTITUTES, *op.cit.*, I, 132 - Calvin claimed the New Jerusalem itself would bear the name *Jehovah*. See, EXPLANATORY NOTES NEW TESTAMENT, *op.cit.*, 1044, for Wesley's view.
21 WORKS, *op.cit.*, VI, 427.
22 *Ibid*, VI, 426-427.
23 *Ibid*, VI, 426.
24 EXPLANATORY NOTES OLD TESTAMENT, *op.cit.*, I, 2. Cf. Malebranche, *op.cit.*, 223 - Malebranche offered a defence for creation *ex nihilo*. See also, NICENE FATHERS, *op.cit.*, II, 208.

25 *Loc.cit.*
26 WORKS, *op.cit.*, VI, 191. Cf. Malebranche, *op.cit.*, 273-274. Wesley again flirts with the Cartesians, especially with Malebranche, but also with Descartes and Spinoza, linking them with this type of Thomistic Aristotelianism.
27 EXPLANATORY NOTES NEW TESTAMENT, *op.cit.*, 899, 1041-1042. Cf. W. T. Jones, *op.cit.*, 222-224, 228-231. Also, WORKS, *op.cit.*, VI, 315. See Chapter XII of this work - THE NEW CREATION.
28 Baker, *op.cit.*, XXV, 186. Cf. Calkins, *op.cit.*, 127. Also, Francis J. McConnell, *JOHN WESLEY* (New York: Abingdon Press, 1939), 326.
29 EXPLANATORY NOTES OLD TESTAMENT, *op.cit.*, I, 2.
30 *Ibid*, I, 3. Cf. Eaton, *op.cit.*, 320.
31 *Loc.cit.*
32 *Loc.cit.*
33 *Loc.cit.* Cf. Eaton, *op.cit.*, 330 - Descartes had a great dislike for the doctrine of primeval chaos.
34 *Loc.cit.*
35 WORKS, *op.cit.*, XII, 210.
36 *Ibid.* XII, 212.
37 EXPLANATORY NOTES OLD TESTAMENT, *op.cit.*, I, 3. Cf. Eaton, *op.cit.*, 318 - Descartes argued that creation took five to six thousand years. See also, Baker, *op.cit.*, XXV, 265 - The young Wesley of 1731 was greatly impressed with the argument of Archbishop King that "all created beings. . . are necessarily imperfect; nay, infinitely distinct from supreme perfection. Nor can they all be equally perfect."
38 WORKS, *op.cit.*, VI, 429.
39 *Ibid*, VI, 207.
40 EXPLANATORY NOTES OLD TESTAMENT, *op.cit.*, I, 3.
41 WORKS, *op.cit.*, VI, 326, 427. Cf. ENCYCLOPEDIA OF PHILOSOPHY, *op.cit.*, I, 143. See also, Wiener, *op.cit.*, xxxix - Leibniz attacked the Cartesian doctrine of the conservation of motion, which doctrine Wesley held, because it totally ignored the existence of the eternal, dynamic interplay of natural forces, such as monads.
42 *Ibid*, VI, 427.
43 *Ibid*, VI, 242, 326.
44 EXPLANATORY NOTES OLD TESTAMENT, *op.cit.*, 1, 3.
45 *Loc.cit.*
46 *Loc.cit.*
47 *Loc.cit.*
48 *Loc.cit.*
49 *Loc.cit.* Cf. W. T. Jones, *op.cit.*, 224. Also, Ross, *op.cit.*, 51, 57.
50 *Loc.cit.*
51 *Loc.cit.*
52 *Loc.cit.* Cf. WORKS, *op.cit.*, VI, 209-210 - Wesley spoke of the benefits of the night: "Night - By this the *springs* of the animal machine were wound up

from time to time, and kept always fit for the pleasing labour for which man
was designed by his Creator."

53   *Ibid*, 1, 4. Cf. NICENE FATHERS, *op.cit.*, II, 208 - Augustine commented
on the "days" of Genesis I - "What kind of days these were it is extremely difficult, or perhaps impossible for us to conceive."

54   *Loc.cit.*

55   WORKS, *op.cit.*, VI, 210, 316 - Wesley placed "magazines of fire, hail, snow,
vapour, winds, and storms" in this atmosphere.

56   EXPLANATORY NOTES OLD TESTAMENT, *op.cit.*, I, 4.

57   WORKS, *op.cit.*, VI, 210-211.

58   *Ibid*, VI, 211.

59   *Loc.cit.*

60   EXPLANATORY NOTES OLD TESTAMENT, *op.cit.*, I, 4.

61   Ibid, I, 5. Cf. WORKS, *op.cit.*, VI, 208.

62   WORKS, *op.cit.*, VI, 208; III, 385-386 - Wesley believed that the Antedilu-
vian earth was completely flat, "without high or abrupt mountains, and without sea, being one uniform crust, enclosing the great abyss. . .that the flood
was caused by the breaking of this crust, and its sinking into the abyss of waters. . . and. . . that the present state of the. . . earth. . . shows it to be the ruins of the former earth." Cf. JOURNAL, *op.cit.*, V, 351.

63   EXPLANATORY NOTES OLD TESTAMENT, *op.cit.*, I, 5.

64   WORKS, *op.cit.*, XIII, 495.

65   *Loc.cit.*

66   EXPLANATORY NOTES OLD TESTAMENT, *op.cit.*, I, 220 - Aaron
struck the dust of Egypt with his rod and the dust became lice.

67   John Wesley, *A COMPENDIUM OF NATURAL PHILOSOPHY: BEING
A SURVEY OF THE WISDOM OF GOD IN THE CREATION* (London:
Thomas Tegg and Son, 1836), III, 127.

68   WORKS, *op.cit.*, VI, 202.

69   JOURNAL, *op.cit.*, IV, 195, 210; V, 104. Cf. WORKS, *op.cit.*, VI, 339;
XIII, 395-400.

70   *Ibid*, IV, 210 - Wesley cited Rodger's *ESSAY ON THE LEARNING OF
THE ANCIENTS* for his documentation. He also claimed that some of the
ancients possessed the microscope as well as the telescope.

71   EXPLANATORY NOTES NEW TESTAMENT, *op.cit.*, 968.

72   EXPLANATORY NOTES NEW TESTAMENT, *op.cit.*, I, 5-6.

73   JOURNAL, *op.cit.*, V, 400 - Wesley was impressed by Dr. Pye's tract entitled, *A DIALOGUE BETWEEN MOSES AND LORD BOLINGBROKE*, in
which Pye defended the Genesis account of Creation but with honest reser-
vations, the solar system's inclusion in that account being one of his reserva-
tions.

74   WORKS, *op.cit.*, VII, 168.

75   *Loc.cit.*

76   JOURNAL, *op.cit.*, V, 400. Cf. WORKS, *op.cit.*, VI, 339 - Wesley held that
the Milky Way consists only of fixed stars.

77   WORKS, *op.cit.*, VII, 168.

78 *Loc.cit.* Cf. WORKS, *op.cit.*, X, 361.
79 *Ibid*, VI, 209.
80 *Loc.cit.*
81 *Ibid*, VI, 210, 340.
82 *Ibid*, VI, 340.
83 *Loc.cit.*
84 *Ibid*, XIII, 395-396; VII, 169.
85 *Ibid*, XIII, 398. Cf. John Wesley, *A SURVEY OF THE WISDOM OF GOD IN THE CREATION: OR A COMPENDIUM OF NATURAL PHILOSOPHY* (Third American Edition, New York: N. Bangs and T. Mason, 1823), II, 139.
86 EXPLANATORY NOTES OF TESTAMENT, *op.cit.*, I, 6.
87 WORKS, *op.cit.*, VI, 211.
88 Telford, *op.cit.*, V, 283.
89 WORKS, *op.cit.*, VII, 172-173. Cf. JOURNAL, *op.cit.*, IV, 354 -Wesley read Christian Huygens's *CONJECTURES* on September 20, 1759. Huygens (1629-1695) was a Dutch mathematician.
90 JOURNAL, *op.cit.*, IV, 354. Cf. WORKS, op.cit., XIII, 396-400.
91 WORKS, *op.cit.*, VI, 339-340, 326 - Wesley referred to comets as "amazing bodies...that shoot in every direction through the immeasurable fields of ether."
92 *Ibid*, VI, 211.
93 *Loc.cit.*
94 EXPLANATORY NOTES OLD TESTAMENT, *op.cit.*, I, 6.
95 *Loc.cit.*
96 *Loc.cit.* Cf. WORKS, *op.cit.*, VI, 342.
97 WORKS, *op.cit.*, VI, 212.
98 John Wesley, *A SURVEY OF THE WISDOM OF GOD IN THE CREATION: OR A COMPENDIUM OF NATURAL PHILOSOPHY* (London: J. Fry and Company, 1777), II, 255.
99 WORKS, *op.cit.*, VI, 212.
100 COMPENDIUM (Tegg Edition), *op.cit.*, III, 127.
101 WORKS, *op.cit.*, VI, 212.
102 *Loc.cit.*
103 *Ibid*, VI, 342.
104 SURVEY (Fry Edition), *op.cit.*, II, 255. Cf. COMPENDIUM (Tegg), *op.cit.*, III, 127.
105 WORKS, *op.cit.*, VI, 212.
106 EXPLANATORY NOTES OLD TESTAMENT, *op.cit.*, I, 6.
107 *Loc.cit.*
108 SURVEY (Fry), *op.cit.*, II, 255.
109 COMPENDIUM (Tegg), *op.cit.*, III, 127.
110 *Loc.cit.* Cf. SURVEY (Fry), *op.cit.*, II, 255.
111 EXPLANATORY NOTES OLD TESTAMENT, *op.cit.*, I, 7.
112 WORKS, *op.cit.*, VI, 212.
113 EXPLANATORY NOTES OLD TESTAMENT, *op.cit.*, I, 7.

114   *Ibid*, II, 1635.
115   *Ibid*, I, 7.
116   *Loc.cit.*
117   *Loc.cit.* Cf. WORKS, *op.cit.*, VII, 344.
118   *Loc.cit.* Cf. WORKS, *op.cit.*, VII, 137, 345.
119   *Loc.cit.*
120   *Ibid*, I, 8.
121   *Loc.cit.*
122   J. M. Evans, *PARADISE LOST AND THE GENESIS TRADITION*
      (Oxford: The Clarendon Press, 1968), 43.
123   EXPLANATORY NOTES OLD TESTAMENT, *op.cit.*, I, 8.
124   *Ibid*, I, 7.
125   *Ibid*, I, 8.
126   *Loc.cit.*
127   *Loc.cit.*
128   *Loc.cit.*
129   *Loc.cit.*
130   *Loc.cit.*
131   *Loc.cit.*
132   WORKS, *op.cit.*, VI, 212.
133   *Loc.cit.*
134   EXPLANATORY NOTES OLD TESTAMENT, *op.cit.*, I, 8-9.
135   *Ibid*, I, 9.
136   *Loc.cit.*
137   *Loc.cit.*
138   *Loc.cit.*
139   WORKS, *op.cit.*, VI, 213. Cf. Robert Southey, *THE LIFE OF WESLEY*
      (Oxford: Oxford University Press, 1925), II, 72-73.
140   EXPLANATORY NOTES OLD TESTAMENT, *op.cit.*, I, 9.
141   *Loc.cit.*
142   *Ibid*, I, 10.
143   *Loc.cit.*
144   *Loc.cit.*
145   *Loc.cit.*
146   *Loc.cit.* Cf. NICENE FATHERS, *op.cit.*, II, 209 - Wesley's rationale for
      God resting without being weary was borrowed from Augustine.
147   *Loc.cit.*
148   EXPLANATORY NOTES NEW TESTAMENT, *op.cit.*, 7.
149   EXPLANATORY NOTES OLD TESTAMENT, *op.cit.*, I, 10-11. Cf.
      Baker, *op.cit.*, XXV, 164 - Susanna Wesley wrote to her son John (1725)
      about the composite nature of man.
150   WORKS, *op.cit.*, VII, 225.
151   *Loc.cit.* Cf. VI, 138, 140.
152   Eaton, *op.cit.*, 350-352.
153   WORKS, *op.cit.*, VII, 226.
154   Eaton, *op.cit.*, 351, 360. Cf. Malebranche, *op.cit.*, 91.

155 COMPENDIUM (Tegg), *op.cit.*, I, xiii-xiv.
156 WORKS, *op.cit.*, VII, 225.
157 *op.cit.*, VII, 350.
158 WORKS, *op.cit.*, VI, 427-428; VII, 227. Cf. JOURNAL, *op.cit.*, VI, 22 - Wesley attacked the theory of man as a clock, advanced by Lord Kames.
159 COMPENDIUM, *op.cit.*, V, 158.
160 WORKS, *op.cit.*, VII, 227 - This argument originated in Malebranche's SEARCH, and Wesley was obviously impressed by it. See also, WORKS VI, 458; SURVEY (Bangs edition), *op.cit.*, I, 113; and O. A. Johnson, *ETHICS* (New York: Holt, Rinehart, Winston), 172.
161 *Ibid*, VII, 226, 320.
162 *Ibid*, VII, 345.
163 *Ibid*, 171 - Earlier in this sermon, Wesley quoted Augustine on this point, disagreeing with him. Man is - in Augustine's words - "*aliqua portio creaturae tuae* (some portion of thy creation) but *quantula portio* (how amazingly small a portion!)." See also, WORKS, *op.cit.*, XI, 447-448.
164 *Ibid*, VI, 203.
165 SURVEY (Bangs), *op.cit.*, I, 113-114 - Wesley followed the argument of Malebranche here. God created the soul of man from his own divine substance so that man can participate in God's substance. "His substance is truly representative of the soul, because it contains its eternal model or archetype." See also, Malebranche, *op.cit.*, 319. Also, ENCYCLOPEDIA OF PHILOSOPHY, *op.cit.*, III, 338 - Henry More, often cited by Wesley, also emphasized the soul as the agent that activates bodily movements.
166 WORKS, *op.cit.*, VI, 137.
167 *Ibid*, VII, 345; X, 362.
168 *Ibid*, VII, 227.
169 *Ibid*, VII, 232.
170 *Ibid*, VII, 307.
171 *Ibid*, XI, 367.
172 EXPLANATORY NOTES OLD TESTAMENT, *op.cit.*, III, 1869.
173 SURVEY (Bangs), *op.cit.*, I, 55ff.
174 *Ibid*, I, 39. Cf. WORKS, *op.cit.*, VII, 343.
175 *Ibid*, I, 114-115. Cf. WORKS, *op.cit.*, VI, 219 - Wesley surely had Augustine in mind here - "The corruptible body presses down upon the soul... It very frequently hinders the soul in its operations...Yet the soul cannot dispense with its services, imperfect as it is; For an embodied spirit (soul) cannot form one thought but by the mediation of its bodily organ."
176 Ross, *op.cit.*, 191ff.
177 Meagher, *op.cit.*, I, 942.
178 JOURNAL, *op.cit.*, IV, 486 note.
179 EXPLANATORY NOTES NEW TESTAMENT, *op.cit.*, 848.
180 Meagher, *op.cit.*, III, 3555.
181 JOURNAL, *op.cit.*, IV, 486. Cf. WORKS, *op.cit.*, III, 80.
182 *Ibid*, V, 37-39.
183 *Ibid*, V, 395-396.

184   SURVEY (Bangs), *op.cit.*, II, 352.
185   JOURNAL, *op.cit.*, IV, 82.
186   EXPLANATORY NOTES NEW TESTAMENT, *op.cit.*, 342.
187   WORKS, *op.cit.*, VI, 191; VII, 228.
188   *Ibid*, XIII, 498.
189   *Ibid*, VI, 143.
190   SURVEY (Bangs), *op.cit.*, I, 129; II, 191 - "The soul which is only endued
      with sense, occupies the lowest degree in the scale." See also, WORKS,
      op.cit., VI, 244 - Wesley held a position hard to be reconciled with the
      SURVEY. Here he argued that the difference between man and beast is
      not reason, since, he observed that brutes have both reason and under-
      standing. He claimed the difference lies in man alone being "capable of
      God." Inferior creatures are not. In this passage, he even went so far as to
      attribute immortality to the brutes. However, such immortality reduces to
      the eternity *a parte post* of matter from which they were made. Most brutes
      do not have personal immortality, but only those who are living at the com-
      ing of the new creation. See Chapter XII, THE NEW CREATION.
191   WORKS, *op.cit.*, VI, 213. Cf. SURVEY (Bangs), *op.cit.*, II, 192 - Wesley
      said, "A thick cloud conceals from our sight the noblest parts of this im-
      mense chain, and admits us only to a slight view of some ill-connected links...
      but not withstanding our knowledge of the chain of beings is so very imper-
      fect, it is sufficient at least to inspire us with most exalted ideas of that
      amazing and noble progression and variety which reigns in the universe."
192   EXPLANATORY NOTES OLD TESTAMENT, *op.cit.*, I, 10.
193   SURVEY (Bangs), *op.cit.*, II, 205.
194   *Ibid*, II, 206.
195   *Loc.cit.*
196   *Loc.cit.*
197   *Ibid*, II, 207.
198   *Ibid*, II, 211. Cf. WORKS, *op.cit.*, X, 362.
199   *Ibid*, II, 208. See also, the PREFACE to this work, I, v, where Wesley justi-
      fies his reason for writing so many amazing things.
200   *Ibid*, II, 212.
201   Meagher, *op.cit.*, III, 2920.
202   *Loc.cit.*
203   *Ibid*, III, 2921.
204   SURVEY (Bangs), *op.cit.*, II, 212.
205   *Loc.cit.*
206   *Loc.cit.*
207   *Ibid*, II, 213.
208   *Loc.cit.*
209   *Loc.cit.*
210   WORKS, *op.cit.*, VI, 190.
211   *Ibid*, VI, 191.
212   *Ibid*, VI, 370. Cf. EXPLANATORY NOTES NEW TESTAMENT, *op.cit.*,
      928 - Wesley observed that the term "archangel" appears but twice in the

New Testament, and no one knows if there is more than one. See also, Southey, *op.cit.*, II, 72-73.
213 *Ibid*, XIII, 487.
214 *Ibid*, VII, 232ff.
215 *Ibid*, VI, 362.
216 *Loc.cit.*
217 *Ibid*, VI, 363.
218 *Loc.cit.*
219 *Ibid*, VI, 364.
220 *Loc.cit.*
221 *Ibid*, VI, 365.
222 *Loc.cit.*
223 *Loc.cit.*
224 *Ibid*, VI, 366.
225 Telford, *op.cit.*, VII, 94.
226 EXPLANATORY NOTES NEW TESTAMENT, *op.cit.*, 742.
227 EXPLANATORY NOTES OLD TESTAMENT, *op.cit.*, II, 1611.
228 *Ibid*, I, 2.
229 *Ibid*, I, 3.
230 NICENE FATHERS, *op.cit.*, II, 209.
231 *Ibid*, II, 210.
232 EXPLANATORY NOTES OLD TESTAMENT, III, 1773.
233 *Ibid*, III, 1961.
234 *Ibid*, III, 1985.
235 WORKS, *op.cit.*, V, 435.

Chapter Four

The Fall of Angels, Man, and the Cosmos

"He (God) is one, infinite in nature and power, free, intelligent, and omniscient; that, consequently, he proposes to himself an end in every one of his actions; and that the end of the creating the world was, the exercise of his power, and wisdom, and goodness; which he therefore made as perfect as it could be made by infinite goodness, and power, and wisdom.
. . .But, if so, how came evil into the world?"[1]

The problem of theodicy is the inescapable dilemma of religion. How can the existence and phenomenology of evil be explained, especially when superlative attributes involving beneficence and wisdom are posited for the first cause of all things? The Christian religion grew out of a religion that had already developed for itself a meaningful understanding of the origin and cause of evil. Early Christianity borrowed and reflected the theodicy of Judaism, notably of the rabbinical variety. In Catholic theology, St. Augustine proved most definitive, arguing against the two extremes of Manichaeanism and Pelagianism. He not only carried the day for Catholic Orthodoxy at this point, but he carried the centuries that followed. The sixteenth century reformers - Luther, Calvin, and Bucer especially - revived Augustine's description of the origin and cause of evil, as did the Church of England. John Wesley was a spiritual son of Augustine in many respects, particularly in reference to theodicy. A review of Augustine's explanation of evil will provide a helpful context for Wesley's treatment of the subject.

Augustine rejected a number of simplistic solutions, such as dualism - in which there are two deities, one good and the other evil. He also rejected the idea that the one God is essentially good but lacking in power or wisdom so that he is a bumbler. He rejected outright the popular notion that God is the author of both good and evil, engaging himself in some type of cosmic chess-game, proving that his power is arbitrary. What did Augustine offer in the place of these rejected views? He advanced the following argument -

> "By the Trinity, thus supremely and equally and unchangeably good, all things were created; and these are not supremely and equally and unchangeably good, but they are good, even taken separately. Taken as a whole, however, they are very good, because their ensemble constitutes the universe in all its wonderful order and beauty. . . What is called evil in the universe is but the absence of good. . . All beings were made good, but not perfectly good, are liable to corruption."[2]

Since the creation was made good, but not perfectly good, the occasion for corruption of the good was present. This, Augustine argued, does not make God the "progenitor of evil things, neither has he made any evil nature." God, being both "incorruptible and incontaminable," has created a universe unlike himself, but not an evil universe. It was a universe susceptible or "liable" to corruption under one particular circumstance - the "voluntary sin of the soul, to which God gave free will."[3] He gave souls with free will to only angels and men.[4] Evil, then, is not a "substance" which has a metaphysical undergirding like one of Plato's forms or archetypes.[5] Evil is a condition arising from "the perversion of the will."[6] As such, it is contrary to nature, for nature is good - it is a "disagreement hostile" to natural substance.[7] Evil is the corruption of a previous good.[8] For this reason "there can be no evil where there is no good."[9] God's wisdom is to be recognized in his creation of the universe after this manner and in his making "a good use even of evil wills."[10]

Whose will was first freely exercised in sin against the Creator? Augustine held that it was Lucifer, a cherub, whose soul first became proud shortly after his creation on the first day of the week of Genesis I -

"Isaiah. . . represents the devil under the person of the king of Babylon, 'How art thou fallen, O Lucifer, son of the morning!'. . . Ezekiel says, 'Thou hast been in Eden, the garden of God. . . Thou wast perfect in thy ways' . . . It is not to be supposed that he sinned from the beginning of his created existence, but from the beginning of his sin, when by his pride he had commenced to sin."[11]

Pride was the "sin of the will" committed by Lucifer. Augustine affirmed, "Pride is the beginning of all sin... It was this which overthrew the devil, from whom arose the original sin." Afterwards, the devil pursued man, "who was yet standing in his uprightness," and "subverted him in the same way in which he himself fell."[12] Centuries later, Wesley added the following observation to Augustine's argument - "Pride was the sin that turned angels into devils."[13] In Augustine's theodicy "the devil is the author and source of all sin."[14] Consequently, "the devil is the mediator of death."[15] Hence, God caused

"the devil (good by God's creation, wicked by his own will) to be cast down from his high position, and to become the mockery of His angels... and because God, when He created him, was certainly not ignorant of his future malignity, and foresaw the good which He Himself would bring out of his evil."[16]

Lucifer's sin of pride was contagious and other angels joined him willingly, opposing the will of their Creator. They were expelled from heaven along with Lucifer -

". . .We understand that the angels were created when the first light was made, and that a separation was made between the holy and the unclean angels, when, as is said, 'God divided the light from the darkness; and God called the light Day, and the darkness He called Night.' For He alone could make this distinction, who was able also before they fell, to foreknow that they would fall, and that, being deprived of the light of truth, they would abide in the darkness of pride."[17]

Moreover, Augustine continued -

"Though there is sin, all things are not therefore full of sin, for the great majority of the heavenly inhabitants preserve their nature's integrity. And the sinful will, though it violated the order of its own nature, did not on that account escape the laws of God, who justly orders all things for good. For as the beauty of a picture is increased by well-managed shadows, so, to the eye that has skill to discern it, the universe is beautiful even by sinners, though, considered by themselves, their deformity is a sad blemish."[18]

Lucifer and the wicked angels, then, were cast down from the heavenly expanse to "the lowest parts of the world, where they are, as it were, incarcerated till their final damnation in the day of judgment."[19] St. Peter "very plainly says, 'God spared not the angels that sinned, but cast them down to hell, and delivered them into chains of darkness to be reserved into judgment.'"[20] Like Lucifer, these angels rejected truth, heaven, and their original goodness although the Holy Spirit imbued them with preserving love.[21] Their pride, as self-love, brought them finally down to hell, from whence they are permitted to forage onto the earth's surface, leading men into pride. The story of Adam and Eve, being tempted by the devil in the guise of a serpent, must be understood in this context, Augustine reasoned. Adam and Eve were so created as to be able to choose either good or evil.[22] God "foresaw that man would make a bad use of his free will, that is, would sin." Therefore, "God arranged His own designs rather with a view to do good to man, even in his sinfulness."[23]

WESLEY ON THE ORIGIN AND NATURE OF EVIL

As a Fellow of Lincoln College, young Wesley wrote home to his father on December 19, 1729. As so often in writing to his father, Wesley spoke of theological matters which were of mutual interest. In this particular letter, the issue was the origin of evil. John had recently read Ditton's *DISCOURSE ON THE RESURRECTION OF CHRIST*, and he was surprised to see a brief essay on evil at the conclusion of it. He suggested that his father read the essay, if he had not already done so. The arguments of the essay, John reported, were those of Augustine. Assuming that Samuel Wesley had not read the essay, son John outlined these arguments. It is obvious that young Wesley subscribed completely to these Augustinian ideas concerning the origin of evil -

"From the nature of liberty and free-will, we may deduce a very possible and satisfactory (perhaps the only possible just) account of the origin of evil. ...It noway derogated from any one perfection of an infinite Being, to endow other beings which he made with such a power as we call liberty; that is, to furnish them with such capacity, dispositions, and principles of actions, that it should be possible for them either to observe or to deviate from those eternal rules and measures of fitness and agreeableness, with respect to certain things and circumstances, which were so conformable to the infinite rectitude of his own will, and which infinite reason must necessarily discover. Now, evil is a deviation from those measures of eternal, unerring order and reason; not to choose what is worthy to be chosen, and is accordingly chose by such a will as the divine. And to bring this about, no more is necessary, than the exerting certain acts of that power we call free-will, by which power we are enabled to choose or refuse, and to determine ourselves to action accordingly. Therefore, without having recourse to any ill principle, we may fairly account for the origin of evil, from the possibility of a various use of our liberty; even as that capacity or possibility itself is ultimately founded on the defectibility and finiteness of a created nature."[24]

In a later letter to his father, Wesley again treated the subject of evil's origin. On December 11, 1730, his letter criticized the well-known work of Archbishop King - *DE ORIGINE MALI* - saying of it - "I was strangely disappointed, finding it the least satisfactory account of any given by any author whom I ever read in my life."[25] While the work was considered unique, Wesley found it contradicting every "man that ever writ on the subject."[26] The first principle cited by Wesley was most un-Augustinian - "Natural evils flow naturally and necessarily from the essence of matter," so that divine intervention cannot prevent them - a Manichaean notion. Another principle was immediately attacked by Wesley - Creation lacked divine power so that matter's nature is deficient, insuring evil's existence as a reality of nature. Wesley rejected these principles of the Archbishop because of their variance with the Augustinian tradition.[27] A month later, in another letter to his father, Wesley treated another one of Ditton's books but without any criticism. However, he did not recommend the reading of this work.[28]

Following the theology of Augustine, Wesley refused to credit God as the author of evil. In his *THOUGHTS UPON NECESSITY*, Wesley openly clashed with the Calvinists who seemed happy to have God as the Sovereign God creating evil for his own glory. Wesley accused Jonathan Edwards of this non-Augustinian idea.[29] He lamented -

> "It is not easy for a man of common understanding, especially if unassisted by education, to unravel these finely-woven schemes, or show distinctly where the fallacy lies. But he knows, he feels, he is certain, they cannot be true; That the Holy God cannot be the author of sin. The horrid consequence of supposing this may appear to the meanest understanding."[30]

Wesley's sermon, *THE END OF CHRIST'S COMING*, brings the principle behind this controversy into sharp focus, re-enforcing the Augustinian quality within his theodicy. The sermon affirms -

> "Every spirit in the universe, as such, is endued with understanding, and, in consequence, with a will, and with a measure of liberty; and that these three are inseparably united in every intelligent nature. And observe: *Liberty necessitated*, or over-ruled, is really no liberty at all. It is a contradiction in terms. It is the same as *unfree freedom*; that is, downright nonsense. . . It may be further observed. . . That where there is no liberty, there can be no moral good or evil, no virtue or vice."[31]

Wesley's point - that "liberty" of the creature's will is absolutely essential before evil can be evil, and good can be good - is the foundation of his understanding of the introduction of evil into the created order. In his sermon on *THE END OF CHRIST'S COMING*, he elaborated upon this point -

> "*Unde malum*? How came evil into the world? It came from 'Lucifer, son of the morning.' It was the work of the devil. 'For the devil,' saith the Apostle, 'sinneth from the beginning;' that is, was the first sinner in the universe, the author of sin, the first being who, by the abuse of his liberty, introduced evil into the Creation. He. . . was self-tempted to think too highly of himself. He

freely yielded to the temptation; and gave way, first to pride, then to self-will. He said, 'I will sit upon the sides of the north; I will be like the most High.'"[32]

Consequently, Lucifer was the creature who introduced evil into the created order. God, in no wise, must be considered as its originator. The origin and nature of evil are the results of Lucifer's pride and self-will.

LUCIFER AND THE FALLEN ANGELS

When Lucifer sinned, becoming the enemy and adversary of God, he was given other names - Satan and the Devil, the Dragon and the Serpent. Wesley's commentary on Revelation XII, 9, describes this result of the first rebellion -

"He (Satan) was cast out of heaven; and at this the inhabitants of heaven rejoiced. He is termed the *great dragon . . .the ancient serpent* - an allusion to his deceiving Eve in that form. Dragons are a kind of large serpent. *Who is called the Devil and Satan* - These are words of exactly the same meaning; only the former is Greek; the latter, Hebrew; denoting the grand adversary of all saints. . . *He has deceived the whole world* - not only in their first parents, but through all ages, and in all countries, into unbelief and all-wickedness; into the hating and persecuting faith and all goodness. *He was cast out unto the earth* - He was cast out of heaven; and being cast out thence, himself came to earth. Nor had he been employed on the earth before, although his ordinary abode was in heaven."[33]

In addition to being the adversary of God, Satan is also the adversary of man, from generation to generation. He stalks "poor souls" as a "lion," and "leads them captive at his will." Moreover, "he dwelleth in them and walketh in them. . . keeping possession of their hearts, setting up his throne there, and bringing every thought into obedience to himself."[34] He works in them by his "mighty energy, transforming them into his own likeness, effacing all the remains of the image of God, and preparing them for every evil word and work."[35] For this reason, Satan is also called "the prince of this world."[36] His kingdom, Wesley claimed, is "the kingdom of hell."[37]

It extends over all the earth, into the atmosphere, and deep into the bowels of the earth.

Originally, all the angels of heaven were of the same nature, until Lucifer introduced evil and gained the support of other angelic beings, becoming separated from the rest who remained obedient to God. Until then all the angels were "pure ethereal creatures, simple and incorruptible; if not wholly immaterial, yet certainly not encumbered with gross, earthly flesh and blood."[38] They were endued with understanding, affections, and liberty - "a power of self-determination; so that it lay within themselves, either to continue in their allegiance to God, or to rebel against him."[39] When some of them fell from this original state, they immediately made Lucifer their chief. Together with him, they are fallen stars, and they number "a third part" of all the heavenly host.[40]

These rebellious angels suffered immediate loss for their sin - "What an astonishing change was wrought within when angels became devils!" They lost all goodness, contracting hateful tempers, becoming envious of their fellow creatures who did not sin. Their actions with humans became cruel. They long to inspire humans with the same wickedness with themselves, and to involve them in the same misery.[41] They take their orders from Satan, who arranges them in ranks and assigns them positions and tasks.[42] They have their den in the bowels of the earth where Satan is the "angel of the bottomless pit."[43] Their greatest loss, however, was that of heaven, and they were cast down into hell (II Peter II, 4), "a place of unknown misery, with the strongest chains in a dungeon of darkness, to be reserved unto the judgment of the great day. Though still those chains do not hinder their walking up and down seeking whom they may devour."[44]

A brief observation concerning the bottomless pit is in order here. John Wesley believed that hell - the bottomless pit in the bowels of the earth - was created on the third day of the first week when God made the earth. The angelic rebellion had already taken place on the first day. What did God do with these wicked angels until hell was created on the third day? Wesley gave no answer. One possibility - clearly speculative - is that Wesley took a leaf out of Hesiod's myth of the fall of the Titan gods from the highest heaven to earth to dank, dark Tartarus below. That fall took time, according to Hesiod. Let it be remembered that Wesley knew and quoted the literature of Hesiod, even in his sermons. Wesley also knew that the word "Tartarus" appears in the Greek text of II Peter II, 4. Wesley also noted the great immensity of space between the inhabited heavens and the earth. Perhaps, Wesley might argue, God cast the evil angels from heaven on the first day, immediately after their rebellion, and they fell the rest of that day, all of the second day, and landed in Tartarus on the third day, immediately after it was created for them.[45] In his commentary on Jude 6 - "And the angels who kept not their first dignity, but left their own habitation, he hath reserved in everlasting chains under darkness to the judgment of the great day" - Wesley observed -

> "When these fallen angels came out of the hands of God, they were holy; else God made that which was evil; and being holy, they were beloved by God; else He hated the image of His own spotless purity. But now he loves them no more; they are doomed to endless destruction (for if He loved them still, He would love what is sinful): and both His former love, and His present righteousness and eternal displeasure towards the same work of His own hands, are because He changeth not; because He invariably loveth righteousness, and hateth iniquity."[46]

A frequent point of New Testament eschatology, emphasized by Wesley, makes the post-fall abode of the evil angels only a temporary holding place until the day of judgment. Then the devil and his angels "are cast into the everlasting fire" in "outer darkness."[47] The hell (Tartarus) in the bowels of the earth is that temporary abode. The "outer darkness" is what Wesley also called the "nethermost hell."[48] The "nethermost hell" is likewise called "the lake of fire" into which, after a thousand year day of judgment, Satan, his evil angels, and all the nations they have deceived will be cast forever.[49] But until then, the hell under the earth is a terrifying place. Wesley, as a Christian Vergil, led his congregation down into its fiery depths -

"Regions of sorrow, doleful shades (souls), where peace and rest can never dwell. . . Look down! What a prison is there! 'Twixt upper, nether, and surrounding fire!' And what inhabitants! What horrid, fearful shapes, emblems of the rage against God and man, the envy, fury, despair, fixed within, - causing them to gnash their teeth at Him they so long despised."[50]

Furthermore, the demonic inhabitants of this earthly hell continue their "howling and blaspheming, cursing and looking upward, till they are cast into the everlasting fire."[51] Paradoxically, God frequently uses the inhabitants of hell under the earth to "do his gloomy errands in the deep," and "to inflict vengeance on wicked men" whose souls are sent there awaiting the great judgment day.[52] While this hell is their temporary abode and prison, evil angels, led by Satan, are given temporary ability to roam over the face of the earth, and even hover above the earth in the air as "powers of the air." This ability, however, is considerably limited - "so far as God permits!" - but tremendous evil is generated by them.[53] An important instance of this divine permissiveness is found in the book of Job where Satan appears before God with the "sons of God." He has been roaming over the earth, and God gives him permission to afflict Job. Wesley could not understand God's reasoning in this matter.[54] In his sermon *OF EVIL ANGELS*, Wesley outlined the activities of fallen angels upon the face of the earth. He recognized fifteen specific activities - (1) Evil angels act as "governors of the world" and "rulers of the darkness of this age." Satan and his angels spread "all the ignorance, all the error, all the folly, and particularly all the wickedness of men, in such a manner as may most hinder the kingdom of God, and most advance the kingdom of darkness."[55] (2) An evil angel, supposedly, accompanies every man, in addition to a guardian angel - the one to incite to evil and the other to preserve in goodness. Wesley, however, was not fully convinced of this ancient Christian belief and openly argued against taking it too seriously, but he included it in this list of demonic activities anyway.[56] (3) Satan and his angels watch every man, looking for an opportunity to tempt towards evil, noticing every "slip we make. . . they are also 'about our bed, and about our path, and spy out all our ways.'"[57] (4) These malign spirits further darken the minds of "those that know not God" by obscuring the light of truth with clouds of unbelief. Consequently, faith and love decay in the soul.[58] (5) Satan attacks man's love for his neighbor by sowing seeds of private and public suspicions, animosities, resentment, quarrels, and the like, by which the peace of families and nations is destroyed, plunging all into "the pit of destruction."[59] (6) The devilish host seek to keep man from doing good, if they cannot "prevail upon (him) to do evil," and they have many devices to "lessen, if not destroy, that love, joy, peace... which our Lord works by his loving Spirit in them that believe."[60] (7) Satan is especially skillful in infusing "evil thoughts of every kind into the hearts of men, shooting in" in an unnatural manner.[61] (8) Satan attempts to awaken evil passions or tempers in our souls - such as, "unbelief, atheism, ill-will, bitterness, hatred, malice, envy . . . fear, sorrow, anxiety, worldly care. . . impatience, ill-nature, anger, resentment. . . fraud, guile, dissimulation. . . love of the world, inordinate affection, foolish desires."[62] (9) As no man can perform good without the assistance of God, so no man can perform evil without the assistance of Satan.[63] (10) To all who seek to be the children of God, Satan is a special tempter, more than to those who are already his children.[64] (11) Satan "will torment whom he cannot destroy" - "If he cannot entice men to sin, he will, so far as he is permitted, put them to pain. . . he is the occasion, directly or indirectly, of many of the pains of mankind. . . And innumerable accidents. . . are undoubtedly owing to his agency."[65] (12) "Diabolical agency" accounts for "many diseases. . . both of the acute and chronical kind."[66] (13) Lunacy has its origin in demonic possession.[67] (14) Sudden diseases are thrust upon persons like Job, "by divine permission."[68] And (15) "Many little inconveniences we suffer" are the work of Satan and his evil helpers, attempting to hinder us in every way, both great and small.[69] Evil spirits have an abundance of work to do![70] Unfortunately for man, Satan often appears as "an angel of light," deceiving even the righteous.[71]

THE FALL OF MAN

Why is there pain in the world if God is "loving to every man, and his mercy is over all his works?" Wesley's answer to this poignant question was short and incisive - "Because there is sin: Had there been no sin, there would have been no pain."[72] Another important question follows immediately - Why is there sin in the world? Wesley's response to this query is not so short, and it bears the stigmata of St. Augustine and Rabbinic Judaism, with some help from the Cartesians. Wesley's introductory response deserves quotation -

> "Because man was created in the image of God. Because he is not mere matter, a clod of earth, a lump of clay, without sense or understanding; but a spirit like his Creator, a being endued not only with sense and understanding, but also with a will exerting itself in various affections. To crown all the rest, he was endued with liberty; a power of directing his own affections and actions; a capacity of determining himself, or of choosing good or evil. Indeed, had not man been endued with this, all the rest would have been of no use: Had he not been a free as an intelligent being, his understanding would have been as incapable of holiness, or any kind of virtue, as a tree or a block of marble. And having this power, a power of choosing good or evil, he chose the latter: He chose evil. Thus 'sin entered into the world,' and pain of every kind, preparatory to death."[73]

The occasion for this unfortunate choice was provided by Satan, the fallen cherub. In his sermon *THE END OF CHRIST'S COMING*, Wesley flashed back into salvation-history to the original context of Adam's tragic decision -

> "(Satan) did not fall alone, but soon drew after him a third part of the stars of heaven; in consequence of which they lost their glory and happiness, and were driven from their former habitation. . . Having great wrath, and perhaps envy, at the happiness of the creatures whom God had newly created, it is not strange that he should desire and endeavour to deprive them of it. In order to this, he concealed himself in the serpent, who was the most subtle, or intelligent of all the brute creatures; and, on that account, the least liable to raise suspicion. Indeed, some have (not improbably) supposed that the ser-

pent was then endued with reason and speech. Had not Eve known he was so, would she have admitted any parley with him?"[74]

Where was God when all this was developing? Why did he not intervene and thwart Satan's design, thus preventing Adam and Eve from making such a serious mistake? Wesley argued that God could certainly have prevented the fall, seeing he has all power in heaven and earth, but because of his eternal knowledge of all things, God recognized that "to permit the fall of the first man was far best for mankind in general; that abundantly more good than evil would accrue to the posterity of Adam by his fall; that if 'sin abounded' thereby over all the earth, yet 'grace would much more abound.'"[75] This optimistic evaluation seems radically naive to twentieth century thinkers. However, Wesley held that since all creation is designed to move up the ladder of perfection to final, ultimate created perfection, the lapses or backslidings, while not absolutely necessary, give God greater occasions for bringing goodness out of evil. Such occasions, though, should not be engineered by man so that by sinning grace may abound. Man should not sin, ever, and need not sin at any time. Grace is sufficient for him so that he need not sin. If he sins, he sins in the presence of grace, and that needlessly. The tragedy of man's sin is that it comes forth in the presence of enabling grace, and not in its absence. Nevertheless, when grace has been ignored, and man has willfully sinned, God has ingenious ways of extracting good from that phenomenon. It is only in this setting that the biblical story of the fall had any validity for Wesley. Without this explanation the account of Genesis III would have simply been a quaint piece of ancient, oriental mythology, lacking any significance to other cultures and ages. Instead of myth, the Genesis III fall of Adam was an historical fact for Wesley, applicable to the universal condition of mankind. While Wesley often addressed this subject in sermons, letters, treatises, and magazine articles, his most complete treatment of it is recorded in the *EXPLANATORY NOTES UPON THE OLD TESTAMENT*. This treatment will concern us here, but other Wesleyan works will be incorporated into it when appropriate.

The beginning of the story of Adam's great transgression actually occurs in Genesis II. Wesley's commentary of verses 8 through 25 needs careful consideration because it sets the stage for chapter III. Wesley divided this passage into four units, which we shall now examine -

(1) Genesis II, 8 - 15. Man was made a composite creature, consisting of body and soul. His body was made from the earth, and his soul was a rational and immortal spirit from God. Man was thus made for his complete happiness.[76] The student of historical theology recognizes this emphasis on created happiness as originating with Augustine. Indeed, Wesley was much indebted to Augustine for his understanding of creation and fall. Wesley's commentary on both elements reveals this indebtedness. Wesley argued - Man's body was made with *senses* (sight, hearing, tasting, smelling, and touching), and it was given a soul to inhabit it. Being made happy, it was placed in *the paradise-of God*. Paradise offered to the human body the most satisfaction for the senses. It offered the most happiness to the soul as well, since by virtue of possessing a soul, man was in a covenant relationship with God.[77] In his sermon *THE NEW BIRTH*, Wesley maintained that the soul has spiritual senses that parallel the physical senses of the body.[78] Spiritual senses are linked with spiritual sense-organs - eyes of the soul to see the magnificent works of God, ears to hear God's voice, nostrils to detect the incense of divine presence, a palate to taste the satisfying bread of heaven, and a system of spiritual nerve-fibers by which divine impressions create the most rewarding "feelings" of wholesomeness and well-being. It was a complete, composite creature that God formed and placed in his paradise. This first man was capable of total happiness, physical and spiritual. The stage is now set for the unfolding drama of man's fall! (a) The place - Paradise. God created paradise to be the "palace" of the "prince" (Adam). The palace was not an "ivory house" but a "garden." Wesley's reason for mixing metaphors here is of concern. He argued that before the fall, there was no need for clothing or house,

since the climate was consistently fair and beneficent. Consequently, the garden of Eden was, for Adam, a natural palace -

"The heaven was the roof of Adam's house, and never was any roof so curiously ceiled and painted; the earth was his floor, and never was any floor so richly inlaid: the shadow of the trees was his retirement, and never were any rooms so finely hung: Solomon's and all their glory were not arrayed like them."[79]

The "furniture" of the garden or palace was "the immediate work of God's wisdom and power." God placed this furniture on the third day when the earth was made.[80] He then called the palace "Eden" which name means "delight and pleasure." According to Wesley, Moses specifically located Eden for the benefit of "those who knew that country."[81] As for others, Moses advised them to seek the heavenly paradise instead of trying to find the earthly Eden. Behind this digression from the actual text was Wesley's encounter with a group of simplistic persons who advertised that they were close to discovering the original garden of Eden.[82] If Wesley were still living, what would he say about those simplistic souls who are always on the brink of finding Noah's ark, or the ark of the covenant, or the burial shroud of Christ? (b) The trees - Created on the third day, when the garden was planted, fruit trees of the "best and choicest" varieties were placed by God in the palace of the prince -

"It was beautiful with every tree that was pleasant to the sight - It was enriched with every tree that yielded fruit grateful to the table, and useful to the body. But. . . it had two extraordinary trees peculiar to itself, on earth there were not their like. . . There was *the tree of life* in the midst of the garden - Which was not so much a natural means to preserve or prolong life; but was chiefly intended to be a sign to Adam, assuring him of the continuance of life and happiness, upon condition of his perseverance in innocency and obedience. . . There was *the tree of the knowledge of good and evil* - So called, not because it had any virtue to beget useful knowledge, but because there was an express revelation of the will of God concerning this tree, so that by it he might know good and evil. What is good? It is good not to eat of this tree; What is evil? To eat of this tree."[83]

(c) The rivers - Four rivers watered the garden (verses 10-14). Wesley thought there was only one river, but it had four branches. Its flow contributed much to the pleasantness and fruitfulness of Eden.[84]

(2) Genesis II, 16 - 17. These two verses form a unit - "And the Lord commanded the Man, saying, Of every tree of the garden thou mayest freely eat. But of the tree of the knowledge of good and evil, thou shalt not eat of it: for in the day thou eatest thereof thou shalt surely die." Wesley observed that God, the all-powerful and all-wise Creator, then became the great "ruler and lawgiver."[85] This imperative is the very first command given in the duration known as time. As ruler, or governor, God never uses his power to force or coerce.[86] This command to Adam was both wise and just because Adam was free to obey or flout it. It could have been neither wise or just if Adam had been forced to obey it or disobey it. Moreover, God showed his wisdom and justice by adding a warning to the command. The warning revealed the seriousness of violating the law. The warning - "Thou shalt surely die" - implied "thou shalt lose all the happiness thou hast either in possession or prospect; and thou shalt become liable to death, and all the miseries that preface and attend it."[87] According to Wesley, the warning fixed the time of death - "In the day thou eatest, thou shalt surely die." It would be unwise and unjust to warn without being precise concerning the time of punishment. Adam, being very intelligent, knew that disobedience would bring immediate mortality and spiritual death.[89] Having been educated by God, Adam was free from force or coercion. He could freely choose - to obey or disobey.

(3) Genesis II, 18 - 20. This passage contains one of the most neglected phrases in all biblical commentaries, including Wesley's. The obvious is simply neglected - "It is not good that man should be alone" (verse 18), reflected God. The deity had made all other creatures to be mated, but Adam was both male and female in one body. The mating of all other creatures was "good," but Adam's loneliness was "not good." The subsequent creation of woman was, therefore, a remedial act. It was designed to rectify a flaw by pro-

ducing something better, a "help-meet" for Adam. Wesley ignored this obvious observation. Instead he wrote -

> "Though there was an upper world of angels, and a lower world of brutes, yet there being none of the same rank of beings with himself, he might truly be said to be alone. And *every beast of the field*, and *every fowl of the air* God brought to Adam - Either by the ministry of angels, or by a special instinct that he might *name them*, and so might give a proof of his knowledge, the names he gave them being expressive of their inmost natures."[90]

(4) Genesis II, 21 -22. The taking of the woman from Adam's side took place, according to Wesley, on the sixth day, although this passage is from the second creation account, as noted earlier. Wesley viewed this passage as an elaboration of Genesis I, 27.[91] In it, God, the great physician, separated male and female from the first human body *via* a surgical procedure. He first induced "deep sleep," the patient being prepared for "the opening of his side" and the removal of a rib. Adam felt no pain because as yet there was no pain since there was no sin, pain being the immediate result of sin.[92] Why, if this is true, was the deep sleep necessary? Wesley took an amazing position - The sleep was not induced to minimize pain, but to protect Adam's mental health from the shock of being opened up and having some part of his body removed.[93] If, however, Adam had already sinned, he would have experienced pain.[94] Upon removing the rib, Yahweh closed up the wound, and then made woman around the rib.

(5) Genesis II, 23 - 25. The first marriage followed the awakening of Adam. Wesley referred to the bride as a "lovely creature." She was "a piece" of Adam, destined to be his companion and wife by divine institution. Marriage was, therefore, an Order of Creation, and not a trial added to human kind in consequence of the fall. Wesley knew the Rabbinic traditions of Judaism very well. He surely knew the teaching that our marriages are made in heaven before we are born. He may have known the rabbinic notion that since the sixth day of creation, God sits in heaven and arranges marriages.[95] He might have agreed with Rabbi Eleazar that God was the "best man" at Adam and Eve's wedding.[96] Wesley's exege-

sis emphasized Adam's acceptance of Eve as his wife, naming her *Isha* (woman) as a token of the marriage.[97] The term *Isha* also means "she-man," that is, "made of man, and joined to man."[98] Once an integral part of man, then separated from him through marriage she was made an integral part of man once again - "Therefore shall a man leave his father and mother, and shall cleave unto his wife; and they shall be one flesh" (verse 24).[99] Besides companionship, Wesley argued, marriage was designed to advance the "preservation of mankind." Children are the primary fruit of marriage, other benefits are secondary.[100] The last verse of this passage noted the nakedness of bride and groom at the first marriage, but excused it on the ground of their innocency. Wesley added another reason for nakedness then - The climate of the garden was so ideal that clothes were unnecessary.[101]

With the stage of Genesis II set, Wesley moved his commentary along into the great fall chapter of the Bible - Genesis III. He saw this chapter as the most tragic and influential in the Old Testament since it relates the entrance of human sin into the affairs of mankind and the universe. While it explicitly describes the beginning and consequence of that original sin, it also reveals divine grace at work in seeking the fallen couple, in clothing them, and in promising them a future deliverance from the power of evil through the "seed of *Isha*."[102] Wesley divided the twenty-four verses of this chapter into sixteen points of exegesis. These points are -

(1) Genesis III, 1 - 5. "We have here an account of the temptation wherewith Satan assaulted our first parents, and which proved fatal to them." Satan appeared as a serpent. Wesley held that in doing so, Satan took the "shape" of a serpent, rather than possessing a serpent. In this disguise Satan became the tempter of Adam and Eve. Why this disguise? Wesley's answer - "Because it is a subtile creature. It is not improbable, that reason and speech were then known properties of the serpent. And therefore Eve was not surprised at his reasoning and speaking, which otherwise she must have been."[103] In his sermon on *THE FALL OF MAN*, Wesley expanded this description of the wily serpent -

"'Now the serpent was more subtil,' or intelligent, 'than any beast of the field which the Lord God had made;'. . . endued with more understanding than any other animal in the brute creation. Indeed, there is no improbability in the conjecture of an ingenious man, that the serpent was endued with reason, which is now the property of man. And this accounts for a circumstance which, on any other supposition, would be utterly unintelligible. How comes Eve not to be surprised, yea, startled and affrighted, at hearing the serpent speak and reason; unless she knew that reason, and speech in consequence of it, were the original properties of the serpent? Hence, without showing any surprise, she immediately enters into conversation with him."[104]

The serpentine approach of Satan to Eve, Wesley argued, began by denying there was any sin and danger in her eating the forbidden fruit. Instead of danger, Satan reasoned, much advantage would come from it - "God doth know, that in the day ye eat thereof, then your eyes shall be opened: and ye shall be as gods, knowing good and evil."[105] Wesley noted that the phrase - "Your eyes shall be opened" - was a false promise of increased intellectual power and pleasure, bringing incisive views such as never before. Likewise the phrase - "Ye shall be as gods" - was false, promising the omniscience and omnipotence of *Elohim*.[106] The promise of knowing good and evil was equally deceptive, perverting the name of the tree - "He (Satan) perverts the sense of it, and wrests it to their destruction, as if this tree would give them a speculative notional knowledge of the natures, kinds, and originals of good and evil."[107] Satan's entire temptation is reducible to this - "In the day you eat thereof - You will find a sudden and immediate change for the better."[108] Returning to Wesley's sermon on *THE FALL OF MAN*, we are treated to a greater discourse on the wiles of the lying devil and the deception of Eve -

"See how he, who was a liar from the beginning, mixes truth and falsehood together! Perhaps on purpose, that she might be the more inclined to speak, in order to clear God of the unjust charge. Accordingly, the woman said unto the serpent. . . 'We may eat of the fruit of the trees of the garden: But of the fruit of the tree in the midst of the garden, God hath said, Ye shall not eat of it, neither shall ye touch it, lest ye die.' Thus far she appears to have been clear of blame. But how long did she continue so? 'And the serpent said unto the woman, Ye shall not surely die: For God doth that in the day ye eat thereof, your eyes shall be opened, and ye shall be as gods, knowing good and evils.'. . . Here sin began: namely, unbelief. 'The woman was deceived,' says the Apostle. She believed a lie: She gave more credit to the word of the devil, than to the word of God. And unbelief brought forth actual sin; 'When the woman saw that the tree was good for food, and pleasant to the eyes, and to be desired to make one wise, she took of the fruit, and did eat;' and so completed her sin."[109]

(2) Genesis III, 6 - 8. "God tried the obedience of our first parents by forbidding them *the tree of knowledge,* and Satan doth as it were join issue with God, and in that very thing undertakes to seduce them into a transgression; and here we find how he prevailed, God permitting it for wise and holy ends."[110] The woman was the ring-leader, Wesley held. She first ate the fruit, then gave it to her husband "with the same arguments that the serpent had used with her." She added her testimony - that "she herself had eaten of it, and found it so far from being deadly that it was extremely pleasant."[111] Believing a lie, she was deceived. However, her sin did not end with eating the forbidden fruit. She amplified her sin by urging her husband "to join in the transgression." Without any hesitation, Adam took the fruit from Eve and ate it. While Eve ate because she had been deceived, as the Apostle noted, Adam "sinned with his eyes open. . . He rebelled against his Creator."[112] In that act, Adam died spiritually - "The life of God was extinguished in his soul. The glory departed from him. He lost the whole moral image of God, - the righteousness and true holiness."[113] Wesley called this couple "criminals," who were immediately seized by "shame and fear."[114] The exact description of Adam's fallen, unhappy state is best given in Wesley's sermon on *THE END OF CHRIST'S COMING* -

"He was unholy: he was unhappy: he was full of sin; full of guilt and tormenting fears. Being broke off from God, and looking upon him now as an angry Judge, 'he was afraid.' But how was his understanding darkened, to think he could 'hide himself from the presence of the Lord among the trees of the garden!' Thus was his soul utterly dead to God! And in that day his body likewise began to die, - became obnoxious to weakness, sickness, pain; all preparatory to the death of the body, which naturally led to eternal death."[115]

The exposition given Genesis III, 7, in Wesley's *EXPLANA-TORY NOTES UPON THE OLD TESTAMENT,* deserves our attention here. The verse reads - "And the eyes of them both were opened, and they knew that they were naked: and they sewed fig-leaves together, and made themselves aprons." The commentary reads -

"Their hearts smote them for what they had done. Now when it was too late, they saw the happiness they were fallen from, and the misery they were fallen into. They saw God provoked, his favour forfeited, his image lost; they felt a disorder in their own spirits, which they had never before been conscious of; they saw a law in their members arising against the law of their minds, and captivating them both to sin and wrath; they saw that they were naked, that is, that they were stripped, deprived of all the honours and joys of their paradise state, and exposed to all the miseries that might justly be expected from an angry God. . . And they sewed fig-leaves together, and, to cover, at least, part of their shame one from another, made themselves aprons."[116]

When in the cool of the day God came down to commune with Adam, our first parents were in hiding "from the presence of the Lord." According to Wesley, "God" or the "Lord" was none other than Christ, the pre-existent Son of God. Seeking out fallen kind, he appeared to them "in the form of man, and conversed with them face to face."[117] Christ came in human form "to convince and humble them (and) not to amaze and terrify them."[118]

(3) Genesis III, 9. "Where art thou?" The call of Christ to hidden man must be viewed as "a gracious pursuit in order to his recovery," Wesley explained.[119] The call was an expression of "inexpressible tenderness and lenity" on the part of the almighty Creator. It was a merciful invitation to return from rebellion. Without the opportunity to return, man would have no other choice but to "eternally" flee from God.[120] In that case, Adam's condition would have been the same as the fallen angels.[121]

(4) Genesis III, 10. "I heard thy voice in the garden: and I was afraid, because I was naked; and hid myself." Wesley claimed that Adam had good reason to be afraid of God.[122] He refused to acknowledge his fault, and, as Wesley observed, he showed no sense of humiliation for it.[123] But Christ used "astonishing tenderness" in bringing Adam to that acknowledgement.

(5) Genesis III, 11. And Christ said, "Who told thee thou wast naked? Hast thou eaten of the tree, whereof I commanded thee that thou shouldest not eat?" Adam was thus humbled by the Christ that knows everything about us, and the God who requires a confession from the sinner.[124] Wesley then made Adam the recipient of a stern lecture from Christ - "I commanded thee not to eat of it. I thy maker, I thy master, I thy benefactor, I commanded thee to the contrary."[125]

(6) Genesis III, 13. Christ then asked, "What is this thou hast done?" Adam's answer represented an evasion of blame for the sin - "The woman whom thou gavest to be with me, she gave me of the tree, and I did eat." Wesley observed that this response shifts the blame to Eve and God.[126] Eve followed suit, blaming the serpent - "the serpent beguiled me."[127] Wesley summarized the matter to this point -

> "The prisoners being found guilty by their own confession, besides the infallible knowledge of the Judge, and nothing material being offered in arrest of judgment, God immediately proceeds to pass sentence, and in these verses begins (where the sin began) with the serpent. God did not examine the serpent, nor ask him what he had done, but immediately sentenced him."[128]

This sentence was immediate and forthright because, as Satan, "he (the serpent) was already convicted of rebellion against God," and because he "was forever excluded from pardon." Wesley then asked, "Why should any thing be said to convince and humble him, who was to find no place for repentance?"[129]

(7) Genesis III, 14. "Thou art cursed above all cattle, and above every beast of the field: upon thy belly thou shalt go, and dust thou shalt eat all the days of thy life." This divine curse upon the serpent was well deserved, Wesley thought. However, it was a curse on the

serpent and not Satan. Hence, all serpents are cursed - this serpent being the federal head of the species.[130]

(8) Genesis III, 15. The curse on the serpent was expanded to include enmity between the serpent and the woman, between his seed and hers - "And I will put enmity between thee and the woman, and between thy seed and her seed: it shall bruise thy head, and thou shalt bruise his heel." Following Augustine, in his *CIVITAS DEI*, Wesley spoke of this enmity in terms of a perpetual struggle "between the kingdom of God and the kingdom of the devil among men." The "seed of the woman" refers to Christ as incarnate yet to come after many centuries. Wesley saw Revelation XII, 7, as an explicit reference to this struggle.[131] That text reads - "Now war arose in heaven, Michael and his angels fighting against the dragon (Satan)." This struggle involves more than Christ and the devil. It also involves the hosts of heaven and the host of hell, God's people and Satan's, between good and evil.[132] A paradox exists in Genesis III, 15. The curse is actually a promise. The curse against the serpent is also a promise of man's deliverance from Satan's power. Wesley's commentary on the promise reads -

"A gracious promise is here made of Christ as the deliverer of fallen man from the power of Satan. By faith in this promise, our first parents, and the patriarchs before the flood, were justified and saved; and to this promise, and the benefit of it, instantly serving God day and night they hoped to come. Notice is here given them of three things concerning Christ. (1.) His incarnation, that he should be the seed of the woman. (2.) His suffering and death, pointed at in Satan's bruising his heel, that is, his human nature. (3.) His victory over Satan thereby, Satan had now trampled upon the woman, and insulted over her; but the seed of the woman should be raised up in the fullness of time to avenge her quarrel, and to trample upon him, to spoil him, to lead him captive, and to triumph over him."[133]

(9) Genesis III, 16. The sentence passed upon the woman read - "I will greatly multiply thy sorrow and thy conception; in sorrow thou shalt bring forth children: and thy desire shall be to thy husband, and he shall rule over thee." Sorrow in childbearing and subjection to her husband is a terrible sentence! All Eve's daugh-

ters share her sentence.[134]   Wesley saw it as "necessary correction."[135]   At her creation, woman was equal to man, but with this
sentence she became inferior.[136]

   (10) Genesis III, 17. God's reason for placing a curse on Adam
is stated here - "Because thou hast hearkened to the voice of thy
wife." In his commentary, Wesley stressed that it was Adam's de-
liberate choice to eat the forbidden fruit and not Eve's persuasion
that constituted his sin. Consequently, God cursed the ground for
Adam's sake. As Eve's curse affected her vocation - the bearing of
children - so Adam's curse affected his vocation - the tilling of the
ground. The paradisiacal condition would degenerate to "thorns
and thistles."[137]   Wesley identified this condition with St. Paul's
cursed cosmos being made "subject to vanity" (Romans VIII, 20).
"Adam only made it liable to the sentence which God pronounced;
yet not without hope."[138]   Thus most of the ground, once serviceable to man's comfort and happiness, became barren as a suitable
punishment for Adam's part in the original sin. Instead of eating
the "delicious fruits of paradise," Adam's diet would henceforth be
the "herbs of the field. . . coarse and vile."[139]

   (11) Genesis III, 19. "In the sweat of thy face shalt thou eat
bread." Wesley rightly observed that "work" was not a curse. It was
instituted before the fall - Adam kept and dressed the garden. His
curse changed the nature of work - "His business before he sinned
was a constant pleasure to him; but now his labour shall be a
weariness."[140]   Postlapsarian work, therefore, was marked by useless and hurtful productions, bringing frustration and pain. Adam
would find no relief until his body and soul should forsake one another in death, and, as Wesley so aptly put it, "become itself a lump
of dust, and then it shall be lodged in the grave, and mingle with
the dust of the earth."[141]   God instructed Adam concerning his
fallen nature: "For dust thou art, and unto dust shalt thou return."
Wesley was amazed at the remarkable body of dust -

> "'Dust thou art:' But how fearfully and wonderfully wrought into innumer-
> able fibers, nerves, membranes, muscles, arteries, veins, vessels of various
> kinds! And how amazingly is this dust connected with water, with inclosed,

circulating fluids, diversified a thousand ways by a thousand tubes and strainers! Yea, and how wonderfully is air impacted into every part, solid or fluid, of the animal machine; air not elastic, which would tear the machine in pieces, but as fixed as water under the pole! But all this would not avail, were not ethereal fire intimately mixed both with this earth, air, and water. And all these elements are mingled together in the most exact proportion; so that while the body is in health, no one of them predominates, in the least degree, over the others. Such was man, with regard to his corporeal part, as he came out of the hands of this Maker. But since he sinned, he is not only dust, but mortal, corruptible dust. And by sad experience we find, that this 'corruptible body presses down the soul.'"[142]

(12) Genesis III, 20. God had earlier given man the name "Adam" from "red earth." He was taken from the red earth and in death he was now destined to return. And Adam named his wife "Eve," which means "the mother of all living." Wesley made a novel observation: "Adam bears the name of the dying body, Eve of the living soul."[143] Then, Wesley recounted, God blessed the sinful pair, "Be fruitful and multiply." It would be extremely difficult for Adam to be fruitful with cursed ground, and for Eve to bear children because of great pain and sorrow. Nevertheless, God's blessing, Wesley reasoned, was a confirmation of the promise that one day "the seed of this woman, should break the serpent's head" and also break the curse of sin.[144]

(13) Genesis III, 21. "Unto Adam also and to his wife did the Lord God make coats of skins, and clothed them." Such compassion for them was not without a fresh revelation of the seriousness of sin. It was necessary to slay the beasts for their skins. Adam and Eve now realized what death is. God slew the beasts before their eyes. The animals provided more than skins, however. They were also slain for sacrifice, "to typify the great sacrifice which in the later end of the world should be offered once for all. Thus the first thing that died was a sacrifice, or Christ in a figure."[145]

(14) Genesis III, 22. "Behold, the man is become as one of us, to know good and evil." Ironically, Wesley observed, man received more than he anticipated when he ate of the forbidden fruit - "What advantages!"[146] This was said, Wesley explained, to humble

Adam and Eve and bring them to a sense of their sin. In hearing this, the guilty pair saw their folly in allowing themselves to be wretchedly deceived by the devil.[147]

(15) Genesis III, 23. "He sent him out." God sent Adam and his wife from the garden, because they were no longer fit to occupy it. But, they were not willing to depart from it.[148]

(16) Genesis III, 24. "God drove him out." Where did God send him? "He might justly have chased him out of the world, but he only chased him out of the garden; he might justly have cast him down to hell, as the angels that sinned were, when they were shut out from the heavenly paradise." But, Wesley retorted, "Man was only sent to till the ground out of which he was taken. He was only sent to a place of toil, not to a place of torment." Moreover, "He was sent to the ground, not to the grave; to the work-house, not to the dungeon, not to the prison-house; to hold the plough, not to drag the chain."[148] Our first parents were not abandoned to despair - "God's thoughts of love designing them for a second state of probation upon new terms."[149] Then, Wesley held, God stationed "a detachment of cherubim, armed with a dreadful and irresistible power, represented by flaming swords which turned every way. . .to keep the way that led to the tree of life."[150]

THE FALL OF THE COSMOS

"There is a serious mistake in supposing 'the world is now in the same state it was at the beginning' . . .the world, at the beginning, was a totally different state from that wherein we find it now. . .God Almighty. . .did not make it as it is now. He himself made it better, unspeakably better, than it is at present. He made it without any blemish, yea, without any defect. He made no corruption, no destruction, in the inanimate creation. He made not death in the animal creation; neither its harbingers, - sin and pain."[151]

John Wesley was convinced that the Bible teaches that the original sin brought serious and far-reaching consequences to the whole created universe. The heavens, the earth, and the seas have been shot-through with defects because of Adam's disobedience. They are inextricably flawed, and, to quote St. Paul, they "groan" under their subjection to "vanity."[152]

Wesley understood the ancient Jewish tradition that "the heavens" are composed of three specific layers.[153] Since St. Paul spoke of his visionary visit to the "the third heaven" (II Corinthians XII), Wesley was quite happy to embrace the belief in multiple heavens. For Wesley, however, the third heaven, where God sits enthroned above his angels - as popular tradition describes it - is actually an anthropomorphism: "It is this, the third heaven, which is usually supposed to be the more immediate residence of God; so far as any residence can be ascribed to his omnipresent Spirit, who pervades and fills the whole universe. It is here (if we speak after the manner of men) that the Lord sitteth upon his throne, surrounded by angels and archangels."[154] In biblical and rabbinic traditions, the sin of Adam did not adversely affect the third heaven, and Wesley claimed that "this Palace of the Most High was the same from eternity, and will be, world without end."[155] It must be noted, at this point, that Wesley's knowledge of the literature of Rabbinic Judaism was quite extensive, although the TALMUD had not yet been translated from its ancient text. Wesley knew that the rabbis had taught that the lower heavens, beneath the third heaven, were indeed flawed by the sin of the first man.

The second heaven, Wesley held, was the starry heaven. Upon the occasion of the first sin, some of the unmovable stars were thrust into erratic orbits, an idea especially common in rabbinic writings (Jubilees, The Apocalypse of Baruch, 4 Ezra, and later Midrashic literature). These stars, according to Wesley, began to blaze and wander as "half-formed planets, in a chaotic state."[156] Wesley thought of these stars as the "comets" which are portents of judgment upon the sins of men and nations. Comets were not included in creation as such. They came into being after Adam's sin, being perverted stars, or, "ruined worlds, - worlds that have undergone a general conflagration."[157] Furthermore, with the original sin, the starry heaven lost its "exact order and harmony."[158] Originally the sun "was situated at the most exact distance from the earth, so as to yield a sufficient quantity of heat (neither too little nor too much) to every part of it. God had not yet

> Bid his angels turn askance
> This oblique globe.

There was no violent winter, or sultry summer; no extreme, either of heat or cold. No soil was burned up by the solar heat; none uninhabitable through the want of it."[159]

However, with the first sin the relationship of sun to earth was drastically altered for the worse.

The lowest heaven did not escape corruption either. Called the "region of the air" by Wesley, the first heaven was instantaneously flawed. Originally, it was tranquil -

"The element of air was then always serene, and always friendly to man. In contained no frightful meteor, no unwholesome vapours, no poisonous exhalations. There were no tempests, but only cool and gentle breezes. . . fanning both man and beast, and wafting the fragrant odours on their silent wings."[160]

With the fall of man, however, the first heaven was suddenly "torn with hurricanes. . .agitated by furious storms. . .destructive tempests. . .(and) pernicious meteors."[161] The atmosphere lost its clarity and became clogged with clouds and fog.[162] Poisonous "damps" set in everywhere. The Sirocco and other great winds swept the earth, parching the ground, destroying vegetation, and suffocating living creatures.[163] Not only did winds sweep over the earth, but fire also. As one of the four elements used by God in the creation of the universe, fire was a positive force in nature, adding heat to various entities as God intended. But the fall turned fire into a "destroyer."[164] From then onward, conflagrations broke out all over the earth, destroying life in many forms.

The first sin adversely affected the waters of the world, both rivers and seas. Originally, all water was fresh and pure, but confined within the great abyss for "there was no external sea in the paradisiacal earth; none until the great deep burst the barriers which were originally appointed for it."[165] While there was no sea at first, because the earth completely covered it, there were rivers on the earth, sufficient enough to water and keep the ground fertile and plenteous.[166] Moreover, there were no lakes of putrid, turbid, or stagnate water. The fall of Adam changed most of this. The once pure and clear water of creation became unhealthful and unpleasing - a poisonous mixture which polluted stream and lake.[167]

The earth was wracked with a great many defects because of the original sin. It was immediately convulsed with earthquakes and volcanic eruptions.[168] Concerning earthquakes, Wesley said, "God was the author, and sin was the moral cause."[169] As a result, agitations and violent convulsions within the "bowels of the globe" continue to bring earthquakes, volcanic eruptions, and burning mountains.[170]

The features of the earth's surface also underwent drastic changes. Originally, the earth's crust was beautiful, fertile, and possessed gentle hills and mountains, separated by broad valleys. The original sin brought a diminishing of earth's beauty, a loss of fertility, and a violent upheaval of hills and mountains, making them steep and rugged.[171] Wild deserts replaced broad valleys.[172] Consequently, many parts of the earth became incapable of ever being inhabited.[173] Vast areas of vegetation died and barren sands resulted. Other areas became impassable morasses and unfruitful bogs.[174] Overall, these changes brought a great amount of "inequalities on the surface of the earth."[175]

The earth's climate was changed from its balmy and paradisiacal ideal to radical extremes of cold and heat.[176] As a result, Adam and Eve needed clothing, Wesley argues.[177] Before the fall, "spring and summer went hand in hand."[178] After, however, they were distinctly separated seasons, and autumn and winter gave a declining and frigid condition to the earth. Man's clothing served more than modesty's end, it provided protection from the summer's blazing heat and humidity and from the winter's chilling blasts. The earth, which once provided an inexhaustible sustenance to its living creatures, now, because of the changes in physical and climatic features, was greatly diminished in productivity.[179] Furthermore, it began to put forth radically new forms of vegetation which had never existed before - thorns or briers, thistles, fetid weeds, and poisonous plants of all sorts.[180] Creation was not finished. The first sin set in motion a new wave of created things, evil things to afflict man and cosmos: "A whole army of evils, totally new, totally unknown till then, broke in upon rebel man, and all other creatures, and overspread the face of the earth."[181]

In his sermon entitled *THE NEW CREATION*, Wesley addressed this subject at considerable length. Excerpts follow -

> "In the living part of the creation were seen the most deplorable effects of Adam's apostasy. The whole animated creation, whatever has life, from leviathan to the smallest mite, was thereby made subject to such vanity, as the inanimate creatures could not be. . . They were subject to that fell monster, DEATH, the conqueror of all that breathe. . . Also to Pain, death's forerunner. . . (From then onward) how many millions of creatures in the sea, in the air, and on every part of the earth can only survive by taking away the lives of others; by tearing in pieces and devouring their poor innocent, resisting fellow-creatures."[182]

Wesley recognized several serious consequences of Adam's sin on the brute creation: (1) death; (2) loss of native powers; (3) change of disposition; and (4) subjection to vanity. Concerning (1), originally the brute creatures were made immortal, not knowing pain.[183] But, when Adam sinned and lost his immortality, the brute creatures lost their immortality too. Pain, by virtue of the degenerating process of the body called mortality, set in immediately. Some of them died at once to be a sacrifice for Adam's sin. (2) All brute creatures lost a great amount of their native powers, both physical and intellectual. Wesley's sermon on the General Deliverance explicitly treats this dimension. He was indebted to Dr. Hildrop's famous work, *FREE THOUGHTS ON THE BRUTE CREATION*,[184] for the passage which follows.

> "They sustained much loss, even in the lower faculties; their vigour, strength, and swiftness. But undoubtedly they suffered far more in their understand-

ing; more than we can easily conceive. Perhaps insects and worms had then as much understanding as the most intelligent brutes have now. Whereas millions of creatures have present, little more understanding than the earth on which they crawl or the rock to which they adhere. They suffered still more in their will, in their passions; which were then variously distorted, and frequently set in flat opposition to the little understanding that was left them. Their liberty was greatly impaired; yea, in many cases, totally destroyed. They are still utterly enslaved to irrational appetites, which have full dominion over them."[185]

Before leaving this point of the loss of native powers, it must be noted that Wesley believed that before the fall many of the brutes had the power of speech. Clearly, he reasoned, the serpent did, and Eve was not alarmed because he spoke to her.[186] But the higher brutes also had the same ability to speak. However, the fall changed all that. In exegeting Numbers XXII, 28, Wesley observed the Balaam's ass was granted "the power of speech and reasoning for that time."[187] What was universally lost at the fall, was at least restored temporally to Balaam's ass. The serpent, before the fall, also enjoyed the power of reason and walking upright. Wesley may have known the rabbinic tradition at this point. Rabbi Joshua taught that before the fall the serpent walked and talked like a man. But after the fall, this changed. "What did God do unto him? He severed his feet and cut off his tongue, so that he should no longer be able to speak."[188] Wesley's version of the serpent's loss of native powers reads, "Upon thy belly thou shalt go - No longer upon feet, or half erect, but thou shalt crawl along, thy belly cleaving to the earth.[189] (3) With Adam's apostasy, all the brute creatures suffered a negative change in their dispositions. All brutes were vegetarians before the fall, and they "breathed, in their various kinds, the benevolence of their great Creator."[190] There were no birds or beast of prey among them. Even the insects did not prey on other creatures. "The spider was then as harmless as the fly, and did not then lie in wait for blood."[191] With the first sin, however, all brute creatures were changed, in a moment, in a twinkling of an eye. Fierce competition for survival, taking the lives of others, and tearing and devouring one another became the new way of life within the brute creation.[192] (4) Consequently, all creatures of the air, the earth, and the sea were made subject to vanity because of Adam's sin: "The intercourse between God and the inferior creatures being stopped (by Adam's transgression), those blessings could no longer flow in upon them. And then it was that 'the creature,' every creature, 'was subjected to vanity,' to sorrow, to pain of every kind...by the wise permission of God, determining to draw eternal good out of the temporary evil."[193] Because man is to blame for the brute's tragic lot, "the far greater part of them flee from him, studiously avoiding his hated presence."[194] Moreover, they can blame man for their outward appearance. Before the fall, the animals had "beauty" stamped upon their images by the Creator. Since the fall, however, "they are shocking to behold! Nay, they are not only terrible and grisly to look upon, but deformed and that to a high degree."[195]

Wesley's summation of the fallen state of brutes is best stated in his treatise on original sin -

> "It is by reason of man's apostasy that even brute animals suffer. 'The whole creation groaneth together' on his account, 'and travaileth together in pain to this day.' For the brute 'creation was made subject to vanity,' to abuse, pain, occupation, death, 'not willingly,' not by any act of its own, 'but by reason of Adam's sin, whom he had appointed lord of the whole lower world, for his sake pronounced this curse, not only on the ground, but on all which was before under his dominion. The misery, therefore, of the brute creation is so far from being an objection to the apostasy of man, that it is a visible standing demonstration thereof: If beast suffer, then man is fallen."[196]

Wesley was convinced that God knows the pains of these creatures, and, as St. Paul suggested, he is "bringing them nearer and nearer to the birth, which shall be accomplished in its season." Wesley continued, "The whole animal creation waiteth for that final manifestation of the Sons of God; in which they themselves also shall be delivered (not by annihilation; annihilation is not deliverance) from the present bondage of corruption, into a measure of the glorious liberty of the children of God."[197] The promise of a new heaven and a new earth, as described in Revelation XXI,

Wesley held, pertains not just to mankind's destiny but equally to the animals' destiny. "Behold, I make all things new - There is no restriction in the text - but 'on every creature according to its capacity: God shall wipe away all tears from their eyes. And there shall be no more death.'" Furthermore, Wesley claimed, "delivered animals" shall inherit the new earth together with "delivered people." The Wesleyan account of this forthcoming event is stated in the sermon, *THE GENERAL DELIVERANCE* -

"The whole brute creation will then, undoubtedly, be restored, not only to the vigour, strength, and swiftness which they had at their creation, but to a far higher degree of each than they ever enjoyed. The will be restored, not only to that measure of understanding which they had in paradise, but to a degree of it as much higher than that, as the understanding of an elephant is beyond that of a worm. And whatever affections they had in the garden of God, will be restored with vast increase; being exalted and refined in a manner which we ourselves are not now able to comprehend. The liberty they then had will be completely restored, and they will be free in all their motions. They will be delivered from all irregular appetites, from all unruly passions, from every disposition that is either evil in itself, or has any tendency to evil. No rage will be found in any creature, no fierceness, no cruelty, or thirst for blood. So far from it, that 'the wolf shall dwell with the lamb, the leopard shall lie down with the kid' the calf and the young lion together; and a little child shall lead them. The cow and the bear shall feed together; and the lion shall eat straw like the ox. They shall not hurt nor destroy in all my holy mountain. . . Thus, in that day, all the vanity to which they are now helplessly subject will be abolished; they will suffer no more, either from within or without; the days of their groaning are ended. At the same time, there can be no reasonable doubt, but all the horridness of their appearance, and all the deformity of their aspect, will vanish away, and be exchanged for their primeval beauty. And with their beauty their happiness will return; to which there can then be no obstruction."[198]

In the future state, all the redeemed animals will enjoy an eternal and perennial spring, devoid of extremes of heat and cold, and storms and tempests. Instead of painful experiences, God's wisdom and goodness will create happy experiences for them.[199] "As a recompence for what they once suffered, while under the bondage of corruption, . . .they shall enjoy happiness suited to their state, without alloy, without interruption, and end."[200]   Wesley further noted that God, the Father of All, while making "large amends" to the brutes for what they suffered "under the present bondage," did not regard animals and men equally. God regards man much more. Nevertheless, Wesley conjectured, in the future state, God, the all-gracious Creator, may elevate the brutes to a higher "scale of beings." At the same time, men will be made "equal to angels," while the brutes will be made like men are now.[201] Until then, God advances a special care for all animals.[202] For this reason, Wesley often championed the cause of humane treatment for the animals of England.

The future state will witness a new heaven and a new earth, both without flaw and imperfections. "But the most glorious of all will be the change which then will take place on the poor, sinful, miserable children of men." These had fallen into "a lower depth, than any other part of the creation." But in the future state, they will be elevated to equality with angels, and God will be their God and they will be his people.[203]

St. Augustine argued that evil is the perversion of some good, and that God uses every occasion of evil to create a greater good. Where sin abounds, grace abounds even more. The Homily of the Church of England, entitled "The Misery of All Mankind," used this Augustinian principle to instill hope and anticipation in the people of the Church. Wesley, from this childhood onward, knew this sermon quite well. Its points and phraseology run throughout Wesley's sermons, treatises, and letters with great frequency. In fact, Wesley held the Homilies to be the most important authority after the Bible,[204] and the best of "all our sermons."[205]   The Homily on the misery of all mankind, sermon two, summarizes the whole story of the fall of angels, men, and the cosmos accordingly - "The Scripture shutteth up all under sin, that the promise by the faith of Jesus Christ should be given unto them that believe."[206] As for man's part in this tragedy, the Homily states -

"let us recognize before God that we are miserable and wretched sinners. . . that we are full of imperfections. . .we do not love God so much as we are bound to do, with all our heart, mind, and power; we do not fear God so much as we ought to do; we do not pray to God. . .we give, forgive, believe, live and hope imperfectly; we speak, think, and do imperfectly, we fight against the devil, the world, and the flesh imperfectly."[207]

Nevertheless, God's love abounds, bringing forth grace upon grace out of man's sin. Of all his sermons, none is as explicit on this point as Wesley's *GOD'S LOVE TO FALLEN MAN.* The text was Romans V, 15 - "not as the offence, so also is the free gift." The arguments unfold as follows: (1) By Adam's willful rebellion against God sin entered into the world, and as many as were then in the loins of the forefather, were made sinners, being deprived of the favour of God and his image, of all virtue, righteousness, and true holiness. They sank into the image of the devil, in pride, malice, and "all other diabolical tempers." They also inherited the image of the brute, exhibiting brutal passions and appetites. Consequently, death entered the cosmos, "with all his forerunners and attendants - pain, sickness, and a whole train of uneasy, as well as unholy, passions and tempers."[208] (2) For this great heritage we may all thank Adam as has every generation and nation since his day. Instead of rising up and calling him blessed, mankind has severely condemned Adam because he "Brought death into the world, and all our woe!"[209] (3) God's mercy and justice have been questioned by many for permitting this disobedience and its consequences. "Was it not easy for the Almighty to have prevented it?" Wesley answered -

"He certainly did foresee the whole. This cannot be denied: For 'known unto God are all his works from the beginning of the world;' rather, from all eternity, as the words απ αιωνος properly signify. And it was undoubtedly in his power to prevent it; for he hath all power both in heaven and earth. But it was known to him, at the same time, that it was best, upon the whole, not to prevent it. He knew that 'not as the transgression, so is the free gift;' that the evil resulting from the former was not as the good resulting from the latter, - not worthy to be compared with it. He saw that to permit the fall of the first man was far best for mankind in general; that abundantly more good than evil would accrue to the posterity of Adam by his fall; that if 'sin abounded' thereby over all the earth, yet grace 'would much more abound;' yea, and that to every individual of the human race, unless it was his own choice."[210]

(4) It is most unfortunate, Wesley argued, that the vast majority of Christians do not understand that grace out-performs evil. Wesley wanted his Methodists to appreciate this truth. He made this point in other writings, always insisting that "the wise Being. . .knows how to extract good out of evil,"[211] and that "there is no evil in any place but the hand of the Lord is in it."[212]

The end result is, Wesley affirmed, that fallen mankind has received, by Adam's sin, a capacity that was never known before the first sin. "First, of being more holy and more happy on earth, and, Secondly, of being more happy in heaven, than otherwise they could have been!"[213]

In the first place, Wesley announced, mankind in general gained a capacity of attaining "more holiness and happiness on earth" than if Adam had not fallen. The reason for this claim is obvious: "For if Adam had not fallen, Christ had not died." There are numerous aspects to this basic truth -

"Unless all the partakers of human nature had received that deadly wound in Adam, it would not have been needful for the Son of God to take our nature upon him. Do you not see that this was the very ground of his coming into the world?. . .Was it not to remedy this very thing that 'the Word was made flesh,' that 'as in Adam all died, so in Christ all' might be made alive? Unless, then, many had been made sinners by the disobedience of one, by the obedience of one many would not have been made righteous. . .So there would have been no room for that amazing display of the Son of God's love to mankind: There would have been no occasion for his being 'obedient unto death, even the death of the cross.' It could not then have been said, to the astonishment of all the hosts of heaven, 'God so loved the world,' yea, the ungodly world, which had no thought or desire of returning to him, 'that he gave his Son' out of his bosom, his only begotten Son, 'to the end that whosoever believeth on him should not perish, but have everlasting life.' Neither could we then have said, 'God was in Christ reconciling the world to himself;' or, that he 'made him to be sin,' that is, a sin-offering, 'for us, who knew no sin, that we might be made the righteousness of God through him.' There would have been no such occasion for such 'an Advocate with the Father,' as

'Jesus Christ the righteous;' neither for his appearing 'at the right hand of God, to make intercession for us.'"[214]

Moreover, without the fall there could be no such thing as faith in God, or in the Son of God who gave himself for us. Nor could there be faith in the Holy Spirit who renews the image of God within us, and raises "us from the death of sin unto the life of righteousness."[215] Without the capacity for faith, justification by faith is an impossibility, and, as a result, there can be no redemption in the blood of Christ. Furthermore, without faith Christ would not be our "wisdom, righteousness, and sanctification."[216] Without the capacity for faith, our lives would evidence a "grand blank." Indeed, Wesley argued, something good and supreme would be lacking within us. We would be like Adam before the fall! But the capacity granted the descendants of Adam, in consequence of the fall, has room for love as well as faith. As faith existed before the fall, but in a minimal way, so did love. However, it was love of God as Creator and Preserver, but "we could not have loved him under the nearest and dearest relation, - as delivering up his Son for us all." It is only by virtue of the fall that we can love Christ as Saviour and Redeemer, being made conformable to his death, and partakers of the power of his resurrection. It is possible, since the fall, to love the Holy Spirit, as the revealer of the Father and Son, bringing us from spiritual darkness into spiritual light, renewing the image of God within us, and sealing us unto the day of redemption.[217] The capacity for faith and love, then, gives Adam's children an "unspeakable advantage" over their first parents in Paradise. Then too, both faith and love are subject to the spiritual law of growth. Love, the greater of the two, has a dynamic extension, both vertically and horizontally -towards God the Trinity, and towards our neighbours.[218] Moreover, "this motive to brotherly love (would be) totally wanting if Adam had not fallen."[219]

Wesley's sermon suddenly takes a surprising turn - the pain and suffering resulting from Adam's sin, earlier described as a universal tragedy, must be seen as the justice of God and the "unspeakable goodness of God." Furthermore, Wesley asserted, "For how much good does he continually bring out of this evil! How much holiness and happiness out of pain!"[220] It is immediately apparent that Wesley would reject out of hand all contemporary approaches to divine healing that emphasize that it is not God's will that anyone should ever suffer pain. He stoutly affirmed that pain provides God with an opportunity for greater good, without the permanent removal of pain. Wesley believed that the removal of pain for mankind comes only when these mortal bodies put on immortality, not before. In fact, even faith healers suffer pain and finally die! Wesley deserves a serious hearing at this point -

> "How innumerable are the benefits which God conveys to the children of men through the channel of sufferings! - so that it might well be said, 'What are termed afflictions in the language of men, are in the language of God styled blessings.' Indeed, had there been no suffering in the world, a considerable part of religion, yea, and, in some respects, the most excellent part, could have had no place therein; since the very existence of it depends on our suffering; so that had there been no pain, it could have had no being. Upon this foundation, even our suffering, it is evident all our passive graces are built; yea, the noblest of all Christian graces, - love endureth all things. Here is the ground for resignation to God, enabling us to say from the heart in every trying hour, 'It is the Lord: Let him do what seemeth him good... Shall we receive good at the hand of the Lord, and shall we not receive evil!' And what a glorious spectacle is this! Did it not constrain even a Heathen to cry out, *Ecce spectaculum Deo dignum*! 'See a sight worthy of God;' a good man struggling with adversity, and superior to it. Here is the ground for confidence in God, both with regard to what we should fear, were it not that our soul is calmly stayed on Him. What room could there be for trust in God if there was no such thing as pain or danger? Who might not say then, 'The cup which my Father hath given me, shall I not drink it?' It is by sufferings that our faith is tried, and, therefore, made more acceptable to God. It is in the day of trouble that we have occasion to say, 'Though he slay me, yet will I trust in him.' And this is well pleasing to God, that we should own him in the face of danger; in defiance of sorrow, sickness, pain, or death."[221]

Furthermore, according to Wesley, if there had never been any natural or moral evil in the world, there could not have been any experiences of patience, meekness, gentleness, and longsuffering. Using logic, Wesley deduced that these responses could have no "being" unless they "have evil for their object."[222] If evil had not entered into the world, patience, meekness, gentleness, and long-suffering could have no place within it. How could anyone return good for evil, had there been "no evil-doer" in the universe? Even if God had infused these graces apart from the existence of evil, there would have been no use or exercise for them. Their usefulness and exercise only have significance in relation to the existence of evil. In relation to evil, the more they are exercised, "the more all our graces are strengthened and increased."[223] By these graces holiness and happiness come into the life of man, and, in consequence, good works are produced, "which otherwise could have had no being."[224]

Pain and suffering among the descendants of Adam provide the opportunity for good works, "good of every kind, and in every degree." Wesley observed that the more good we perform, in alleviating pain and suffering in others, the happier we become. What specifically are the good works to be performed?

Wesley used the good works of the Gospel of Matthew: distributing bread to the hungry, covering the naked with clothing, and relieving the strangers by visiting them in their sickness and when in prison.[225] "The more kind offices we do to those that groan under the various evils of human life, - the more comfort we receive even in the present world, the greater the recompense we have in our own bosom."[226]

Wesley's argument that pain and suffering, caused by original sin, gives God an occasion for greater good, leads to the conclusion that holiness and happiness also result when one, in the face of pain and suffering, performs moral good for the benefit of others. Adam's sin, therefore, gives man the opportunity of "being more holy," of doing innumerable good works, which "otherwise could not have been done," and "by putting it into our power to suffer for God. . .(these) may be of such advantage to the children of men, even in the present life, as they will not thoroughly comprehend till they attain life everlasting."[227] But, Wesley, affirmed, these advantages which accrue to one's earthly life also reap benefits to be received later in eternal life. The earthly benefits of bringing good out of pain and suffering, for both others and self, lay up treasures of good in heaven, to be inherited later. Commenting on St. Paul's description of the resurrection yet to come, Wesley observed that "one star differeth from another star in glory, so also is the resurrection of the dead." For Wesley, the stars are different kinds of persons who inherit in eternity the kind of destiny they have prepared for during the earthly life. "The most glorious stars will undoubtedly be those who are the most holy, who bear most of that image of God wherein they were created; the next in glory to these will be those who have been most abundant in good works; and next to them, those that have suffered most, according to the will of God."[228] Behind Wesley's identification of stars as the children of the resurrection, speaking metaphorically, laid his understanding of Daniel XII, 2-3. In the *EXPLANATORY NOTES UPON THE OLD TESTAMENT*, Wesley renders these verses accordingly -

> "And many of them that sleep in the dust of the earth shall awake, some to everlasting life, and some to shame and everlasting contempt. And they that be wise, shall shine as the brightness of the firmament, and they that turn many to righteousness, as the stars for ever and ever."[229]

The spiritual stars, according to Wesley, are those who turn many to righteousness, both by applying the passive virtues for one's self and by "ministering to the needs" of others, "relieving the distressed in every kind: And hereby innumerable stars will be added to their eternal crown."[230] It is strange that Wesley should here change his metaphor from people as stars to stars as rewards for one's crown. Nevertheless, Wesley's point is that "there will be an abundant reward in heaven for suffering as well as for doing the will of God." Borrowing from St. Paul, Wesley affirmed, "These light afflictions, which are but for a moment, work out for us a far more exceeding and eternal weight of glory."[231] Consequently, the sin that brought pain and suffering also "occasioned to all the children of God an increase of glory to all eternity."[232] All sufferings will end at the resurrection of the flesh, but the "joys occasioned thereby shall never end, but flow at God's right hand for ever-more."[223]

The most important truth in this context of grace out-bounding sin, as Wesley described it, is -

"If God had prevented the fall of man, 'the Word' had never been 'made flesh;' nor had we ever 'seen his glory as of the only-begotten of the Father.' Those mysteries never had been displayed 'which the very angels desire to look into.' Methinks this consideration swallows up all the rest, and should never be out of our thoughts. Unless 'by one man judgment had come upon all men to condemnation,' neither angels nor men could ever have known 'the unsearchable riches of Christ."[234]

Therefore, Wesley exclaimed, "See, then, upon the whole, how little reason we have to repine at the fall of our first parent; since herefrom we may derive such unspeakable advantages in time and eternity."[235] No one should, therefore, question God's mercy in allowing the original sin. God's mercy clearly exceeds man's opinion that God is to blame for poor Adam's sin and its consequences. Wesley raised a rhetorical question, "Should we not rather bless him from the ground of the heart, for therein laying the grand scheme of man's redemption, and making way for that glorious manifestation of his wisdom, holiness, justice, and mercy?" But, as Wesley indicated, many persons blame God for locking mankind into the worst possible situation by his eternal decrees. One of Wesley's finest statements against popular Calvinism and its fixation on decrees is given at the end of this sermon. Its citation here is justified -

"If, indeed, God had decreed, before the foundation of the world, that millions of men should dwell in everlasting burnings, because Adam sinned hundreds or thousands of years before they had a being, I know not who could thank him for this, unless the devil and his angels; Seeing, on this supposition, all those millions of unhappy spirits would be plunged into hell by Adam's sin, without any possible advantage from it. But blessed by God, this is not the case. Such a decree never existed. On the contrary, every one born of a woman may be an unspeakable gainer thereby: and none ever was or can be a loser but by his own choice."[236]

Wesley's summary view of fallen man contains the following points: (1) God made man in his own image; (2) man initially possessed understanding and liberty; (3) man abused that liberty and produced moral evil; (4) Adam's sin brought pain and suffering into the cosmos; (5) God permitted the sin, evil, pain and suffering in order to reveal his wisdom, justice, and mercy, by bestowing these on all who would receive them by choice, and thus become infinitely happy, receiving more after the fall than what Adam lost in the fall.[237] Where sin abounded, grace did much more abound. In Christ, believing man receives more than Adam lost in the fall. Augustine and Aquinas were right when they affirmed, "Since God is supremely good, he would not allow any evil thing to exist in his works were he not able by his omnipotence and goodness to bring good out of evil."[238]

Notes

1 WORKS, *op.cit.*, XII, 3.
2 Schaff, NICENE. *op.cit.*, III, 240.
3 *Ibid*, IV, 119. Augustine said, "He who sins not voluntarily, sins not at all."
4 *Ibid*, IV, 100.
5 *Ibid*, IV, 72.
6 *Ibid*, IV, 111.
7 *Ibid*, IV, 72; II, 214. Augustine added that evil "has its origin not in the creation, but in the will."
8 *Ibid*, IV, 147.
9 *Ibid*, IV, 241.
10 *Ibid*, II, 214.
11 *Ibid*, II, 213.
12 *Ibid*, V, 132.
13 EXPLANATORY NOTES OLD TESTAMENT, *op.cit.*, I, 17.
14 Schaff, NICENE, *op.cit.*, V, 403.
15 *Ibid*, III, 76.
16 *Ibid*, II, 214.
17 *Ibid*, II, 215.
18 *Ibid*, II, 218.
19 *Ibid*, II, 224.
20 *Loc.cit.*
21 *Ibid*, II, 231.
22 *Ibid*, IV, 271. Augustine added, "In the future life, the choice of evil will be impossible."
23 *Loc.cit.*
24 WORKS, *op.cit.*, XII, 1-3. CF. Frank Baker, *op.cit.*, XXV, 240-242.
25 Frank Baker, *op.cit.*, XXV, 258.
26 *Loc.cit.*
27 *Loc.cit.*
28 *Ibid*, XXV, 267. Cf. WORKS, *op.cit.*, XII, 3-6.
29 WORKS, *op.cit.*, X, 463.
30 *Loc.cit.*
31 *Ibid*, VI, 270.
32 *Ibid*, VI, 271; 372.
33 EXPLANATORY NOTES NEW TESTAMENT, *op.cit.*, 996. Cf. EXPLANATORY NOTES OLD TESTAMENT, *op.cit.*, III, 1985; 2361.
34 WORKS, *op.cit.*, V, 480.
35 *Loc.cit.*
36 *Loc.cit.*

37 EXPLANATORY NOTES NEW TESTAMENT, *op.cit.*, 955.
38 WORKS, *op.cit.*, VI, 371-372.
39 *Ibid*, VI, 372.
40 *Loc.cit.* Cf. EXPLANATORY NOTES NEW TESTAMENT, *op.cit.*, 996. The tail of the great dragon swept one third of the stars (angels) to earth with him.
41 *Ibid*, VI, 373.
42 *Ibid*, VI, 374.
43 *Loc.cit.*
44 EXPLANATORY NOTES NEW TESTAMENT, *op.cit.*, 894.
45 *Ibid*, 121-122. Here Wesley quotes from Matthew where hell is described as a place for Satan and his angels.
46 *Ibid*, 927-928.
47 WORKS, *op.cit.*, VII, 327.
48 *Ibid*, VII, 234.
49 EXPLANATORY NOTES NEW TESTAMENT, *op.cit.*, 1037-1038.
50 WORKS, *op.cit.*, VII, 323.
51 *Ibid*, VII, 327.
52 *Ibid*, VII, 328.
53 *Ibid*, VI, 374.
54 EXPLANATORY NOTES OLD TESTAMENT, *op.cit.*, II, 1518-1519.
55 WORKS, *op.cit.*, VI, 374.
56 *Ibid*, VI, 374-375.
57 *Ibid*, VI, 375.
58 *Ibid*, VI, 375-376.
59 *Ibid*, VI, 376.
60 *Loc.cit.*
61 *Loc.cit.*
62 *Ibid*, VI, 376-377.
63 *Ibid*, VI, 377.
64 *Loc.cit.*
65 *Ibid*, VI, 378.
66 *Loc.cit.*
67 *Loc.cit.*
68 *Ibid*, VI, 378-379.
69 *Ibid*, VI, 379.
70 *Ibid*, XII, 301-302. Cf. EXPLANATORY NOTES NEW TESTAMENT, *op.cit.*, 721.
71 *Ibid*, VI, 380.
72 *Ibid*, VI, 215.
73 *Loc.cit.*
74 *Ibid*, VI, 271.
75 *Ibid*, VI, 232, 234. Wesley linked the atonement with this advantage.
76 EXPLANATORY NOTES OLD TESTAMENT, *op.cit.*, I, 11.
77 *Loc.cit.*
78 WORKS, *op.cit.*, VI, 70.

79   EXPLANATORY NOTES OLD TESTAMENT, *op.cit.*, I, 11.
80   *Loc.cit.*
81   *Ibid.,* I, 12.
82   *Loc.cit.*
83   *Loc.cit.* Cf. Evans, *op.cit.*, 45. The rabbinic tradition claimed that a journey of 500 years was necessary to encompass the tree of life, and that the fruit of the other tree, the forbidden tree, was the fig.
84   *Loc.cit.*
85   *Loc.cit.*
86   WORKS, *op.cit.*, X, 220; VI, 318.
87   EXPLANATORY NOTES OLD TESTAMENT, *op.cit.*, I, 12.
88   *Loc.cit.*
89   *Loc.cit.*
90   *Ibid,* I, 13.
91   *Loc.cit.*
92   *Loc.cit.*
93   *Loc.cit.*
94   WORKS, *op.cit.*, VI, 215.
95   A. Cohen, *EVERYMAN'S TALMUD* (New York: Schocken Books, 1975), 163.
96   Evans, *op.cit.*, 45.
97   EXPLANATORY NOTES OLD TESTAMENT, *op.cit.*, I, 13.
98   *Loc.cit.*
99   *Loc.cit.*
100 *Loc.cit.*
101 *Loc.cit.*
102 *Ibid,* I, 14.
103 *Loc.cit.*
104 WORKS, *op.cit.*, VI, 216.
105 EXPLANATORY NOTES OLD TESTAMENT, *op.cit.*, I, 14.
106 *Loc.cit.*
107 *Loc.cit.*
108 *Ibid,* I, 14-15.
109 WORKS, *op.cit.*, VI, 216-217.
110 EXPLANATORY NOTES OLD TESTAMENT, *op.cit.*, I, 15.
111 *Loc.cit.*
112 WORKS, *op.cit.*, VI, 217.
113 *Ibid,* VI, 272.
114 EXPLANATORY NOTES OLD TESTAMENT, *op.cit.*, I, 15.
115 WORKS, *op.cit.*, VI, 272.
116 EXPLANATORY NOTES OLD TESTAMENT, *op.cit.*, I, 15-16. One might expect Wesley to incorporate the word "breeches" (britches) instead of "aprons" in this passage. The Geneva Bible, used by Wesley's Puritan forefathers, employed that translation. See *THE GENEVA BIBLE* (London: 1615), 3; also, Luther A. Weigle, *THE GENESIS OCTAPLA* (New York: Thomas Nelson and Sons), 14-15.

117   WORKS, *op.cit.*, VI, 273. Wesley further cited similar encounters of the
      pre-existent Christ with Noah, Abraham, Isaac, Jacob, and Moses.
118   EXPLANATORY NOTES OLD TESTAMENT, *op.cit.*, I, 16.   Cf.
      WORKS, op.cit., VI, 272ff.
119   *Loc.cit.*
120   WORKS, *op.cit.*, VI, 217.
121   EXPLANATORY NOTES OLD TESTAMENT, *op.cit.*, I, 16.
122   *Loc.cit.*
123   WORKS, *op.cit.*, VI, 217.
124   EXPLANATORY NOTES OLD TESTAMENT, *op.cit.*, I, 16.
125   *Loc.cit.*
126   *Ibid*, I, 17.
127   *Loc.cit.*
128   *Loc.cit.*
129   *Loc.cit.*
130   *Loc.cit.*
131   *Loc.cit.*
132   *Loc.cit.*
133   *Ibid*, I, 17-18. Cf. Evans, *op.cit.*, 52. The rabbis held that "because the wis-
      dom of the serpent was so great, therefore was the penalty inflicted upon it
      proportionate to its wisdom...consequently he was cursed above all cattle
      and all the beasts of the field."
134   *Ibid*, I, 18
135   *Loc.cit.*
136   *Loc.cit.* Cf. WORKS, *op.cit.*, VI, 218.
137   *Loc.cit.*
138   EXPLANATORY NOTES NEW TESTAMENT, *op.cit.*, 549.
139   WORKS, *op.cit.*, VI, 218.
140   EXPLANATORY NOTES OLD TESTAMENT, *op.cit.*, I, 18.
141   *Loc.cit.*
142   WORKS, *op.cit.*, VI, 219
143   EXPLANATORY NOTES OLD TESTAMENT, *op.cit.*, I, 18-19.
144   *Ibid*, I, 19.
145   *Loc.cit.*
146   *Loc.cit.*
147   *Loc.cit.*
148   *Loc.cit.*
149   *Ibid*, I, 20.
150   *Loc.cit.*
151   WORKS, *op.cit.*, VI, 213.
152   EXPLANATORY NOTES NEW TESTAMENT, *op.cit.*, 549.
153   WORKS, *op.cit.*, VI, 289.
154   *Ibid*, VI, 290.
155   *Loc.cit.*
156   *Loc.cit.*
157   *Ibid*, VI, 211.

158 *Ibid*, VI, 290. Cf. SURVEY, *op.cit.*, II, 90-91. Wesley described meteors as coming into being as a result of this disharmony.
159 *Ibid*, VI, 209.
160 *Loc.cit.*
161 *Ibid*, VI, 291.
162 *Loc.cit.*
163 *Loc.cit.*
164 *Loc.cit.*
165 *Ibid*, VI 208.
166 *Ibid*, VI, 208-209.
167 *Ibid*, VI, 292.
168 *Ibid*, VI, 294.
169 *Ibid*, VII, 387.
170 *Ibid*, VI, 208.
171 *Loc.cit.*
172 *Ibid*, VI, 293.
173 *Loc.cit.*
174 *Ibid*, VI, 294.
175 *Loc.cit.*
176 *Ibid*, VI, 293.
177 EXPLANATORY NOTES OLD TESTAMENT, *op.cit.*, I, 13.
178 WORKS, *op.cit.*, VI, 56.
179 *Loc.cit.*
180 *Ibid*, VI, 294, 210-211.
181 *Ibid*, VI, 214.
182 *Ibid*, VI, 294-295.
183 *Ibid*, VI, 245.
184 *Ibid*, XIV, 290.
185 *Ibid*, VI, 245-246.
186 EXPLANATORY NOTES OLD TESTAMENT, *op.cit.*, I, 14.
187 *Ibid*, I, 538.
188 Evans, *op.cit.*, 47.
189 EXPLANATORY NOTES OLD TESTAMENT, *op.cit.*, I, 17.
190 WORKS, *op.cit.*, VI, 213.
191 *Ibid*, VI, 212.
192 *Ibid*, VI, 294-295.
193 *Ibid*, VI, 245.
194 *Ibid*, VI, 246.
195 *Ibid*, VI, 247.
196 *Ibid*, IX, 389.
197 *Ibid*, VI, 247-248.
198 *Ibid*, VI, 249.
199 *Loc.cit.*
200 *Ibid*, VI, 250.
201 *Loc.cit.*
202 *Ibid*, VI, 241ff, 319. Cf. JOURNAL, *op.cit.*, IV, 125, 176.

203   *Ibid*, VI, 295.
204   *Ibid,,* VII, 204, 461.
205   Frank Baker, *op.cit.*, XXV, 645. Cf. WORKS, *op.cit.*, I, 164, 224, 259; V, 61, 239; VII, 204; VIII, 23, 31, 54, 55, 74, 103-105, 129, 130, 473, 474. Also, JOURNAL, *op.cit.*, I, 454n; II, 101, 275, 326; IV, 425.
206   *THE HOMILIES* (London: The Prayer Book and Homily Society, 1833), 8.
207   *Ibid*, 10.
208   WORKS, *op.cit.*, VI, 231.
209   *Loc.cit.*
210   *Ibid*, VI, 232.
211   *Ibid*, VII, 464.
212   *Ibid*, VII, 500.
213   *Ibid*, VI, 232.
214   *Ibid*, VI, 233.
215   *Loc.cit.*
216   *Ibid*, VI, 234.
217   *Loc.cit.*
218   *Ibid*, VI, 235.
219   *Loc.cit.*
220   *Loc.cit.*
221   *Ibid*, VI, 235-236.
222   *Ibid*, VI, 236.
223   *Loc.cit.*
224   *Ibid*, VI, 237.
225   *Loc.cit.*
226   *Loc.cit.*
227   *Loc.cit.*
228   *Ibid*, VI, 238.
229   EXPLANATORY NOTES OLD TESTAMENT, *op.cit.*, III, 2464-2465.
230   WORKS, *op.cit.*, VI, 238.
231   *Loc.cit.*
232   *Loc.cit.*
233   *Loc.cit.*
234   *Ibid*, VI, 239.
235   *Loc.cit.*
236   *Ibid*, VI, 240.
237   *Loc.cit.*
238   A.M. Fairweather, *op.cit.*, XI, 56.

Chapter 5

The Pilgrimage from Paradise Lost to Paradise Improved: The Pilgrim's Lot

The Abundance of His Grace

Ho! every one that thirsts draw nigh,
'Tis God invites the fallen race:
Mercy and free salvation buy;
Buy wine, and milk, and gospel grace.

Come to the living waters, come!
Sinners, obey your Maker's call;
Return, ye weary wanderers, home.
And find his grace is free for all.

See from the Rock a fountain rise;
For you in healing streams it rolls;
Money ye need not bring, nor price,
Ye laboring, burdened, sin-sick souls.

Nothing ye in exchange shall give;
Leave all you have and are behind;
Frankly the gift of God receive;
Pardon and peace in Jesus find.[1]

- John Wesley

By the disobedience of Adam all men are sinners, mortal, and aliens from God and Paradise. By the obedience of Jesus Christ all men are redeemed, reconciled to God, and enabled to embark on the pilgrimage which leads to an eternal paradise far surpassing that which was lost. Unfortunately, Wesley believed, not every redeemed soul sets forth on this pilgrimage. And those who do are not guaranteed teleological success for simply starting. The goal is reached only after grace abounds more and more (the divine side) and human effort is expended in "working out salvation" (the human side). The way of the pilgrim means faith, hope, love, charity, obedience, tribulation, patience, gentleness, kindness, prayer, fasting, acts of mercy and compassion, generosity and hospitality, honesty, justice, holiness of heart and life, and avoidance of the devil, the world, and the passions of flesh.

Wesley used two terms almost interchangeably, although he distinguished between them - sojourner and pilgrim. In his commentary on First Peter II, 11, where these terms appear, he treated them semantically. Sojourners, he claimed, referring to the original Greek, means "those who are in a strange house." As for the term pilgrim, it literally means "those who are in a strange country." He concluded, "You sojourn in the body; you are pilgrims in this world."[2] Our souls are sojourners in a strange house. Our original house, or created body, was immortal and without flaw or pain. Our present bodies are mortal, flawed and subject to various pains, making a "strange house" for our souls. Moreover, as composite creatures, we now live in a strange country, this fallen cosmos. We are not at home within it. We cannot be at home within it. Like Abraham, Isaac, and Jacob we are "strangers" within it, seeking our "own country."[3] The search is long and arduous, dangerous but rewarding -

"The time of our eternal redemption draweth nigh. Let us hold out a little longer, and all tears shall be wiped from our eyes, and we shall never sigh nor sorrow any more. And how soon shall we forget all we endured in this earthly tabernacle, when once we are clothed with that house which is from above! We are but on our journey towards home, and so must expect to struggle with many difficulties; but it will not be long ere we come to our journey's end, and that will make amends for all. We shall then be in a safe harbour, out of the reach of all storms and dangers. We shall then be at home in our Father's house, no longer exposed to the inconveniences which, so long as we abide abroad in these tents, we are subject to."[4]

Following Malebranche's design of a Christian pilgrim, Wesley saw the development involving (1) faith in Christ, whose atonement is the sure foundation for salvation; and (2) the work of salvation, bringing removal of guilt of sin and cancellation of the power of sin, "and being restored both to the favour and image of God." The end result is for the pilgrim to "know, love, and serve his great Creator."[5] Furthermore, this design is God's plan for "every man upon the face of the earth." In his sermon, *THE FALL OF MAN*, Wesley elaborated upon this theme -

"Remember! You were born for nothing else. You live for nothing else. Your life is continued to you upon earth, for no other purpose than this, that you may know, love, and serve God on earth, and enjoy him to all eternity. Consider! You were not created to please your senses, to gratify your imagination, to gain money, or the praise of men; to seek happiness in any created good, in anything under the sun. All this is 'walking in a vain shadow;' it is leading a restless, miserable life, in order to a miserable eternity. On the contrary, you were created for this, and for no other purpose, by seeking and finding happiness in God on earth, to secure the glory of God in heaven."[6]

The pilgrim is the person who now lives to God, and in eternity shall live with God - "none shall enjoy the glory of God in heaven, but he that bears the image of God on earth."[7] And, Wesley continued, "none can see the kingdom of God above, unless the kingdom of God be in him below." The pilgrim must exhibit the mind of Christ, enabling him to "walk as Christ also walked."[8] A famous heathen author once said, "*sancti recessus mentis, et incoctum generoso pectus honesto*; 'a virtuous, holy mind, and an heart deep-dyed with generous honesty.'" Such a mind belonged to Jesus Christ, and it must also belong to every pilgrim who would enter into life everlasting with God. God requires nothing less than this possession.[9] Furthermore, the pilgrim knows that his holiness must be more than the doing of no harm, or doing good, or going to church, and partaking of the sacrament of the table. Such holiness is only "skin-deep" and "superficial."[10] Pilgrims know that true holiness, without which no one can see God, is a matter of the life of

God within the soul - "it is the mind which was in Christ Jesus; it is 'righteousness, and peace, and joy in the Holy Ghost.'"[11]

Also, John Wesley argued that true religion involves personal holiness as well as the imputed righteousness of Christ. He simply refused to accept the popular view of the day which stressed that "men are holy, without a grain of holiness in them! holy in Christ, however unholy in themselves; they are in Christ, without one jot of the mind that was in Christ."[12] The pilgrim life is an upward path of holiness, imputed and personal, leading to the spiritual perfection of Love, attainable in this life by those who believe and obey all the enablements of grace.

The pilgrim may easily be deceived since there are numerous expressions of religion. False religions, Wesley maintained, are those which have no place for "giving the heart to God." One such false religion is orthodoxy. "Into this snare fall thousands of those who profess to hold 'salvation by faith;' indeed, all of those who, by faith, mean only a system of Arminian or Calvinian opinions."[13] The key words are "system" and "opinions." Wesley was systematically an Arminian, and even published a magazine by that name. However, he did not believe that his salvation rested on the correctness of Arminian doctrine as many others believed. It was Wesley's firm conviction that his salvation rested upon the grace of Christ and his faith response of giving all his heart to God through Christ. Arminian doctrine, for Wesley, was a descriptive attempt to explain the far-reaching implications of the salvation experienced in Christ. It was inadequate to fully relate the deep meaning of salvation experienced in human terms. Such an attempt, however, is necessary and significant, even though it is hardly infallible. But woe unto those Arminians, or Calvinists or Papists, who equate "correct" doctrine with the foundation of salvation! As for "opinion," Wesley meant an assent to a rational proposition that has only a "probable" status of reality, rather than an actual status.[14] He would reduce most theological doctrines to the status of "opinions." He refused to think of such probabilities as being orthodox or correct. A "correct probability" is illogical! Let the pilgrim beware of taking up the false religion of orthodoxy. Let the pilgrim find the true religion which helps one to give his heart to God. When it comes to opinions, the pilgrim should think and let think![15]

Another false religion, attractive to many pilgrims, is that religion of outward forms, ceremonies, and pageantry which never takes the worshipper beyond the confines of the earthly temple. The expectation of final salvation, in this type of religion, rests upon habitual attendance of the place of worship.[16] Let the pilgrim find the true religion in which God is worshipped in Spirit and in truth, not separated from the services of the Church.

A third kind of false religion, according to Wesley, is the religion of works.[17] The quest in this religion is the finding of God's favor by performing good works. Working finally brings wages. The false assumption is that one can earn his way into heaven by laboring for salvation. The good that is done is, therefore, done for the wrong reasons - not to do good to all men, but to save one's soul, and that alone. The pilgrim must find salvation as a gift, received in faith, and then do good to all men because salvation has made him good!

A last and fatal religion of deception is, as Wesley termed it, "a religion of Atheism."[18] Atheistic religion is any religion that has a foundation other than God. Wesley, if he could visit the twentieth century, might include, in this category of false religion, secular humanism, and dialectical materialism with its opposite - capitalistic materialism. Let the pilgrim beware of fervent, ideological movements which crusade for just causes, generating spiritual heat, but lacking God as their sole foundation.

In spite of the existence of many false religions, the pilgrim may be assured of one, true religion. The foundation of this religion is God alone, the Alpha and Omega, who was in Christ, reconciling the world to himself. God is the beginning and end of this true religion. He is the first and the last, the God who fills eternity and time, the immensity of space, and the hearts of those who give him their hearts in response to his grace. More specifically -

"True religion is right tempers towards God and man. It is, in two words, gratitude and benevolence; gratitude to our Creator and supreme Benefactor, and benevolence to our fellow creatures. In other words, it is the loving God with all our heart, and our neighbour as ourselves."[19]

Our gratitude towards God produces benevolence towards neighbors. Christian benevolence means that we do no harm or ill to neighbors, but, more especially, that we be "useful" and productive of good works, always being "patterns to all of true, genuine morality. . .of justice, mercy and truth."[20] Such benevolence is fueled by the constant love of God shed abroad in the heart by the Holy Spirit, making the pilgrim humble, meek, and gentle. This constant love also makes the pilgrim perceptive of what is right and what is good. Wesley called this kind of religion "pure and undefiled religion."[21] Wesley sounded a solemn warning against "taking half of this religion for the whole." The whole is summed up in the command - "Thou shalt love the Lord. . .and thy neighbour." To take only half, love of God, is a perversion of true religion. Furthermore, there can be no actual love of neighbor without love for God. The wise pilgrim will practice true religion with Wesley's words ringing in his heart - "So shall you 'inherit the kingdom prepared for you from the beginning of the world!'"[22]

However, before the pilgrim can claim his place in that kingdom, his sojourn on earth must be marked by progress toward the restoration of the moral image of God within him. That which was lost in the first sin, must now progressively be restored. It is restorable by the work of "Him that bruises the serpent's head." Jesus Christ not only restores what was lost, delivering the pilgrim from sin, but he fills the sojourning soul with "the fulness of God."[23] This is true religion! Wesley then exhorted,

"Beware of taking anything else, or any thing less than this, for religion! Not *any thing else*: Do not imagine an outward form, a round of duties, both in public and private, is religion! Do not suppose that honesty, justice, and whatever is called *morality*. . .is religion. And least of all dream that orthodoxy, right opinion, (vulgarly called faith) is religion. Of all religious dreams, this is the vainest; which takes hay and stubble for gold tried in the fire! Take no less for his religion, than the 'faith that worketh by love;' all inward and outward holiness. Be not content with any religion which does not imply the destruction of all the works of the devil; that is, of all sin. . .this is the work. . .which the Son of God was manifested to destroy in this present life. He is able, he is willing, to destroy it now, in all that believe in him. . .Do not distrust his power, or his love! Put his promise to the proof!"[24]

THE PILGRIM'S WAY HOME

The pilgrimage from Paradise Lost to Paradise Improved is difficult and somewhat complicated. There are no short-cuts, nor broad highways with smooth passage assured. Wesley's understanding of the pilgrim's way was definitely influenced by John Bunyan's *PILGRIM'S PROGRESS*. Wesley wanted all his Methodists to read Bunyan's famous work, but that was not practical. Consequently, he abridged the work, reducing it to but 49 pages.[25] The abridgement was widely circulated among the Methodist societies. Wesley often borrowed words, phrases, and imagery from it. In a letter to Elizabeth Padbury (August 1, 1783), Wesley alluded to Bunyan's "doldrums" - "I apprehend when you find those seasons of dryness and heaviness, this is serving either to the agency of the devil, who can easily cloud our mind when God permits, or to the corruptible body pressing down the soul. But believe and conquer all."[26] As in Bunyan's work, Wesley recognized that the pilgrim must take certain paths, following route directions, charting a course through unfamiliar country-sides, avoiding dangers hidden to the naked eye, and enjoying a sense of providence along the way. The pilgrim need not stumble from point to point on the Path to Perfection. No one needs to move through the pilgrim life as a bungler. Indeed, each pilgrim may move with a great degree of effectiveness, *if* the pilgrim will give strict attention to the divine map of salvation. Follow the map of Scripture, Wesley asserted, and it will bring you to heaven -

"I am a creature of a day, passing through life as an arrow through the air. I am a spirit come from God, and returning to God: Just hovering over the great gulf; till, a few moments hence, I am no more seen; I drop into an un-

changeable eternity! I want to know one thing, - the way to heaven; how to
land safe on that happy shore. God himself has condescended to teach the
way: For this very end he came from heaven. He hath written it down in a
book. O give me that book! At any price, give me the book of God!"[27]

The map of Scripture contains important places, connected by a
road, which the pilgrim must visit. The road is straight and narrow,
and it begins at the place of birth. But, for Wesley, the place of
birth is also the place of the Atonement. The two overlap - to be
born is to be covered by the benefits of Christ's death. The pilgrimage to heaven begins at birth and at the Cross. Starkey is correct when he observes that Wesley taught -

"All men are sons of Christ as well as sons of Adam in so far as all fallen men
participate in the results of the Atonement. All men are debtors to Christ in
that their original guilt is absolved and their free will and conscience is restored by the atoning work of the second Adam. This gift of Christ is bestowed as the presence of the Holy Spirit granted at birth."[28]

In the Atonement, Wesley believed, fallen man receives more
through restoration than what he lost.[29] Moreover, the atoning
Christ becomes "a second general Parent and representative of the
whole human race."[30] As such, Jesus Christ imparts particular
benefits of his death to all men. In his commentary on St. John I:9,
Wesley spoke of conscience as being one of these benefits - "9.
Who lighteth every man - By what is vulgarly termed natural conscience, pointing out at least the general lines of good and evil, and
this light, if men did not hinder, would shine more and more to the
perfect day."[31] Wesley identified this gift of conscience, granted at
birth, as a supernatural gift of God.[32] The operation of the Holy
Spirit upon the conscience, moving it to either commend or condemn, creates "preventing grace."[33] But the Holy Spirit simultaneously gives other gifts too. A degree of liberty and a free will are
given by the Spirit at birth.[34] Collectively, under the inspiration
and guidance of the Spirit, the conscience, liberty, and the free will
constitute what Wesley termed "preventing grace." Preventing
grace is the beginning of the pilgrimage toward eternal salvation,

according to Wesley. In some circumstances it actually means salvation -

"No man living is without some preventing grace, and every degree of grace is a degree of life. . .therefore no infant ever was, or ever will be, sent to hell for the guilt of Adam's sin, seeing it is cancelled by the righteousness of Christ, as soon as they are sent into the world."[35]

As children grow in years, the Holy Spirit teaches them to "know themselves" and to "feel the burden of sin," creating within them a "desire to flee from the wrath to come."[36] Wesley spoke of preventing grace as "the first dawn of light. . .(with) some degree of salvation; the beginning of deliverance. . .there is no man, unless he has quenched the Spirit that is wholly void of the grace of God. . . conscience is more properly termed preventing grace."[37]

The goal of preventing grace is faith as a spirit-inspired response to God by man. Man's cooperation with the Holy Spirit is essential. The type of faith related to preventing grace was termed "preliminary faith" by Wesley. It should be noted here that Wesley distinguished between three types of faith - preliminary faith, justifying faith, and sanctifying faith. The first of these is the most basic type of faith, the starting point of faith. Preliminary faith is preparatory for justifying faith. As preliminary faith is related to preventing grace, justifying faith is related to convincing grace. But, justifying faith is also preparatory for sanctifying faith, the highest degree of faith. Sanctifying faith is related to sanctifying grace. The Christian pilgrim must grow in faith and grace, from the lowest to the highest, for "without faith it is impossible to please God."[38] The nature of preliminary faith, as Wesley understood it, as the spirit-inspired response of man under the influence of preventing grace, forms an unusual application of empiricism. As the human body possesses empirical senses - sight, hearing, smelling, tasting, and touching - so does the soul have spiritual eyes to see the invisible realities of God, spiritual ears to hear the still small voice of God, spiritual nostrils to detect the aroma of the divine presence, a spiritual palate to taste the sweets of eternal love, and a spiritual nervous system by which the soul knows that it has been touched by its Creator and Saviour.[39] The Atonement unlocks these spiritual senses, and the Holy Spirit brings sights, sounds, aromas, tastes, and feelings to the pilgrim's soul. Preliminary faith, then, is one's spiritual response to these empirical stimulations. To see with the eye of the soul what is invisible to the eye of the body is a facet of preliminary faith. To hear the voice of God, inaudible to the ear of the body, is a facet of preliminary faith. To smell the fragrance of the Spirit's presence, apart from the functioning of the nose of the body, is another facet of preliminary faith. To taste the good things of God, bypassing the palate of the body, is equally a facet of preliminary faith. And, most importantly, "feeling" the many impulses of God's loving grace towards the soul, as an element of preliminary faith, far surpasses all corporeal feelings - a kind of "Feel Divine, all feels excelling!" This principle of soul-empiricism undergirds the other types of Wesleyan faith, both justifying and sanctifying faith. It must be kept in mind when considering the upper reaches of the pilgrim's pathway to heaven.

So, the pilgrimage begins on the divine map at birth and the Atonement. The beginning is positive and dynamic, but a successful end is not guaranteed. Such an end is conditional, and many factors are involved.

The pilgrim road leading upward from the starting point of birth and the Atonement may well be called the *Via Gratiae*, the Way of Grace. Indeed, it is a way of grace from its beginning to its *telos* in eternity. Along its way the pilgrim must experience many blessings, trials, and temptations. But along the way a provident God intersperses spiritual places, as cities of vital grace, where pilgrims experience extraordinary workings of God's love, enabling them to move upward, closer to the prize of their high calling in Christ Jesus.[40]

From birth onward, the true pilgrim moves upward along the *Via Gratiae* of preventing grace, the Holy Spirit providing inward stimulations to the soul, in order to create preliminary faith. When faith is born, and the pilgrim nears the twin cities of Justification and Regeneration, he is allowed to enter only by the single gate marked *Sola Fide*, by "Faith Alone." His good works do not entitle him to enter into justification or regeneration. Entrance is gained only through the evidence of faith - faith as the creative gift of the Spirit, and as an act of total commitment by the pilgrim of himself to God through Christ. Preliminary faith has matured, becoming what Wesley termed "justifying faith."[41] It must be observed, however, that the metamorphose from preliminary faith to justifying faith takes place in Wesley's scheme before the pilgrim gets to the mighty gate. In the outlying region through which the *Via Gratiae* leads the pilgrim, there is a sort of force-field generated by the Holy Spirit, which Wesley called "convincing grace."[42] Convincing grace, as the inward working of the Spirit in the pilgrim, has three impulses: (1) a deep conviction of personal sin and the need of a saviour;[43] (2) a growing desire to please God;[44] and (3) a burgeoning spirit of repentance.[45] When the pilgrim yields to these Spirit-inspired impulses, his faith increases to the quality of justifying faith. He may now enter the gate into the realities of justification and regeneration.

While preventing grace, by virtue of the Atonement, grants a temporary justification to all persons until the first "actual" sin, entering into the city of justification provides the pilgrim with a pardon for "actual" sins committed since birth,[46] and as such it has an enduring nature, but not an indestructible nature. The meaning of justification, according to Wesley, resides in the pilgrim being forgiven and accepted by God -

> "All believers are forgiven and accepted, not for the sake of anything in them, or of anything that ever was, that is, or ever can be done by them, but wholly and solely for the sake of what Christ hath done and suffered for them. . . 'Not for works of righteousness which we have done, but of his own mercy he saved us. . . - not of works, lest any man should boast.'. . .And this is the doctrine which I have constantly believed and taught, for near eight and twenty years. . .extracted from the *HOMILIES* of our Church."[47]

Wesley's mature understanding of justification was explicitly Anglican. Writing to the Bishop of Exeter, in 1751, he defended the traditional nature of his understanding of justification - "I learned it from the Eleventh and Twelfth Articles and from the Homilies of our Church."[48]   One affirmation from the Eleventh Article declares, ". . . We are justified by faith only...a most wholesome Doctrine, and very full of comfort, as more largely is expressed in the Homily of Justification."[49] The Twelfth Article declares, ". . . Good works, which are the fruits of Faith, and follow after Justification, cannot put away our sins, and endure the severity of God's judgement; yet are they pleasing and acceptable to God in Christ, and do spring out necessarily of a true and lively Faith."[50]

What does justification mean? Wesley's answer includes several dimensions: (1) It is a divine activity which God offers man through his son;[51] (2) It establishes an objective, relational change whereby persons of faith are accepted into God's favor;[52] (3) It means the pardon of sins;[53] and (4) It often produces "a sense of pardon" as "a distinct, explicit assurance that. . .sins are forgiven."[54] This last dimension needs examination. Shortly after his Aldersgate experience, Wesley began to preach the absolute necessity of having the direct assurance of sins forgiven in justification. Without such assurance, he argued, one is not justified but still under the curse of sin. Late in life, Wesley rejected this foolish view -

"When fifty years ago my brother Charles and I, in the simplicity of our hearts, told the good people of England, that unless they knew their sins forgiven, they were under the wrath and curse of God, I marvel, Melville, they did not stone us! The Methodists, I hope, know better now. We preach assurance as we always did, as a common privilege of the children of God; but we do not enforce it under the pain of damnation, denounced on all who enjoy it not."[55]

Writing in 1745, Wesley explained his revised position, which, incidentally, was thoroughly Anglican:

"I allow (1.) That there is such an explicit assurance. (2.) That it is the common privilege of real Christians. (3.) That it is the proper Christian faith, which 'purifieth the heart,' and 'overcometh the world.'

But I cannot allow, that justifying faith is such an assurance, or necessarily connected therewith. Because, if justifying faith necessarily implies such an explicit assurance of pardon, then, every one who has it not, and every one so long as he has it not, is under the wrath and under the curse of God. But this is a supposition contrary to Scripture, as well as to experience. . .Again: The assertion, 'that justifying faith is a sense of pardon,' is contrary to reason; It is flatly absurd. For how can a sense of our receiving pardon be the condition of our receiving it?"[56]

Wesley was accused by some of having abandoned "a clear belief of justification by faith alone." He retorted, "I say, A man may be saved, who is not clear in his judgement concerning it."[57] He remembered the position of Count Zinzendorf at this point - That the justified pilgrim may not "know he is justified, till long after; For the assurance of it is distinct from justification itself."[58] Nevertheless, Wesley insisted that the assurance of justification is "the common privilege of the children of God," and that it will come, if not at the moment of justification, at some point of the earthly pilgrimage after justification.

For Wesley, justification is more than an event. Once it has taken place as an objective fact, it creates a "state" in which the believer lives, moves, and has his being. As such, it is an "inexpressibly great and glorious" state.[59] In the Annual Conference of 1745, Wesley was asked, "Do we ordinarily represent a justified state so great and happy as it is?" He answered, "Perhaps not. A believer, walking in the light, is inexpressibly great and happy."[60] The reason for this blessed state, he reasoned, lies not in the fact of pardon and reconciliation with God, but with the impartation of the Holy Spirit at the very moment of justification.[61] The Spirit continues to proffer the state of justification as long as the pilgrim continues to live by faith, obeying rather than quenching the Spirit's promptings and inspirations.

According to Wesley, the pilgrim must be aware of the fact that in addition to the justification at the beginning of the Christian life, as one travels further up the *Via Gratiae*; there are other degrees of justification. In 1768, in debate, Wesley asserted his allegiance to a traditional Anglican view of justification - "There are innumerable degrees both in a justified and sanctified state, more than it is possible for us exactly to define."[62] While some churchmen interpreted the Articles and Homilies of the Church of England to teach a doctrine of a "two-fold justification," - one at the beginning of the Christian life and the other at the end - Wesley interpreted the Articles and Homilies to teach that there is but one justification, spanning the entire Christian life from beginning to end.[63] In debate with Hervey, Wesley responded to the assertion that "justification is complete the first moment we believe, and is incapable of augmentation" - Wesley said, "Not so: There may be as many degrees in the favour as in the image of God (justification and sanctification)."[64] Justification for Wesley, then, was one progressive work of grace, with various degrees, from the beginning of the Christian life to its end at death. Lindstrom traces the development of Wesley's position accurately. In 1738, he contends, Wesley tended to depreciate any concept of a subsequent justification following evangelical conversion. This, of course, meant a denial of the doctrine of final justification. However, John Wesley became embroiled in controversy with the Antinomians who argued that since justification is once and for all, and imperishable, God is bound to accept the justified believer no matter how unrighteously he lives. In opposition to these Antinomians, Wesley began to speak as an Anglican, referring to "our acquittal at the last day."[65] Then he used the argument of degrees of justification as his chief weapon against these opponents.[66] He gave final justification the status of "the culmination of the order of salvation."[67] In so doing, he reconciled St. Paul with St. James - faith and works. Paul spoke of justification by faith alone as the beginning of the Christian life, and James spoke of justification at the point of judgment.[68] Therefore, the Christian pilgrim must enter into the city of justification and its encompassing state, being assured by the divine promise that its realities will abide with him as he faithfully continues to climb up the *Via Gratiae* to higher spiritual ground. Between the first degree of justification and the last, there are innumerable instances of justification.

When the pilgrim enters the city of justification, he also enters the twin city of regeneration. These two cities, side by side, and inextricably linked by convincing grace, represent the two great branches of Wesleyan salvation, both possessing progressive elements after their initial beginnings. The first branch (justification) relates to God's objective act of granting pardon and acceptance to the pilgrim,[70] while the second branch (regeneration) relates to God's special act within the soul of the pilgrim, bringing an actual renewal of his fallen nature.[71] Wesley understood regeneration as having two dimensions: (1) as a single act of God in which a "new birth" occurs, being the first radical change wrought by the Holy Spirit within the soul;[72] and (2) as a continuing, progressive work of the Spirit within the soul, designed to bring the full restoration of the moral image of God to man.[73] He called the first the "new birth," and the other "sanctification." When the pilgrim enters the twin cities by the merits of Christ received in faith, he is justified, born anew, and sanctification begins. In the new birth, the spiritual senses of his soul are fully awakened so that he may see, hear, smell, taste, and feel the numerous tokens of convincing grace.[74] The Holy Spirit brings the spiritual experience of "feeling" grace received. Wesley frequently used the term "feel." In relation to the new birth, the pilgrim "feels" that he is truly a child of God, and "feels" the love of God shed abroad in his heart.[75] It should be observed that the place of "feeling" was indigenous to traditional Anglicanism. In his famous *A FURTHER APPEAL TO MEN OF REASON AND RELIGION*, Wesley quoted feeling-passages from the standard Homilies on Rogation Week, Faith, and Scripture.[76] It is, he held, quite appropriate to feel these tokens when the new birth occurs. However, the new birth is only the beginning of being made actually righteous. He is born of the Spirit, but there is more to life than birth. In the treatise *THE PRINCIPLES OF A METHODIST*, written in 1740, Wesley treated the incomplete nature of the new birth, calling it "imperfect." He meant "imperfect" to bear the grammatical meaning, that is, a thing imperfect is in force but not completed (perfected). The text reads -

"The moment a man comes to Christ (by faith) he is justified, and born again; that is, he is born again in the imperfect sense, for there are two, if not more, degrees of regeneration, and he has power over all the stirrings and motions of sin, but not a total freedom over them. Therefore he hath not yet, in the full and proper sense, a new and clean heart. But being exposed to various temptations he may and will fall from this condition if he doth not attend to a more excellent gift. . .Sanctification (is) the last and highest state of perfection in this life. For then are the faithful born again in the full and perfect sense. Then is there given unto them a new and clean heart; and the struggle between the old and the new man is over."[77]

As Wesley held to "degrees of Justification," he also held a doctrine of "degrees of regeneration" - In this case, the new birth and sanctification. It should be noted that sanctification, when completed, according to Wesley, is also the new birth, but in the "full and perfect sense." Wesley reminded objectors to this position that "the dealings of God with man are infinitely varied, and cannot be confined to any general rule: Both in justification and sanctification He often acts in a manner we cannot account for."[78] The gradual, progressive work of sanctification, nevertheless, has a general course to follow. It seems to be a universal course according to the pilgrims of all ages who kept the faith. Wesley described this course -

"From the time of our being born again, the gradual work of sanctification takes place. We are enabled by the Spirit to mortify the deeds of the body of our evil nature and as we are more and more dead to sin, we are more and more alive to God. We go on from grace to grace, while we are careful to abstain from all appearance of evil and are zealous of good works, as we have opportunity, doing good to all men; while we walk in all His ordinances blameless, therein worshipping Him in spirit and in truth; while we take up our cross, and deny ourselves every pleasure that does not lead us to God."[79]

Moreover, Wesley recognized an instantaneous side to sanctification. The gradual usually precedes the instantaneous as preparatory.[80] Two important benefits are imparted with the instantaneous: (1) the power and root of sin are then destroyed within the pilgrim; and (2) the moral image of god is fully and perfectly restored to the pilgrim.[81] As a result of this experience, often termed "entire sanctification" by Wesleyan disciples, perfect love (agape) possesses the pilgrim, affecting his whole nature. Perfect love is the fulfilling of the Great Commandment. It is love filling the heart, love filling up the entire capacity of the soul, love rejoicing evermore, love praying without ceasing, and love giving thanks in all things.[82] Entire sanctification, or perfect love, can be attained by the devout pilgrim in this present life, long before death. However, in case it is not attained before death, it is always imparted as a gift at death. Wesley stated the case explicitly in his remarkable *BRIEF THOUGHTS ON CHRISTIAN PERFECTION* -

> "I believe this perfection is always wrought in the soul by a simple act of faith; consequently, in an instant. But I believe a gradual work, both preceding and following that instant. . .As to the time. I believe this instant generally is the instant of death, the moment before the soul leaves the body. But I believe it may be ten, twenty, or forty years before. . .I believe it is usually many years after justification, but that it may be within five years or five months after it. I know no conclusive argument to the contrary."[83]

The pilgrim does not remain for long in the twin cities, but passes through them, not leaving by the gate he entered. Instead, he takes the *Via Gratiae* upward, progressing in the state of justification and sanctification, not looking back nor downward, but always upward toward the prize before him. Little does he realize what lies before him, but he is confident that he who has begun the good work within him will continue it until the day he meets Christ the Prize.

THE PILGRIM'S LOT UNTIL HE GETS HOME

> "O Thou, to whose all-searching sight
> The darkness shineth as the light,
> Search, prove my heart, it pants for Thee;
> O burst these bonds, and set it free.
>
> Wash out its stains, refine its dross,
> Nail my affections to the cross;

Hallow each thought; let all within
Be clean, as Thou, my lord, art clean.

If in this darksome wild I stray,
Be Thou my light, be Thou my way:
No foes, no violence I fear,
No fraud, while Thou, my God, art near.

When rising floods my soul o'erflow,
When sinks my heart in waves of woe,
Jesus, Thy timely aid impart,
And raise my head, and cheer my heart.

Saviour, where'er Thy steps I see,
Dauntless, untired, I follow Thee;
O let Thy hand support me still,
And lead me to Thy holy hill.

If rough and thorny be the way,
My strength proportion to my day;
Till toil, and grief, and pain shall cease,
Where all is calm, and joy, and peace."84
                    - Gerhard Tersteegen, Translated by John Wesley

The Christian *Viator*, having put justified and regenerated feet upon the *Via Gratiae*, may expect the immediate temptations of Satan. The pilgrim surely follows his Lord in this experience. The pattern is the same. In his commentary on Matthew IV: 1-11, Wesley rehearsed how Jesus, following his baptism and anointing by the Holy Spirit, was tempted by the devil after Jesus fasted for forty days and nights. Wesley observed that the fasting brought "more abundant spiritual strength from God." Following this, Jesus was tempted.[85] Speaking to Christian pilgrims, Wesley exhorted, "Let us expect the sharpest temptations."[86] While Wesley reminded his Methodist pilgrims that Jesus never enjoined "either fasting, alms-deeds, or prayer,"[87] he clearly gave an example of how fasting and prayer bring an abundant spiritual strength with which to combat temptations. Consequently, the Christian pilgrim should proceed on the upward way while practicing both fasting and prayer.

Wesley's understanding of fasting was rooted in Sermon XVI of the Homilies of the Church of England. In that Homily, the nature of fasting was carefully explained and encouraged. Fasting is a "good work" which the Christian should practice, not because it brings grace, but because grace brings "good works."[88] Moreover, according to the Homily, there are two kinds of fasting - one outward for the body, and the other inward for the heart and mind. The outward requires abstinence from meat, drink, all "natural food," and "delicious pleasures;" and the inward requires abstinence from all thoughts that do not have God as their referent.[89]

Wesley, in his series of sermons from the Sermon on the Mount, spelled out the various dimensions of fasting for the Methodist pilgrim. Within his sermon, Wesley quoted significantly from the Homily on fasting, affirming the correctness of its line of reasoning.[90] But he exceeded the treatment of the Homily in his explanation of this discipline. Wesley thought the pilgrim should know the advantages of fasting before engaging in its regular practice. His sermon treats the basics in such a way that one gets the impression that his congregation knew next to nothing about the practice. For instance, the preacher introduces the subject in the context of Satan's devices, especially the device of separating inward from outward religion.[91] Many pilgrims have been deceived by this device in reference to fasting. Obviously, Wesley saw the outward and inward dimensions of fasting, as taught in the Homily, as inseparable. If they are separated, fasting is a worthless waste of time, and Satan rejoices.

According to Wesley, the word "to fast" simply means "to not eat, to abstain from food."[92] However, like many things, Wesley saw "degrees or measures of fasting."[93] There are degrees of length - from forty days and nights to the most common scriptural length of one day, "from morning till evening."[94] In the Primitive Church, Wesley observed, there was a half-day fast known as the *Semijejunia*.[95] Tertullian reported that the half-day fasts were kept by the Christians of his day every Wednesday and Friday throughout the year. Those keeping the half-day fast took no food until three o'clock in the afternoon, after the close of the afternoon public service. Wesley acknowledged another degree of fasting, involving quantity of food allowable in the fast. Under some conditions, complete fasting may not be wise. Consequently, Wesley insisted, the Church has always allowed a partial fasting, called *abstinence*. Sickness and physical weakness are valid reasons for engaging in this lesser fasting.[96] It should be noted that by "abstinence" Wesley did not mean total abstinence, but, rather, "eating little; the abstaining in part; the taking a smaller quantity of food than usual."[97] Another degree of fasting for Wesley involved the quality of food. Wesley referred to this degree as the "lowest kind of fasting." It means abstaining from "pleasant food," such as meat and fine wine during the Lenten season.[98] As in the Old Testament Church there were regular seasons of fasting, so the early Christian Church observed stated fasts, both annual and weekly. Fasting, therefore, has a long and illustrious history. Every new pilgrim should practice it, as did millions of pilgrims before him. More especially, the pilgrim who desires "to walk humbly and closely with God, will find frequent occasion for private seasons. . . of fasting."[99]

Wesley believed that the justified and regenerated pilgrim has a sensitive memory of his former life, how he once sinned "by excess of food," by lack of temperance, and by indulgence in sensual appetites.[100] Such a history of sinning, Wesley reasoned, impairs physical health and mental (soul) health. The wise pilgrim, with this background, will practice fasting on a regular basis "to remove, therefore, the effect" by removing "the cause." He will also "keep a distance from all excess...(being) temperate in all things."[101] Wesley also allowed for pilgrims to practice fasting as a "holy revenge upon themselves, for their past folly and ingratitude, in turning the things which should have been for their health into an occasion of falling."[102] However, a greater reason for fasting involves its special relationship to prayer. Wesley held that fasting is a definite help to prayer, "especially when we set apart larger portions of time for private prayer." When united this way in the piety of earnest pilgrims, many of them have experienced the transcending of the soul above "the things of earth," a "third heaven" type of experience.[103] The union of the two disciplines also brings the following Wesleyan advantages: a "seriousness of spirit, earnestness, sensibility and tenderness of conscience, deadness to the world, and consequently the love of God, and every holy and heavenly affection."[104]

The pilgrim should remember that fasting and prayer, in the Bible, often turned away the impending wrath of God, as well as being a means of "obtaining whatever blessings we stand in need of."[105] Then too, the Bible indicates that the Apostles "always joined fasting with prayer when they desired the blessing of God on any important undertaking."[106]

The Christian pilgrim, climbing the upward *Via Gratiae*, can only make progress by the sincere practice of fasting and prayer. He must never allow pride to set in, nor the idea that fasting brings a special merit with God.[107] Since the body can be "afflicted too much, so as to be unfit for the works of our calling," the pilgrim must fast wisely in order to preserve good health.[108]

It will be remembered that the Homily on Fasting spoke of fasting of two kinds: for body and for soul. So far, this discussion of Wesley's understanding has treated fasting that is related to the body. His sermon on fasting also treats fasting and the soul. The whole meaning of this kind of fasting is best summarized as follows -

"Let us take care to afflict our souls as well as our bodies. Let every season, either of public or private fasting, be a season of exercising all those holy affections which are implied in a broken and contrite heart. Let it be a season of devout mourning, of godly sorrow for sin; such a sorrow as that of the Corinthians, concerning which the Apostle saith, 'I rejoice, not that you were made sorry, but that ye sorrowed to repentance. . .' - the sorrow which is according to God, which is a precious gift of his Spirit, lifting the soul to God from whom it flows."[108]

Martin Luther's contention, in his Ninety-five Theses, of the Christian life as a lifetime of repentance, undergirded Wesley's theology of fasting. He argued, In fasting "let our sorrowing after a

godly sort work in us the same inward and outward repentance. . .
Let it work in us the same carefulness to be found in him, without
spot and blameless."[109] The Christian pilgrim, therefore, has many
good reasons for fasting and praying. They are a vital part of his
lot!

The place of prayer in the pilgrimage toward the new creation
needs specific attention at this point. Fasting is the spiritual context or atmosphere for Christian prayer. Wesley used the Lord's
Prayer and its accompanying injunctions (Matthew VI, 6-15) as the
bases for instructing the pilgrims in the piety of prayer.[110] Pilgrims
are to pray in private, then God will reward them. Prayers are not
to be repetitious, but carefully thought out and worded to say what
one means and to mean what one says. All prayers should be uttered "in the language of the heart." Do not pray "to inform God of
our wants," for he is omniscient and knows all our needs before we
know them, but pray in order to accept God's grace in confronting
our needs. When the pilgrim prays, he should follow the pattern of
the perfect prayer - the prayer that incorporates all the foregoing
injunctions - The Lord's Prayer. Since portions of the Lord's
Prayer have already been treated in this work, and others remain to
be treated in subsequent chapters, a treatment of it here is not
needed. Let it be sufficient to note that the pilgrim, in praying, is
to recite this perfect prayer, and he is to frame his own prayers according to its pattern.

Wesley was appalled that so many of his Methodist pilgrims did
not pray. To Miss Bishop, for instance, he wrote, "My Dear Sister;
You look inward too much, and upward too little."[111] There were
many persons like Miss Bishop in the Methodist societies. So
Wesley provided numerous volumes on prayer for his pilgrims. In
his CHRISTIAN LIBRARY, he included the famous work on
prayer by Dr. Palmer, *Prayers For Families*.[112] He also wrote his
own manuals of prayer, such as *A Collection of Forms of Prayers for
Every Day in the Week*,[113] and *Prayers for Children*.[114] One such
prayer treats the young child as a pilgrim on the *Via Gratiae* -

"I bless thee for my creation, preservation, and all the blessings of this life; but above all, for thy great love in the redemption of the world by our Lord Jesus Christ. I bless thee for preserving me in the night past, and bringing me safe to the beginning of a new day. Defend me with the same with thy mighty power, and grant that this day I fall into no sin, neither run into any kind of danger; but let all my doings be so ordered by thy governance, that I may do always that which is righteous in thy sight, through Jesus Christ my Redeemer. Grant me such grace, that I may be able to withstand the temptations of the world, the flesh, and the devil, and with a pure heart and mind to follow the steps of my gracious Redeemer. Keep me, I beseech thee, O Lord, from all things hurtful to my soul or body, and grant me thy pardon and peace, that, being cleansed from all my sins, I may serve thee with a quiet mind, bring forth plenteously the fruit of good works, and continue in the same unto my life's end, through Jesus Christ, my Saviour and Redeemer. Amen.
'Our Father...etc.'[115]

The pilgrim's lot, therefore, means a constant engagement of fasting and prayer. The pilgrim's life is not a dream, nor a phantasy, but a battle. The pilgrim must realize that when Satan fights for his kingdom, "the best method to be used in this exegence is fasting and prayer."[116]

From beginning to end, the pilgrim's lot on the *Via Gratiae* is a spiritual battle with Satan. Such a theme is overwhelmingly present in all Wesley's writings from Oxford to his last days. This battle is extensive. On one side there is the pilgrim, who is not alone but part of an army led by Jesus Christ. On the other side are many humans, who are not pilgrims, led by Satan. Both armies have active generals, angel participants, and human personnel. The battle has been going on since the beginning of human history, but one day it will end when one of the generals - riding on a white horse, called Faithful and True, with eyes like a flame of fire, wearing many diadems upon his head, clothed in vestments dipped in blood, also called the Word of God, and heralded as the KING OF KINGS AND LORD OF LORDS - will lead his hosts, all on white horses, to complete victory over the army of Satan.[117] But, Wesley held, that final battle is not yet! Nevertheless, daily battles are unavoidable, being instigated by Satan, but Christ is always present with the pilgrim to give the victory. Satan's attacks are not always obvious to unwary pilgrims. He frequently disguises himself as an angel of light and deceives them, gaining the advantage over them. Satan's devices are multitudinous, and he employs many evil angels and evil men to accomplish his ends. The Christian pilgrim must know these tactics, and he must also know Christ's power to counterattack Satan's devices.

In his sermon, *SATAN'S DEVICES*, Wesley warned his pilgrim followers that the 'subtle god of this world labours to destroy the children of God - or at least to torment whom he cannot destroy, to perplex and hinder them in running the race which is set before them."[118] Satan's devices are numerous, like the stars of the heavens and the sands of the sea-shore. It is not enough to warn that they are many. The pilgrim must know precisely what these devices are and how they are used against him.

The first "grand device of Satan" involves his attack upon the "first work of God in the soul." God's first work refers to justification by faith which brings great joy to the soul. Satan endeavors to dampen this joy by reminding each pilgrim of his own vileness, sinfulness, and unworthiness so that he begins to "think lightly of the present gifts of God," while longing for greater gifts yet to be received. Satan shoots the fiery dart of accusation - "God is holy: You are unholy...How is it possible that you, unclean as you are, should be in a state of acceptance with God?" Another dart immediately follows: "You see indeed the mark, the prize of your high calling; but do you not see it is afar off?" Still another is launched: "How can you presume then to think that all your sins are already blotted out? How can this be, until you are brought nearer to God, until you bear more resemblance to him?" If this device is effective, the pilgrim thinks himself back at the prejustification state. Satan then has gained a victory.[119] To counter this device, Wesley advised, let the pilgrim examine himself to see if he possesses the fruits of justification - possession of the mind of Christ, and a soul that is dead to sin and alive to righteousness.[120] If he does, then Satan's darts are diverted with the shield of faith.

When sickness and pain overtake the pilgrim, Satan usually begins his deadly assault upon the soul. On this occasion, Wesley observed, 'he will press this with all his might. . .You are not holy; you know it well; you know that holiness is the full image of God; and how far is this above, out of your sight? You cannot attain unto it. Therefore, all your labour has been in vain."[121] The Satanic conclusion is bitter to the pilgrim - "You are yet in your sins, and must therefore perish at the last."[122] But, exhorted Wesley, the pilgrim must keep the eye of the soul fixed steadily upon Christ, then Satan's assault will be emptied of its force. He will no more be able to take the pilgrim's peace than his joy.[123]

Satan's third device involves the pilgrim's righteousness received at justification. He accomplishes the diminishing of man's righteousness by first dampening his joy, as observed earlier. Joy, from being justified, "is a precious means of promoting every holy temper; a choice instrument of God, whereby he carries on much of his work in a believing soul." Consequently, should he succeed in dampening the pilgrim's joy, he will succeed in diminishing his righteousness also.[124] There are two dimensions to this righteousness (holiness) - one inward and the other outward. The inward relates to the promotion of every "holy temper" and the moral image of God restored within the pilgrim's soul. The outward relates to the works of the pilgrim's hands "to go on in the work of faith, and in the labour of love."[125] When Satan "shakes our joy," Wesley noted, "he hinders our holiness also." Therefore, "lift up the hands that hang down, and confirm the feeble knees!"

Another clever device, used effectively by Satan, involves the shaking of the pilgrim's peace by instilling doubts and fears within the mind. If they take root and grow there, as choking weeds, they weaken and destroy the pilgrim's faith.[126] As long as faith is strong, doubts and fears cannot take root. Hence the way of avoiding this device of Satan is to grow in faith, not casting away one's confidence in Christ.[127]

The pilgrim may slip unwares into another device of the devil, unless, of course, he takes due caution - paying too much thought for tomorrow, "so as to neglect the improvement of today."[128]

While this device represents a temptation to count one's chickens before they hatch in the material realm, it has a more important application in the spiritual realm. Wesley argued, "We may so expect perfect love, as not to use that which is already shed abroad in our hearts...(some) have greatly suffered thereby. They were so taken up with what they were to receive hereafter, as utterly to neglect what they had already received." Expecting to receive five talents more, these pilgrims "buried their own talent in the earth."[129] As a result, Satan won that battle too. Wesley's exhortation must stand as one of the most eloquent appeals of all times to pilgrims tempted with the radical preoccupation of tomorrowitis -

"Redeem the time. Improve the present moment. Buy up every opportunity of growing in grace, or of doing good. Let not the thought of receiving more grace tomorrow, make you negligent today. You have one talent now: If you expect five more, so much the rather improve that you have. And the more you expect to receive hereafter, the more labour for God now. . .Now approve yourself a faithful steward of the present grace of God. Whatever may be tomorrow, give all diligence today, to 'add to your faith courage, temperance, patience, brotherly kindness, and the fear of God, 'till you attain that pure and perfect love!"[130]

These are the standard devices of Satan, used systematically against the Christian pilgrim. Because they are so widely used, with great effectiveness, Wesley treated them in one sermon. However, they represent only a few of Satan's "fiery darts" in his vast arsenal. There are "innumerable" devices in addition to these. Since so little attention has been given this subject in Wesleyan studies, and since the problem was so momentous for Wesley's pilgrim's progress, a further examination is justified.

One of the most unusual devices of Satan, Wesley believed, was the imposition of "fits" or "seizures" by Satan just as a sinner was becoming a pilgrim at the gates of justification and regeneration. The victim would "drop down as dead" but after awhile revive and rejoice in salvation. Some victims would be torn with violent convulsions and be carried away.[131] This phenomenon was very common during Wesley's evangelistic meetings between January and

July of 1739. He immediately attributed it to the work of the Holy Spirit.[132] As time passed, Wesley was forced to rethink its significance. In November 1759, he distinguished between two kinds of fits: (1) those that are the legitimate work of the Holy Spirit, and (2) those that are spurious imitations caused by Satan.[133] The fits caused by the Holy Spirit, Wesley held, are not to be despised nor belittled. However, it should be observed that Wesley sometimes confused this neat distinction. For instance, in March 1743, Wesley researched the incidents of fits among his societies in the north near Newcastle. His conclusions are illuminating:

". . .all of them were persons in perfect health; and had not been subject to fits of any kind, till they were thus affected." The fits came upon them suddenly, without any warning. They were either hearing the Word being preached, or they were contemplating it. Immediately they fell down, "lost all their strength, and were seized with violent pain." Some said afterward that the pain was "as if a sword was running through them." Others spoke of the pain as a great weight being laid upon them, "as if it would squeeze them into the earth." Others were choked, "so that they could not breathe." Others, "that their hearts swelled ready to burst." Others reported that their inward parts were "tearing all to pieces." Wesley's next conclusion is surprising -

"These symptoms I can no more impute to any natural cause than to the Spirit of God. I can make no doubt but it was Satan tearing them, as they were coming to Christ. And hence proceeded those grievous cries, whereby he might design both to discredit the work of God and to affright fearful people from hearing that word whereby their souls might be saved."[134]

Wesley further referred to such fits as "being bewitched." He then gave the following assessment of fits as witchcraft -

"Why should they not call it so now? Because the infidels (intellectuals) have hooted witchcraft out of the world; and the compliasant Christians, in large numbers, have joined with them in the cry. I do not so much wonder at this - that many of these should talk like infidels. But I have sometimes been in-

clined to wonder at the pert, saucy, indecent manner wherein some of those
trample upon men far wiser than themselves; at their speaking so dogmati-
cally against what not only the whole world, heathen and Christian, believed
in past ages, but thousands, learned as well as unlearned, firmly believe at this
day."[135]

How can these two radically different views of the origin of fits
be reconciled in Wesley's thought? Wesley gives the solution in his
letter to Dr. Rutherforth on March 28, 1768. Rutherforth, one of
Wesley's critics, demanded to know why "You ascribe the same
symptoms sometimes to the one (Holy Spirit), and sometimes to
the other (Satan)." Wesley responded, "I do not: I always ascribe
these symptoms to Satan tearing them." Rutherforth asserted, "Mr.
W. sometimes denies that he considers these fits as signs of the new
birth." Wesley answered, "I always deny it, if you mean by signs
anything more than something which may accidentally attend it."
Fits, wrought by Satan, are sometimes present when one is born
anew, but the new birth does not depend upon having fits. The
new birth is the result of the inward operation of the Holy Spirit.
Fits are "outward symptoms" of Satan's attempt to hinder the new
birth from taking place.[136] It was obvious to Wesley that some
Methodist pilgrims had come to salvation inspite of Satan's device
of fits, but such an experience did not necessarily make them better
pilgrims. Nor did Wesley insist that such an experience should be
universalized. Satan attacks whom he wills, and should never be
invited to attack a seeking sinner so he may have a special experience, greater than that brought by Christ alone.

Another device of Satan, which proved to be a thorn in Wesley's
flesh because of its degenerating effect in the societies, involved
emotional extravagances -

"It is chiefly among these enormous mountains that so many have been
awakened, justified, and soon after perfected in love; but, even while they are
full of love, Satan strives to push many of them to extravagance. This appears in several instances: (1) Frequently three or four, yea, ten or twelve,
pray aloud all together. (2) Some of them, perhaps many, scream all together as loud as they possibly can. (3) Some of them use improper, yea, in-

decent, expressions in prayer. (4) Several drop down as dead; and are as stiff as a corpse; but in a while they start up, and cry, 'Glory! glory!' perhaps twenty times together. Just so do the French prophets, and very lately the Jumpers in Wales, bring the real work into contempt."[137]

There are other devices of Satan which the pilgrim will surely encounter before his journey is completed. Wesley's works abound with references and descriptions of them. An almost endless listing can be made -

- Afflicting a person by speaking inwardly to him, cursing, swearing and blaspheming, inciting that person to commit evil.[138]

- Convincing a believer that "God had told him" that he was destined for greatness, thus arousing him to a vain and proud enthusiasm.[139]

- To see that the people of a place are only half-awakened to Christ, then left alone so they will fall backwards.[140]

- To encourage drunkenness, tale-bearing, and evil speaking Methodists.[141]

- To raise up bigots in the society who will fight over opinions.[142]

- To strike the gospel preacher with hoarseness and encourage laughter in the congregation.[143]

- To stimulate pride in a pilgrim who has experienced a vision.[144]

- Convincing a believer that self-examination is not necessary.[145]

- Inspiring a Methodist society to engage in disputes.[146]

- Convincing pilgrims to leave the society because of disputes.[147]

- To sift Christian pilgrims as wheat.[148]

- To encourage believers to be satisfied with "naked faith," having no concern for joy, peace, and righteousness.[149]

- To put pilgrims in physical danger from time to time.[150]

- To encourage believers to depart from simplicity.[151]

- To inspire overly optimistic reports at annual conference time.[152]

- When Satan cannot physically hurt the pilgrim, he may afflict the pilgrim's horse.[153]

- To use believers in the disruption of a religious meeting, and thus reward Satan's strivings.[154]

- To buffet believers with a disease like epilepsy.[155]

- To drive Christians to despair.[156]

- Through subtlety perverting all good.[157]

- Bringing a separation and estrangement of brothers.[158]

- Convincing pilgrims to live the life of an Antinomian.[159]

- To encourage Christians to drift wherever the currents of the present world will take them, making "shipwreck" inevitable.[160]

- To make pilgrims subject to the evil angels.[161]

The activities of evil angels include:

The practice of cruelty against the children of men;

The inspiring of God's children to the same wickedness they possess;

The bringing of misery upon all humans;

The observation of every person to find a weakness or opportunity to gain an advantage over him;

The studying of a pilgrim's circumstances in order to find an occasion for tempting him;

The surrounding of the pilgrim's bed and path, so as to spy out all his ways and do him harm;

The transformation of themselves into seeming angels of light in order to deceive and beguile into evil;

The spreading of ignorance, like a cloud, over the human understanding;

The stealing of Christian joy by bringing in doubt the hope of immortality;

The dampening of one's love for God and neighbours;

The exciting of private and public animosities, suspicions, resentments, and quarrels;

The destruction of peace between families and nations, and the banishment of unity and concord from the face of the earth;

The embittering of the poor, miserable children of men against one another;

The hindrance of every good word and work;

The infusion of evil thoughts of every kind into the hearts of mankind;

The awakening of evil passions or tempers in the human soul;

The instilling of unbelief, atheism, ill-will, bitterness, hatred, malice, and envy within all mankind;

The inspiration of impatience, ill-nature, love of the world, inordinate affection, and foolish desires within man;

The preparation of the pilgrim for betraying God, or lying to the Holy Spirit;

The sowing of the seed within the believer to be like other men, wicked men;

The tormenting of those pilgrims who cannot be destroyed by Satan and his evil angels;

To afflict the righteous with sickness and pain;

The causing of accidents - falling horses, the overturning of carriages, etc.;

The destruction of houses by burning, falling, and storms or earthquakes;

Adding discomforts to the pilgrim's daily life;

And, bringing nightmare to sleeping believers.

"But to all these, and a thousand more, this subtle spirit can give the appearance of accidents; for fear the sufferers, if they knew the real agents, should call for help on One that is stronger than him."[162]

Indeed, for Wesley, the pilgrim's lot is not a dream but a battle. The text for his sermon *Of Evil Angels* was Ephesians VI, 12 - "We wrestle not against flesh and blood, but against principalities, against powers, against the rulers of the darkness of this world, against wicked spirits in heavenly places." At the close of this sermon, Wesley exhorted his hearers to "put on the panoply, 'the whole armour of God,' universal holiness."[163] But, the pilgrim-warrior must know more than Satan's arsenal of devices. He must know the divine arsenal of graces, empowerments, promises, gifts, and providential assurances that "if God be for us, who can be against us?"[164] To rephrase St. Paul, this is a matter of where Satan's devices abound, the divine devices much more abound!

The greatest of all divine devices is providence. The Methodist pilgrim should know its dimensions and live within its context without tempting grace. Wesley believed that there is a three-fold circle of divine providence, "above that which presides over the whole universe. . .inanimate creation. . . (and) animal creation."[165] This three-fold providence relates to the children of men, all Adam's posterity, dispersed over the face of the earth.[166] The outermost ring of providence envelops all men, whether heathens, Mahometans, Jews, or Christians. He causes his sun to rise and shine upon all. God gives them rain and fruitful seasons, pouring countless other benefits upon them. In this way he is the God of all - heathens, Mahometans, Jews, and Christians alike.[167] In this circle of providence, God is no respecter of persons. All men are accepted of him, through Jesus Christ, though they may not know Christ nor his written word and ordinances.[168] Wesley affirmed, "His love is not confined: 'The Lord is loving unto every man, and his mercy is over all his works.'"[169] The second circle of providence, moving inward, has the visible Christian Church as its concern. While this circle of providence is smaller than the first, the intensity of providence is greater. Wesley explained -

"He takes more immediate care of those that are comprised in the second, the smaller circle; which includes all that are called Christians, all that profess to believe in Christ. We may reasonably think that these, in some degree, honour him, at least more than the Heathens do: God does, likewise, in some measure, honour them, and has a nearer concern for them. By many instances it appears, that the prince of this world (Satan) has not so full power over these as over the Heathens. The God whom they even profess to serve, does, in some measure, maintain his own cause; so that the spirits of darkness do not reign so uncontrolled over them as they do over the heathen world."[170]

The third circle of divine providence, being the innermost and the smallest, extends the special care of God to "only the invisible Church of Christ."[171] While those who belong to the invisible Church of Christ also belong to the visible Church, not everyone who belongs to the visible Church is included in the invisible. Those who are of the invisible are also of the visible, and they benefit from both circles of providence. The criteria for inclusion in the innermost circle, according to Wesley, are summarized in his sermon ON DIVINE PROVIDENCE -

"Within the third, the innermost circle, are contained only the real Christians; those that worship God, not in form only, but in spirit and in truth. Herein are comprised all that love God, or a least, truly fear God and work righteousness; all in whom is the mind which was in Christ, and who walk as Christ also walked. The words of our Lord above recited peculiarly refer to these. It is to these in particular that he says, 'Even the very hairs of your head are all numbered.' He sees their souls and their bodies; he takes particular notice of all their tempers, desires, and thoughts, all their words and actions. He marks all their sufferings, inward and outward, and the source whence they arise; so that we may well say, 'Thou knowest the pains thy servants feel, Thou hear'st thy children's cry; And their best wishes to fulfil, Thy grace is ever nigh.' Nothing relative to these is too great, nothing too little, for his attention. He has his eye continually, as upon every individual person that is a member of this his family, so upon every circumstance that relates either to their souls or bodies; either to their inward or outward state; wherein either their present or eternal happiness is in any degree concerned."[172]

The Wesleyan pilgrim knows first-hand these dimensions of providence. Once he lived in the outer circle, not knowing Christ, the written Word, or divine ordinances. But the atonement of Christ benefited him anyway. He was then entered into the visible Church by baptism, taught, and nurtured until he was spiritually confirmed into the invisible Church. From providence he goes on to providence, grace abounding. By the most intense and intimate providence, the pilgrim knows the truth uttered by Cicero so long ago - *Deorum moderamine cuncta geri*: "That all things, all events in this world, are under the management of God."[173] Inspite of Satan's devices, through the providence of his innermost circle, God has made all things beautiful in his time. By "beautiful" Wesley meant "convenient" so that a thing performed by God could not be done better.[174] Consequently, all things work together for good for those in the innermost circle, for God providentially does all things through his eternal wisdom.[175]

Providentially, God is omnipresent, knowing all things firsthand. In a real sense, Wesley believed, the pilgrim lives, moves, and has his being in God. What could be more providential? No assault by Satan takes place outside divine presence and concern. When a pilgrim yields to a diabolical prompting, the tragedy is that sin was conceived and born in divine presence, never in its absence.

Another Wesleyan element of pilgrim's providence is the great work of Christ in undoing the nefarious works of Satan. He does this in numerous ways:[176]

By reconciling us to God;

By justifying us and giving peace;

By delivering us from perplexing doubts;

By rescuing us from tormenting fears;

By striking a blow at Satan's grand work of pride, making us humble ourselves in spiritual dust and ashes, because we are sinners on the path to perfection;

By striking a blow at self-will, enabling us to say in all things, "Thy will be done;"

By destroying within us the love of the world and every hurtful desire;

By saving us from seeking happiness in any creature;
By reversing Satan's turning of our hearts from the Creator to the creature.

But, providentially, Christ does not destroy the entire work of Satan in a pilgrim during this earthly life. Wesley elaborated on this theme: "He does not yet destroy bodily weakness, sickness, pain, and a thousand infirmities incident to flesh and blood." Furthermore, "He does not destroy all that weakness of understanding, which is the natural consequence of the soul's dwelling in a corruptible body." Ignorance and error are good for us in the sense that they keep us from pride, making us forever humble in this life.[177] To keep us humble and dependent upon him, Christ "leaves us encompassed with all these infirmities, particularly weakness of understanding; till the sentence takes place, 'Dust thou art, and unto dust shalt thou return.'"[178]

Another important aspect of divine providence, in Wesley's theology, concerns guardian angels. Every Christian pilgrim lives under the protective wings of good angels. In one of his hymns, John Wesley penned this stanza -

> "Angels our servants are,
> And keep in all our ways,
> And in their watchful hands they bear
> The sacred sons of grace;
> Unto that heavenly bliss
> They all our steps attend;
> And God himself our Father is
> And Jesus is our friend."[179]

Both good and evil angels hedge men about, doing their respective and assigned tasks. Such a thing, Wesley asserted, was recognized by ancient heathen writers. For instance, Hesiod, the first Greek philosopher and author of THEOGONY, said, "Millions of spiritual creatures walk the earth unseen."[180] St. Paul spoke of them as "spirits" and not as material beings. Nevertheless, angels do have bodies, but "not gross and earthly like ours, but of a finer substance; resembling fire or flame." The Psalmist intimated this when he queried, "Who maketh his angels spirits, and his ministers a flame of fire?"[181] The good angels, sent by God to minister sight unseen to pilgrims, know the hearts and thoughts of those pilgrims.[182] They also possess an inconceivable degree of wisdom. In the six thousand years of their existence, the wisdom of good angels has increased considerably. This increase is by virtue of observing the ongoing works of God - of creation, of providence, and of grace.[183] They also possess holiness and goodness, plus an astonishing strength which defies human comprehension.[184] On this last point, Wesley was explicit -

> "The angels of God have great power, in particular, over the human body; power either to cause or remove pain and diseases, either to kill or to heal. They perfectly well understand whereof we are made; they know all the springs of this curious machine (the human body), and can doubtless, by God's permission, touch any of them, so as either to stop or restore its motion."[185]

However, the angels of God have a certain amount of power over the soul as well as the body. They are commissioned by God to watch over the whole pilgrim, body and soul. Their specific commission is to fulfill the "numerous offices of protection, care and kindness."[186] Wesley believed that the angels are perfectly qualified for their "high office." What specifically do they do in ministering to the pilgrims of the *Via Gratia*?

(1) Good angels make this a world of mercy. Even evil and ungrateful persons, as long as they have a thought of God or any fear of him, are recipients of their attentive ways of mercy. But such mercy is consistently for the "heirs of salvation. . .those now 'saved by faith,' or at least seeking God in sincerity."[187]

(2) Good angels first minister to the souls of heirs by assisting in the search for truth, by removing doubts and difficulties, by throwing light upon what was previously dark and obscure, and by confirming in pilgrims "the truth that is after godliness."[188] They frequently warn of disguised evil, and they also clarify and amplify what is good, gently moving the human will to embrace the good. From time to time, Wesley held, good angels either quicken or dull

affections. They also inspire holy hope and filial fear, thus assisting pilgrims to love God more ardently.[189] They even answer the prayer of Bishop Ken,

> "O may thy angels, while I sleep,
> Around my bed their vigils keep;
> Their love angelical instil,
> Stop every avenue of ill!
> May they celestial joys rehearse,
> And thought to thought with me converse."[190]

(3) Good angels further minister to Christian pilgrims "with respect of our bodies." This ministry has thousands of facets, and no one can fully comprehend it. They often prevent persons from falling into dangers unawares. God gives these angels charge over us, to bear us up, Wesley argued. Our deliverance from evil, he continued, is not by chance nor by wisdom, but by the holy angels.[191] The angels may also be responsible for unusual cures involving diseases thought incurable. While this allows for direct angelic intervention, it also allows for angels to indirectly suggest, through an unaccountable process, a remedy to either the sick person or someone attending him.[192] Moreover, in dreams, angels are responsible for revealing cures which are unknown to physicians.[193]

(4) Good angels also minister to the heirs of salvation by delivering them from the machinations of evil men. The holy angels learn these plots by attending the beds of the wicked, beds upon which many plans are made. They further attend the paths of evil persons to detect their dark designs. Consequently, the angels of God are sometimes active at the beginning of an evil program to thwart and "blast" it. Other times, they wait until such a plan is near execution, then they move against it. The means used to confuse evil devices are numerous and beyond our finding out.[194] Several means, however, are known to pilgrims: sometimes the angels bring a personal loss of strength and courage to the plotters, turning their wisdom into foolishness; and sometimes the holy an-

gels bring the plans of wicked persons to light, a little at a time, and "show us the traps that are laid for our feet."[195]

(5) "Another grand branch of their ministry is, to counterwork evil angels; who are continually going about, not only as roaring lions, seeking whom they may devour, but, more dangerously still, as angels of light, seeking whom they may deceive."[196] The evil angels, engaged in this nefarious work, are as numerous as the stars of heaven. They are full of subtlety by reason of six thousand years of experience. "How great is their strength! Only inferior to that of the angels of God." As for the strength of men in comparison, men are as grasshoppers before them. Evil angels have an added advantage over men - they are invisible. "But the merciful Lord hath not given us up to the will of our enemies: 'His eyes,' that is, his holy angels, 'run to and fro over all the earth.' And if our eyes were opened, we should see, 'they are more that are for us, than they that are against us.'"[197] Hence the good angels, outnumbering and outmatching the evil spirits of Satan, are "able, willing, ready, to defend us." Wesley then applied the lesson to beleaguered pilgrims - "Who can hurt us while we have armies of angels, and the God of angels, on our side?"[198]

When Wesley preached his two sermons on good and evil angels, he was greeted with an air of skepticism. The Age of Enlightenment produced a type of sophistication which viewed the subject of angels - their existence and ministries - with near contempt. Latitudinarians began to hold traditional doctrines in suspension, favoring newer ones. Their next step was the rejection of the traditional. Wesley's position on angels remained completely traditional. It was inevitable that he would have to defend the existence and ministry of angels against such skepticism. He gave his apology in the sermon on good angels. One powerful objection to a doctrine of angelic activity, like Wesley's, was, that, if God is omnipotent and omnipresent, he should not need any intermediaries to accomplish his work. Wesley met this objection head on -

"But does not the Scripture teach, 'The help which is done upon earth, God doeth himself?'" Most certainly he does. And he is able to do it by his own immediate power. He has no need of using any instruments at all, either in heaven or earth. He wants not either angels or men, to fulfil the whole counsel of his will. But it is not his pleasure so to work. He never did; and we may reasonably suppose he never will. He has always wrought by such instruments as he pleases: But still it is God himself that doeth the work. Whatever help, therefore, we have, either by angels or men, is as much the work of God, as if he were to put forth his almighty arm, and work without any means at all. But he has used them from the beginning of the world: In all ages he has used the ministry both of men and angels. And hereby, especially, is seen 'the manifold wisdom of God in the Church.' Meantime the same glory redounds to him, as if he used no instruments at all."[199]

Wesley was not finished with the skeptics, and he did not want their negativism to infest the minds of Christian pilgrims. Therefore, he made a final appeal in his commentary on Romans VIII, 38-39. The text reads: "For I am persuaded, that neither death, nor life, nor angels, nor principalities, nor powers, nor things present, nor things to come, nor height, nor depth, nor any other creature, shall be able to separate us from the love of God, which is in Christ Jesus our Lord."

"*Neither death* - terrible as it is to natural men: a violent death in particular (verse 36). *Nor life* - With all the affliction and distress it can bring (verse 35); or a long, easy life; or all living men. *Nor angels* - Whether good...or bad with all their wisdom and strength. *Nor principalities, nor powers* - Not even those of the highest rank, or the most eminent power. *Nor things present* - Which may befall us during our pilgrimage; or the whole world, till it passeth away. *Nor things to come* - Which may occur either when our time on earth is past, or when time itself is at an end, as the final judgement, the general conflagration, the everlasting fire. *Nor height, nor depth* - The former sentence respected the differences of times; this, the differences of places. How many great and various things are contained in these words, we do not, need not, cannot know yet. *The height* - In St. Paul's sublime style, is put for heaven. *The depth* - For the great abyss: that is, neither the heights. I will not say of walls, mountains, seas, but, of the heaven itself, can move us; nor the abyss itself, the very thought of which might astonish the boldest creature. *Nor any creature* - Nothing beneath the Almighty; visible enemies He does not even deign to name. *Shall be able* - Either by force (verse 35); or by any legal claim (verse 33). *To separate us from the love of God in Christ* - Which will surely save, protect, deliver us who believe, in, and through, and from, them all."[200]

Wesley's version of the progress of the Christian pilgrim is quite dynamic.   The pilgrim's lot is one of grace and providence abounding, the devices of Satan continuing but not succeeding unless the pilgrim fails to faithfully appropriate the divine devices of grace and providence. The pilgrimage leads through this world and time, taking the high road of the *Via Gratiae*. The road of grace finally leads to the open gates of the eternal City of God, the New Jerusalem, where God and Christ fold "faithful pilgrim" to their breasts.   John Wesley's hymn, *The Pilgrim's Lot*, sets this triumphant theme to liturgical form -

> "How happy is the pilgrim's lot,
> How free from every anxious thought,
> From worldly hope and fear!
> Confined to neither court nor cell,
> His soul distains on earth to dwell,
> He only sojourns here.
>
> This happiness in part is mine,
> Already saved from low design,
> From every creature-love;
> Blest with the scorn of finite good,
> My soul is lightened of its load,
> And seeks the things above.
>
> There is my house and portion fair;
> My treasure and my heart are there,
> And my abiding home;
> For me my elder brother stay,
> And angels beckon me away,
> And Jesus bids me come.
>
> 'I come,' thy servant, Lord, replies,
> 'I come to meet thee in the skies,
> And claim my heavenly rest!
> Now let the pilgrim's journey end;
> Now, O my Saviour, Brother, Friend,
> Receive me to thy breast!"[201]

Notes

1 METHODIST HYMNAL, *op.cit.*, 362.
2 EXPLANATORY NOTES NEW TESTAMENT, *op.cit.*, 878.
3 *Ibid*, 843-844. Cf. WORKS, *op.cit.*, VI, 137 - "Nor is everything properly our own in the land of our pilgrimage. . .till we come to our own country."
4 WORKS, *op.cit.*, VII, 484.
5 *Ibid*, VII, 230.
6 *Loc.cit.* Cf. Malebranche, op.cit., 307-311.
7 *Ibid*, X, 364.
8 *Loc.cit.*
9 *Ibid*, X, 364-365.
10 *Ibid*, X, 365.
11 *Ibid*, X, 366. Cf. JOURNAL, *op.cit.*, III, 81 - Wesley summarized "the one true religion" as "righteousness, and peace, and joy in the Holy Ghost."
12 *Loc.cit.*
13 *Ibid*, VII, 269.
14 *Ibid*, XIV, 179.
15 *Ibid*, XII, 274. Cf. JOURNAL, *op.cit.*, VII, 389.
16 *Ibid*, VII, 269; V, 77-78 - Wesley argued that forms and ceremonies "are good in their place; just so far as they are in fact subservient to true religion...Let no man dream that they have intrinsic worth; or that religion cannot subsist without them."
17 *Loc.cit.*
18 *Loc.cit.*
19 *Loc.cit.* Also, VII, 260; V, 76-77, 79-80.
20 *Loc.cit.*
21 *Ibid*, VII, 277, 324 - Wesley asked, "What is the very root of this religion? 'God in man! Heaven connected with earth! The unspeakable union of mortal with immortal.'"
22 *Ibid*, VII, 273.
23 *Ibid*, VI, 276.
24 *Ibid*, VI, 275-277; V, 77.
25 Luke Tyerman, *THE LIFE AND TIMES OF THE REV. JOHN WESLEY,* M.A., (London: Hodder and Stoughton, 1876), I, 434.
26 Telford, *op.cit.*, VII, 185.
27 WORKS, *op.cit.*, V, 3.
28 Starkey, *op.cit.*, 45. Cf. William R. Cannon, *THE THEOLOGY OF JOHN WESLEY* (New York: Abingdon Press, 1946), 40. Cannon argues that this view came from seventeenth century Anglicanism.
29 WORKS, *op.cit.*, VII, 232ff.

30   *Ibid*, V, 55.
31   EXPLANATORY NOTES NEW TESTAMENT, *op.cit.*, 303.
32   WORKS, *op.cit.*, VII, 187; X, 232.
33   *Ibid*, VII, 189-190; VIII, 52-53.
34   *Ibid*, VII, 345; X, 229-230.
35   *Ibid*, XII, 453; X, 334.
36   *Ibid*, V, 109.
37   *Ibid*, VI, 512.
38   EXPLANATORY NOTES NEW TESTAMENT, *op.cit.*, 842.
39   WORKS, *op.cit.*, VIII, 5, 13. Cf. Starkey, *op.cit.*, 48.
40   EXPLANATORY NOTES NEW TESTAMENT, *op.cit.*, 735.
41   Williams, *op.cit.*, 65.
42   Lee, *op.cit.*, 130.
43   WORKS, *op.cit.*, IX, 306.
44   *Ibid*, VI, 509.
45   *Loc.cit.*
46   *Ibid*, VIII, 277; XII, 453. Cf. Harald Lindstrom, *WESLEY AND SANCTI-FICATION* (Stockholm: Nya Bokforlags Aktiebolaget, 1946), 30.
47   *Ibid*, V, 239 - from Wesley's sermon of Sunday, November 24, 1765.
48   Telford, *op.cit.*, III, 321.
49   *BOOK OF COMMON PRAYER* (New York: Henry Frawde, 1897), 559.
50   *Loc.cit.* Cf. WORKS, *op.cit.*, X, 432 - "I still believe, no good works can be done before justification." (1773).
51   Sugden, *op.cit.*, 119.
52   Lindstrom, *op.cit.*, 84.
53   WORKS, *op.cit.*, V, 239.
54   *Ibid*, XII, 112.
55   Southey, *op.cit.*, 251-252.
56   WORKS, *op.cit.*, XII, 112-113.
57   *Ibid*, X, 403.
58   JOURNAL, *op.cit.*, II, 13.
59   WORKS, *op.cit.*, X, 431.
60   Ibid, VIII, 284
61   Telford, op.cit., V, 215. In 1770, Wesley argued that the reception of the Holy Spirit occurs at justification and not at the time of entire sanctification.
62   WORKS, *op.cit.*, XII, 283.
63   *Ibid*, X, 430-431.
64   *Ibid*, X, 320.
65   Lindstrom, *op.cit.*, 205. Cf. WORKS, *op.cit.*, VIII, 46.
66   Robert C. Monk, *JOHN WESLEY: HIS PURITAN HERITAGE* (Nashville: Abingdon Press, 1966), 123.
67   *Ibid*, 122, 123, 127-128.
68   *Ibid*, 123. Cf. WORKS, *op.cit.*, VIII, 68-69, 277.
69   WORKS, *op.cit.*, VI, 65; VIII, 285.
70   *Ibid*, V, 224.
71   *Ibid*, VI, 65.

72 *Ibid*, VI, 509. Cf. Starkey, *op.cit.*, 33.
73 *Loc.cit.* Cf. Lindstrom, *op.cit.*, 123.
74 *Ibid*, V, 225.
75 *Ibid*, VI, 70.
76 *Ibid*, VIII, 104ff.
77 *Ibid*, VIII, 373-374.
78 *Ibid*, XII, 290.
79 *Ibid*, VI, 46, 509; VIII, 285.
80 *Ibid*, VIII, 279; XI, 387.
81 *Ibid*, VI, 509.
82 *Ibid*, VI, 46.
83 *Ibid*, XI, 446.
84 METHODIST HYMNAL, *op.cit.*, 496.
85 EXPLANATORY NOTES NEW TESTAMENT, *op.cit.*, 25.
86 *Loc.cit.*
87 *Ibid*, 39.
88 HOMILIES, *op.cit.*, II, 190.
89 *Ibid*, II, 191.
90 WORKS, *op.cit.*, V, 349.
91 *Ibid*, V, 344.
92 *Ibid*, V, 345.
93 *Ibid*, V, 346.
94 *Loc.cit.*
95 *Loc.cit.*
96 *Loc.cit.*
97 *Loc.cit.*
98 *Ibid*, V, 347.
99 *Ibid*, V, 348.
100 *Ibid*, V, 349-350.
101 *Ibid*, V, 350.
102 *Loc.cit.*
103 *Ibid*, V. 351.
104 *Loc.cit.*
105 *Ibid*, V, 352. Cf. JOURNAL, *op.cit.*, VI, 167 - In August 1777, Wesley said, "I desired as many as I could to join together in fasting and prayer, that God would restore the spirit of love and of a sound mind to the poor deluded rebels in America."
106 *Loc.cit.*
107 *Ibid*, V, 358.
108 *Ibid*, V, 359.
109 *Loc.cit.*
110 EXPLANATORY NOTES NEW TESTAMENT, *op.cit.*, 36-39.
111 WORKS, *op.cit.*, XIII, 20.
112 John Wesley, *A CHRISTIAN LIBRARY* (London: T. Cordeux, 1819), XII, 223-249.
113 WORKS, *op.cit.*, XI, 203-259.

114   *Ibid*, XI, 259-272.
115   *Ibid*, XI, 262. For other dimensions of Wesleyan prayer, consult JOUR-NAL, *op.cit.*, I, 309, 374, 449, 449n; II, 147, 283, 298, 301, 302, 404, 455, 516, 535; III, 56, 267, 487; IV, 112, 156, 197, 198, 256, 326, 482; V, 160, 472; VI, 214, 392, 334, 349, 350, 412; VII, 336; VIII, 103.
116   Telford, *op.cit.*, VIII, 27.
117   EXPLANATORY NOTES NEW TESTAMENT, *op.cit.*, 1034-1035.
118   WORKS, *op.cit.*, VI, 32 - Wesley's text was II Corinthians II, 11 - "We are not ignorant of Satan's devices."
119   *Ibid*, VI, 33-34.
120   *Ibid*, VI, 35.
121   *Loc.cit.*
122   *Loc.cit.*
123   *Loc.cit.*
124   *Loc.cit.*
125   *Loc.cit.*
126   *Ibid*, VI, 36.
127   *Ibid*, VI, 36-37.
128   *Ibid*, VI, 38.
129   *Loc.cit.*
130   *Ibid*, VI, 42-43.
131   JOURNAL, *op.cit.*, V, 56, 33-34, 73, 375.
132   *Ibid*, II, 122, 131, 147, 148, 180-184, 186-187, 189, 190, 192, 198-199, 248.
133   *Ibid*, IV, 359-360.
134   *Ibid*, III, 69; V, 32-35, 56. Cf. WORKS, *op.cit.*, IX, 27, 189.
135   *Ibid*, V, 375.
136   WORKS, *op.cit.*, XIV, 356-358.
137   JOURNAL, *op.cit.*, VII, 153.
138   *Ibid*, III, 29.
139   *Ibid*, III, 54.
140   *Ibid*, III, 71.
141   *Ibid*, III, 380.
142   *Ibid*, IV, 76.
143   *Ibid*, IV, 337.
144   *Ibid*, IV, 360.
145   *Ibid*, V, 110.
146   *Ibid*, V, 148.
147   *Ibid*, V, 196.
148   *Ibid*, V, 448.
149   *Ibid*, VI, 18.
150   *Ibid*, VI, 27-28.
151   *Ibid*, VI, 144.
152   *Ibid*, VI, 167.
153   *Ibid*, VII, 282.
154   *Ibid*, VII, 153.
155   Telford, *op.cit.*, VII, 226.

156 *Ibid*, VII, 329.
157 WORKS, *op.cit.*, XII, 345, 96, 130, 218, 286, 323.
158 *Ibid*, XII, 130.
159 *Ibid*, XII, 296-297; VIII, 278.
160 *Ibid*, XII, 96.
161 *Ibid*, VI, 370-380. Cf. Southey, *op.cit.*, II, 73.
162 *Ibid*, VI, 378.
163 *Ibid*, VI, 379.
164 EXPLANATORY NOTES NEW TESTAMENT, *op.cit.*, 552.
165 WORKS, *op.cit.*, VI, 318-319.
166 *Ibid*, VI, 319.
167 *Ibid*, VI, 319, 428.
168 EXPLANATORY NOTES NEW TESTAMENT, *op.cit.*, 435.
169 WORKS, *op.cit.*, VI, 319.
170 *Ibid*, VI, 319, 428.
171 *Ibid*, VI, 428.
172 *Ibid*, VI, 315.
173 *Ibid*, VI, 313.
174 EXPLANATORY NOTES OLD TESTAMENT, *op.cit.*, III, 1902.
175 EXPLANATORY NOTES NEW TESTAMENT, *op.cit.*, 550-551.
176 WORKS, *op.cit.*, VI, 275.
177 *Loc.cit.*
178 *Ibid*, VI, 276.
179 METHODIST HYMNAL, *op.cit.*, 356.
180 WORKS, *op.cit.*, VI, 362.
181 Psalms CIV, 4. Cf. WORKS, *op.cit.*, VI, 362.
182 WORKS, *op.cit.*, VI, 363.
183 *Ibid*, VI, 364.
184 *Ibid*, VI, 364-365.
185 *Ibid*, VI, 365.
186 EXPLANATORY NOTES NEW TESTAMENT, *op.cit.*, 813.
187 WORKS, *op.cit.*, VI, 366.
188 *Loc.cit.*
189 *Loc.cit.*
190 *Loc.cit.* Cf. W. Benham, *THE PROSE WORKS OF THE RIGHT REV-
EREND THOMAS KEN* (London: Griffith, Farran, Okeden and Welsh),
260. Wesley took liberties in citing Ken. The quotation was not a prayer,
but a verse and a half from Ken's AN EVENING HYMN. Wesley made
several alterations in the text, as a comparison reveals. Ken's text reads:

> O may my Guardian while I sleep,
> Close to my head his vigils keep,
> His love angelical instil,
> Stop all the avenues of ill.
>
> May he celestial joy rehearse,

And thought to thought with me converse
Or in my stead, all the night long,
Sing to God a grateful song."

191   *Ibid*, VI, 367.
192   *Loc.cit.*
193   *Loc.cit.*
194   *Ibid*, VI, 367-368.
195   *Ibid*, VI, 368.
196   *Loc.cit.*
197   *Loc.cit.* Cf. EXPLANATORY NOTES OLD TESTAMENT, *op.cit.*, II, 1203 - Wesley here cited the prophet Elisha's experience at Dothan (II Kings VI).
198   *Loc.cit.*
199   *Ibid*, VI, 369.
200   EXPLANATORY NOTES NEW TESTAMENT, *op.cit.*, 553-554. Cf. Telford, *op.cit.*, VIII, 28 - In a letter (1787), Wesley stated that Satan "is in a great measure bound already; he is not now permitted to deceive the nations, as in the past ages."
201   METHODIST HYMNAL, *op.cit.*, 1078.

Chapter Six

The Pilgrimage from Paradise Lost to Paradise Improved: The Pilgrim's Praxis - Holiness and Stewardship

THE PILGRIM'S HOLINESS

The primary praxis of the pilgrim is holiness, without which he cannot possibly see the face of God in glory.

In his attack on Antinomianism, entitled a *BLOW AT THE ROOT*, Wesley carefully defined the necessity of holiness -

"'Without holiness no man shall see the Lord,' shall see the face of God in glory. Nothing under heaven can be more sure than this; 'for the mouth of the Lord hath spoken it. And though heaven and earth pass away, yet his word shall not pass away.' . . .No, it cannot be; none shall live with God, but he that now lives to God; none shall enjoy the glory of God in heaven, but he that bears the image of God on earth; none that is not saved from sin here can be saved from hell hereafter; none can see the kingdom of God above, unless the kingdom of God be in him below. Whosoever will reign with Christ in heaven, must have Christ reigning in him on earth. He must have 'that mind in him which was in Christ, enabling him to walk as Christ also walked."[1]

His sermon, *TRUE CHRISTIANITY DEFENDED*, gives additional insight into the nature of this holiness. Analyzing the popular prayer - "Cleanse the thoughts of our hearts by the inspiration of thy Holy Spirit, that we may perfectly love thee, and worthily magnify thy holy name" - Wesley detected two aspects to holiness. The first, denoted by the petition "Cleanse the thoughts of our hearts," relates to the "negative branch of inward holiness; the height and depth of which is purity of heart, by the inspiration of God's Holy Spirit." The second, denoted by the clause "that we may perfectly love thee," relates to the positive branch of outward holiness.[2] The pilgrim must possess and practice this holiness, in both inward and outward realities. To have the one and not the other is to lack true holiness.[3] True holiness is one holiness, with both inward and outward manifestations. As such, Wesley referred to it as "the true wedding garment," and "the only qualification for glory."[4] He frequently termed the inward "holiness of heart," and the outward "holiness of conversation." Semantically, "conversation" meant "manner of living," involving ethics. Wesley held that holiness of conversation results from holiness of heart, "for a good tree will bring forth good fruit. And all inward holiness is the immediate fruit of the faith that worketh by love."[5] The progression is, therefore, faith, inward holiness, and outward holiness, in that order.

Wesley saw pilgrims in peril of slipping into Antinomianism and consequently losing salvation altogether. His commentary on Antinomianism in his age could also fit the last half of the Twentieth Century -

> "Bishop Brown thought Arianism and Socinianism were the flood which the dragon is in this age pouring out of his mouth to swallow up the woman: Perhaps it may; especially with Dr. Taylor's emendation. But still the main flood in England seems to be Antinomianism. This has been a greater hindrance to the work of God than any or all others put together. But God has already lifted up His standard, and He will maintain his own cause. In the present dispensation, He undoubtedly is aiming at that point, to spread holiness over the land. . .inward and outward holiness. A thousand things will be presented by men and evils to divert us from our point."[6]

The appeal of eighteenth century Antinomianism stressed the believer's completeness in Christ, as had Simon Magus in the first century: Christ has completed all things for salvation, and since his righteousness is imputed to us, we need none of our own. Christ has so much righteousness and holiness, we need none of our own.

"To think that we have any, or to desire or seek any, is to renounce Christ." From "the beginning to the end of salvation, all is in Christ, nothing in man; and. . .those who teach otherwise are legal Preachers, and know nothing of the gospel."[7] Wesley's teaching of holiness, considered legalistic by the Antinomians, began in 1725[8] and continued without alteration until his death in 1791. His sermon at St. Mary's, Oxford University, on January 1, 1733, embodied the biblical theme of holiness under the title, *THE CIRCUMCISION OF THE HEART*. The text was Pauline (Romans II, 29) - "Circumcision is that of the heart, in the Spirit, and not in the letter." While many passages are worthy of citation, the following best shows the heart of the doctrine -

> "In general, we may observe, it is that habitual disposition of soul which, in the sacred writings, is termed holiness; and which directly implies, the being cleansed from sin, 'from all filthiness both of flesh and spirit;' and, by consequence, the being endued with those virtues which were also in Christ Jesus; the being so 'renewed in the spirit of our mind,' as to be 'perfect as our Father in heaven is perfect.'"[9]

Years later, in March 1774, Wesley preached one of his many holiness sermons at Wednesbury. The text was from the Epistle to the Hebrews II, 3 - "How shall we escape if we neglect so great a salvation?" The sermon concluded with this question - "If we do not 'go on to perfection,' how shall we escape lukewarmness, Antinomianism, hell-fire?" Wesley believed that neglect of holiness in the pilgrim life guarantees a degenerative process - from holiness to lukewarmness to Antinomianism to Gehenna (hell-fire).[10] A few days later, Wesley preached another holiness sermon to a congregation meeting at five o'clock in the morning. "I explained that important truth that God trieth us every moment, weighs all our thoughts, words, and actions, and is pleased or displeased with us according to our works." The JOURNAL commentary on this sermon is interesting. "I see more and more clearly that there is a great gulf fixed between us and all those who, by denying this, sap the very foundation both of inward and outward holiness."[11] Alas, for Wesley, Antinomianism had infiltrated his Methodist societies and the biblical doctrine of holiness was being denied in pilgrim living. When he preached holiness at his society in Trewergy, a Methodist Antinomian cried out in protest, "Damnable doctrine!" Wesley's response was worthy of sanctified status - "True; it condemns all those who hear and do not obey it!"[12]

One of Wesley's biblical foundations for the pilgrim's life being rooted in holiness was Isaiah XXXV - "The wilderness and the solitary place shall be glad...the desert shall rejoice and blossom as the rose. . .the parched ground shall become a pool. . .the thirsty land springs of waters...an highway shall be there, and a way, and it shall be called the way of holiness, the unclean shall not pass over it, but it shall be for those, the way-faring men. . .the redeemed shall walk there. . .the ransomed of the lord shall return and come to Zion, with songs, and everlasting joy upon their heads. . .sorrow and sighing shall flee away." Wesley found an allegorical meaning to this passage as well as the historical meaning. The wilderness, allegorically, is the Church, God's people, having been ravaged by the enemy. However, God's goodness and power will transform this present wilderness by the working of the Incarnate God. It is He who will open the eyes of the blind, the ears of the deaf, and the mouths of the dumb, bringing them to spiritual life. He will provide them with streams of mercy as they live within the transformed wilderness. He will build a highway for them to walk upon - "even a causey (causeway), which is raised ground." Moreover, "the people (walking in it) shall be all righteous. . .The way shall be so plain and strait, that even the most foolish travellers cannot easily mistake it."[13] Wesley held that Christ, the Incarnate God, has already transformed the wilderness, or Old Testament Church, into a virtual paradise with its raised highway of holiness. Unfortunately, Wesley maintained, the Antinomians would reduce the Church of God back into a virtual wilderness. Changing metaphors, Wesley referred to this retrogression as "a blow at the root," whereby Christ is "stabbed in the house of his friends."[14] Addressing the Antinomians of his societies, Wesley asked, "O when will ye understand, that to oppose either inward or outward holiness, under the colour of exalting Christ, is directly to act the part of Judas, 'to betray the Son of man with a kiss?'"[15]

The most complete description of biblical holiness in Wesleyan literature is *A PLAIN ACCOUNT OF CHRISTIAN PERFECTION*. The remainder of the title reads, "as believed and taught by the Reverend Mr. John Wesley, from the year 1725, to the year 1777." In it, Wesley traces the history of the doctrine in his ministry, revealing that he held this to be "the truth as it is in Jesus." An important observation at this point - In 1725, Wesley resolved to dedicate all his "life to God," with all his "thoughts, and words, and actions."[16] The years 1726, 1727, 1728, 1729, 1730, 1733, 1735, and 1736 (the pre-Aldersgate years) are specifically mentioned by Wesley as decisive in his understanding and experience of holiness. In his description of 1738, Wesley completely omitted any reference to the Aldersgate experience. It did not directly relate to his holiness motif. It should also be noted that while Wesley's references to Aldersgate became non-existent after a short time, his commitment to holiness never waned. Indeed, it was the constant theme of his ministry in the societies until his dying day.

The *PLAIN ACCOUNT* further informs us that Wesley's first tract on holiness was entitled "The Character of a Methodist." This title was chosen because it seemed less likely to evoke controversy than a title involving perfection. Nevertheless, the tract described "a perfect Christian."[17] Wesley extracted from the Bible all the ideals and virtues of sainthood, which are enjoined upon the people of God as obligatory. With these, he blended spiritual qualities of heart and life which spring from inner motivations that cannot be legislated. For instance -

> "A Methodist is one who loves the Lord his God with all his heart, with all his soul, with all his mind, and with all his strength. God is the joy of his heart, and the desire of his soul. . .he is therefore happy in God. . .having in him a well of water springing up unto everlasting life, and overflowing his soul with peace and joy. Perfect Love having now cast out fear, he rejoices evermore . . . his joy is full. . .and he. . .in everything giveth thanks. . .knowing this is the will of God in Christ Jesus concerning him. . .he cheerfully receives all. . . whether he giveth or taketh away, equally blessing the name of the Lord.

Whether in ease or pain, whether in sickness or health, whether in life or death, he giveth thanks from the ground of the heart to Him who orders it for good; into whose hands he hath wholly committed his body and soul. . .He is therefore anxiously careful for nothing. . .resting on Him, after making his request known to Him with thanksgiving."[18]

The perfect pilgrim, according to Wesley, further prays without ceasing in the "language of his heart." Whether in retirement, business, company, or leisure, the person of holiness constantly lifts his heart to the Lord in prayer, and he has "the loving eye of the soul fixed on Him. . .seeing Him that is invisible."[19] Moreover, loving God so wondrously, the perfect Methodist "loves his neighbour as himself." He loves every man as his own soul - brother, neighbour, and enemy. In this love his heart is pure - free from envy, malice, wrath, and every unkind temper. He is cleansed from pride, having "put on bowels of mercies, kindness, humbleness of mind, meekness, longsuffering." Such love is also known as "purity of heart."[20] It has its being by virtue of the "great gift of God" - the salvation of our souls, or, in another figure of speech, "the image of God stamped on our hearts."[21] There is both a gradual and an instantaneous side to the experience of this holiness or perfect love.[22]

Wesley referred to the personal experience of holiness as sanctification. It begins the "moment a man is justified." In an Augustinian way, the power of sin (Wesley's "seed of sin") remains in justified man until he is thoroughly sanctified. But, from the moment he is justified, sanctification, as a gradual process, brings a death to sin and the believer grows in grace.[23] However, in an instant the believer may be "entirely sanctified" by which Wesley meant a complete cleansing by the Holy Spirit of the soul, "rooting out the seeds of sin," and perfecting love.[24] It is possible to have such an experience in this present life. In fact, "Now" is always the appropriate time for the experience. This theme is eloquently expressed in Wesley's hymnal of 1749 -

"From this inbred sin deliver,
Let the yoke Now be broke;
Make me Thine forever.

Partner of Thy perfect nature,
Let me be Now in Thee,
A new, sinless creature."[25]

These hymn words were from the pen of Charles Wesley. While John agreed with the theme of entire sanctification now, he objected to the last line's affirmation of a "sinless creature."[26]

The pilgrim must set his feet on the highway of holiness in consequence of having his heart subjected to the sanctifying work of the Holy Spirit. His holiness must be both inward and outward. Wesley translated an anonymous hymn from the German. It is the prayer of a sincere pilgrim for entire sanctification and holiness -

O Thou who all things canst control,
Chase this dread slumber from my soul;
With joy and fear, with love and awe,
Give me to keep Thy perfect law.

O may one beam of Thy blest light
Pierce through, dispel the shade of night;
Touch my cold breast with heavenly fire;
With holy, conquering zeal inspire.

For zeal I sigh, for zeal I pant;
Yet heavy is my soul, and faint;
With steps unwavering, undismayed,
Give me in all Thy paths to tread.

With outstretched hands, and streaming eyes,
Oft I begin to grasp the prize;
I groan, I strive, I watch, I pray;
But ah! my zeal soon dies away.

The deadly slumber that I feel
Afresh upon my spirit steal;
Rise, Lord, stir up Thy quickening power,
And wake me that I sleep no more.[27]

The Methodist pilgrim, Wesley maintained, is on the Way of Grace (Via Gratiae) which is also the Way of holiness (Via Sancti). Sanctifying faith, in response to the workings of the Spirit, produces inward holiness of heart. This in turn produces the fruit of outward holiness. In his *GENERAL RULES OF THE UNITED SOCIETIES* (May 1, 1743), Wesley reduced outward holiness to three basic principles, with explicit examples of each:

(1) "Doing no harm" - avoiding evil of every kind, such as taking the name of God in vain; the profaning of the Lord's Day, either by performing ordinary work thereon, or by buying or selling. Also avoiding drunkenness, the buying or selling of "spirituous liquors, or drinking them, unless in cases of extreme necessity." Fighting, quarreling, and brawling are contrary to the spirit of outward holiness because they violate the principle of "doing no harm." When brother goes to court against brother, when one returns evil for evil, and when one rails back at another, then the spirit of holiness is shattered and much evil ensues. Using many words in buying and selling indicates an evil intent to gain an advantage over another person. Hence, this too must be avoided. Smuggled goods should not be purchased by pilgrims, nor should they charge or pay usury (unlawful interest). Moreover, uncharitable and unprofitable conversation - such as speaking evil of magistrates or of ministers - must always be avoided. The pilgrim is further obliged to avoid "doing to others as (he) would not they should do unto (him)." Under this heading of "doing no harm," Wesley also added a prohibition against "putting on of gold or costly apparel," as commanded by the Apostle Peter (I Peter III, 3). Other prohibitions follow: engaging in diversions which "cannot be used in the name of the Lord Jesus;" singing songs and reading books which "do not tend to the knowledge or love of God;" softness and "needless" self-indulgence; "laying up treasures on earth;" borrowing without any prospect of repayment; and shop-lifting.[28] All of these acts, Wesley believed, bring harm to someone - always to the doer and most frequently to an innocent recipient. Outward holiness, then, first means "doing no harm."

(2) "Doing good" - The pilgrim is to practice doing good, out of a merciful motivation, making use of every opportunity. In reference to the bodies of men, the pilgrim is expected to feed the hungry, clothe the naked, and visit those that are sick or in prison. In reference to the souls of men, the pilgrim is expected to teach, reprove, and exhort all persons encountered along life's way, "trampling under foot that enthusiastic doctrine of devils, that 'we are not to do good unless our hearts be free to it.'" Furthermore, the holy pilgrim must practice charity and hospitality to those of the household of faith, preferring them above all others. This preference should show itself in pilgrims buying from other Christians, and in "helping each other in business." Wesley's rationale for this advice was simply that "the world will love its own, and them only." The poor, struggling Christian, he believed, will have a long wait for the world to bring charity to his door. Hence, all Christians must respond to the needs of Christians, exceeding those few acts of mercy suggested above. Personal frugality will enable a pilgrim to have sufficient means at any one time to come to the aid of another Christian in dire need. Wesley's doctrine of economic frugality was treated in his sermon *CAUSES OF THE INEFFICACY OF CHRISTIANITY*, in which he equated gaining and saving all the money possible, without giving it away to needy believers, as a grieving of the Holy Spirit of God.[29] A diligent practice of frugality and charity will keep the gospel from being scandalized. By doing good to both Christian and non-christian, a faithful pilgrim will be taking up his cross daily because he surely will be reproached.[30] The outward holiness of doing good must be a habit (praxis) - a strong, positive way of life, approximating that lived earlier by Jesus of Nazareth.

(3) Attend "all the ordinances of God" - These are several: the public worship of God; the ministry of the word, either read or expounded; the Lord's Supper; family and private prayer; searching the Scriptures; and fasting.[31]

The Antinomians accused Wesley of being a legalist. In his defense, however, one should observe that ethical principles, as "do no harm," or "do good," are meaningless and abstract unless they can be related to specific acts. Wesley chose the ethical principles of the New Testament. Likewise he used the New Testament acts, cited as illustrative of those principles by the New Testament authors. He was no more nor no less legalistic than the authors of the New Testament. Remove from thence everything considered legalistic by the Antinomians and all that remains is a corpus of values that has no concrete connection with specific acts - acts which constitute the flow of daily life. Make one value relevant by connecting it with an act performed in a special "situation" which may never again be permissible, and you have made a "new law" for just one occasion. Such a position is the ultimate in legalism because it fills the universe of morality with singular laws which are deemed "meaningful" but may not ever be repeated. O the tediousness of all forms of Antinomianism! Wesley was considerably less legalistic than his Twentieth Century followers in America, who, every four years, submit to General Conference more proposed legislation than can reasonably be considered. Even then, every quadrennium sees a growing corpse of legalism, much of it inspired by the secular interpretation that democratic politics is about to restore Paradise - a Paradise lost long ago by the practice of legalistic religion like that of John Wesley's. Little wonder that values are gone - They had no acts with which to live and move and have any concrete being!

In 1789, Wesley held conversations with a number of his preachers. One of the questions asked of Wesley was, What was the rise of Methodism, so called? The answer is significant:

> "In 1729, two young men, reading the Bible, saw they could not be saved without holiness, followed after it, and incited others so to do. In 1737 they saw holiness comes by faith. They saw likewise, that men are justified before they are sanctified; but still holiness was their point. God then thrust them out, utterly against their will, to raise a holy people. When Satan could no otherwise hinder this, he threw Calvinism in the way; and then Antinomianism, which strikes directly at the root of all holiness."[32]

THE PILGRIM'S STEWARDSHIP

The practitioner of biblical holiness pays careful attention to the stewardship of life in all its dimensions. He knows that he is a sojourner and pilgrim, a visitor in a strange house and a strange country.[33] He does not own the house nor the country. He simply lives within both for a short time. God the Creator has provided the house of the human body. He has also provided the country of the world.[34] Man sojourns in the body and is a pilgrim in the world. But, he is also a sinful, fallen creature whom God redeems. Man is, therefore, a "debtor to his Creator."[35] However, prior to the fall, man was made a steward of God's created order. Since the fall, man is both a debtor and a steward.

Wesley's sermon, *THE GOOD STEWARD*, dated May 14, 1768, explains the difference between debtor and steward. A debtor is obligated to return what he has received, "yet until the time of payment comes, he is at liberty to use it as he pleases." All humans are "indebted to Him for all we have." On the other hand, the steward is not at liberty to use "what is lodged in his hands as he pleases." He can only use things according to the will of his master. The steward is not the proprietor of anything, not even his own life or soul. Things are entrusted to the steward on the condition that he disposes of them in strict accordance with the master's will.[36]

A seeming difficulty arises with Wesley's distinction since he affirmed that man is both debtor and steward at the same time. Actually, there is no contradiction, for Wesley saw man a debtor in reference to the gift of salvation and a steward in relation to things (*ta idia*) of the created order. Consequently, Wesley summarized the case as follows -

"We are not at liberty to use what he has lodged in our hands as we please, but as He pleases who alone is the possessor of heaven and earth, and the Lord of every creature. We have no right to dispose of anything we have, but according to His will, seeing we are not proprietors of any of these things; they are all. . .belonging to another person; nor is anything properly our own, in the land of our pilgrimage. We shall not receive *ta idia*, our own things, till we come to our own country. Eternal things only are our own; With all these temporal things we are barely entrusted by another; the Disposer and Lord of all. And He entrusts us with them on this express condition, - that we use them only as our Master's goods, and according to the particular directions which he has given us in His word."[37]

In particular, Wesley affirmed, our Creator has entrusted us with our souls, bodies, goods, and talents. His sermon provides a helpful sketch of each. (1) Souls - immortal spirits, made in the image of God with the faculties of understanding, imagination, memory, will, affections like love and hatred, joy and sorrow, desire and aversion, and hope and fear.[38] God has entrusted us with these faculties of soul, "not that we may employ them according to our own will, but according to the express orders He has given us." Our understanding, imagination, and memory (the rational trinity in Descartes's TREATISE ON MAN) are to be used exclusively for God's glory. Our will is to be given up entirely to God, and our affections are "to be regulated as He directs."[39] (2) Bodies are "those exquisitely wrought machines," so fearfully and wonderfully made, "with all the powers and members thereof." God has entrusted us with sense organs - of seeing, hearing, smelling, tasting, and touching (John Locke's empirical senses). But, Wesley argued, these are not "given us as our own, to be employed according to our own will." God has placed restrictions on these senses, and the Bible is replete with directions concerning what we may look upon, hear, and so forth.[40] In addition to these, the tongue, with its talent of speech, is a special trust. God gave it so that it would move in praise to Him. Hence, those who speak are held accountable for every word. Likewise our hands and feet, and all other members of the body, are entrusted to us to be used for performing good, "not as instruments of unrighteousness unto sin, but as instruments of righteousness to God."[41] (3) Worldly Goods - food, raiment, shelter are the necessities. But God also entrusts us with conveniences. Included in this category Wesley treated money - an "unspeakably precious" commodity.[42] Because money was so very important to Wesley, its treatment will be reserved for later in this chapter. (4) Talents - "talents which do not properly come under any of these heads" - bodily strength, health, pleasing personality, an "agreeable address," learning and knowledge, influence over others, power to help or hinder persons, time, and most importantly, the grace of God.[43]

Before moving on to Wesley's description of a future accounting of each steward before God, consideration must be given two important themes in his doctrine of stewardship - money and time.

1. *Money* - While the subject of money runs throughout Wesley's writings with great frequency, his most explicit statement on the subject is found in the sermon *THE USE OF MONEY*. The text of the sermon was Luke XVI, 9 - "I say unto you, Make to yourselves friends of the mammon of unrighteousness; that, when ye fail, they may receive you into everlasting habitations." This text, considered traditionally as one of the "hard sayings" of Jesus, was a good starting point for his sermon. "There was a certain rich man, who had a steward, and he was accused to him of wasting his goods. And calling him, he said, Give an account of thy stewardship, for thou canst be no longer steward." Jesus recounted the method used by the evil steward to cover his thefts and added the words, "His Lord commended the unjust steward." The observation of Jesus was that "the children of the world are wiser in their generation than the children of light." A hard saying, indeed! However, Wesley interpreted Jesus's observation in the following manner -

"Those who seek no other portion than this world 'are wiser' (not absolutely; for they are, one and all, the veriest fools, the most egregious madmen under heaven; but, 'in their generation,' in their own way; they are consistent with themselves; they are truer to their acknowledged principles; they more steadily pursue their end) 'than the children of light;' than they who see 'the light of the glory of God in the face of Jesus Christ.' Then follows the words above recited: 'And I,' - the only-begotten Son of God, the Creator, Lord, and Possessor of heaven and earth and all that is therein; the Judge of all, to whom ye are to 'give an account of your stewardship,' when ye 'can be no longer stewards;' 'I say unto you,' - learn in this respect, even of the unjust steward, - 'make yourselves friends,' by wise, timely precaution, 'of the mammon of unrighteousness.' 'Mammon' means riches, or money. It is termed 'the mammon of unrighteousness,' because of the unrighteous manner wherein it is frequently procured and wherein even that which is honestly procured, is generally employed. 'Make yourself friends' of this, by doing all possible good, particularly to the children of God; 'that, when ye fail,' - when ye return to dust, when ye have no more place under the sun, - those of them who are gone before 'may receive you,' may welcome you, into the everlasting habitations.'"44

Having established a clear meaning for this hard saying, Wesley concluded, "An excellent branch of Christian wisdom is here inculcated by our Lord on all his followers, namely, the right use of money; - a subject largely spoken of, after their manner, by men of the world; but not sufficiently considered by those whom God hath chosen out of the world."45 Christians do not understand the nature of money. Gold and silver are not to blame for the corruption that is in the world. It is not money that is the root of evil, but, as the Apostle Paul affirmed, "the love of money is the root of all evil." Money may be used ill or well. Its good usage is indispensible for the stability of a civilized nation. It is a "most compendious instrument of transacting all manner of business, and (if we use it according to Christian wisdom) of doing all manner of good."46 An excellent illustration of Christian wisdom, Wesley held, in using money for good, was the Church at Jerusalem (Acts II, IV, V). Filled with the Holy Ghost, so that "no man counted any thing he had his own, distribution was made to every one as he had need.47 Money, "in the present state of mankind," is "an excellent gift of God." In the hands of Christians it means food for the hungry, drink for the thirsty, clothing for the naked, lodging for the stranger, supply for the widow and orphan, defence for the oppressed, "a means of health to the sick," ease to those in pain, eyes to the blind (eyeglasses), feet to the lame (artificial limbs) - "Yea, a lifter up from the gates of death!"48 Money in the hands of the children of God must always be used for good. How may one determine the proper usage? Wesley laid down three "plain rules" by which, if exactly followed, the Christian may prove a faithful steward of the mammon of unrighteousness: (a) *"Gain all you can"* - This is a "bounden duty" without paying too dearly for it, without endangering life and health for it, and without robbing us of "proper seasons for food and sleep."[49] (1) Wesley continued, we must not gain all we can at the expense of our minds either. "We must preserve, at all events, the spirit of an healthful mind. Therefore, we may not engage or continue in any simple trade; any that is contrary to the law of God, or of our country."[50] A good conscience will not allow robbing and defrauding the king of his customs. To gain money, contrary to Christian conscience, is to lose our souls. (2) "We must gain all we can, without hurting our neighbour." For Wesley any acquisition of a neighbor's substance, houses and lands, by means of gambling is a totally unchristian act. To gain the substance of a neighbor by foreclosure on debts that have been allowed to escalate beyond reason is equally despicable. In this latter instance, doctors and lawyers generally enrich themselves at the expense of their clients![51] All persons are victimized by moneylenders who charge usury. Pawn-brokers are notorious for gaining much at others' expense. No Methodist should ever engage in putting out money at usury rates or in pawn-broking. As for selling, no Methodist business man should sell goods "below the market-price; we cannot study to ruin our neighbour's trade, in order to advance our own."[52] Nor is it a Christian act to entice away workmen or servants from a neighbor. Wesley concluded, "None can gain by swallowing up his neighbour's substance, without gaining the damnation of hell!"[53] (3) Moreover, Wesley argued, we are not to gain an advantage over a neighbor by hurting his body. For instance, "we may not sell any thing which tends to impair health. . .Such is, eminently, all that liquid fire, commonly called drams, or spirituous liquors."[54] It is true, he insisted, that such spirits may have a place in medicine under certain conditions, but generally those who distill and sell spirits are "poisoners" and nothing less. "They murder His Majesty's subjects by wholesale, neither does their eye pity or spare. They drive them to hell like sheep. And what is their gain? Is it not the blood of these men?" Wesley described the future of distillers and sellers of liquors -

"Who then would envy their large estates and sumptuous palaces? A curse is in the midst of them: The curse of God cleaves to the stones, the timber, the furniture of them! The curse of God is in their gardens, their walks, their groves; a fire that burns to the nethermost hell! Blood, blood is there; The foundation; the floor, the walls, the roof, are stained with blood! And canst thou hope, O thou man of blood, though thou art 'clothed in scarlet and fine linen, and farest sumptuously every day;' canst thou hope to deliver down thy fields of blood to the third generation? Not so, for there is a God in heaven; Therefore, thy name shall soon be rooted out. Like as those whom thou hast destroyed, body and soul, 'thy memorial shall perish with thee!"[56]

Closely associated in guilt with distillers and sellers of spirituous liquors, but in a lesser degree, are surgeons, physicians, and apothecaries, because they often "play with the lives or health of men, to enlarge their own gain." These professions often "purposely lengthen the pain or disease, which they are able to remove speedily." Physicians especially, Wesley believed, "protract the cure of their patient's body, in order to plunder his substance."[57] (4) Furthermore, we are not to gain an advantage over our neighbor by hurting him in his soul. This may be done directly or indirectly by encouraging him to intemperance and unchastity by attending "taverns, victualling-houses, opera-houses, play-houses, or any other places of public, fashionable diversion." Knowing that his position was controversial, Wesley reduced his argument to this final stage: "If these profit the souls of men, you are clear; your employment is good, and your gain innocent; but if they are either sinful in themselves, or natural inlets to sin of various kinds, then, it is to be feared, you have a sad account to make." If the latter is the case, he continued, "O beware, lest God say in that day. 'These have perished in their iniquity, but their blood do I require at thy hands!'"[58] (5) "Gain all you can by honest industry. Use all possible diligence in your calling. Lose no time. If you understand yourself, and your relation to God and man, you know you have none to spare."[59] A Christian business, Wesley maintained, will fill up "every day and every hour," leaving no time for "silly, unprofitable diversions. . .You have always something better to do, something that will profit you." Whatever a Christian hand finds to do, in the way of employment, it is to be done with all one's might. "Do it as soon as possible: No delay!" Procrastination has no place in the pilgrim's praxis of employment. Furthermore, Wesley exhorted, "Do it as well as possible. Do not sleep or yawn over it; Put your whole strength to the work. Spare no pains. Let nothing be done by halves, or in a slight and careless manner."[60] (6) "Gain all you can by common sense." In business, the Christian must apply all the knowledge imparted to him by God to improve the business. Wesley believed that time brings new methods and techniques to the marketplace, and these are better than those which preceded them. He lamented, "How men run on in the same dull track with their forefathers...It is a shame for a Christian not to improve upon them (methods and techniques), in whatever he takes in hand."[61] The rest of Wesley's admonition should be emblazoned across the heavens so every Methodist pilgrim would always have it before and above him -

"You should be continually learning, from the experience of others, or from your own experience, reading, and reflection, to do everything you have to do better to-day than you did yesterday. And see that you practice whatever you learn, that you may make the best of all that is in your hands."[62]

(b) Wesley's second rule concerning the pilgrim's use of money is "*Save all you can.*" Money must never be thrown into the sea of idle expenses, nor should it be used to gratify the desires of eyes and flesh, nor the pride of life. Wesley elaborated upon this rule by offering the following considerations: (1) Monetary expenditures for sensual pleasures are misguided and consistently should be avoided. In matters of eating, gluttony is not the only sensual habit that is wrong. "There is a regular, reputable kind of sensuality, an elegant epicurism, which does not immediately disorder the stomach, nor impair the understanding; and yet it cannot be maintained without considerable expense."[63] The latter is as wrong as the former. Pilgrims are admonished to take note - "Cut off all this expense!"[64] (2) Avoid wasting money, pleasing the eyes by purchasing costly apparel, or adorning houses. Expensive and superfluous furniture, pictures, paintings, gildings, books, formal gardens, and the like are inappropriate objects for Christians to purchase. "Let your neighbours, who know nothing better, do this." But let the Christian follow Christ![65] (3) Spend no money to gratify the pride of life, that is, "to gain the admiration or praise of men." Wesley believed that extravagance in diet, clothing, and housing feeds both the desire of the eyes and the pride of life, making extravagance doubly sinful. Generosity and hospitality do not atone for sinful extravagance.[66] (4) Do not throw away money on your children by providing them with "delicate food, gay or costly apparel, (and) superfluities" of all kinds. To do this is to "purchase for them more pride or lust, more vanity, or foolish and hurtful desires."[67] Children do not need any more pride, lust, or vanity. Fallen nature has given them an ample supply already. To purchase them more is an evil thing. (5) Moreover, do not leave them money upon your departure from this life if "you have good reason to believe they would waste what is now in your possession, in gratifying, and thereby increasing, the desire of the flesh, the desire of the eye, or the pride of life; at the peril of theirs and your own soul, do not set these traps in their way."[68] To do so is to offer up the children to Belial. Wesley was amazed that some parents could "never leave their children enough." Late in his *JOURNAL* Wesley recorded the following: "At Darlington Mr. _____ died, and left many thousand pounds to an idle spendthrift, but not one groat to the poor. O unwise steward of the mammon of unrighteousness! How much better for him had he died a beggar!"[69] What should a wealthy parent do with his money? Wesley was explicit in answering this query -

"If I had one child, elder or younger, who knew the value of money, one who, I believed, would put it to the true use, I should think it my absolute, indispensable duty, to leave that child the bulk of my fortune; and to the rest just so much as would enable them to live in the manner they had been accustomed to do."[70]

But, asked an objector, "What if all your children were equally ignorant of the true use of money?" Wesley answered that he would then distribute equally to them, but just enough to keep them "above want," and have the rest of the estate given to a charitable work of God.[71]

(c) Wesley's third rule concerning the use of money is *"Give all you can!"* Wesley's rationale for this rule is based upon his understanding of the creation of man. When God made Adam, He made him a steward and not a proprietor. Adam's children are forever stewards too. As such, they are entrusted with goods of various kinds, but only for a season of time. The sole ownership of these goods is God's. In addition to the goods one has in stewardship trust, one's body and soul are equally held in stewardship. Then too, money in particular belongs to God as all else. Wesley added this reminder, "He has told you, in the most clear and express terms, how you are to employ it for him, in such a manner, that it may be all an holy sacrifice, acceptable through Christ Jesus."[72] There are specific directions for the distribution of God's money by the faithful steward: (1) The steward must first use money to adequately satisfy his own needs for food, clothing, shelter as nature requires - no more and no less - preserving the body in health and strength. The well-being of his wife and children, and other household members, must be included in this budgetary management. After their well-being has been secured, Wesley argued, whatever is "an overplus" should be given away where it will do the greatest good. "In so doing, you will give all you can; nay, in a sound sense, all you have: For all that is laid out in this manner is really given to God."[73] (2) Should one have doubts about how to make distribution, he should ask the following questions: "In expending this, am I acting according to my character?" "Am I acting herein, not as a proprietor, but as a steward of my Lord's goods?" "Am I doing this in obedience to his word?" "In what scripture does he require me so to do?" "Can I offer up this action, this expense, as a sacrifice to God through Jesus Christ?" In addition to this method of settling doubts, Wesley advised frequent prayer. A model prayer is offered by Wesley. Its main petitions are: "Lord, Thou seest I am going to expend this sum on that _____ . . .Thou knowest, I act therein with a single eye, as a steward of Thy goods. . . Thou knowest I do this in obedience to Thy word

. . .Let this, I beseech Thee, be an holy sacrifice, acceptable through Jesus Christ!. . .Give me a witness in myself, that for this labour of love I shall have a recompence when Thou rewardest every man according to his works." Wesley's "holy sacrifice" means more than a proper expenditure. It also means "give all you can to God, or, in other words, give all you have to God...not a tenth, not a third, not half, but all that is God's."[74]

The pilgrim, then must be a good steward of money. He must gain all he can, save all he can, and give all that is "superplus" away with the greatest degree of charity and wisdom. He must avoid getting rich by gaining and saving only. It is imperative that he practices step three - giving all away to the glory of God. In his sermon entitled ON RICHES, Wesley stated the New Testament dictum: "How hardly shall they that have riches enter into the kingdom of God! It is easier for a camel to go through the eye of a needle, than for a rich man to enter into the kingdom of God" (Matthew XIX, 24). But, how does one define the term "rich" in the New Testament sense? Wesley saw the meaning to exceed having a treasure trove of gold or silver. It also means the condition of "any one that possesses more than the necessaries and conveniences of life." Moreover, it applies to "one that has food and raiment sufficient for himself and his family, and *something over*."[75] Such a condition is a hindrance to holiness, and it is an occasion for many temptations to sin. To be specific, being rich tends to lead one to trust in the things he possesses. Faith is thus diverted from God to riches. As a result, love - the first fruit of faith - is diverted from God and one's neighbor to riches. The love of God produces humility, but since love has been displaced to riches, true humility cannot have any reality in those who are rich. Meekness cannot exist without humility, and the rich think more highly of themselves than they ought to think. They elevate themselves above others. They refuse to submit to anyone, and they are no longer "easy to be entreated." It is difficult to find patience in those who are rich, "unless there is a counterbalance of long and severe affliction...as an antidote to their riches."[76] In such cases, God usually sends pain, sickness, and other great crosses. The end to be attained is

patience, until "they are perfect and entire, lacking nothing."
These are the hindrances of riches to holiness. The temptations
occasioned by riches are many, but a few should be cited: There is
a temptation to Atheism when one is rich - "an entire forgetfulness
of God, as if there were no such Being in the universe;"[77] There is
a subsequent temptation to idolatry - "from the worship of no God
to the worship of false gods. . .the works of his hands...to how many
species of idolatry is every rich man exposed!;"[78] There are the
temptations to the "desire of the eyes" - "to seek happiness in beautiful houses, in elegant furniture, in curious pictures, in delightful
gardens. . .rich, gay apparel. . .in every new thing, little or great,
which fashion, *the mistress of fools*, recommends. . .to seek happiness. . .in poetry, history, music, philosophy, or curios arts and sciences;"[79] There are the temptations related to the "pride of life" -
not merely the pomp that accompanies being rich, but also the
"honour that cometh of men. . .whether it be deserved or not. . .A
rich man is sure to meet with this: It is a snare he cannot escape,
and who can bear general applause without being puffed up, without being insensibly induced to think of himself more highly than
he ought to think. . .a better man than those who have not these
advantages;"[80] and there is the temptation to indulge the self-will
which is born in every child of man - "to beget and nourish every
temper that is contrary to the love of God. . .(and) of our neighbour. . .Resentment[81]

In his popular sermon, *DIVES AND LAZARUS*, Wesley summarized his general position on the danger of riches -

"It is no more sinful to be rich than to be poor. But it is dangerous beyond
expression. Therefore, I remind all of you that are of this number, that have
the conveniences of life, and something over, that ye walk upon slippery
ground. Ye continually tread on snares and deaths. Ye are every moment
on the verge of hell!"[82]

And warn the Methodist pilgrims he did! His *JOURNAL* abounds
with numerous references to Wesley's preaching upon this subject.
His entry for September 19, 1763, states -

"I gave our brethren a solemn caution not to 'love the world, neither the things of the world.' This will be their grand danger; as they are industrious and frugal, they must needs increase in goods. This appears already. In London, Bristol, and most other trading towns, those who are in business have increased in substance sevenfold, some of them twenty, yea, and hundredfold. What need, then, have these of the strongest warnings, lest they be entangled therein, and perish!"[83]

In Aughrim (Ireland) on Tuesday, June 20, 1769, Wesley preached a strong sermon on the text from Luke XII, 20 - "Thou Fool, this night thy soul shall be required of thee!" He described his hearers as "a money-loving people." His post-mortem on the encounter reads, "I am afraid that many of them are sermon-proof."[84]

Wesley's warning always ended with an appeal to "give all you can." Such an appeal meant alms-giving, and that systematically. He knew first-hand the ravages of poverty. He consistently visited the poor in their sufferings and squalor -

"I began visiting those of our society who lived in Bethnal Green hamlet. Many of them I found in such poverty as few can conceive without seeing it. Oh why do not all the rich that fear God constantly visit the poor? Can they spend part of their spare time better? Certainly not. So they will find in that day when every man shall receive his own reward according to his own labour. Such another scene I saw the next day, in visiting another part of the society.

I have not found any such distress, no, not in the prison of Newgate. One poor man was just creeping out of his sick-bed to his ragged wife and three little children, who were more than half naked, and the very picture of famine; when, one bringing in a loaf of bread, they all ran, seized upon it, and tore it in pieces in an instant. Who would not rejoice that there is another world?"[85]

Why should the poor have to wait for "another world" in which to be full and satisfied? Because, Wesley believed, the wealthy do not have a heart of charity. How widespread did he think this condition was among the rich? In a letter to Miss Bishop, dated November 16, 1777, after she had inherited a fortune, Wesley wrote: "Two-thirds of those who are grown rich are greatly degenerated. They do not, will not save all they can in order to give all they can. And without doing this they cannot grow in grace; nay, they continually grieve the Holy Spirit of God".[86] What kind of giving did Wesley have in mind for the rich? In his sermon *THE DANGER OF INCREASING RICHES*, Wesley gave this illustration of acceptable giving -

> "I am pained for you that are rich in this world. Do you give all you can? Ye who receive five hundred pounds a year, and spend only two hundred, do you give three hundred back to God? If not, you certainly rob God of that three hundred. You that receive two hundred and spend but one, do you give God the other hundred? If not, you rob him of just so much...It is not your own. It cannot be, unless you are Lord of heaven and earth."[87]

In his sermon, *WORLDY FOLLY*, Wesley had a rich man cry out for God's mercy, asking, "What shall I do?" Wesley responded, "Why, disperse abroad, give to the poor. Feed the hungry, clothe the naked. Be a father to the fatherless, and a husband to the widow. Freely thou hast received; freely give."[88] The rich do not have far to go to find the poor - they are so plentiful that the rich will "never want something to do."[89] Wesley would never accept the notion of "trickle-down economics" because so little ever actually trickles down. God requires the rich to give more to the poor than a trickle. To keep wealthy Methodist pilgrims from thinking in terms of a "trickle," Wesley instructed them to pray this prayer -

> "Lord, save me or I perish! See my riches increase; let me not set my heart upon them! Thou seest I stand upon slippery ground; do Thou undertake for me! . . .See, Lord, how greatly my substance increases! Nothing less than Thy almighty power can prevent my setting my heart upon it, and being crushed lower than the grave."[90]

In the sermon, *THE INEFFICACY OF CHRISTIANITY*, Wesley lamented that the history of the Church is the general story of the rich neglecting to give to the poor - a history of grieving God's Spirit.[91] However, this was not true in the first Church at

Jerusalem. There "was not any among them that lacked; but distribution was made to everyone according as he had need."[92] Wesley acknowledged that such a practice was not the result of following a positive commandment, but the result of love permeating the entire Church.[93] Fortunately, there have been some in every generation of the Church motivated to the same practice. But these have been preciously few in number. In his inefficacy sermon, Wesley stated, "And we have full proof that it may be so still. It is so among the people called Quakers. Yea, and among the Moravians, so called. And why should it not be so with us (Methodists)?"[94] If only the wealthy in Methodism would "love" all others and "give" all they can, Wesley reasoned, "with two thousand pounds, and not much less, we could supply the present wants of all our poor, and put them in a way of supplying their own wants for the time to come."[95]   Concerning this kind of economic practice, Wesley equated it with being a "Bible Christian" - "I am determined to be a Bible Christian, not almost, but altogether. Who will meet me on this ground? Join me on this, or not at all."[96] It should be noted that Wesley wrote this ideal for almsgiving into his *DIRECTIONS GIVEN TO THE BAND SOCIETIES* (December 25, 1744) - "II. Zealously to maintain good works; in particular, - 1. To give alms of such things as you possess, and that to the uttermost of your power . . .3. To be patterns of diligence and frugality, of self-denial, and taking up the cross daily."[97]

One should not think that Wesley arrived at this doctrine of stewardship of money on his own. He was a son of the Church of England and an admirer of the *HOMILIES*. He spoke of the *HOMILIES* as "being next to Scripture."[98] From childhood Wesley knew each select sermon, having heard his father and other priests of the church deliver them. Long before he could preach them as a priest, he knew them by heart. Later in life, with the world as his parish, Wesley composed many of his sermons upon the foundation of the *HOMILIES*, working their texts, words, and phrases into his own. *HOMILY XXIII - ON ALMSGIVING -* is a case in point. Its emphasis on the "duty of love" undergirds Wesley's full presentation. Its use of Matthew XXV, Deuteronomy XV, I Thessalonians

V, Hebrews XIII, and Tobit IV, among other sources, can not be overlooked in Wesley's treatment. Wesley's condemnation of possessing and wearing "gay apparel" is clearly rooted in the HOMILY with its attack upon those who allow such apparel to puff them up "with pride and divers vanities."[99] The reasoned emphasis on the theme of not "pampering the flesh" can be seen as the source of Wesley's frequent exhortations to his Methodists.

2. *Time* - Wesley's doctrine of stewardship of time was founded on the commandment of Ephesians V, 16 - "Redeem the time, because the days are evil." In his *EXPLANATORY NOTES UPON THE NEW TESTAMENT*, Wesley explained this commandment -

> "With all possible care redeeming the time - Saving all you can for the best purposes; buying every possible moments out of the hands of sin and Satan; out of the hands of sloth, ease, pleasure, worldly business; the more diligently, because the present are evil days, days of the grossest ignorance, immorality, and profaneness."[100]

In fact, Wesley frequently preached a prepared sermon on this text from Ephesians. His introduction was the statement above, taken verbatim from his *EXPLANATORY NOTES UPON THE NEW TESTAMENT*. In addition to biblical sources for this sermon, Wesley explicitly cited Jeremy Taylor and Richard Baxter as worthy of consideration in relation to the stewardship of time.[101] Of these two, Taylor's treatment of time and the pilgrim seems more important to Wesley. A brief survey of Taylor's position will help clarify Wesley's position.

Taylor's famous work, *HOLY LIVING AND DYING*, begins with a description of the care of our time. God has given to man a short time "here on earth, and yet on this short time eternity depends." After we become persons "capable of laws, knowing good from evil," God holds us accountable for every hour of our life, and He will judge us according to our employment thereof.[102] God has previously determined how time should best be used. Therefore, he has "given every man work enough to do, that there shall be no room for idleness; and yet hath so ordered the world, that there shall be space for devotion."[103] There is a special grace at work in man when he uses time for his God-given vocation -

> "So long as idleness is quite shut out from our lives, all the sins of wantonness, softness, and effeminacy, are prevented, and there is little room left for temptation; and, therefore, to a busy man, temptation is fain to climb up together with his business, and sins creep upon him only by accidents and occasions; whereas, to an idle person, they come in a full body, and with open violence and the impudence of a restless importunity."[104]

In other words, the idler's mind is the devil's workshop! Taylor calls idleness "the sin of Sodom and her daughters...the burial of a living man."[105]

Bishop Taylor gave specific rules for "employing" our time: (a) Upon awakening in the morning, think immediately of God and His service for the day, and at night "let Him close thine eyes." (b) Be diligent in the performance of your vocation, "So as not lightly or without reasonable occasion to neglect it." (c) "Let all the intervals or void spaces of time be employed in prayers, reading, meditating, works of nature, recreation, charity, friendliness, and neighbourhood, and means of spiritual and corporal health; ever remembering so to work in our calling, as not to neglect the work of our high calling; but to begin and end the day with God."[106] (d) Do not use the Christian Sabbath and the festival days of the Church for idleness - "but let them be spent in the works of the day, that is, of religion and charity, according to the rule appointed." (e) Avoid the company of drunkards and busy bodies, "and all such as are apt to talk much to little purpose; for no man can be provident of his time, that is not prudent in his choice of his company." (f) Never be triflingly employed, "merely to pass the time away; for every day well spent may become a day of salvation; and time rightly employed is an acceptable time." (g) During your daily employment of vocation, "often retire to God in short prayers and ejaculations." (h) Let your business be suited to a "reasonable" person, not that fit for a child or "distracted people." Let it be fit for your age and understanding.[107] (i) Fit your employment to your person and calling - "Some there are, that employ their time in affairs infinitely below the dignity of their person...Nero went up and down Greece, and challenged the fiddlers at their trade." (j) Let your employment be fitting for a Christian - "in no sense, mingled with sin, for he that takes pains to serve the ends of covetousness, or ministers to another's lust, or keeps a shop of impurities or intemperance, is idle in the worst sense."[108] (k) The women of noble birth and wealth should spend their time nursing their children, care for the house, visit poor cottages and relieve their necessities, being courteous to the neighborhood, "learn in silence of their husbands," read good books, pray often and speak little.[109] (1) Let recreation not be excessive in consuming time - "Choose such which are healthful, short, transient, recreative, and apt to refresh you; but at no hand dwell upon them, or make them your great employment."[110]

Bishop Taylor saw the Christian sabbath as a special unit of time, requiring a special stewardship. He gave three general rules for keeping the Lord's Day holy: (a) "Abstain from all servile and laborious work, except such, which are matters of necessity, of common life, or of great charity."[111] (b) The Lord's Day must be a day of joy, festivity, spiritual rejoicing, and thanksgiving - "Let your devotions spend themselves in singing or reading psalms, in recounting the great works of God; in remembering his mercies, in worshipping his excellencies, in celebrating his attributes, in admiring his person."[112] (c) Be at the public houses of prayer, "entering early and cheerfully, attending reverently and devoutly, abiding patiently during the whole office, piously assisting at the prayers, and gladly also hearing the sermon; and, at no hand, omitting to receive the holy communion, when it is offered."[113]

Wesley knew Taylor's position concerning the stewardship of time. In fact, he recounted Taylor's main points in his conversations with his preachers - "never be idle, or triflingly employed."[114] In describing sabbath observance, Wesley used Taylor's three rules. Wesley's treatment, however, was an expansion of these rules -

"On this day, above all, cry aloud, and spare not, to the God who heareth prayer. This is the day he hath set apart for the good of your soul, both in this world and that which is to come. Never more disappoint the design of His love, either by worldly business or idle diversions. Let not a little thing keep you from the house of God, either in the forenoon or afternoon. And spend as much as you can of the rest of the day, either in repeating what you have heard, or in reading the Scripture, or in private prayer, or talking of the things of God."[115]

The sermon *ON REDEEMING THE TIME* has a most unusual thesis. Wesley accepted all of Taylor's principles concerning the use of time. But, it must be noted, they apply only to the awakened person. When one is asleep, they have no relevancy. Hence, Wesley argued, the Christian pilgrim must keep sleeping time to a bare minimum - no more than is absolutely necessary, and no less than is needed to maintain proper health. Because of this surprising idea, no study of Wesley's understanding of the stewardship of time should omit an analysis of this sermon.

According to Wesley, Richard Baxter (A.D. 1615-1691) held that four hours of sleep in twenty-four is enough for any man. But, Wesley retorted, "a human body can scarce continue in health and vigour, without, at least, six hours' sleep in four-and-twenty. . .I never found either man or woman that retained vigorous health for one year, with a less quantity of sleep than this."[116] Wesley observed that women require a "little more sleep than men." He attributed this condition to the woman's "weaker, as well as moister, habit of body."[117] Generally, men need "above six hours sleep, healthy women, a little above seven in four-and-twenty."[118]

How may a person determine how much sleep is actually needed? Wesley observed that when one gets too much sleep, there is a period of sleeplessness during the night. Try awaking at six in the morning and that night go to bed at the usual time. If sleeplessness still occurs, reset the "alarum" (alarm-clock) for five o'clock. The next night retire at the usual time. If sleeplessness still persists, reset the alarm for four o'clock. This experiment brought Wesley to awake each morning at four, and his periods of nocturnal sleeplessness ceased altogether. "By the same experiment, rising earlier and earlier every morning, may one find how much sleep he really wants."[119]

What bearing does this have upon Christian stewardship? Why should anyone go to all this trouble? "What harm is there in doing as our neighbours do?" Wesley greeted these questions with one of his own - "Do you really desire to know what harm there is in not redeeming all the time you can from sleep. . .Suppose in spending therein an hour a day more than nature requires?" First, in doing this, one "hurts" his substance (living) by "throwing away six hours a week, which might turn to some temporal account."[120] Secondly, excessive sleep "hurts your health." This is an empirical fact of life. Excessive sleep "lays the foundation of many diseases. It is the chief real cause of all nervous diseases in particular."[121] Moreover, by "soaking" so long "between warm sheets, the flesh, as it were, (is) parboiled, and becomes soft an flabby."[122] Excessive sleep also brings weakness of sight. Wesley claimed knowledge of this through his own personal experience. It was not until he began the habit of rising at four each morning that his eye-sight strengthened, after very poor vision during his childhood.[123] But worst of all, excessive sleep "hurts the soul." It sows the seeds of foolish and hurtful desires. It breeds intemperance, "an universal softness and faintness of spirit, making us afraid of every little inconvenience, unwilling to deny ourselves any pleasure, or to take up or bear any cross."[124]

Wesley's sermon includes a lengthy quotation from William Law on this subject of excessive sleep. The quotation does not throw any new ideas into the sermon, but it fortifies what Wesley had already affirmed. Nevertheless, there are some classical statements, worthy of our notice: "Sleep is such a dull, stupid state of existence, that, even among mere animals, we despise them most which are most drowsy;" "A person who is a slave to this idleness is in the same temper when he is up;" and "Like any more moderate course of indulgence, (sleep) silently, and by smaller degrees, wears away the spirit of religion, and sinks the soul into dulness and sensuality;"[125] Wesley concluded this sermon with an appeal for his hearers to place their faith in God who enables all who would redeem time to continue in the way of holiness. God will strengthen, and the pilgrim must hold fast to his holy habit of redeeming time -

"Go on, in a full pursuit of all the mind that was in Christ, of inward and then outward holiness; so shall you by not almost but altogether a Christian; so shall you finish your course with joy: You shall awake up after his likeness, and be satisfied."[126]

Wesley, the pilgrim, was not always satisfied with his redemption of time. In a letter to a friend (December 15, 1772), he exclaimed, "I often cry out, Vitae me redde priori!" - that is, "My former happy life restore!" He continued, "Let me be again an Oxford Methodist! I am often in doubt whether it would not be best for me to resume all my Oxford rules, great and small. I did then walk closely with God, and redeem the time. But what have I been doing these thirty years?"[127] Five years later, Wesley wrote to another friend (December 10, 1777) and explained how his redemption of time presently compared with the Oxford days -

"Though I am always in haste, I am never in a hurry; because I never undertake any more work than I can go through with perfect calmness of spirit. It is true, I travel four or five thousand miles in a year. But I generally travel alone in my carriage; and, consequently, am as retired ten hours in a day, as if I was in a wilderness. On other days, I never spend less than three hours (frequently ten or twelve) in the day alone. So there are few persons in the kingdom who spend so many hours secluded from all company. Yet I find time to visit the sick and the poor; and I must do it, if I believe the Bible, if I believe these are the marks whereby the Shepherd of Israel will know and judge his sheep at the great day; therefore, when there is time and opportunity for it, who can doubt but this is matter of absolute duty? When I was at Oxford, and lived almost like a hermit, I saw not how any busy man could be saved. I scarce thought it possible for a man to retain the Christian spirit amidst the noise and bustle of the world. God taught me better by my own experience. I had ten times more business in America. . .than ever I had in my life. But it was not hindrance to silence of spirit."[128]

For the older Wesley, the stewardship of time was elastic and dynamic, beyond rules. His itinerary and oversight of the societies placed him in a special category, separate from his preachers and lay followers. They were obligated to the stewardship of time according to his rules and regulations, while Wesley gave them a nearly flawless example of how to use every segment of time for the glory of God.

The Christian pilgrim, therefore, must be a faithful and good steward of all things, especially money and time. But, this commitment is very difficult to maintain because there are many diversions in the present life. Most of these diversions are thrown into the pilgrim's path by Satan and his evil hosts. Consequently, they are quite alluring and not easily ignored. Yet the pilgrim has divine grace at his disposal so he may practice self-denial in reference to the diversions. Wesley saw self-denial in reference to the diversions. Wesley saw self-denial as "the more excellent way" for the pilgrim to take.[129] Borrowing from Clement of Alexandria, Wesley identified "two orders of Christians" - (1) Those leading an innocent life, conforming in all things not sinful, "to the customs and fashions of the world, doing many good works, abstaining from gross evils. . .(having) a conscience void of offence in their behaviour, but (they do) not aim at any particular strictness;" and (2) those who do all these things and more, and yet use "all diligence to attain the whole mind that was in Christ," laboring to walk "in a constant course of universal self-denial."[130] Whatever pleasure they consciously recognize as hindering them from the pleasure of God, these Christians trample under foot, gladly and voluntarily. This is the higher path for the Christian, while the first is the lower. Wesley believed that the Holy Spirit gives the choice of taking either the higher or the lower to each justified soul. The Spirit, however, "sets before him 'the more excellent way.'" The Holy Spirit "incites him to walk therein." The more excellent way of self-denial is the narrow way of holiness that brings the "entire image of God" to the faithful pilgrim.[131] Wesley disclaimed the notion that the other Christians, on the lower path, are on the broad road that leads to hell. But, he added, "This much I must affirm, they will not have so high a place in heaven as they would have had if they had chosen the better part."[132] If the pilgrim chooses to walk in the one, he must quit the other. He cannot walk in both simultaneously.[133] It is the Spirit's desire that he selects the more excellent way.

The way of self-denial means the rejection of alluring diversion in favor of the pleasure of God. Wesley's sermon *ON A SINGL. EYE* makes this point quite explicit from beginning to end.[1: Moreover, in his sermon *THE MORE EXCELLENT WAY*, there a listing if diversions to be avoided by the pilgrim taking the highe way - (1) those of the sportsmen: hunting, shooting, and fishin (not for necessity's sake); (2) those of a public nature: races, mas querades, plays, assemblies, and balls; and (3) those employed i private houses: cards, dancing, music, and the "reading of play; novels, romances, newspapers, and fashionable poetry".[135] Wesle was realistic enough to know that the majority of his Methodist pil grims would not consistently resist these diversions. But he con stantly spoke of the virtue of self-denial in regard to these, and he made his societies the places where Methodists gave an account o their virtue or lack of it.[136] Wesley desired that all his follower: walk on the path of self-denial, avoiding the snares of these diver sions. To do so is part of being a faithful and good steward of body soul, mind, things, and time.

Wesley's evaluation of some of these diversions demands a hearing -

"Let those who have nothing better to do, still run foxes and hares out of breath. Neither much be said about horse-races, till some man of sense will undertake to defend them. It seems a great deal more may be said in de-fence of seeing a serious tragedy. I could not do it with a clear conscience; at least not in the English theatre, the sink of all profaneness and debauchery; but possibly others can. I cannot say quite so much for balls or assemblies, which, though more reputable than masquerades, yet must be allowed by all impartial persons to have exactly the same tendency. So, undoubtedly, have all public dancings. And the same tendency they must have, unless the same caution obtained among modern Christians which was observed among the ancient Heathens. With them, men and women never danced together, but always in separate rooms. This was always observed in ancient Greece, and for several ages at Rome, where a woman dancing in company with men would have at once been set down for a prostitute. Of playing cards I say the same as of seeing plays. I could not do it with a clear conscience. But I am not obliged to pass any judgement on those that are otherwise minded. I leave them to their own Master: To Him let them stand or fall."[137]

Some scholars of Wesley think it strange that he would preach the above position when his mother had raised him differently. Susanna Wesley played cards with her children and even hired a dancing instructor for them.[138] Wesley never spoke a disparaging word about his mother's method of child-rearing. In fact, Wesley often used it as a model for Methodist parents to follow. As for card playing between parent and child, such an activity accomplishes two notable objectives: (1) it establishes familiarity between parent and child, which is absolutely necessary for successful Christian nurture; and (2) it enables a child to think and react quickly, which skill is needed in all of life. Card-playing in child-rearing has its place, but in the life of the serious pilgrim it is a diversion best avoided. As regards Susanna's use of a dancing instructor, it must be observed that dancing for pleasure was not the object. Susanna wanted her children to learn the grace of movement, and for that reason the instructor was employed for awhile at the Epworth parsonage. However, Wesley would not allow Miss Bishop to use dancing at her girls' school, although some of the girls' parents demanded it and withdrew their daughters when it was not offered. In a short time these students sought readmission, and Wesley made this comment -

"It seems God himself has already decided the question concerning dancing. He hath shown his approbation of your conduct, by sending those children to you again. If dancing be not evil in itself, yet it leads young women to numberless evils. And the hazard of these on the one side, seems far to overbalance the little inconveniences on the other. Therefore thus much may certainly be said, You have chosen the more excellent way."[139]

Wesley's sermon *ON PUBLIC DIVERSIONS* attacked the English love-affair with horse-racing. The basis of his criticism was that horse-racing, like all other diversions, destroys the stewardship of possessions and time.[140] The argument proceeds along this line -

"Is there poison in this diversion which is supposed to be harmless in itself? To clear this up, let us, First, observe the notorious lying that is always joined with it; The various kinds of over-reaching and cheating; the horrid oaths and curses that constantly accompany it, wherewith the name of our Lord God, blessed for ever, is blasphemed. When or where was this diversion ever known without these dreadful consequences? . . .And surely these alone, had we no other ill consequences to charge upon this diversion, are enough, till a way is found to purge it from them, to make both God and all wise men abhor it. But, over and above these, we charge it, Secondly, with affording the fairest means to exercise and to increase covetousness. This is done by the occasion it gives to all who please to lay wagers with one another, which commonly brings so strong a desire of possessing what is another's, as will hardly cease when that one point is decided; but will be exceedingly likely to leave such a thirst in the mind, as not all the winning in the world will satisfy. And what amends can the trifling sport of a thousand people make for one soul thus corrupted and ruined? Therefore, on this account too, till a way is known to secure all that frequent it from this danger, well may this sport itself be an abomination to Him who values one soul more than the whole world. May we not well fear, that it is an abomination to the Lord, because of a Third effect of it? because it is so apt to inflame those passions which he so earnestly commands us to quench? because many people are so heated on such occasions, as they never ought to be on any occasion? supposing it possible that a man might be angry and not sin; yet hardly upon such occasions, or in such a degree as those who are angry on such occasions commonly are. This consequence, too, let him separate from such a diversion, who would prevent its being displeasing to God.[141]

According to Wesley, it is not valid to ask, "What harm is there in a horse-race?" There are so many reasons for not attending one that the question is without merit. The most reasonable of these are: (1) If you are a young person, you attend either to see or be seen, "to admire other fine sights, or to be admired yourself." This condition may be called "the desire of the eye, and the pride of life." The horse-race, with all its attending embellishments, "strengthens those affections which are already too strong." Diversions like the races are "the noblest instruments the devil has to fill the mind with earthly, sensual, and devilish passions; to make you a light and trifling spirit. . .to make you a lover of pleasure more than a lover of God."[142] (2) If you are advanced in years, and have been attending the races for some time, "hath it not done you hurt enough, if it has hindered any of you from partaking of the blessed

sacrament?" Serious examination and private devotion before partaking of the sacrament are required, but the race-course is not
conducive to them. Consequently, "it has occasioned your neglecting to come to this holy table. . .losing all those inestimable
advantages which are reached out to them who obey him."[143] (3) If
you are rich, having attended the races, you have "given something
towards it. . .you have thrown away a part of that talent, which had
you rightly improved, you might have been an everlasting gainer by
it." Wesley here emphasized the stewardship motif by alluding to
the parable of the talents (Matthew XXV, 18). He continued this
theme by adding, "You have utterly lost what God himself, had you
lent it to him, would richly have repaid you. For you have given it
to those (gamblers) who neither need, nor perhaps thank you for
it." On the other hand, "if you had bestowed upon your helpless
brethren, your blessed Redeemer would have esteemed it as done
unto himself, and would have treated you accordingly at the great
day."[144] (4) If you are a poor man who has "given anything to this
diversion," you have been hurt most of all! Wesley's exact words
are sharp and biting -

> "It has made you throw away, for an idle sport abroad, what your wife and
> family wanted at home. If so, you have denied the faith, and are far worse
> than an infidel. But suppose it cost you no money, was it not hurt enough if it
> cost you any of your time? What had you to do to run after trifling diver-
> sions, when you ought to have been employed in honest labour? Surely if the
> rich think, that God hath given them more than they want, (though it will be
> well if they do not one day think otherwise) yet you have no temptation to
> think so. Sufficient for your day is the labour thereof."[145]

The conclusion of Wesley's sermon *ON PUBLIC DIVERSIONS*
is an appeal to all who "formerly erred" in this matter, but "are now
resolved, by the grace of God, to return no more to the error of
their ways." The appeal is for these persons to avoid and earnestly
oppose such diversions because they are contrary to the will of
God. In particular, the young people should scorn "all employ-
ments that are useless, but much more if they are sinful." Elderly
persons should employ their time in preparing for the better life

yet to come - "for your day is far spent, and your night is at hand. Redeem therefore the little time you have left." The rich should labour and give so as to lay up treasures in heaven - "For you are they to whom much is given, not to throw away, but to use well and wisely; and of you much shall be required." The poor should work with their hands to provide for their own households the "necessaries of nature." But it is not enough for individuals to avoid and oppose such diversions. There must be a collective response "to wipe off the past scandal from our town and people." Such a response, Wesley held, must have two purposes: (1) To educate people on the nature of "this unhappy diversion" and so "hinder its coming among us any more;" and (2) To implement a practical program of mercy, "as God hath prospered us," by which our "afflicted neighbour" are the recipients.[146] A universal awakening of true religion would insure the demise of this diversion.[147]

Another diversion treated by Wesley as a danger to pilgrims was that of the theatre. As noted earlier, Wesley regarded the English theatre as "the sink of all profaneness and debauchery." It gave Wesley great delight when "a play-house" went out of business. In April of 1754, Wesley preached at Sadler's Wells, in a converted play-house. He cheerfully commented, "I am glad when it pleases God to take possession of what Satan esteemed his own ground."[148] But for every one lost by Satan, Wesley found, he erects another. On December 20, 1764, Wesley wrote to the mayor and members of the Corporation of the City of Bristol, objecting to the building of a new theatre there. The letter cites reasons against its being completed: (1) most of the stage-entertainments "sap the foundation of all religion, as they naturally tend to efface all traces of piety and seriousness out of the minds of men;" (2) such plays hurt a great trading city by misleading youth into gay and trifling lifestyles, so that industry and business suffer by their neglect; and (3) drinking and debauchery of every kind are "attendants on these entertainments, with indolence, effeminacy, and idleness, which affect trade in a high degree."[149] Wesley added that these very reasons caused the Corporation of Nottingham to reject the building of a new theatre there, "being determined to encourage nothing of the kind."[150] One should not think Wesley a barbarian on this issue. He believed that profane, drunken plays belong to Satan. There are, however, some plays worth attending. In the evening of December 14, 1768, he saw the Westminster scholars act the ADELPHI by Terence. Wesley was laudatory, calling the performance of this Latin play "an entertainment not unworthy of a Christian." Compared with the English plays the Latin ones are superior. Wesley exclaimed, "O how do these heathens shame us! Their very comedies contain both excellent sense, the liveliest pictures of men and manners, and so fine strokes of genuine morality as are seldom found in the writings of Christians."[151] The Christian pilgrim should avoid the play-houses that cater to the low and profane. Like Wesley, however, the pilgrim should carefully select those plays and their theatres that enlarge one's mental, moral and spiritual sensitivities. Following this principle, the pilgrim will not become an habitual theatre-goer, sliding farther and farther from the kingdom of God.

One more diversion remains for the self-denying pilgrim to avoid - drunkenness. The sermon *ON PUBLIC DIVERSIONS* treats this subject in the context of stewardship - the stewardship of brotherliness -

"You see the wine when it sparkles in the cup, and are going to drink of it. I tell you there is poison in it! and, therefore, beg you to throw it away. You answer, 'The wine is harmless in itself.' I reply, Perhaps it is so; but still if it be mixed with what is not harmless, no one in his senses, if he knows it at least, unless he could separate the good from the bad, will once think of drinking it. If you add, 'It is not poison to me, though it be to others;' then I say, Throw it away for thy brother's sake, lest thou embolden him to drink also. Why should thy strength occasion thy weak brother to perish, for whom Christ died?"[152]

Wesley was not outlawing the drinking of wine, as some have hastily supposed. He admitted that wine is harmless in itself, but that it becomes poison if it "be mixed with what is not harmless." When wine is mixed with anger, tragedy follows. When mixed with jealousy, murder results. When excessive consumption occurs, all sorts of evil proceed. The evil lies not in the wine, but in the heart. The heart harbors the "evil thoughts, murders, adulteries, fornications, thefts, false witness, railing: These are the things which defile a man."[153] Drunkenness unlocks the evil within the human heart. No man is so strong as to get drunk and keep the evil stored within. the sight of an apparent "strong man" doing so is illusory, giving the "weaker brother" a false example. *Und dass ist Vorboten*!

Wesley was convinced that drunkenness is a device of Satan, and that its habitual practice will keep one out of the kingdom of God.[154] He knew the biblical injunctions against this device, and he knew *HOMILY XVII (On Drunkenness)* of the Church of England. Wesley's claim that drunkenness hurts the body, infects the mind, and wastes the substance, came directly from this *HOMILY*.[155] Yet, wine is not the culprit. Wesley could not accept the argument of Dr. Cadogan who condemned wine *toto genere*. Wesley affirmed wine to be "one of the noblest cordials in nature."[156] It should be noted that this affirmation was made in 1771, when Wesley was quite mature. Wine has other redeeming qualities, other than medicinal ones. Wesley acknowledged its value in joyous celebration - For instance, his commentary on Jesus turning water into wine at Cana (John II:lff) reads -

> "Christ does not take away human society, but sanctifies it. Water might have quenched thirst, yet our Lord allows wine; especially at a festival solemnity."[157]

The cup of the Lord's Supper contains wine by which we celebrate the remission of sins by Christ's death.[158] "As our bodies are strengthened by bread and wine, so are our souls by these tokens of the body and blood of Christ."[159] Wesley would never consent to the substitution of grape-juice for wine in the Eucharist. Nor would he allow drunkenness among his Methodist pilgrims as his sermons and society rules explicitly show. The ideal was for his followers to "be not drunken with wine, wherein is excess, but be ye filled with the Spirit." His commentary on the phrase "wherein is excess" is crucial: "That is, which leads to debauchery of every kind."[160] Drunkenness was, for Wesley, the same as debauchery. The drinking of wine in moderation, for proper reasons, Wesley held, is quite compatible with the Spirit-filled life and self-denial. To help convince his Methodists of this, Wesley placed Dr. Goodman's *WINTER EVENING CONFERENCE* in his *CHRISTIAN LIBRARY* for their benefit.[161]

The pilgrim's praxis, then, is clearly holiness and stewardship, without which no one sees God.

Notes

1 WORKS, *op.cit.*, X, 364.
2 *Ibid*, VII, 456.
3 *Ibid*, VII, 316.
4 *Loc.cit.*
5 *Ibid*, VI, 100. Cf. EXPLANATORY NOTES NEW TESTAMENT, *op.cit.*, 863 - "Works do not give life to faith, but faith begets works, and then is perfected by them."
6 *Ibid*, XII, 296-297. Brown's reference to the "dragon" who attempts to "swallow up the woman" is from Revelation XII, 1ff. It was a popular Anglican interpretation that the dragon was Satan and the woman the Church.
7 *Ibid*, X, 366. See also 266ff.
8 *Ibid*, X, 373.
9 *Ibid*, V, 203.
10 JOURNAL, *op.cit.*, VI, 12. Cf. EXPLANATORY NOTES NEW TESTAMENT, *op.cit.*, 813.
11 *Loc.cit.*
12 *Ibid*, VI, 38.
13 EXPLANATORY NOTES OLD TESTAMENT, *op.cit.*, III, 2039-2040.
14 WORKS, *op.cit.*, X, 366.
15 *Ibid*, X, 367-368.
16 *Ibid*, XI, 366.
17 *Ibid*, XI, 370-371.
18 *Ibid*, XI, 371.
19 *Loc.cit.*
20 *Ibid*, XI, 372.
21 *Ibid*, XI, 378.
22 *Ibid*, XI, 380.
23 *Ibid*, XI, 387. Also, VIII, 285.
24 *Ibid*, XI, 392.
25 *Loc. cit.*
26 *Ibid*, XI, 391.
27 METHODIST HYMNAL, *op.cit.*, 560.
28 WORKS, *op.cit.*, VIII, 270.
29 *Ibid*, VII, 286.
30 *Ibid*, VIII, 270-271.
31 *Ibid*, VIII, 271.
32 *Ibid*, VIII, 300.
33 EXPLANATORY NOTES NEW TESTAMENT, *op.cit.*, 878.
34 *Loc.cit.*

35 WORKS, *op.cit.*, VI, 136.
36 *Ibid*, VI, 137; VIII, 328 - Wesley required that each preacher distribute his sermon on The Good Steward to all the Methodists.
37 *Loc.cit.*
38 *Ibid*, VI, 137-138.
39 *Ibid*, VI, 138.
40 *Loc.cit.*
41 *Ibid*, VI, 139.
42 *Loc.cit.*
43 *Loc.cit.*
44 *Ibid*, VI, 124-135; V, 380.
45 *Ibid*, VI, 125.
46 *Ibid*, VI, 126. Cf. EXPLANATORY NOTES NEW TESTAMENT, *op.cit.*, 785.
47 *Loc.cit.*
48 *Loc.cit.*
49 *Ibid*, VI, 127.
50 *Loc.cit.*
51 *Ibid*, VI, 128.
52 *Loc.cit.*
53 *Loc.cit.*
54 *Loc.cit.*
55 *Ibid*, VI, 129.
56 *Loc.cit.*
57 *Loc.cit.*
58 *Ibid*, VI, 130.
59 *Loc.cit.*
60 *Loc.cit.*
61 *Loc.cit.*
62 *Loc.cit.*
63 *Ibid*, VI, 131.
64 *Loc.cit.*
65 *Loc.cit.*
66 *Loc.cit.*
67 *Ibid*, VI, 132. Cf. HOMILIES, *op.cit.*, 214. The standard sermon of the Church of England on almsgiving, Homily XXIII, emphasized all that Wesley affirmed here. One important line reads, "Wearers of gorgeous apparel are commonly puffed up with pride and divers vanities." Another reads, "Cut away all ambition, pride and vain pomp in apparel."
68 *Loc.cit.*
69 JOURNAL, *op.cit.*, VII, 169.
70 WORKS, *op.cit.*, VI, 132.
71 *Loc.cit.*
72 *Ibid*, VI, 133.
73 *Ibid*, VI, 134.
74 *Ibid*, VI, 135.

75   *Ibid*, VII, 215.
76   *Ibid*, VII, 217.
77   *Loc.cit.*
78   *Ibid*, VII, 218.
79   *Ibid*, VII, 218-219.
80   *Ibid*, VII, 219-220.
81   *Ibid*, VII, 220.
82   *Ibid*, VII, 250; 355.
83   JOURNAL, *op.cit.*, V, 30-31.
84   *Ibid*, V, 322.
85   *Ibid*, VI, 136-137.
86   Telford, *op.cit.*, VI, 288-289.
87   WORKS, *op.cit.*, VII, 362; 309.
88   *Ibid*, VII, 306.
89   *Ibid*, VII, 307.
90   *Ibid*, VII, 308.
91   *Ibid*, VII, 286.
92   *Loc.cit.*
93   EXPLANATORY NOTES NEW TESTAMENT, *op.cit.*, 402.
94   WORKS, *op.cit.*, VII, 286-287ff.
95   *Ibid*, VII, 287; XII, 200 - Wesley declared, "I love the poor."
96   *Loc.cit.*
97   *Ibid*, VIII, 274.
98   *Ibid*, VII, 204, 461.
99   HOMILIES, *op.cit.*, 214.
100 EXPLANATORY NOTES NEW TESTAMENT, *op.cit.*, 718.   Cf.
     WORKS, *op.cit.*, VII, 67.
101 WORKS, *op.cit.*, VII, 68.
102 Jeremy Taylor, *HOLY LIVING AND DYING WITH PRAYERS*, (New
     York: Appleton and Company, 1847), 7.
103 *Ibid*, 8.
104 *Ibid*, 9.
105 *Loc.cit.*
106 *Ibid*, 9-10.
107 *Ibid*, 10.
108 *Ibid*, 11.
109 *Ibid*, 12.
110 *Ibid*, 13.
111 *Ibid*, 192.
112 *Ibid*, 193.
113 *Ibid*, 193-194.
114 WORKS, *op.cit.*, VIII, 304; XI, 367; VII, 421; JOURNAL, *op.cit.*, I, 51;
     Lee, *op.cit.*, 27.
115 *Ibid*, XI, 166.
116 *Ibid*, VII, 68.
117 *Loc.cit.*

118   *Ibid*, VII, 69, 29.
119   *Loc.cit.*
120   *Loc.cit.*
121   *Ibid*, VII, 70.
122   *Loc.cit.*
123   *Loc.cit.*
124   *Ibid*, VII, 71. Cf. EXPLANATORY NOTES NEW TESTAMENT, *op.cit.*, 891.
125   *Ibid*, VII, 71-72.
126   *Ibid*, VII, 75.
127   *Ibid*, XII, 140-141.
128   *Ibid*, XII, 304.
129   *Ibid*, VII, 28.
130   *Loc.cit.*
131   *Loc.cit.*
132   *Ibid*, VII, 29.
133   *Ibid*, VI, 107.
134   *Ibid*, VII, 297ff.
135   *Ibid*, VII, 34.
136   *Ibid*, VIII, 272-274.
137   *Ibid*, VII, 34-35.
138   Rita F. Snowden, *SUCH A WOMAN*, (London: The Epworth Press, 1963), 22.
139   WORKS, *op.cit.*, XIII, 39.
140   *Ibid*, VII, 507.
141   *Ibid*, VII, 505.
142   *Ibid*, VII, 506.
143   *Loc.cit.*
144   *Loc.cit.*
145   *Ibid*, VII, 506-507.
146   *Ibid*, VII, 507.
147   *Ibid*, VII, 507-508.
148   JOURNAL, *op.cit.*, IV, 93-94.
149   WORKS, *op.cit.*, XII, 128.
150   *Loc.cit.*
151   JOURNAL, *op.cit.*, V, 294-295.
152   WORKS, *op.cit.*, VII, 504-505.
153   EXPLANATORY NOTES NEW TESTAMENT, *op.cit.*, 78.
154   *Ibid*, 601.
155   HOMILIES, *op.cit.*, 207ff.
156   JOURNAL, *op.cit.*, V, 430.
157   EXPLANATORY NOTES NEW TESTAMENT, *op.cit.*, 308.
158   *Ibid*, 620.
159   WORKS, *op.cit.*, VII, 148.
160   EXPLANATORY NOTES NEW TESTAMENT, *op.cit.*, 718.
161   CHRISTIAN LIBRARY, *op.cit.*, XX.